36: *British Novelists, 1890-1929: Modernists,* edited by Thomas F. Staley (1985)

37: *American Writers of the Early Republic,* edited by Emory Elliott (1985)

38: *Afro-American Writers After 1955: Dramatists and Prose Writers,* edited by Thadious M. Davis and Trudier Harris (1985)

39: *British Novelists, 1660-1800,* 2 parts, edited by Martin C. Battestin (1985)

40: *Poets of Great Britain and Ireland Since 1960,* 2 parts, edited by Vincent B. Sherry, Jr. (1985)

41: *Afro-American Poets Since 1955,* edited by Trudier Harris and Thadious M. Davis (1985)

42: *American Writers for Children Before 1900,* edited by Glenn E. Estes (1985)

43: *American Newspaper Journalists, 1690-1872,* edited by Perry J. Ashley (1986)

44: *American Screenwriters,* Second Series, edited by Randall Clark, Robert E. Morsberger, and Stephen O. Lesser (1986)

45: *American Poets, 1880-1945,* First Series, edited by Peter Quartermain (1986)

46: *American Literary Publishing Houses, 1900-1980: Trade and Paperback,* edited by Peter Dzwonkoski (1986)

47: *American Historians, 1866-1912,* edited by Clyde N. Wilson (1986)

48: *American Poets, 1880-1945,* Second Series, edited by Peter Quartermain (1986)

49: *American Literary Publishing Houses, 1638-1899,* 2 parts, edited by Peter Dzwonkoski (1986)

50: *Afro-American Writers Before the Harlem Renaissance,* edited by Trudier Harris (1986)

51: *Afro-American Writers from the Harlem Renaissance to 1940,* edited by Trudier Harris (1987)

52: *American Writers for Children Since 1960: Fiction,* edited by Glenn E. Estes (1986)

53: *Canadian Writers Since 1960,* First Series, edited by W. H. New (1986)

54: *American Poets, 1880-1945,* Third Series, 2 parts, edited by Peter Quartermain (1987)

55: *Victorian Prose Writers Before 1867,* edited by William B. Thesing (1987)

56: *German Fiction Writers, 1914-1945,* edited by James Hardin (1987)

57: *Victorian Prose Writers After 1867,* edited by William B. Thesing (1987)

58: *Jacobean and Caroline Dramatists,* edited by Fredson Bowers (1987)

59: *American Literary Critics and Scholars, 1800-1850,* edited by John W. Rathbun and Monica M. Grecu (1987)

60: *Canadian Writers Since 1960,* Second Series, edited by W. H. New (1987)

61: *American Writers for Children Since 1960: Poets, Illustrators, and Nonfiction Authors,* edited by Glenn E. Estes (1987)

62: *Elizabethan Dramatists,* edited by Fredson Bowers (1987)

63: *Modern American Critics, 1920-1955,* edited by Gregory S. Jay (1988)

64: *American Literary Critics and Scholars, 1850-1880,* edited by John W. Rathbun and Monica M. Grecu (1988)

65: *French Novelists, 1900-1930,* edited by Catharine Savage Brosman (1988)

66: *German Fiction Writers, 1885-1913,* 2 parts, edited by James Hardin (1988)

67: *Modern American Critics Since 1955,* edited by Gregory S. Jay (1988)

68: *Canadian Writers, 1920-1959,* First Series, edited by W. H. New (1988)

69: *Contemporary German Fiction Writers,* First Series, edited by Wolfgang D. Elfe and James Hardin (1988)

70: *British Mystery Writers, 1860-1919,* edited by Bernard Benstock and Thomas F. Staley (1988)

continued on back endsheets

Dictionary of Literary Biography
Yearbook: 1988

8018

Dictionary of Literary Biography
Yearbook: 1988

Edited by
J. M. Brook

A Bruccoli Clark Layman Book
Gale Research Inc. • Book Tower • Detroit, Michigan 48226

Copyright © 1989
GALE RESEARCH INC.

Manufactured by Edward Brothers, Inc.
Ann Arbor, Michigan
Printed in the United States of America

Library of Congress Catalog Card Number 82-645187
ISSN 0731-7867
ISBN 0-8103-1836-9

To Virginia Brook, my mother

Contents

Obituaries

Plan of the Series

. . . Almost the most prodigious asset of a country, and perhaps its most precious possession, is its native literary product—when that product is fine and noble and enduring.

Mark Twain*

The advisory board, the editors, and the publisher of the *Dictionary of Literary Biography* are joined in endorsing Mark Twain's declaration. The literature of a nation provides an inexhaustible resource of permanent worth. We intend to make literature and its creators better understood and more accessible to students and the reading public, while satisfying the standards of teachers and scholars.

To meet these requirements, *literary biography* has been construed in terms of the author's achievement. The most important thing about a writer is his writing. Accordingly, the entries in *DLB* are career biographies, tracing the development of the author's canon and the evolution of his reputation.

The purpose of *DLB* is not only to provide reliable information in a convenient format but also to place the figures in the larger perspective of literary history and to offer appraisals of their accomplishments by qualified scholars.

The publication plan for *DLB* resulted from two years of preparation. The project was proposed to Bruccoli Clark by Frederick G. Ruffner, president of the Gale Research Company, in November 1975. After specimen entries were prepared and typeset, an advisory board was formed to refine the entry format and develop the series rationale. In meetings held during 1976, the publisher, series editors, and advisory board approved the scheme for a comprehensive biographical dictionary of persons who contributed to North American literature. Editorial work on the first volume began in January 1977, and it was published in 1978. In order to make *DLB* more than a reference tool and to compile volumes that individually have claim to status as lit-

erary history, it was decided to organize volumes by topic, period, or genre. Each of these freestanding volumes provides a biographical-bibliographical guide and overview for a particular area of literature. We are convinced that this organization—as opposed to a single alphabet method—constitutes a valuable innovation in the presentation of reference material. The volume plan necessarily requires many decisions for the placement and treatment of authors who might properly be included in two or three volumes. In some instances a major figure will be included in separate volumes, but with different entries emphasizing the aspect of his career appropriate to each volume. Ernest Hemingway, for example, is represented in *American Writers in Paris, 1920-1939* by an entry focusing on his expatriate apprenticeship; he is also in *American Novelists, 1910-1945* with an entry surveying his entire career. Each volume includes a cumulative index of subject authors and articles. Comprehensive indexes to the entire series are planned.

With volume ten in 1982 it was decided to enlarge the scope of *DLB*. By the end of 1986 twenty-one volumes treating British literature had been published, and volumes for Commonwealth and Modern European literature were in progress. The series has been further augmented by the *DLB Yearbooks* (since 1981) which update published entries and add new entries to keep the *DLB* current with contemporary activity. There have also been *DLB Documentary Series* volumes which provide biographical and critical source materials for figures whose work is judged to have particular interest for students. One of these companion volumes is entirely devoted to Tennessee Williams.

We define literature as the *intellectual commerce of a nation:* not merely as belles lettres but as that ample and complex process by which ideas are generated, shaped, and transmitted. *DLB* entries are not limited to "creative writers" but extend to other figures who in their time and in their way influenced the mind of a people. Thus the series encompasses historians, journalists, publishers, and screenwriters. By this means readers of *DLB* may be aided to perceive litera-

*From an unpublished section of Mark Twain's autobiography, copyright © by the Mark Twain Company.

ture not as cult scripture in the keeping of intellectual high priests but firmly positioned at the center of a nation's life.

DLB includes the major writers appropriate to each volume and those standing in the ranks immediately behind them. Scholarly and critical counsel has been sought in deciding which minor figures to include and how full their entries should be. Wherever possible, useful references are made to figures who do not warrant separate entries.

Each DLB volume has a volume editor responsible for planning the volume, selecting the figures for inclusion, and assigning the entries. Volume editors are also responsible for preparing, where appropriate, appendices surveying the major periodicals and literary and intellectual movements for their volumes, as well as lists of further readings. Work on the series as a whole is coordinated at the Bruccoli Clark Layman editorial center in Columbia, South Carolina, where the editorial staff is responsible for accuracy of the published volumes.

One feature that distinguishes DLB is the illustration policy–its concern with the iconography of literature. Just as an author is influenced by his surroundings, so is the reader's understanding of the author enhanced by a knowledge of his environment. Therefore DLB volumes include not only drawings, paintings, and photographs of authors, often depicting them at various stages in their careers, but also illustrations of their families and places where they lived. Title pages are regularly reproduced in facsimile along with dust jackets for modern authors. The dust jackets are a special feature of DLB because they often document better than anything else the way in which an author's work was perceived in its own time. Specimens of the writers' manuscripts are included when feasible.

Samuel Johnson rightly decreed that "The chief glory of every people arises from its authors." The purpose of the Dictionary of Literary Biography is to compile literary history in the surest way available to us–by accurate and comprehensive treatment of the lives and work of those who contributed to it.

                                        The DLB Advisory Board

Foreword

The *Dictionary of Literary Biography Yearbook* is guided by the same principles that have provided the basic rationale for the entire *DLB* series: 1) the literature of a nation represents an inexhaustible resource of permanent worth; 2) the surest way to trace the outlines of literary history is by a comprehensive treatment of the lives and works of those who contributed to it; and 3) the greatest service the series can provide is to make literary achievement better understood and more accessible to students and the literate public, while serving the needs of scholars. In keeping with those principles, the *Yearbook* has been planned to augment *DLB* by reflecting the vitality of contemporary literature and summarizing current literary activity. The librarian, scholar, or student attempting to stay informed of literary developments is faced with an endless task. The purpose of *DLB Yearbook* is to serve these readers while at the same time enlarging the scope of *DLB*.

The format of the *Yearbook* has been modified with this volume. The book is now divided into two sections: articles about the past year's literary events or topics; and obituaries and tributes. The updates and new author entries previously included as supplements to published *DLB* volumes have been omitted. (These essays will appear in future *DLB* volumes.) However, the *Yearbook* has ex-panded its treatment of the year's literary activities. Included are articles commemorating the centenary of the births of Raymond Chandler, T. S. Eliot, and Eugene O'Neill, and extended discussions of the year's work in fiction, poetry, drama, and literary biography. The *Yearbook* continues two surveys begun last year, an overview of new literary journals, and an in-depth examination of the practice of book reviewing in America. In addition, the *Yearbook* features an article on the 1988 Nobel Prize in Literature, including Najīb Maḥfūẓ's Nobel lecture.

The death of a literary figure prompts an assessment of his achievements and reputation. The Obituaries section marks the passing of Raymond Carver, Charles E. Feinberg, Nancy Hale, and Marguerite Yourcenar.

Each *Yearbook* includes a list of literary prizes and awards, a necrology, and a checklist of books about literary history and biography published during the year.

From the outset, the *DLB* series has undertaken to compile literary history as it is revealed in the lives and works of authors. The *Yearbook* supports that commitment, providing a useful and necessary current record.

Acknowledgments

This book was produced by Bruccoli Clark Layman, Inc. Karen L. Rood is senior editor for the *Dictionary of Literary Biography* series.

Production coordinator is Kimberly Casey. Art supervisor is Susan Todd. Penney L. Haughton is responsible for layout and graphics. Copyediting supervisor is Joan M. Prince. Typesetting supervisor is Kathleen M. Flanagan. William Adams, Laura Ingram, and Michael D. Senecal are editorial associates. The production staff includes Brandy H. Barefoot, Rowena Betts, Charles D. Brower, Joseph M. Bruccoli, Amanda Caulley, Teresa Chaney, Patricia Coate, Mary Colborn, Sarah A. Estes, Cynthia Hallman, Judith K. Ingle, Kathy S. Merlette, Sheri Beckett Neal, and Virginia Smith. Jean W. Ross is permissions editor.

Walter W. Ross and Jennifer Toth did the library research with the assistance of the reference staff at the Thomas Cooper Library of the University of South Carolina: Daniel Boice, Cathy Eckman, Gary Geer, Cathie Gottlieb, David L. Haggard, Jens Holley, Dennis Isbell, Jackie Kinder, Marcia Martin, Jean Rhyne, Beverly Steele, Ellen Tillett, Carol Tobin, and Virginia Weathers.

Dictionary of Literary Biography
Yearbook: 1988

Dictionary of Literary Biography

The 1988 Nobel Prize in Literature
Najīb Maḥfūẓ

(11 December 1911-   )

Roger Allen
University of Pennsylvania

BOOKS: *Hams al-junūn* (Cairo: Maktabat Miṣr., 1939);

ʿ*Abath al-aqdār* (Cairo: Maktabat Miṣr., 1939);

Radūbīs (Cairo: Maktabat Miṣr., 1943);

Kifāḥ Ṭība (Cairo: Maktabat Miṣr., 1944);

Al-Qāhira al-jadīda (Cairo: Maktabat Miṣr., circa 1945);

Khān al-Khalīlī (Cairo: Maktabat Miṣr., circa 1946);

Zuqāq al-Midaqq (Cairo: Maktabat Miṣr., 1947); translated by Trevor Le Gassick as *Midaq Alley* (Beirut: Khayat, 1966; London: Heinemann Educational Books Ltd./Washington, D.C.: Three Continents Press, 1975);

Al-Sarāb (Cairo: Maktabat Miṣr., circa 1948);

Bidāya wa-nihāya (Cairo: Maktabat Miṣr., circa 1949); translated by Ramses Awad as *The Beginning and the End* (Cairo: American University in Cairo Press, 1985);

Bayn al-qaṣrayn (Cairo: Maktabat Miṣr., 1956);

Qaṣr al-shawq (Cairo: Maktabat Miṣr., 1957);

Al-Sukkariyya (Cairo: Maktabat Miṣr., 1957);

Al-Liṣṣ wa-al-kilāb (Cairo: Maktabat Miṣr., 1961); translated by Le Gassick and Mustafa Badawi as *The Thief and the Dogs* (Cairo: American University in Cairo Press, 1984);

Al-Summān wa-al-kharīf (Cairo: Maktabat Miṣr., 1962); translated by Roger Allen as *Autumn Quail* (Cairo: American University in Cairo Press, 1985);

Dunyā Allāh (Cairo: Maktabat Miṣr., 1962);

Al-Ṭarīq (Cairo: Maktabat Miṣr., 1964); translated by Mohamed Islam as *The Search* (Cairo: American University in Cairo Press, 1987);

Bayt sayyiʾ al-sumʿa (Cairo: Maktabat Miṣr., 1965);

Al-Shaḥḥādh (Cairo: Maktabat Miṣr., 1965); translated by Kristin Walker Henry as *The Beggar* (Cairo: American University in Cairo Press, 1986);

Tharthara fawq al-Nīl (Cairo: Maktabat Miṣr., 1966);

Awlād ḥāratinā, (Beirut: Dār al-Ādāb, 1967); translated by Philip Stewart as *Children of Gebelawi* (London: Heinemann Educational Books Ltd., 1981);

Mīrāmār (Cairo: Maktabat Miṣr., 1967); translated by Fatma Moussa-Mahmoud (London: Heinemann Educational Books Ltd., 1978);

Khamārat al-qiṭṭ al-aswad (Cairo: Maktabat Misr., 1969);

Taḥta al-maẓalla (Cairo: Maktabat Miṣr., 1969);

Ḥikāya bi-lā bidāya wa-lā-nihāya (Cairo: Maktabat Miṣr., 1971);

Shahr al-ʿasal (Cairo: Maktabat Miṣr., 1971);

Al-Marāyā (Cairo: Maktabat Miṣr., 1972); translated by Allen as *Mirrors* (Minneapolis: Bibliotheca Islamica, 1977);

Al-Ḥubb taḥta al-maṭar (Cairo: Maktabat Miṣr., 1973);

Al-Jarīma (Cairo: Maktabat Miṣr., 1973);

Al-Karnak (Cairo: Maktabat Miṣr., 1974); translated by Saad al-Gabalawy in *Three Contemporary Egyptian Novels,* edited by al-Gabalawy

(Fredericton, New Brunswick: York Press, 1984); translated by Allen as *Karnak Cafe* (forthcoming, 1989);

God's World, translated by Akef Abadir and Allen (Minneapolis: Bibliotheca Islamica, 1974)—comprises "God's World," "The Happy Man," "A Photograph," "An Extraordinary Official," "The Whisper of Madness," "Child's Paradise," "Shahrazad," "The Drug Addict and the Bomb," "The Singing Drunkard," "The Barman," "A Dream," "Passersby," "The Black Cat Tavern," "Under the Bus Shelter," "Sleep," "The Heart Doctor's Ghost," "The Window on the Thirty-Fifth Floor," "The Prisoner of War's Uniform," "An Unnerving Sound," and "The Wilderness";

Ḥikāyāt ḥaratinā (Cairo: Maktabat Miṣr., 1975); translated by Soad Sobhy, Essam Fattouh, and James Kenneson as *Fountain and Tomb* (Washington, D.C.: Three Continents Press, 1988);

Qalb al-layl (Cairo: Maktabat Miṣr., 1975);

Ḥaḍrat al-muhtaram (Cairo: Maktabat Miṣr., 1975); translated by Rasheed El-Enany as *Respected Sir* (London: Quartet Books, 1986);

Malḥamat al-Ḥarāfīsh (Cairo: Maktabat Miṣr., 1977);

Al-Ḥubb fawqa haḍbat al-haram (Cairo: Maktabat Miṣr., 1979);

Al-Shayṭān yaʿiẓ (Cairo: Maktabat Miṣr., 1979);

ʿAsr al-ḥubb (Cairo: Maktabat Miṣr., 1980);

Afrāḥ al-Qubba (Cairo: Maktabat Miṣr., 1981); translated by Olive Kenny as *Wedding Song* (Cairo: American University in Cairo Press, 1984);

Layālī alf layla (Cairo: Maktabat Miṣr., 1982);

Raʾaytu fī-mā yarā al-nāʾim (Cairo: Maktabat Miṣr., 1982);

Al-Bāqī min al-zaman sāʿa (Cairo: Maktabat Miṣr., 1982);

Amām al-ʿarsh (Cairo: Maktabat Miṣr., 1983);

Riḥlat ibn Faṭūma (Cairo: Maktabat Miṣr., 1983);

Al-Tanẓīm al-sirrī (Cairo: Maktabat Miṣr., 1984);

Al-ʿĀʾish fī al-ḥaqīqa (Cairo: Maktabat Miṣr., 1985);

Yawm qutila al-zaʿīm (Cairo: Maktabat Miṣr., 1985);

Ḥadīth al-ṣabāḥ wa-al-masāʾ (Cairo: Maktabat Miṣr., 1987);

Ṣabāḥ al-ward (Cairo: Maktabat Miṣr., 1987).

TRANSLATIONS OF SHORT STORIES: "The Mosque in the Narrow Lane" and "Hanzal and the Policeman," in *Arabic Writing Today: The Short Story*, edited by Mahmoud

Manzalaoui (Cairo: American Research Center in Egypt, 1968), pp. 117-136;

"The Tavern of the Black Cat," translated by A. F. Cassis, *Contemporary Literature in Translation*, 19 (Summer-Fall 1974): 5-8;

"Zaabalawi," translated by Denys Johnson-Davies, in *Modern Arabic Short Stories*, Arab Authors Series 3 (London: Heinemann Educational Books Ltd., 1974), pp. 137-147;

"The Conjurer Made Off with the Dish," translated by Johnson-Davies, in *Egyptian Short Stories*, Arab Authors Series 8 (London: Heinemann Educational Books Ltd., 1978), pp. 61-67;

"Investigation," translated by Roger Allen, *Edebiyat*, 3 (1978): 27-44;

"An Old Photograph," translated by Allen, *Nimrod*, 24 (Spring-Summer 1981): 91-100;

"A Man and a Shadow," "Under the Bus Shelter," and "The Time and the Place," in *Flights of Fantasy*, edited by Ceza Kassem and Malek Hashem (Cairo: Elias Publishing House, 1985), pp. 47-52, 91-98, 207-216;

"The Mummy Awakes," translated by Allen, in *The Worlds of Muslim Imagination*, edited by Alamgir Hashmi (Islamabad: Gulmohar, 1986), pp. 15-33, 212-215.

TRANSLATIONS OF PLAYS: *The Chase*, translated by Roger Allen, *Mundus Artium*, 10, no. 1 (1977): 134-162;

Harassment, translated by Judith Rosenhouse, *Journal of Arabic Literature*, 9 (1978): 105-137.

Najīb Maḥfūẓ (sometimes transliterated as Naguib Mahfouz) has brought the genre of the novel to a state of genuine maturity in the Arab world. With an educational background in philosophy, an intimate knowledge of the major cities of his homeland, a ready wit, and a carefully developed craft, he has devoted himself over the past four decades to the process of providing, through a succession of novels and short stories, a mirror of the concerns and aspirations of the Egyptian people and of the emerging nations of the Arab region in general. If the vicissitudes of politics, both international and regional, have occasionally brought with them campaigns of orchestrated opprobrium against Maḥfūẓ and his writings, they are quite incapable of diminishing either the nature of his literary achievement or the regard in which he is held by students of Arabic fiction. He has taken risks, both literary and po-

Najīb Maḥfūẓ (Fouad EL KOURI/SIPA PRESS)

litical, and he has worked with a concentration and consistency that no other Arab writer of fiction can match. In this regard he is a great pioneer. The award of the Nobel Prize in Literature is a recognition of his single-minded dedication to the fostering and expansion of a tradition of modern Arabic fiction, and as such, is an acknowledgement of the emergence of modern Arabic literature in general.

Maḥfūẓ was born on 11 December 1911 in one of the older quarters of Cairo near the Mosque of al-Ḥusayn. The narrator of *Al-Marāyā* (1972; translated as *Mirrors*, 1977) describes a childhood very similar to that of Maḥfūẓ himself: a family move from the Ḥusayn quarter to the more suburban ʿAbbāsiyya neighborhood, school days, and then a university degree in philosophy. Maḥfūẓ acknowledges that during this period he was greatly influenced by the writings of prominent Egyptian authors such as Ṭāhā Ḥusayn (1889-1973), ʿAbbās Maḥmūd al-ʿAqqād (1889-1964), Tawfīq al-Ḥakīm (1902?-1986), Yaḥyā Ḥaqqī (b. 1905), and Maḥmūd Taymūr (1894-1973). It was while still a student at the University of Cairo in the early 1930s that Maḥfūẓ began writing short stories, much encouraged in this endeavor by Salāma Mūsā (d. 1958), a Coptic socialist intellectual and editor of the magazine, *Al-Majalla al-Jadīda*. Many of these stories were to be gathered in the 1939 collection *Hams al-junūn* (Whisper of Madness). However, Maḥfūẓ's first published work was *Miṣr al-qadīma* (1932), a translation of James Balkie's *Ancient Egypt* (London, 1912).

It may have been this interest in the earliest history of his homeland that led Maḥfūẓ to plan a whole series of novels set in that period. However, such were the political and social circumstances of Egypt during World War II, when the European powers considered all agreements made with the nations of the Arab world since 1918 to be essentially on hold, that Maḥfūẓ turned his attention to the present. In the period between 1944 and the Egyptian revolution of 1952, Maḥfūẓ laid the foundations for a social-realist fiction in Arabic which was to provide writers of fiction in the postrevolutionary 1950s and 1960s with ready models for the genre. Beginning with *Al-Qāhira al-jadīda* (circa 1945) and culminating in the enormous, three-volume *Al-Thulāthiyya* (Trilogy, 1956-1957), Maḥfūẓ presents a series of portraits of families and communities from the middle and lower classes of Egyptian society struggling to climb the social ladder and even to survive while the country witnesses a period of domestic and international struggle and turmoil.

Following the publication of *Al-Thulāthiyya,* the award of the Egyptian State Prize for Literature to Maḥfūẓ in 1957 gave a tremendous boost to his reputation, and he has been regarded as the doyen of Arabic fiction since that period. However, following the 1952 revolution, Maḥfūẓ did not write any fiction for several years (*Al-Thulāthiyya* was actually completed in April of 1952 but not published until 1956-1957). Many critics have attributed this silence to a sense of unfamiliarity with the new political and societal situations resulting from such a profound change. While that may be at least partially the case, it is important to note that, until his retirement, Maḥfūẓ combined a writing career with the demands of a position within the Ministry of Culture, with special attention to the cinema. In fact the years from 1952 until 1959 were particularly full of activity involving the composition of scenarios for the burgeoning Egyptian film industry. When he did resume the writing of fiction, it was with a work first published in the Cairo newspaper *Al-Ahrām* in 1959, *Awlād ḥāratinā* (Children of Our Quarter, 1967; translated as *Children of Gebelawi,* 1981), which has acquired a great notoriety. Tracing mankind's religious heritage and the frequent recourse to violence, it strongly suggests that science has superseded religion. It is banned in Egypt and several other Arab nations.

In the 1960s Maḥfūẓ published a series of novels in which he portrays attitudes to the Egyptian revolution in what emerges as a crescendo of disillusion and dissatisfaction. A group of individuals within Egyptian society are shown to be lost, alienated, and often oppressed personally and politically. These feelings are expressed through a minimal sketching of background and a close penetration into the consciousness of the individual characters. In this manner Maḥūẓ makes use of all the narrative techniques available to modern novelists, most particularly the interior monologue and stream of consciousness. In *Al-Summān wa-al-kharīf* (The Quail and the Autumn, 1962; translated as *Autumn Quail,* 1985) a former civil servant fired for corruption has his rejectionist attitudes to new political and social realities finally jolted by the Tripartite Invasion of his homeland in 1956. If the disillusion is strongly heard in *Tharthara fawq al-Nīl* (Chatter on the Nile, 1966)

in the context of Egypt's cultural life, it is shown at its clearest within the microcosm of the Miramar Pension in Alexandria in *Mīrāmār* (1967; translated in 1978), where the suicide of Sirḥān, the rising star in the Arab Socialist Union, points out the corruption and atmosphere of terror which characterized this unfortunate era in modern Egyptian political life, one which was brought to an abrupt end by the June War of 1967, known in Arabic as *al-naksa* (the "setback").

Arab authors reacted to this tragedy in various ways, including anger, silence, and exile. Maḥfūẓ chose to express himself in a series of short stories which made their way into collections published in 1969 and 1971. These stories were extremely symbolic and often cyclical in nature. They all reflect the sense of questioning, challenge, and recrimination which were characteristic of this period. When, in 1972, he turned his attention to the longer form again, it was in *Al-Marāyā,* in which the narrator surveys through a retrospect on his own life and career the recent history of Egypt and its people in all walks of life. Many of the subjects of these vignettes comment with extreme frankness about politics, including the Egyptian revolution itself, international relations, and the continuing dilemma regarding the fate of the Palestinian people in their struggle with Israel. Maḥfūẓ continued his retrospective mode in an even more direct manner in another of his most notorious works (made into a highly successful film), *Al-Karnak* (1974; translated, 1984; translated again as *Karnak Cafe,* forthcoming), in which the major topic is the brutal way in which the secret police suppressed political debate during the 1960s. During this phase of his career (the early 1970s), Maḥfūẓ was not shy about expressing his extreme disquiet over the ever widening economic gap between the wealthy and the poor in his homeland. At one point, his views on the subject were apparently sufficient to lead the regime, in what was clearly an unwise gesture, to remove Maḥfūẓ from the rolls of the Writers' Union, thus officially preventing him from publication. Tawfīq al-Ḥakīm, the well-known Egyptian dramatist, Yūsuf Idrīs, arguably the finest writer of Arabic short stories, and Louis 'Awad, the literary critic, were dealt with in the same way. However, the counterproductive nature of this decision was soon realized, and the order was quickly rescinded.

Maḥfūẓ's most recent works have continued to reveal his abiding interest in the reflection of broad philosophical and sociopolitical issues, all within the context of the Egyptian society that he knows and describes with such sympathy and accuracy. Thus, *Ḥaḍrat al-muḥtaram* (1975; translated as *Respected Sir*, 1986) traces the cynical rise to authority of a civil servant whose whole life is spent on that very quest. *Afrāḥ al-Qubba* (1981; translated as *Wedding Song*, 1984) deals with the graft and corruption of the cinema industry through a multinarrator technique encountered (with greater sophistication) in the earlier *Mīrāmār*. While the role of Maḥfūẓ's earlier (pre-1967) novels in the development and fostering of the novelistic tradition in Arabic is clear and generally acknowledged, the place of the series of recent fictional works listed above will have to await the passage of time. Their significance as commentaries by a now world-famous *penseur* on continuing developments in Egyptian society (and especially changes in societal alignments brought about by the "opening up" [*infitah*] of economic markets) is undeniable. However, with the emergence of new generations of younger novelists throughout the Arab world, the assessment of his recent works relative to the larger perspective of Arabic fiction as a whole will need to avail itself of greater temporal distance than is currently possible.

Maḥfūẓ, who is married to ʿInayat Allah and has two daughters, has throughout his career been an extremely private and humble person. He continues to live in a relatively small apartment in ʿAgūza, a suburb on the West Bank of the Nile. Since his retirement from government service he has commuted regularly on Thursdays to the building of *Al-Ahrām*, to which he has contributed columns on a wide variety of subjects.

Throughout Maḥfūẓ's works his intense love for his homeland is obvious. In spite of his wide repute in the Arab world, he has rarely traveled outside his homeland (he did make a short official visit to Yugoslavia). When he does travel, it is to Alexandria (depicted in detail in some of his novels), where he spends the summer months. There, as in Cairo, he maintains a clearly defined schedule. In his writing, as in his civil service career, he has always been a meticulous planner. Such a methodology has also been forced on him to some degree not only by the conflicting demands of a bureaucratic position but also by an eye condition which makes it difficult for him to function in bright light. He prefers to write at certain hours of the day when the sunlight is not at its strongest; and, consequently, he spends much

Cover for an English-language translation of Maḥfūẓ's 1961 novel that marked a shift away from realistic fiction in its emphasis on symbolism and psychology

of his time in heavily shuttered rooms. He has always been particularly receptive to visits from Western scholars studying his works and regularly uses such occasions to turn questions from them concerning his works into sessions in which he is as much the questioner as the interviewee. On Thursday evenings such discussions can be continued at one of the cafés to which he regularly resorts for exchanges of views and good company.

Within the context of his native Egypt, Maḥfūẓ is a superb illustration of Lionel Trilling's phrase concerning the novel, that it is "an especially useful agent of the moral imagination." He has set out to describe the urban Egyptian society in which he himself has grown up and lived and to reflect the many crises and concerns which have characterized the era of massive social upheaval and change contemporaneous with his own writing career. Political freedom, religious and humanistic values, oppression and injustice, the search for consolation from life's pressures, these have been the recurring themes in his works, whether in the form of novels or short stories (and even more rarely, short plays). His literary style has shown distinct progressions, although they are not as abrupt as the writings of many critics would suggest. Clearly, his social-realist works of the 1940s and 1950s demanded a descriptive style which was both evocative and precise. More recently, a resort to a greater use of symbolism, something which may be seen as not only an artistic choice but also a means of conveying unpalatable messages in a way which may escape excessive scrutiny from the censors, has shown an anticipatable move away from "telling" towards "showing." Description has become more terse, economical, and symbolic. Dialogue in turn has become more prolific, laconic, and colorful. Many of his recent works not only reflect Maḥfūẓ's wit but also display a willingness to lend local color through the incorporation of words from the colloquial dialect into a narrative fabric which is otherwise a model of clear and precise modern Arabic literary style.

It was the publication of *Al-Thulāthiyya* that brought Maḥfūẓ to the attention of a broad reading public in the Arab world. This huge work of over fifteen hundred pages traces the dramatic changes in Egyptian life in the period between the two world wars as seen through the life and trials of the ʿAbd al-Jawwād family. Each of the three novels is set in a different quarter of the city which gives the individual volume its title: *Bayn al-qaṣrayn, Qaṣr al-shawq,* and *Al-Sukkariyya.* The first volume begins shortly before the end of World War I and introduces the reader to the members of the family. The father emerges as a complex and somewhat tyrannical personality, willing to confine his wife to the home while he philanders with a woman of low virtue. At the conclusion of the first volume, the eldest son of the family is killed in the rebellion of 1919. This brings to the foreground the second son, Kamāl. In the second volume, Kamāl goes to Teachers' College where he is introduced to Darwinism and other aspects of the modern scientific approach. There is a bitter clash with his father over the question of traditional beliefs and modern education. By the third volume, secular university education is available for members of the younger generation, and indeed the two sexes mingle freely within that context (a theme also referred to later in *Al-Marāyā*). Two grandsons of

the family reflect some of the divisions within the society at large which were to surface again in the wake of the 1952 revolution. One joins the Muslim Brethren, a fundamentalist religious group, while the other becomes a member of the Communist party. As the work concludes, both are in prison, a more than apt reflection of the political and social divisions which were to culminate in the Egyptian revolution itself. It is clearly impossible to do justice in a brief summarization to the detailed and intricate narrative web which Maḥfūẓ creates in this work. He apparently spent some five years researching the topic and in the process of writing. When the volumes were published in the early years after the revolution, the Egyptian people saw, probably for the first time in a work of Arabic fiction, a minutely detailed reflection of their recent political and social life, authentic not only in its portrayal of place and time but also in its depiction of trends and attitudes as reflected in the various members and generations of the ʿAbd al-Jawwād family. And, in that the 1950s were to see revolutions and processes of political and social change in other Arab countries as well, it is hardly surprising that *Al-Thulāthiyya* was read throughout the Arab world and acknowledged as a masterpiece of Arabic fiction. Even thirty years later it retains its immense popularity. A French translation is available, and an English one is in press.

If *Awlād ḥāratinā* gave the impression that Maḥfūẓ might be shifting away from some of the more traditional dictates of realistic fiction, then that was confirmed by his next work, *Al-Liṣṣ wa-al-kilāb* (1961; translated as *The Thief and the Dogs,* 1984), arguably his greatest work. The idea for the plot of this novel seems to have come from an actual series of events which occupied the newspaper columns for several weeks. A man emerges from prison bent on vengeance on his wife and her lover. By mistake he kills the wrong man and is hunted down by the police. In the process he becomes something of a popular hero, until he is finally hounded down and captured. This is also the fate of Saʿīd Mahrān, the main character in *Al-Liṣṣ wa-al-kilāb,* although Maḥfūẓ, with his usual skill, manages to incorporate within the framework of the narrative far more than a mere cops-and-robbers adventure. There are many interesting characters: the aged mystic Shaykh who had been a good friend of Saʿīd's father and whose comments provide a telling religious commentary on the events of the novel and, by implication, on what lies behind them; the prostitute, Nūr, who provides Saʿīd with his only refuge in his hour of greatest need and whose home looks out on the cemetery; and Ra'ūf ʿIlwān, the prominent journalist and former helper of Saʿīd, whose sudden rise to wealth and prominence stimulates Saʿīd's wrath against society and those who have tricked him. As noted above, the theme of exploitation and opportunism implicit in Maḥfūẓ's portrayal of Ra'ūf ʿIlwān was to recur in several of the novels which he wrote in the 1960s. A feature of this novel (and others which were to follow it) is an extreme economy in the depiction of place, at least by contrast with Al-Thulāthiyya, and a copious use of symbolism to convey atmosphere. Within such an environment there is a greater focus on the psychology of the principal character, a process which involves an increased use of interior monologue. The year 1961 marks the beginning of an unhappy period in modern Egyptian history: Syria seceded from the United Arab Republic, and a series of Draconian laws regarding personal rights and freedoms was introduced. Maḥfūẓ's novel caught the uncertain mood of the times with both accuracy and artistry. With its skillful control of narrative techniques it clearly ranks among his most distinguished contributions.

These techniques are employed to equal effect in Tharthara fawq al-Nīl (Chatter on the Nile, 1966). From the detailed and varied venues of Al-Thulāthiyya, via the more restricted scenes of Al-Liṣṣ wa-al-kilāb, readers are now introduced to a particular microcosm of the larger Egypt, a group of members of the cultural and intellectual elite who meet regularly on a houseboat. This group has given up all hope of working within the system. As a means of expressing their sense of alienation and in search of consolation, they resort to the houseboat of Anīs Zakī, an indolent civil servant given to drug-induced reveries and excursions into ancient history. Under the tutelage of Anīs's servant, an apparently timeless individual named ʿAbduh, who serves not only as imam at the local mosque but also as procurer for the group, they meet to talk about contemporary issues, to smoke hashish, and to engage in sex. This atmosphere of je m'en foutisme applies as much to the female as to the male participants in the nightly gathering. Even the arrival of a new participant, Sammāra Bahjat, a woman journalist who announces her intention of embarking on a study of the group, fails to stir them from their apathy. Indeed, she too is co-opted to the group. When they are all involved in a fatal traffic acci-

dent, it appears that Anīs Zakī has at last been shaken into action and a sense of responsibility, but, as ʿAbduh brings him a cup of laced coffee, the final conversation between Sammāra and Anīs is once again a model of total non-communication.

The sense of disillusion in this novel is almost complete. Bringing a large cast of characters together into a restricted space full of personal tensions, Maḥfūẓ manages to create a fictional world which, along with Mīrāmār, is a disarmingly accurate mirror of attitudes among Egyptian intellectuals immediately before the June War of 1967. While the two novels differ in both setting and narrative technique, each can reveal to the careful analyst Maḥfūẓ's anxieties about the course of development of the socialist revolution in his country, feelings which were soon to become more explicit.

The short story "Taḥta al-maẓalla" (1967; translated as "Under the Bus Shelter" in God's World, 1974) was one of a set of shorter works composed in the wake of the June War. It paints a surreal picture of a group of people waiting in a bus-shelter in the pouring rain. They watch in amazement as a whole series of illogical and inexplicable events take place: an insane car chase, people dancing naked and making love in the middle of the street, another group apparently making a film with a strange character who seems to serve as director. The group under the shelter keeps wondering, asking each other what is going on and who is in charge. But their sense of initiative stops there; no one goes beyond asking questions to the process of actually finding out. Eventually a policeman appears and asks for their identity cards; why, he wonders, are they holding a meeting? When they fail to respond, he shoots and kills them. Such apparently is the penalty for those who prefer merely to "stand and stare." This highly symbolic and often cryptic mode of story writing was used by Maḥfūẓ in a large outpouring of similar works, some of considerable length, in the late 1960s and early 1970s. With the passing of President Gamāl ʿAbd al-Nāṣir in 1970, many aspects of Egyptian society underwent considerable change during the presidency of Anwar al-Sādāt. The events of 1967 were, and have continued to be, topics for debate and discussion. Along with them now came a reconsideration of the events of ʿAbd al-Nāṣir's period in power and a fair amount of recrimination, both socially and politically. Al-Marāyā; Al-Ḥubb taḥta al-maṭar (Love in the Rain, 1973), with

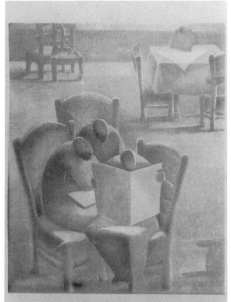

Covers for English-language translations of four of Maḥfūẓ's novels

its concern with the "phony war" at the Suez Canal preceding the 1973 conflict; and *Al-Karnak*, with its frank treatment of secret police violence, were all part of Maḥfūẓ's contribution to these debates.

During the last decade or so, Maḥfūẓ's works of fiction have concentrated to a large degree on issues particular to Egypt. Indeed, in the wake of the Camp David accords with Israel and Maḥfūẓ's guarded support of the direction in which they appear to lead, there have been those government officials and critics in other Arab countries who have initiated or advocated a ban on his works. However such gestures seem too readily prepared to ignore the major contribution which Maḥfūẓ has made to the entire tradition of modern Arabic fiction, and have thus not engendered wide support. Furthermore, such is the amorphous and generally chaotic situation regarding the distribution of books throughout the region that such attempts have been essentially futile in any case. During these years Maḥfūẓ has revived some of his former interests, as in *Malḥamat al-Ḥarāfīsh* (The Epic of the Gutter-Snipes, 1977), in which we see in more elongated form another saga about generations within a popular quarter and the succession of violence by which some semblance of "order" is maintained, an echo of not only *Awlād ḥāratinā* but also the later *Ḥikāyāt ḥāratinā* (Stories of Our Quarter, 1975; translated as *Fountain and Tomb*, 1988). In other works Mahfuz reflects the tendency of several contemporary novelists writing in Arabic by invoking the titles and techniques of earlier narrative collections. *Layālī alf layla* (Nights of the 1000 Nights, 1982), for example, devotes sections to characters from the famous medieval collection: Shahrayār, Qūt al-Qulūb (the beloved slave-girl of Hārūn al-Rashīd), the porter, and Maʿrūf the cobbler. The title *Riḥlat ibn Faṭūma* (The Journey of Ibn Fatūma, 1983) will inevitably bring to the mind of an Arabic reader the well-known geographical narrative of Ibn Baṭṭūta (d. 1377). While Maḥfūẓ continues to reflect in these and other recent works his own concerns and those of the Egyptian people, the local appeal has led to somewhat of a diminution of interest in his writings outside of his homeland.

Najīb Maḥfūẓ had developed his narrative craft at a particular point in the history of modern Arabic fiction so as to be poised to reflect in his writings the aspirations and frustrations of the Arab world during one of the most crucial and exciting periods in that troubled region's modern history. In a vast outpouring of painstakingly crafted fiction, he has reflected on the society that he knows best, the Egyptian bureaucratic middle class, in its encounter with crushing forces, both internal and external. He has insisted on acquainting himself with fictional trends throughout the world and on adjusting his own techniques accordingly. He has addressed, often at some risk to himself, the controversies of the day and many larger philosophical questions that beset modern man. In so doing, Mahfūz has pioneered the development of the modern Arabic novel and become its first genuine master. Political maneuvering aside, that is a verdict on which Arab and Western scholars are overwhelmingly in accord. That he is the first Arab winner of the Nobel Prize in Literature is thus a fitting and long-awaited tribute.

References:

Jareer Abu-Haydar, "*Awlad Haratina* by Najib Mahfūz: An Event in the Arab World," *Journal of Arabic Literature*, 26 (1985): 119-131;

Roger Allen, *The Arabic Novel: An Historical and Critical Introduction* (Syracuse: Syracuse University Press, 1982), pp. 55-62, 101-107;

Allen, " 'Mirrors' by Najib Mahfūz," *Muslim World* (April 1972): 115-125; (Jan. 1973): 15-27;

Allen, *Modern Arabic Literature* (New York: Ungar, 1987), pp. 192-204;

Allen, "Some Recent Works of Najib Mahfuz: A Critical Analysis," *Journal of the American Research Center in Egypt*, 14 (1977): 101-111;

J. Brugman, *An Introduction to the History of Modern Arabic Literature in Egypt* (Leiden: E. J. Brill, 1984): 293-306;

ʿAli Jad, *Form and Technique in the Egyptian Novel 1912-1971* (London: Ithaca, 1983);

H. Kilpatrick, *The Modern Egyptian Novel* (London: Ithaca, 1974), pp. 71-92, 94-113;

Trevor Le Gassick, "An Analysis of Al-Hubb Taht al-Matar (Love in the Rain), a novel by Najib Mahfuz," in *Studies in Modern Arabic Literature*, edited by R. C. Ostle (Warminster: Aris & Phillips, 1975), pp. 140-151;

Le Gassick, "The *Trilogy* of Najib Mahfuz," *Middle East Forum*, 39, no. 2 (1963): 31-34;

Mohamed Mahmoud, "The Unchanging Hero in a Changing World: Najib Mahfuz's *Al-Liss wa 'l-Kilab*," *Journal of Arabic Literature*, 15 (1984): 58-75;

Menahem Milson, "An Allegory on the Social and Cultural Crisis in Egypt," *International*

Journal of Middle East Studies, 3 (1972): 324-347;

Milson, "Nagib Mahfuz and the Quest for Meaning," *Arabica*, 17 (1970): 178-186;

Milson, "Reality, Allegory and Myth in the Work of Najib Mahfuz," *Asian and African Studies*, 11 (Autumn 1976): 157-179;

Fatma Moussa-Mahmoud, *The Arabic Novel in Egypt (1914-1970)* (Cairo: General Egyptian Book Organisation, 1973), pp. 47-54, 63-70;

Mattityahu Peled, *Religion My Own: The Literary Works of Najib Mahfuz* (New Brunswick & London: Transaction Books, 1984);

Donald M. Reid, "The 'Sleeping Philosopher' of Nagib Mahfuz's *Mirrors*," *Muslim World*, 74 (January 1984): 1-11;

Gretchen Ronnow, "The Oral vs. the Written: A Dialectic of Worldviews in Najib Mahfuz's *Children of Our Alley*," *Al-ʿArabiyya*, 17 (Spring-Autumn 1984): 87-118;

Hamdi Sakkut, *The Egyptian Novel and Its Main Trends From 1913-1952* (Cairo: American University in Cairo Press, 1971), pp. 72-76, 114-142;

Sakkut, "Najib Mahfuz's Short Stories," in *Studies in Modern Arabic Literature*, edited by R. C. Ostle (Warminster: Aris & Phillips, 1975), pp. 114-125;

Nur Sharif, *About Arabic Books* (Beirut: Beirut Arab University, 1970), pp. 74-81;

Sasson Somekh, *The Changing Rhythm: A Study of Najib Mahfuz's Novels* (Leiden: E. J. Brill, 1973);

Somekh, " 'Zaʿbalawi'--Author, Theme and Technique," *Journal of Arabic Literature*, 1 (1970): 24-35.

NOBEL LECTURE 1988

Najīb Maḥfūẓ

Translated from the Arabic
by Mohammed Salmawy

Ladies and Gentlemen:

To begin with I would like to thank the Swedish Academy and its Nobel committee for taking notice of my long and perseverant endeavours; and, I would like you to accept my talk with tolerance. For it comes in a language unknown to many of you. But it is the real winner of the prize. It is, therefore, meet that its melodies should float for the first time into your oasis of culture and civilization. I have great hopes that this will not be the last time either, and, that literary writers of my nation will have the pleasure to sit with full merit amongst your international writers who have spread the fragrance of joy and wisdom in this grief-ridden world of ours.

* * *

I was told by a foreign correspondent in Cairo that the moment my name was mentioned in connection with the prize silence fell, and many wondered who I was. Permit me, then, to present myself in as objective a manner as is humanly possible. I am the son of two civilizations that at a certain age in history have formed a happy marriage. The first of these, seven thousand years old, is the Pharaonic civilization; the second, one thousand four hundred years old, is the Islamic one. I am perhaps in no need to introduce to any of you either of the two, you being the elite, the learned ones. But there is no harm, in our present situation of acquaintance and communion, in a mere reminder.

As for Pharaonic civilization I will not talk of the conquests and the building of empires. This has become a worn out pride the mention of which modern conscience, thank God, feels uneasy about. Nor will I talk about how it was guided for the first time to the existence of God and its ushering in the dawn of human conscience. This is a long history and there is not one of you who is not acquainted with the prophet-king Akhenaton. I will not even speak of this civilization's achievements in art and literature, and its renowned miracles: the Pyramids and the Sphinx and Karnak. For he who has not had the chance to see these monuments has read about them and pondered over their forms.

Let me, then, introduce Pharaonic civilization with what seems like a story since my personal circumstances have ordained that I become a story-teller. Hear, then, this recorded historical incident: Old papyri relate that Pharaoh has learned of the existence of a sinful relation between some women of the harem and men of his court. It was expected that he should finish them off in accordance with the spirit of his time. But he, instead, called to his presence the choice of men of law and asked them to investigate what he has come to learn. He told them that he wanted the Truth so that he could pass his sentence with Justice.

This conduct, in my opinion, is greater than founding an empire or building the Pyramids. It is more telling of the superiority of that civilization than any riches or splendour. Gone now is that civilization—a mere story of the past. One day the great Pyramid will disappear too. But Truth and Justice will remain for as long as Mankind has a ruminative mind and a living conscience.

As for Islamic civilization I will not talk about its call for the establishment of a union between all Mankind under the guardianship of the Creator, based on freedom, equality and forgiveness. Nor will I talk about the greatness of its prophet. For among your thinkers there are those who regard him the greatest man in history. I will not talk of its conquests which have planted thousands of minarets calling for worship, devoutness and good throughout great expanses of land from the environs of India and China to the boundaries of France. Nor will I talk of the fraternity between religions and races that has been achieved in its embrace in a spirit of tolerance unknown to Mankind neither before nor since.

I will, instead, introduce that civilization in a moving dramatic situation summarizing one of its most conspicuous traits: In one victorious battle against Byzantium it has given back its prisoners of war in return for a number of books of the ancient Greek heritage in philosophy, medicine and mathematics. This is a testimony of value for the human spirit in its demand for knowledge, even though the demander was a believer in God and the demanded a fruit of a pagan civilization.

It was my fate, ladies and gentlemen, to be born in the lap of these two civilizations, and to absorb their milk, to feed on their literature and art. Then I drank the nectar of your rich and fascinating culture. From the inspiration of all this—as well as my own anxieties—words bedewed from me. These words had the fortune to merit the appreciation of your revered Academy which has crowned my endeavour with the great Nobel Prize. Thanks be to it in my name and the name of those great departed builders who have founded the two civilizations.

* * *

Ladies and Gentlemen:
You may be wondering: This man coming from the third world, how did he find the peace of mind to write stories? You are perfectly right. I come from a world labouring under the burden of debts whose paying back exposes it to starvation or very close to it. Some of its people perish in Asia from floods, others do so in Africa from famine. In South Africa millions have been undone with rejection and with deprivation of all human rights in the age of human rights, as though they were not counted among humans. In the West Bank and Gaza there are people who are lost in spite of the fact that they are living on their own land; land of their fathers, grandfathers and great grandfathers. They have risen to demand the first right secured by primitive Man; namely, that they should have their proper place recognized by others as their own. They were paid back for their brave and noble move—men, women, youth and children alike—by the breaking of bones, killing with bullets, destroying of houses and torture in prisons and camps. Surrounding them are 150 million Arabs following what is happening in anger and grief. This threatens the area with a disaster if it is not saved by the wisdom of those desirous of the just and comprehensive peace.

Yes, how did the man coming from the third world find the peace of mind to write stories? Fortunately, art is generous and sympathetic. In the same way that it dwells with the happy ones it does not desert the wretched. It offers both alike the convenient means for expressing what swells up in their bosom.

* * *

In this decisive moment in the history of civilization it is inconceivable and unacceptable that the moans of Mankind should die out in the void. There is no doubt that Mankind has at least come of age, and our era carries the expectations of *entente* between the superpowers. The human mind now assumes the task of eliminating all causes of destruction and annihilation. And just as scientists exert themselves to cleanse the environment of industrial pollution, intellectuals ought to exert themselves to cleanse humanity of moral pollution. It is both our right and duty to demand of the big leaders in the countries of civilization as well as their economists to affect a real leap that would place them into the focus of the age. In the olden times every leader worked for the good of his own nation alone. The others were considered adversaries, or subjects of exploitation. There was no regard to any value but that of superiority and personal glory. For the sake of this many morals, ideals and values were wasted; many unethical means were justified; many uncounted souls were made to perish. Lies, deceit, treachery, cruelty reigned as the signs of sagacity and the proof of greatness. Today this view needs to be changed from its very source. Today the greatness of a civilized leader ought to be measured by the universality of his vision and his sense of responsibility towards all human kind. The developed world and the third world are but one family. Each human being bears responsibility towards it by the degree of what he has obtained of knowledge, wisdom, and civilization. I would not be exceeding the limits of my duty if I told them in the name of the third world: Be not spectators to our miseries. You have to play therein a noble role befitting your status. From your position of superiority you are responsible for any misdirection of animal, or plant, to say nothing of Man, in any of the four corners of the world. We have had enough of words. Now is the time for action. It is time to end the age of brigands and usurers. We are in the age of leaders responsible for the whole globe. Save the enslaved in the African south! Save the famished in Africa! Save the Palestinians from the bullets and the torture! Nay, save the Israelis from profaning their great spiritual heritage! Save the ones in debt from the rigid laws of economy! Draw their attention to the fact that their responsibility to Mankind should precede their commitment to the laws of a science that Time has perhaps overtaken.

* * *

I beg your pardon, ladies and gentlemen, I feel I may have somewhat troubled your calm. But what do you expect from one coming from the third world? Is not every vessel coloured by what it contains? Besides, where can the moans of Mankind find a place to resound if not in your oasis of civilization planted by its great founder for the service of science, literature, and sublime human values? And as he did one day by consecrating his riches to the service of good, in the hope of obtaining forgiveness, we, children of the third world demand of the able ones, the civilized ones, to follow his example, to imbibe his conduct, to meditate upon his vision.

* * *

Ladies and Gentlemen:
In spite of all what goes on around us I am committed to optimism until the end. I do not say with Kant that Good will be victorious in the other world. Good is achieving victory every day. It may even be that Evil is weaker than we imagine. In front of us is an indelible proof: were it not for the fact that victory is always on the side of Good, hordes of wandering humans would not have been able in the face of beasts and insects, natural disasters, fear and egotism, to grow and multiply. They would not have been able to form nations, to excel in creativeness and invention, to conquer outer space, and to declare Human Rights. The truth of the matter is that Evil is a loud and boisterous debaucherer, and that Man remembers what hurts more than what pleases. Our great poet Abul-ᶜAlaa' Al-Ma'ari was right when he said:

> "A grief at the hour of death
> Is more than a hundred-fold
> Joy at the hour of birth."

I finally reiterate my thanks and ask your forgiveness.

The Year in the Novel

George Garrett
University of Virginia

Much that is today's news may not endure as history, but the news of the literary scene of 1988 concerned itself, as always, with various matters of commerce, the publishing business, with best-sellers and blockbusters, with prizes and awards, and with money—the amounts of money advanced to and earned by both popular and serious writers. The names of the writers of blockbusters were familiar enough: Danielle Steele, *Zoya* (Delacorte); Robert Ludlum, *The Icarus Agenda* (Random House); Jackie Collins, *Rock Star* (Simon and Schuster); Rosamunde Pilcher, *The Shell Seekers* (St. Martin's Press); Sidney Sheldon, *The Sands of Time* (Morrow); Judith Krantz, *Till We Meet Again* (Crown); Joan Collins, *Prime Time* (Simon and Schuster); Richard Bach, *One* (Morrow); and so forth and so on. Somewhat surprising was the continuing triumphant success of what *Newsweek*, in a cover story on Tom Clancy (8 August), dubbed as the "Techno-Thriller," manifest in Clancy's best-selling *The Cardinal of the Kremlin* (Putnam's) and Stephen Coonts's *Final Flight* (Doubleday). Almost astonishing, however, were the distinctly literary books, works of quality fiction which were to be found on the various best-seller lists. Tom Wolfe's *The Bonfire of the Vanities* (Farrar, Straus & Giroux) carried over for months into 1988 for a total of fifty-five weeks on the *New York Times* list, eight weeks as number one. Other best-selling fiction by serious artists included Larry McMurtry's *Anything for Billy* (Simon and Schuster); Anne Tyler's *Breathing Lessons* (Knopf); Gabriel García Márquez's *Love in the Time of Cholera* (Knopf); Elmore Leonard's *Freaky Deaky* (Arbor House); and Michael Chabon's first novel, *The Mysteries of Pittsburgh* (Morrow), which briefly made the lists. And by year's end Anne Rice's latest addition to her ongoing "Vampire Chronicles," *The Queen of the Damned* (Knopf), with the benefit of considerable publicity but with only mixed reviews at best, had found the top spot in the *Publishers Weekly* listing and sat near the top on the other lists. Likewise, at year's end many prizes were awarded and nominations for others announced. The Los Angeles

Dust jacket for the National Book Award-winning novel about the brutal killing of a young black girl by a white man and its effects on a small southern town

Times Book Prize for fiction went to García Márquez for *Love in the Time of Cholera*. The same novel was singled out as one of the two best novels of the year (the other was Anatoli Rybakov's *Children of the Arbat*, published by Little, Brown) from among the 210 books reviewed in the *Wall Street Journal* in 1988. Three novels were among the five works nominated by the National Book Critics Circle for the fiction prize: *Libra* (Viking) by Don DeLillo; *Wheat That Springeth Green* (Knopf) by J. F. Powers; and *Paris Trout* (Random House) by Pete Dexter. This latter, to the surprise of many, in competition with *Breathing Les-*

15

sons, Libra, Wheat That Springeth Green, and Mary McGarry Morris's first novel, *Vanished* (Viking), won the National Book Award. *Paris Trout,* third novel of the forty-three-year-old newspaperman Dexter, is based upon some actual events which occurred in Milledgeville, Georgia (called Cotton Point in the novel), in 1953. The novel deals with the killing by Paris Trout, a white store owner and moneylender, of a teenage black girl and with the trial and the troubles which followed. A strong, quick-moving, unflinching story line, well-turned sentences, and a fine authorial ear for southern speech made this novel stand out among its peers. Australian novelist Peter Carey won Britain's prestigious Booker Prize for 1988 for *Oscar & Lucinda,* published in the United States by Harper & Row. A complex love story set in England and Australia, involving the attempt to build a glass cathedral in the Australian outback, *Oscar & Lucinda* was described by the *Financial Times* as "a cunningly planned, picaresque history of eccentric nineteenth century people." Only a few of Naguib Mahfouz's forty novels have been published in America, but his publisher reported an immediate reaction to the news of his Nobel Prize. The *New York Times* (14 October) reported: "A spokeswoman for Columbia University Press said Mr. Mahfouz's books normally sold up to 200 copies a year. Yesterday alone, the press received orders for about 400 copies."

In the world of dollars and cents there was (public) good news and bad news for American authors. Romance writer Alexandra Ripley was widely reported to have received an advance of something in the neighborhood of $5 million for her forthcoming (1990) sequel to *Gone With the Wind.* Popular fiction writers Lawrence Sanders and Mary Higgins Clark received at auction $2.85 million and $10.1 million respectively for new works. Except for the numbers, which grow higher each year, there is no surprise there. And perhaps the surprise was minimal—though the accompanying national publicity was appropriately extravagant—that Tom Wolfe's *The Bonfire of the Vanities* brought $1.5 million for its paperback advance from Bantam in a spirited auction. For interviewers, Wolfe quoted an adage of Lord Jersey: "Contrary to what the Methodists tell us, money and success are good for the soul." Somewhat more likely to raise blasé eyebrows was the news that the highly regarded literary couple Louise Erdrich and Michael Dorris signed a contract with Harper & Row for an advance of $1.5 mil-

lion for the as-yet-unwritten novel "The Crown of Columbus." And if Simon and Schuster was willing to pay $511,500 for a first novel in the pop-fiction genre by a Honolulu housewife—*A Glimpse of Stocking* by Susan Rusch Libertson—it was breathtaking that Morrow would advance $155,000 for a highly literary novel by a very young author, a recent graduate of a creative writing program. But Michael Chabon's *The Mysteries of Pittsburgh* found itself a place on the best-seller lists, something more than *A Glimpse of Stocking* could manage.

As if to prove that secular justice is not wholly absent from the literary world and that Providence may be at least an efficacious possibility, Jay McInerney's latest contribution to literature, *Story of My Life* (Atlantic Monthly Press), in spite of massive promotion and publicity and Book-of-the-Month Club selection as an alternate, in spite of an initial printing of 103,000 copies, stumbled on its pretentions to popularity and never made any of the best-seller lists. Its reprint rights were sold to Vintage Books for its own original "floor bid"–defined by the *New York Times* as "the minimum guarantee established in advance of an auction which gives the floor holder the opportunity to top any higher offer"–when no other publishers bid. This bittersweet little story, told in first person by twenty-year-old Alison Poole, whose life is mainly concerned with money, cocaine, and sex, received mixed notices at best. Michiko Kakutani, in the *New York Times,* argued that the women in *Story of My Life* were "less like believable women than like a man's paranoid, cartoonlike idea of what such females might be." McInerney's first reaction (see the *Washington Post Book World,* 21 August, p. 15) was to shrug it off–"The only thing Americans like better than success is overturning a success." But by December, in an Associated Press interview story ("McInerney Disturbed By Acquisitive Morality"), he was presenting the novel as an important warning for the national future: "Why should we care about Alison? . . . I say it's because Alison and her cohorts are going to inherit the world." Readers of fiction seemed more concerned about those moneyed few, the ones Tom Wolfe named "masters of the universe," who had already inherited more than their fair share of the world. *Newsweek* (30 May), in "Billionaire Bashing," noted this literary phenomenon and cited the success of Dominick Dunne's *People Like Us* (Crown), a roman à clef in the manner of Wolfe's *The Bonfire of the Vanities,* "portraying the same status-crazed world of the super rich where tycoons vie for invitations to parties, fly their wives to Paris to buy the latest Lacroix fashions and spend $6 million on Monets because they view art as an extension of interior decoration."

Other topics which engaged the literary press included the battle of literary canons in the universities ("I would bet that *The Color Purple* is taught in more English courses than all of Shakespeare's plays combined"–Christopher Clausen); the rise of successful regional and local publishing, particularly in the South; and the continuing effort to ban books from public schools and libraries, an activity wherein, according to the *New York Times* News Service (4 September), the South is also firmly in the lead. There were "inside publishing" stories, dealing with prominent figures–for example Sonny Mehta of Knopf and Robert Gottlieb of the *New Yorker*. The *Boston Globe* ran a two-part series on Knopf editor Gordon Lish in March, "Treating writing like life and death," by Gail Caldwell. The outward and visible world of book publishing was at once more interesting and depressing. Rupert Murdoch absorbed Harper & Row into his multinational conglomerate. His rival, media baron Robert Maxwell, having failed to buy out Harcourt Brace Jovanovich, managed to swallow whole the Macmillan publishing units (including Charles Scribner's Sons). The *Wall Street Journal* devoted serious pieces to the business of bookselling, noting that "B. Dalton Plans/To Shut Out/Small Publishers" (22 April) and "Waldenbooks Peddles/Books a Bit Like Soap,/Transforming Market," (10 October). And the *New York Times* (8 June) quoted Laurence Kirshbaum of Warner Books, publisher of the best-selling eighty-five-page *Leadership Secrets of Attila the Hun* (by California psychologist Wess Roberts), who acknowledged the source of his inspiration to publish the Attila book: "Harry Hoffman, the head of Waldenbooks, is always saying we need more books that can be read in one night. This is one of them."

It is in this world, this arena, that the novelists of 1988 had to stand or fall. All things considered, it is remarkable how many excellent novels were published and found some shelf space in the bookstores.

It was a year in which some of our best-known and most respected novelists produced admirable work. Louis Auchincloss, who has emerged as one of our most productive professionals, presented *The Golden Calves* (Houghton Mifflin), portraying an intense power struggle set in the elegant confines of a small museum on Central Park West. Thomas Berger's *The Houseguest* (Little, Brown), a loosely allegorized novel, his fifteenth so far, somewhat in the manner of *Neighbors*, traces the enigmatic actions of Chuck Burgoyne, at once the ideal houseguest and a force for disorder and disaster.

"Hutch Montberg had heard a rumor that the meek might some day inherit the earth," writes Herbert Gold in *Dreaming* (Donald I. Fine). "Therefore he knew he'd really have to hustle to get his first." In part a kind of sequel, for its cast includes Suki Read, star of *A Girl of Forty* (1986), as well as others from that story, also set in contemporary San Francisco, *Dreaming* centers its story on con man Hutch and his decent brother, Dan, and concerns financial hanky-panky and loss. Another prolific professional, John Updike, gave us *S.*, an epistolary accounting of a mid-life adventure of Sarah Price Worth, a well-to-do Swampscott wife who follows an Indian mystic and guru, Shri Arhat Mandadali ("Art") to his ashram in Arizona. In this deftly satirical send-up (which managed to offend strait-laced feminists) Updike plays a game of allusions and parallels to Hawthorne's *The Scarlet Letter* and *The Blithedale Romance*. At seventy-one J. F. Powers published *Wheat That Springeth Green*, his first novel since *Morte D'Urban*, which won the National Book Award for 1962. Set in the late 1960s, *Wheat That Springeth Green* is the story of Father Joe Hacket, rector of the parish of Saints Francis and Clare. Hacket drinks, is often bored, and has serious baseball dreams. He meditates not upon texts, but on the imaginary fact that "he alone, with his knowledge of batters (encyclopedic), his stuff (world of), his control (phenomenal), had made the Twins a constant threat down the years. Forty-four now, ancient for baseball, he was perhaps best described as a short, fat, white Satchel Paige." But Father Joe is also clear enough in his belief that "the separation of Church and Dreck was a matter of life and death for the world." Thomas Flanagan's *The Tenants of Time* (Dutton), his first work since *The Year of the French* (1979), which won the National Book Critics Circle Award for fiction, is a huge (824 pages of small print) and magnificent achievement. Set chiefly in nineteenth-century Ireland, it is beautifully structured and offers, with a sure and certain authority, a rush of almost cinematic narrative. It could easily outlast most of the works mentioned here.

Louis Auchincloss, whose novel The Golden Calves *portrays a power struggle in a New York museum (© Arnold Newman)*

Another Irish-American, J. P. Donleavy, did not fare well with critics or readers with his latest, *Are You Listening Rabbi Löw* (Atlantic Monthly Press), his first novel in five years. This story of Franz Sigmund (Isadorable) Schultz, misogynistic producer (and a figure in other work by Donleavy), received the coup de grace from Michiko Kakutani in the *New York Times*, who argued that it "marks a new low on Mr. Donleavy's part: the raw energy and linguistic virtuosity that animated his earlier work have given way to an endless succession of tired sketches, and the humor, directed primarily against women and Jews this time, has taken on a disturbing and mean spirited edge." Alice Hoffman did not do much better with reviewers of *At Risk* (Putnam's), the story of a fifth-grade girl gymnast who contracts AIDS. Though it was sold to the Book-of-the-Month Club, had a first printing of one hundred thousand copies, and is scheduled to be filmed by 20th Century-Fox, it was taken to be (at best), in the words of Jonathan Yardley of the *Washington Post*, "a classic instance of good intentions and indifferent execution." Other critics, including Donna Rifkind in the *Wall Street Journal* and

Alan Cheuse on National Public Radio, were considerably less generous. Alice Adams's *Second Chances* (Knopf), dealing with a group of elderly people in northern California, was not well received either. Writing for the *Washington Post*, Barbara Williamson concluded: "Good breeding and politeness diminish Adams' insights and inhibit her characters' expressions of them." Alison Lurie's *The Truth About Lorin Jones* (Little, Brown) pleased some and annoyed others. The witty and satirical story of Polly Alter, thirty-nine-year-old art historian and feminist who is writing a biography of Lorin Jones, a painter who died in 1969, and how, in spite of her rigid preconceptions, she changes herself and her views of the life and art of Lorin Jones, confused some critics who wanted to know where, behind her seven veils of irony, the author stands on the political and social issues of feminism. Some were deeply irritated by Polly's apparent alternative. "She would become an angry, depressed feminist or a selfish, successful career woman."

For her new novel, *Silver* (Farrar, Straus & Giroux), Hilma Wolitzer returns to Paulie Flax and her husband, Howard, who were central to

In the Flesh (1977). They stumble through and manage to survive a major mid-life crisis. Wolitzer's twenty-nine-year-old daughter Meg Wolitzer produced her third novel, a comedy of contemporary manners entitled *This Is Your Life* (Crown), all about the lives of Erica and Opal, the two daughters of a famous and fat comedian named Dottie Engels. Spooky and dream-ridden and mysterious, Kathryn Davis's *Labrador* (Farrar, Straus & Giroux) is also about two sisters, Willie and Kitty Mowbrey, growing up in the mountains of New Hampshire. This first novel was highly praised.

Other novels, written by American novelists of earned distinction, were noteworthy additions to the literature of the year. Carolyn Chute continued her exploration of rural poverty and its human cost with *LeTourneau's Used Auto Parts* (Ticknor & Fields), a story set in Miracle City as well as Egypt, Maine, and featuring a one-man welfare system–Big Lucien LeTourneau. David Plante, in *The Native* (Atheneum), presented the latest addition to his sequence of novels about a French-Canadian family, the Francoeurs, this one chiefly concerned with college-age Antoinette. Mixed reviews greeted Candace Denning's second novel, *The Women in her Dreams* (North Point), which won the Virginia Award for Fiction while still in manuscript. Set in the late 1960s and told in brisk, minimal scenes, it deals with the problems of identical twins. Also granted a mixed reception by reviewers was Ann Hood's second novel, *Waiting to Vanish* (Bantam), following her successful debut with *Somewhere off the Coast of Maine* (1987). *Waiting to Vanish* follows a family brought to the edge of disintegration by a sudden, accidental death. Two novels which received laudatory notices were Tom Lorenz's *Serious Living* (Viking), which continued to examine the life of lower-middle-class Chicago, the world presented in his first novel, *Guys Like Us* (1980); and Richard Russo's *The Risk Pool* (Random House). Russo also follows up on his first novel, *Mohawk* (1986), setting his second in the same upstate New York town and this time moving closer to the autobiographical mode with the story of Ned Hall, who wants to leave Mohawk and become a writer. Other novels of good report this year include Monroe Engel's *Statutes of Limitations* (Knopf); *Of Such Small Differences* by Joanne Greenberg, author of *I Never Promised You a Rose Garden* (1964); Bette Pesetsky's *Midnight Sweets* (Atheneum), whose heroine, Theodora Wate, is an artist with cookies and runs a chain of cookie

boutiques; *Remembering* (North Point) by acclaimed poet and essayist Wendell Berry, described in the *Washington Post Book World* as "an almost perfect fiction, a sublime meditation on how irrevocable loss is redeemed through a renewed sense of kinship with the land and the past."

All past time is history and so, by the time it's published, any novel, except one set in the future, is in fact historical. Yet the genre itself persists, and writers work within its conventions or against them. There were excellent and various historical novels published in this year. Among successful examples of the more conventional execution of the form were Gillian Bradshaw's *Imperial Purple* (Houghton Mifflin), a novel of early Christianity and Byzantium; Joan Wolf's *The Road to Avalon* (New American Library), immersed in Arthurian myth and materials; *The Lords of Vaumartin* by Cecelia Holland, concerning Brittany and Paris in the fourteenth century; Robin McKinley's *The Outlaws of Sherwood* (Greenwillow Books)–Robin Hood and all that; a first novel by Heather Ingram, *The Dance of the Muses: A Novel on the Life of Pierre Ronsard* (Dufour); Jean Plaidy's *The Courts of Love* (Putnam's), the fifth novel in her Queens of England series, this one dealing with Eleanor of Acquitaine, mother of Richard the Lionhearted; Sharon Kay Penman's *Falls the Shadow* (Holt), an account of the life of Simon de Montfort and thirteenth-century England; and Diana L. Paxson's *The White Raven* (Morrow), a recapitulation of the post-Arthurian story of Tristan and Isolde, here known (more accurately) as Drustan and Esselite. Especially well written, with a thorough understanding of the period, is *Armada* (Viking) by Charles Gidley, a former officer of the Royal Navy. Intricately plotted, it is finest in its evocation of the details of sixteenth-century sailing and navigation. *New Yorker* writer Jane Smiley earned attention and encomiums for her large-scale version of the Vikings, isolated from Europe by the plague there and from the native Skraelings (Eskimos) by pride, as their five-hundred-year-old settlement of Greenland began to collapse; *The Greenlanders* (Knopf), richly decorated with lore, folktale, and saga, has as its central character the memorable Margret Asgeirdottir, an outcast survivor. Dorothy Dunnett, in *The Spring of the Ram* (Knopf), continues the series dealing with Renaissance banker Nicholas vander Poele of Burges, following him in this volume as he travels from Europe to Constantinople. Classicist Benita Kane Jaro undertook the tricky story of Gaius Valerius Catullus (83-53 B.C.), the great Roman lyric poet, in *The Key* (Dodd, Mead). Of her achievement critic Doris Grumbach wrote: "If there is to be a worthy successor to Mary Renault, or to Marguerite Yourcenar, it may be Benita Kane Jaro." Unconventional only in scope and ambition, James Michener, in the enormously popular *Alaska* (Random House), true to his own form, undertook to present the history, by fact and fiction, by lecture and dramatization, of the fiftieth state from geological prehistory ("About a billion years ago . . .") until almost the present. The story, as such, cranks up and chugs away with Peter the Great in the first quarter of the eighteenth century and eventually portrays more than one hundred characters, some "real" and some fictional.

Some writers elected to use the past in new or unusual ways. In *Subject to Change* (Farrar, Straus & Giroux), unpredictable Lois Gould, partly as satire and partly as mythmaking, tells of an imaginary kingdom in an imaginary Renaissance. It is mainly the tale of five characters—the King (Henry), his Queen (Catherine), his mistress (Diane), a magician (Cornelius), and a hunchbacked dwarf (Morgantina). There is much that seems magic, sophisticated superstition here and, as it happens, not a quotation mark in the book. Nobel Prize winner Isaac Bashevis Singer wrote in *The King of the Fields* (Farrar, Straus & Giroux) a dark and bloody imaginary history of his native Poland in pre-Christian days. The Poles, led by their king, Kirol Rudy, fight the native Lesniks, led by Cybulla, to the edge of extermination. Ben Dosa, a Jew, brings some sense of civilization even as he witnesses this precursor of the Holocaust. The materials bear out the secular conclusion of Cybulla: "All beliefs were lies. As long as men lived they should enjoy themselves as much as they could. A dead man was no better than a dead frog." Probably the most outrageous use (or misuse) of historical materials for purposes of fiction is to be found in Joseph Heller's *Picture This* (Putnam's), seriously described in the *New York Times* as "a book about the life of Rembrandt and the death of Socrates, the rise of the Netherlands and the fall of Athens" and described by the publisher as "a lighthearted, free-wheeling jaunt through 2500 years of Western civilization which concludes with the startling realization that not much really has changed in all that time." Beginning and ending with the Rembrandt painting of Aristotle contemplating the bust of Homer, it is a wild meditation spoken out loud by the narrator (Heller) which unequivocally and unexceptionally (given the evidence he chooses to give us) concludes, among other things: "You will learn nothing from history that can be applied, so don't kid yourself into thinking you can." Like most of Heller's work, this book is a unique blending of the farcical and the deadly serious.

American history, early and late, continues to fascinate first-rate writers and, it seems, readers also. Charles McCarry, former CIA officer, an editor of *National Geographic*, and the author of five excellent espionage novels, surprised a good many of his regular readers by producing a powerful historical adventure set in the days of the French and Indian Wars—*The Bride of the Wilderness* (New American Library). Intensely imagined, accurate, and honest in large and small details, steady in its requisite suspense, it is also, at times, simply inspired, as in this reaction of its English heroine, Fanny, to the wilderness beyond Boston: "We are at the edge of an enormous place, the largest, the emptiest place on earth and there is nothing in it but silence. It is to the ear what darkness is to the eye." There are a couple of good novels about the American Revolution. Robert H. Fowler's *Jerimiah Martin: A Revolutionary War Novel* (Dodd, Mead) is an undisguised thriller, following the life of a double agent and privateer who somehow manages to witness almost everything. *Redcoat* (Viking), by British writer Bernard Cornwell, makes more serious claims as literature, presenting the British point of view on the war within the framework of the 1777-1778 occupation of Philadelphia. The battlefield scenes are outstanding, gritty, and authentic, as we might expect from Cornwell's previous novels about the Napoleonic Wars. His chief fictional characters—Capt. Christopher Vane and Pvt. Sam Gilpin—are solidly realized and memorable. His portrait of the historical general Sir William Howe is unflattering and perhaps arguable. Another British novel set in American history, one which might even have succeeded had it either been a genuinely experimental narrative or, at best, a Monty Python parody, is Richard Adams's *Traveller* (Knopf), which tries to report the Civil War from the point of view and in the words of Robert E. Lee's famous horse. Adams is usually good with animals, at least in the English milieu. But here the language is clumsy and inauthentic, the history weak and largely outdated. Even the finest opportunities for comedy are lost.

Gabriel
García Márquez

Dust jacket for the English-language translation of García Márquez's 1985 novel written, according to Thomas Pynchon in the New York Times Book Review, *in a style of "maniacal serenity"*

William Kennedy, winner of the Pulitzer Prize and the National Book Critics Circle Award for *Ironweed* (1983), continued his exploration of his hometown, Albany, with what for many reviewers, pro and con, was a surprising direction in *Quinn's Book* (Viking). Told in first person by the orphan boy Daniel Quinn and covering the years 1849-1864, this picaresque tale seems to join together the hard edges and grit of Huck Finn with materials as theatrical, operatic, and fabulous as any Latin American master of "magic realism" could muster. Reviewers were divided between raves and critical assessments, but none denied it was a daring and original venture for one of our most highly regarded novelists.

Novels of the American West, most examples of what critic Michael J. Carroll called "the frontier novel" in the *Los Angeles Times Book Review*, continued to engage the American imagination. Larry McMurtry, who has written frequently about the modern West, but whose one

venture into history, *Lonesome Dove* (1985), won him a Pulitzer Prize, weighed in with *Anything for Billy*, a version of the life of Billy the Kid (1859-1881) as witnessed and told by one Benjamin J. Sippy, a dime novelist for the Wide Awake Library. Sippy follows the klutzy and dangerous outlaw as Billy pines for the female shootist Katie Garza and the English ice-maiden Cecily Snow, gunning down men, women, and children, even animals (as much by accident as anything else) until he, too, is left as another stiff, heels up, alive only in false myth and fading memory. In an interview (*New York Times*, 1 November) McMurtry has said, "I don't think these myths do justice to the richness of human possibility." And in the novel even Ben Sippy can see how things will go: "I suppose they'll argue it forever—or until all the black dirt of life finally washes off Billy and leaves him a pure, clean legend." In her third book, *Mamaw* (Viking), Susan Dodd tells, in a prose that is alive and lyrical, the story of Zerelda Samuel James, the mother of outlaws Frank and Jesse. Old pro Glendon Swarthout was represented by *The Homesman* (Weidenfeld & Nicolson), the story of a frontier woman, Mary Bee Cuddy, who, together with Briggs, an Indian fighter, must take four madwomen back east to Hebron and safety. Winifred Blevins builds *The Yellowstone* (Bantam) around the adventures of twenty-one-year-old trapper Robert Burns Maclean in 1841. Well and widely reviewed was Thomas Savage's thirteenth book, *The Corner of Rife and Pacific* (Morrow), which tells mainly of the Metlen family—John and Lizzie and their son Zack—of Grayling, Montana, beginning with the incorporation of the town in 1890 and ending with the election of Warren Harding to the presidency in 1920. An oddity among the year's westerns was *The Gunslinger* (Plume/New American Library) by the hugely successful Stephen King. This fragmentary work, about a gunfighter named Roland, was written (the author says) while he was still a college student. Often the prose gives this claim credibility: "Volcanoes blurted endless magma like giant pimples on some ugly adolescent's baseball head."

Although it is set, mainly, in April of 1980, Edward Abbey's large new novel, *The Fool's Progress: An Honest Novel* (Holt), is free-ranging in time and space and part of the western tradition. The protagonist, Henry Holyoak Lightcap, and his faithful, dying dog Solstice must travel back east on an old truck, armed with next to no money and an expired driver's license, from Tucson to Stump Creek, West Virginia. Lightcap is a wonderfully realized Abbey character, purely picaresque and learning by doing as he goes. The picture of life, as it is, in these United States is as idiosyncratic and memorable as the finest of Abbey's fiction.

Native Americans, past and present, are at the center of the current work by some of our best novelists. Probably most attention was paid, appropriately, to Louise Erdrich's third novel dealing with her own people, the North Dakota Chippewa. Covering the years 1912-1924, *Tracks* (Holt) is told by Nanapush, a tribal elder who has memories of the good days long gone, and Pauline Puyat, a troubled and confused and visionary Catholic. A good deal of the story is about Nanapush's adopted daughter, Fleur Pillager, a mystic who can at times cast magic spells. Various characters from the earlier *Love Medicine* (1984) reappear, and the prose has the singular lyric quality Erdrich has developed and explored. Another prominent novelist, Jim Harrison, concerns himself with the history of the Sioux in his latest, *Dalva* (Dutton/Seymour Lawrence). The macho Harrison surprised many by telling most of the story in the first-person voice of a forty-five-year-old woman, Dalva Northridge, who as a young woman in Nebraska had an affair with and a child by her Sioux half brother, Duane. Lee Lescaze, in the *Wall Street Journal,* accurately described the essence of Paul West's large and shaggy novel, *The Place in Flowers Where Pollen Rests* (Doubleday), as "a mixture of Hopi myth, porn film making, accidental killings, Vietnam combat, village idiots, idiot-savants, and long, long musings about life, art, the cosmos." Lest that should sound too action-packed, she adds that this story of two Hopi Indians, George and Oswald, is "an almost plotless tale of two men on a mesa musing on their lives and man's fate." West, whose earlier *Rat Man of Paris* (1986) received serious attention, continues to demonstrate an astonishing breadth and depth of imagination. Tony Hillerman, a genre writer of crime fiction who has, like Elmore Leonard, crossed over to be classified as a novelist without giving up the ways and means of his genre, produced his ninth mystery novel, *A Thief of Time* (Harper & Row), concerned with two Navajo detectives, Joe Leaphorn and Jim Chee, first introduced in *The Blessing Way* (1979). The new book appeared on several best-seller lists. Another tale of native American crime and punishment, though not, strictly speaking, a genre novel, was Craig

Strete's *Death in the Spirit House* (Doubleday). Perhaps, from the standpoint of authenticity, the most interesting fictional account of Indian life published in 1988 was Ella Cara Deloria's *Waterlily* (University of Nebraska Press). Written in the early 1940s by a full-blooded Sioux, *Waterlily* depicts life in the nineteenth century among the Sioux. *Publishers Weekly* identified it as "an authoritative, expertly researched account of Sioux beliefs, social conventions and ceremonies."

In a sense, stories which purport to depict the future, especially the near future, belong to the category of history also; they are quite as much period pieces as conventional historical fiction. Among these was Lucius Shepard's *Life During Wartime* (Bantam), picturing a future war in Guatemala in which both sides use psychics for intelligence. Here a couple of psychics, on opposite sides, fall in love. In *Kisses of the Enemy* (Farrar, Straus & Giroux) Australian novelist Rodney Hall creates a grim totalitarian future for an Australia secretly controlled by the CIA. Experimental novelist David Markson offers an even bleaker prospect in *Wittgenstein's Mistress* (Dalkey Archive), in which a woman named Kate, living at the Metropolitan Museum, is apparently the only inhabitant left on earth. Stephen Wright's second novel, *M31: A Family Romance* (Harmony), is contemporary yet points toward the future, telling of the strange lives of a midwestern couple, Dash and Dot, a husband-wife team of authors and lecturers who believe they are the descendants of aliens from the galaxy M31. They live in an abandoned church with a radar dish atop the steeple. There is a homemade spaceship and characters with names like Edsel and Trinity and Dallas. Wright has been compared with American cultural icon Thomas Pynchon.

Fairly recent history, often focusing on significant, discreet events and sometimes, true to the latest fashion, using "real" figures as fictional characters, was represented by a variety of novels. In part because this year was the twenty-fifth anniversary of the assassination of President Kennedy in Dallas, and in part because his last novel, *White Noise* (1985), received the American Book Award, Don DeLillo's ninth novel, *Libra* (Viking), earned extensive critical attention. It offers a massive, and speculative, study of the killing of the president, featuring Lee Harvey Oswald and including at least 125 characters, many of them historical. The facts are accurate and deftly assembled; the speculation—that it was a kind of CIA plot—

Dust jacket for the fictionalized account of the assassination of John F. Kennedy that portrays many historical figures, including Lee Harvey Oswald

remains precisely that. As DeLillo insists in his concluding author's note, it is a work of fiction, of imagination: "While drawing from the historical record, I've made no attempt to furnish factual answers to any questions raised by the assassination." Adroit, witty, satirical, David Slavitt's *Salazar Blinks* (Atheneum) introduces Carlos, a fictional Portuguese poet, to give some shape to the months in 1968 when dictator Antonio Salazar somehow governed his nation and empire in spite of a stroke which had left him speechless and immobile. It is a very funny book, but dark enough for our times as, for example, in these indisputable conclusions of Carlos: "There is no such thing as the dignity of the human condition. There is no such thing as an inalienable human right. There is only good fortune–the lucky chance that you are not at this moment being persecuted. That you and your people are not this week being done to death." South Carolinian

Ben Greer found a way to use a speaking and thinking Lyndon Johnson as a minor, but memorable, character in his large-scale fourth novel, *The Loss of Heaven* (Doubleday). Greer's story, set in 1964, concerns a powerful and successful family matriarch, seventy-year-old Harper Longstreet, and her four grandsons–Ford, a politician; Starkie, a military man; Wick, who is destined for the priesthood; and Blackie, a cat burglar. It is Greer's most ambitious and encompassing novel thus far in a productive career. Some other novels dealing directly and in detail with actual events of recent history and often with real figures of the time are *Mitla Pass* (Doubleday), by Leon Uris, which concerns the life of a writer much like Uris and is built upon the central event of an Israeli paratroop drop during the 1956 Sinai War (as to its literary *quality*, reviewer David Brooks spoke for many others when he wrote in the *Wall Street Journal:* "Perhaps never before has an accomplished author written a book this terrible . . ."); *The Pledge* (Houghton Mifflin), by old pro Howard Fast, who through fictional hero Bruce Bacon, a foreign correspondent, rehearses World War II and the McCarthy years; *Love in the Days of Rage* (Dutton), in which original beatnik, poet, and publisher Lawrence Ferlinghetti writes of the love affair of American painter Annie and French banker Julian, played out in the summer of the 1968 riots in Paris; and *Peking* (Little, Brown), in which British writer Anthony Grey uses as his protagonist the historical missionary Jakob Kellner, who made the Long March with the Chinese Communists in 1934-1935. Michael Kilian's *Dance on a Sinking Ship* (St. Martin's Press), set during an imaginary voyage of the Dutch liner *Wilhelmina* in 1935, probably set some kind of record for the number of "real" characters on the loose in a novel, including Edward VIII and Mrs. Simpson, the Mountbattens, and Charles Lindbergh.

Germany and real and imaginary Germans figure prominently in Jack Gerson's crime novel set in Berlin in 1934, *Death's Head Berlin* (St. Martin's Press). Douglas Unger, author of the highly respected *Leaving the Land* (1984) and *El Yanqui* (1986), presented *The Turkey War* (Harper & Row), set in the town of Nowell, South Dakota, and dealing with German prisoners of war and work at the Safebuy turkey plant. Twenty-three-year-old Paul Watkins caught the attention of many critics with his first novel, *Night Over Day Over Night* (Knopf), the first-person account by a young German narrator, Sebastian, of his life in the Waffen SS in 1944. Authentic in depth as well as in detail, and not violating the imagined limits of its strict point of view, this novel is so stunningly "real" as to seem clearly (and impossibly) autobiographical.

In fact, overt fun and games with autobiographical reality characterized several novels in 1988. With *Last Notes From Home* (Random House) Frederick Exley announced the completion of the trilogy which began with *A Fan's Notes* (1968) and included *Pages From a Cold Island* (1975). This volume, unlike the others, was announced and labeled as a novel. Partly (clearly) fantasy, particularly in its accounts of sexual obsessions and activities, the story also deals with the death of Exley's brother, Col. William R. Exley (1926-1973), and Exley's final visit with him to Hawaii. There are elaborately exaggerated characters, who may or may not have some basis in "reality," but who are plainly fictional in this context: O'Twoomey, the wild Irishman; his Samoan sidekick, Hannibal; Alissa, Exley's psychoanalyst and lover in Watertown, New York; and (above all) Robin Glenn, the incredible airline stewardess whom Exley marries. Considering the whole trilogy, one can see a steady movement for Exley to include more and more fantasy and interior life in his autobiography. Equally autobiographical in its details (if far less easy to read and follow, because of many quotations, its multiple typefaces, and a plethora of footnotes) is Jerzy Kosinski's *The Hermit of 69th Street: The Working Papers of Norbert Kosky* (Seaver/Holt). This complex and massive experimental work, Kosinski's first since the scandal created by the rumors that he had not, in fact, written his earlier novels, is dubbed an "autofiction," and in the Ruthenian writer, Norbert Kosky, he creates a character whose life closely approximates and parallels his own. Without using any of the self-reflexive, postmodern tricks favored by Kosinski, the severely disabled young Irish writer Christopher Nolan has used a somewhat similar device in *Under the Eye of the Clock: The Life Story of Christopher Nolan* (St. Martin's Press). Here, mainly for the sake of being able to write his own story from the slight distance of third-person narration, Nolan calls himself Joseph Meehan: "Baffled by beauty, slow to worry, able only to think, Joseph continued on his lively path through life." Philip Roth's *The Facts: A Novelist's Autobiography* (Farrar, Straus & Giroux) was published as nonfiction. Yet it begins with a letter to fictional character Nathan Zuckerman, protagonist of several Roth novels; and the

short book ends with a thirty-five-page letter from the fictional Zuckerman to Roth, reacting to the "facts" of Roth's book and urging him not to publish it, but to stick to fiction instead. Zuckerman also questions, in detail, the validity of the facts as Roth has presented them. It can be seriously argued that *The Facts* is as much a fiction as most of the novels Roth has written. Even writers not widely known and unable to depend on a public persona to compare to and contrast with a "real" self can create this eccentric postmodern tension by calling attention to likenesses and differences between the two. For example, William Wiser's *The Chile Tour* (Atheneum) tells the story of one Frank White, who assumes the identities of I. M. Gold and Mr. Buddy. The promotional material for the book informs us that like the fictional Frank White, Wiser, too, has not only been "a Navy seaman, a psychiatric-hospital attendant, a writer-in-residence and a hotel bellboy, but he is also accustomed to feeling like an imposter." Another example of this explicitly autobiographical genre is Jan Kerouac's *Trainsong* (Holt). Daughter of Jack Kerouac, she began her story with *Baby Driver* (1981) and seems likely to continue in that mode in the future. A sure sign of the power of this fashion in the creating of public and private self has been the insistence on the part of certain writers that their latest novels are, to some degree, to be *taken* as autobiography. Larry Woiwode's new novel, *Born Brothers* (Farrar, Straus & Giroux), a sequel to his highly praised *Beyond the Bedroom Wall* (1975), continues the story of the Catholic Neumiller family, concentrating especially on the three brothers–Tim, Jerome, and Charles. Interviewed by Mervyn Rothstein of the *New York Times* (5 September), Woiwode flatly declared: "*Born Brothers* is about as autobiographical as I'd ever care to be." Joseph McElroy brought up the subject (in the best advertising/political manner) as it relates to his new book, *The Letter Left To Me* (Knopf). This little story of a letter left as a legacy by a dead father to his fifteen-year-old son, McElroy's most accessible novel to date, has been given more authenticity and plausibility by hints (which McElroy refuses to discuss or elaborate in public) that it is deeply, privately autobiographical. And, as a final example of the power of fashion, consider that past master of public relations, Jay McInerney, quoted in the *Washington Post,* felt it necessary to defend his use of a young woman as the narrative voice and point of view of *Story of My Life* by asserting that his other two novels were patently autobiographical. "I felt for the moment I had exhausted my interest in characters who were stand ins for me." The weakness of McInerney's fiction is suggested in that remark. Absent is any notion of either the exhaustion or ennui of an imaginary reader.

The autobiography of a whole historical period is the ambitious and experimental goal of Geoffrey O'Brien's *Dream Time: Chapters From the Sixties* (Viking). Described by the publisher, with sufficient candor as to be mildly confusing, as "part fiction, part memoir, part cultural criticism, part prose montage," *Dream Time* has stories, fables, essays, and meditations, adding up to an implied narrator and, by inference, the history of himself in his own time. The publisher claims that "*Dream Time* is a brilliant work of cultural archeology that puts its readers deep within the sensibility of the sixties." Fair warning to those readers for whom the real, lived experience of the sixties was enough. And cold comfort to the humble and the lucky who may have lived through the era without giving it much notice.

Out of that period the Vietnam War continues, in various ways and guises, to be the subject of American fiction. Jessica Auerbach's *Painting On Glass* (Norton) is the bittersweet account of the off-again, on-again love affair of a young woman and a man who flees to Canada rather than serve in Vietnam. Paul Hoover's first novel, *Saigon, Illinois* (Vintage), is the story of a conscientious objector doing his alternative service in Chicago in the 1960s. Tim Mahoney's *We're Not Here* (Delta) tells of Bill Lemmen, a career buck sergeant who loves the land ("God Almighty, this is the nicest place I've ever seen") and the people of Vietnam, especially his woman, Hoa Muon, and an orphan boy, Van. It works backward from the present with Lemmen trying to find his people again, now in San Francisco. The recapitulation and reshaping of the 1960s has not, yet, done away with the Vietnam combat novel. One of the well-received examples of that genre was *Knives in the Night* (Ivy Books), by David Sherman, first volume in an announced series dealing with Combined Action Platoon Tango Niner located in Bun Hov village. Reviewing the novel for the *Washington Times*, Dan Cragg called it "good, solid, old-fashioned combat fiction by a talented newcomer, based on the true story of some of the bravest and most resourceful young men America ever sent to war."

Two other worthy military novels, neither set in Vietnam nor the 1960s, were Anthony Price's *A New Kind of War* (Mysterious Press) and Philip F. O'Connor's *Defending Civilization* (Weidenfeld & Nicolson). O'Connor's story is set in England at the American base at Greenham Common in 1955 and told in the first person by young 2d Lt. Thomas V. Hanlon. It is a pertinent cold-war story, primarily concerned with the cover-up of the serious defects of the Skysweeper antiaircraft gun. Price's novel is a British army story, beginning in Greece, then moving to cover three days near the ancient Roman frontier in the Teutoborg Forest as World War II comes to an end. David Audley and Sir Frederick Clinton, introduced in earlier Price books, are present, but the central character is Captain Fattorini, the new man in Special Unit TRR-2.

The crime and suspense novel, in its various contemporary forms, from whodunit to psychological thriller, has simultaneously become increasingly popular and a strong current of mainstream fiction. Many bookstores now shelve the better-known suspense novelists in both the "crime" and "new fiction" sections. Two working writers who have had something to do with that change of status are George V. Higgins and Elmore Leonard, both represented with first-rate books this year. Higgins gives us *Wonderful Years, Wonderful Years* (Holt), his seventeenth book since *The Friends of Eddie Coyle* (1973). This one is lean and quick, swiftly paced, and presents a whole catalog of Higgins characters–crooked politicians, grubby lawyers, sleazy contractors, a covey of interesting women, and an ex-con chauffeur named Bucky Arbuckle, a simple man of great courage and loyalty who is worth reading about and remembering. Elmore Leonard creates memorable and worthwhile characters, too, moving amid a nest of vipers. And in *Freaky Deaky* he brings forward Chris Mankowski, Detroit police detective, formerly of the bomb squad, now of the Sex Crimes Division. The good guys triumph, in spite of elaborate and intricate plotting by the bad ones; and Mankowski, best of show, gives new meaning to the epithet "explosive climax." Some others who have written themselves out of the crime corner include Ruth Rendell, whose *The Veiled One* (Pantheon) puts Chief Inspector Reginald Wexford into his fourteenth novel, though Wexford is in the hospital for a good part of this one, leaving Mike Burden to follow the case; Richard Condon, whose *Prizzi's Glory* (Dutton) carries his well-known crime family into the midst of a Mafia plot to capture the presidency in 1992; and Robert B. Parker, whose *Crimson Joy* (Delacorte) continues the story of the private eye he created, Spenser. Parker, faced with more than usual success, could have been speaking for others when he recently allowed: "Being a celebrity writer is not so intrusive that you can't stand it."

Evidence of the dignified status of the genre is to be found in work by "serious" novelists who have elected to try their luck with the suspense novel. Former Jesuit, now director of the creative writing program at Stanford, John L'Heureux entered the lists with *A Woman Run Mad* (Viking). Well-written, neatly plotted, and elegantly executed, its central failure, noted by some critics, is the absence of any character worth really worrying over or caring about. This one may, indeed, all things considered, win the maximum blurb prize for 1988: Carolyn See's description–"A cross between a Henry James novel and the Texas chain saw massacre"–may be definitive. Less literary, pop writer Edward Stewart's *Privileged Lives* (Delacorte) attempts to cash in on the New York chic scene so effectively exploited by Tom Wolfe, Dominick Dunne, and Truman Capote. That part may be, at its best, expendable; but New York City detective Lt. Vince Cardozo is worth the price of admission. Another New York suspense story, this one more attentive to the downside of life in downtown Manhattan, is Andrew Vachss's *Blue Belle* (Knopf), his third novel featuring the rough-and-ready, street-smart Burke.

Finally, as the genre is more and more developed and refined, pressure is on writers who wish to stand out among the herd to create unusual detectives. Two of the odder entries of 1988 are the lesbian detective in Sarah Schulman's *After Delores* (Dutton) and Zeke Gahagan, the eighty-one-year-old private eye, riddled by bad digestion, arthritic joints, and fading sensory perception, in Vincent McConnor's *The Man Who Knew Hammett* (TOR).

For black American writers the example of Toni Morrison's *Beloved* (1987) must have been encouraging; *Beloved* sat firmly in place on the hardcover best-seller lists for half a year, well into the spring of 1988. In the meantime impressive new works appeared. Gloria Naylor, whose novel *The Women of Brewster Place* won the American Book Award for first fiction in 1983, brought out her third novel, *Mama Day* (Ticknor & Fields). Naylor, who grew up in New York City, here returns to her southern roots as she creates the story of Miranda Day, the matriarch of the sea island community of Willow Springs. Mama Day,

motivated by "pure devilment and curiosity," fights the powers of darkness and twentieth-century development with herbal medicine and magic in a story so rich with folktale and the fabulous that it could accurately be called "down-home magic realism." Poet and screenwriter Al Young is represented by his fifth novel, and his first in eight years, *Seduction by Light* (Seymour Lawrence/Dell). There appears here also a formidable matriarchal figure, the first-person vernacular narrator Mamie Franklin, former movie actress and now a housekeeper in California. Aptly described by its publisher as "this most contemporary metaphysical comedy," the book is perhaps most notable for its triumphant narrator, of whom Ishmael Reed predicts: "She will become one of the most memorable characters in American fiction." The admirable matriarch also figures as the central character and first-person narrator in Clarence Major's sixth novel, *Such Was the Season* (Mercury House). Here Annie Eliza, reigning sovereign of a black Atlanta family, has the first words and the last and in between tells many a tall (some of them very "postmodern") tale. Majors used to write self-reflexive, postmodern fiction. Now he has an outstanding fictional character who does it for him. Thunder's Mouth is a small press, heavily subsidized by the National Endowment for the Arts and devoted to publishing black and politically activist literature. Cyrus Colter's fifth novel, *A Chocolate Soldier*, is built around the characters of black clergyman Meshach Barry and his friend and sometime rival, the martyred Cager Lee. It surprises by presenting these characters with the ambiguity and mixture which makes them human and dimensional as well as representative social figures. Near the end of 1988 a new black writer, still in his early twenties, appeared with a book which caught the attention of many in the jaded literary world. Trey Ellis, in *Platitudes* (Vintage), offers up a relentless and relentlessly funny satire, a send-up based on the stereotypes and clichés of contemporary American black fiction, especially (and most dangerously) the funky group-think of radical feminism. Postmodern to the hilt, he has two people trying to tell the story of Earle Tyner, a middle-class black teenager. One version is by Dewayne Wellington, a nerd who depicts Earle as a preppy and a nerd, and the other by Isshee Ayam, black feminist and the author of such works as *Hog Jowl Junction*, who gives the story a rural setting and a mythopoeic structure and a vernacular lingo never heard yet by man or beast outside the covers of certain black American novels. Ellis may yet end up in trouble, but meanwhile he has appeared on the scene more like a gust than a breath of fresh air.

The South produced a full share, and then some, of the novels of the year. Novelists of all ages and at all stages of their literary careers were well represented. Among the more prominent novelists were Reynolds Price, Bobbie Ann Mason, Lee Smith, Anne Tyler, Rita Mae Brown, Harry Crews, and Ellen Douglas. Price, who has enjoyed a period of intense productivity during recent times, offered in his seventh novel, *Good Hearts* (Atheneum), a surprising and satisfying sequel to his first novel, *A Long and Happy Life* (1962), bringing the life and the love affair of Rosacoke (Mustian) and Wesley Beavers up to date. Rosa and Wesley have been married more than a quarter century (Rosa is a secretary and Wesley is a mechanic) when their enduring relationship suffers a major crisis. Told in varied narration, both omniscient and first person, *Good Hearts* moves through crisis to an appropriate happy and forgiving ending. Even a rapist, Waverly Wilbanks, who doesn't *mean* any harm, is forgiven. Bobbie Ann Mason's *Spence + Lila* (Harper & Row) also deals with a marriage of long standing, forty years, under terrible stress. Lila Culpepper is in the hospital in Paducah for cancer surgery. Mason uses an alternating third-person point of view—Lila in the hospital faced with the strange and extreme procedures of modern medicine; Spence driving to and from their farm, rehearsing their life together. *Spence + Lila* indulges in a happy ending, too, ending with Lila back home, having survived the worst and changed for the better, her face "dancing like pond water in the rain, all unsettled and stirring with aroused possibility." Lee Smith's eighth book, *Fair and Tender Ladies* (Putnam's), following the critically praised *Oral History* (1983) and *Family Linen* (1985), is an epistolary novel. The narrator/author is Ivy Rowe, who begins writing as a child close to the turn of the century and finishes with letters from the mid 1970s. In scope and authenticity this is Smith's most thorough evocation of the Appalachian land and life of southwest Virginia. Anne Tyler's eleventh novel, *Breathing Lessons* (Knopf), is another story of a long marriage (twenty-eight years) that gathers strength from stress and energy from awakened memory. Here we go with Maggie and Ira Moran during a single summer day, to and from the funeral of an old friend at Deer Lick, Pennsyl-

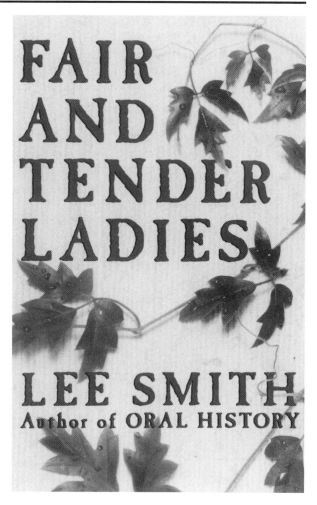

Dust jacket for an epistolary account of life in twentieth-century Appalachia

vania. Rita Mae Brown's *Bingo* (Bantam) returns to Runnymede, Maryland, and to the Hunsenmeir sisters, Julia and Louise, who first appeared in Brown's *Six of One* (1978). The sisters, both in their eighties, are rivals for the affections of Ed Tutweiler, youngish in his seventies. A strong subplot involves Julia's lesbian daughter, Nicole. The indefatigable Harry Crews presented another volume in his singular version of redneck japes and pasquils, this one, *The Knockout Artist* (Harper & Row), being the story (a myth aslant, a metaphor looking for a home) of Eugene Talmedge Biggs, a heavyweight fighter out of rural Georgia cursed with a glass jaw. In New Orleans Biggs turns weakness into strength and show business by knocking himself out for money. Ellen Douglas (pen name for Josephine Haxton), in *Can't Quit You, Baby* (Atheneum), her sixth novel, tells the story of the complex relationship between two story-telling women, Cornelia, a rich white lady, and her black servant, Tweet. Other novels in the southern tradition included *Peachtree Road* (Harper & Row), written by Anne Rivers Siddons at the urging of Pat Conroy and depicting four generations of Atlanta's elite; *Pit Bull* (Weidenfeld & Nicolson), by Scott Ely, the story of Jack Porse and his father, Dexter, and, most interestingly, of Alligator, the most ferocious pit bull in the Mississippi Delta; *Gone The Sun* (Doubleday), by Winston Groom, a New South story of one Beau Gunn, successful playwright and journalist who goes home to run the *Bienville Courier-Democrat*; *The Preacher's Boy* (Algonquin), Terry Pringle's second novel, the story of Michael Page, only son of the Baptist preacher in a small Texas town; *The Horse Hunters* (Random House), by Robert Newton Peck, a tale of hunting the mythical white stallion in the unspoiled central Florida days of the Depression; *Pay the Piper* (Dutton), Joan Williams's fifth novel, a story of a woman's passion and disappointment, set in the 1940s; *Breaking Gentle* (Viking), fifth novel of Beverly Lowry, telling of a family of four; *Alice* (St. Martin's Press), by Sara Flanigan, concerning the treatment of a deaf epileptic girl in rural Georgia fifty years ago as seen and told by young Ellie Perkins and her older brother Sammy; and *The Lively Lives of Crispin Mobey* (Atheneum), by Gabriel Quyth (pseudonym), an epistolary novel about a missionary sent forth by the Southern Primitive Protestant Church of Abysmuth, Mississippi. The South can also boast these days of its very own postmodernists, represented this year by Frederick Barthelme's *Two Against One* (Weidenfeld & Nicolson), another story of a marriage (fifteen years) which probably ought not to survive, but somehow does, in a yuppie-ridden world of clothes and brand names and clumsy sex. These southerners are not victims of their pasts. As protagonist Edward Lasco puts it, "The minute we got married, I forgot everything that happened before that." In contrast, *New Yorker* writer John Gardiner's *In the Heart of the Whole World* (Knopf), set in New South northern Virginia, though it deals with sex and violence, is a quiet and forgiving book. New South and Old are nicely assimilated in Clyde Edgerton's highly praised *The Floatplane Notebooks* (Algonquin), a cheerful, story-rich recounting of several generations of the Copelands of Listre, North Carolina.

An oddity of the year in publishing, one which did not escape the notice of alert critics, was the appearance in fiction of the new, post-

Dust jacket for poet Margaret Diehl's first novel, which portrays a postfeminist heroine who in the end settles for love and monogamy

feminist heroine who is as sexually predatory as any male. In the hip milieu of *Vanity Fair* James Wolcott described the genre as "by, for, and about good girls who want to be bad–literature's answer to *Dirty Dancing*." Several first novels are exemplary. Poet Margaret Diehl's *Men* recounts the adventures, affairs, and one-night stands of young Stella James, who has what is depicted as a very good time until, at the end, she weakens, falls in love, and settles for monogamy. Cynthia Crossen, in the *Wall Street Journal*, cheerfully opined: "It must be a commentary on something that when our heroine falls in love, this book starts getting boring." Carole Mallory's *Flash* (Poseidon) is the story of Mayan Endicott, an X-rated film star who, by roundabout means, becomes a dedicated feminist. Considerable critical attention was lavished upon *Velocity* (Random House) by Kristin McCloy, which, told in the first person by Ellie, combines a story of grief (the death of her mother) and passionate sex with Jesse, described by the publisher as "a Harley-driving half-Cherokee and sometime Hell's Angel, who lives purely and dangerously in the present." It is set in rural North Carolina. Also southern in context and attitudes, though no first novel, is Ellen Gilchrist's *The Anna Papers* (Little, Brown), which, following the life and the death of a prominent southern novelist, Anna Hand, has as much sex, albeit much of it middle-aged, as any of Gilchrist's younger competitors can imagine. More in line with the older ways, though thoroughly cognizant of the complex, free-floating manners (and the lack thereof) of our own age, is Don Hendrie's third novel, *A Survey of the Atlantic Beaches* (Crown), tracing the adventures, many of them sexual, of Devereux Hoopes as he spends the summer traveling down the seaboard from Massachusetts to Florida.

The British have not only continued to buy and develop American publishing companies, but also, in recent years, there has been a renaissance of sorts in British fiction, leading to the regular publication in America of more and more British novels. Some, this year, are old-timers in our literary scene. Graham Greene, now in his eighty-fifth year, shows no signs of slowing down, except when measured against his own prolific standards. His *The Captain and the Enemy* (Viking) is a brief and complex novel with various forms of betrayal as its theme, beginning in misty England in 1957 and ending in turbulent Panama in 1977, a month before the signing of the Canal Zone Treaty. Iris Murdoch's latest is *The Book of Brotherhood* (Viking), all about a close circle of friends in Oxford, held together by fascination with Marxist philosopher David Crimmond. *A Far Cry From Kensington* (Houghton Mifflin), Muriel Spark's eighteenth novel, is a brief (189 pages) excursion in the shabby London literary and publishing world immediately following World War II. John Mortimer's *Summer's Lease* (Viking) is about an eccentric English family during a month's holiday in Italy; while Alan Sillitoe's latest, *Out of the Whirlpool* (Harper & Row), is set in the grimy world of working-class Nottingham. Edna O'Brien's *The High Road* (Farrar, Straus & Giroux), her first novel in more than a decade, places its alienated heroine, Anna, together with other British and Irish women and the Irish poet David Anthony Ignatius Donne in an unnamed Mediterranean resort. Author of the earlier success, *The Shooting Party*, Isabel Colegate, in *Deceits*

of Time (Viking), builds her story around Catherine Hilery, a biographer who (as in Alison Lurrie's *Lorin Jones*) discovers more than she is prepared for in pursuing her subject. Anita Brookner's subtle *A Friend From England* (Pantheon), the story of Rachel Kennedy, who works in a London bookshop, and her friends, the Livingstones and their daughter, Heather, seems to have puzzled reviewers here and earned a somewhat less enthusiastic public response than her earlier works received. Faye Weldon published two books in America during the year–*The Heart of the Country* (Viking) and *The Hearts and Lives of Men* (Viking)–and was given a full-scale critical appreciation by Terrence Rafferty in the *New Yorker* (1 August). Most attention elsewhere went to *The Hearts and Lives of Men*, which was originally written as a serial for *Woman* in 1986. It retells the confused childhood, adventures, and misadventures of (believe it or not) Little Nell, daughter of Helen Lally and Clifford Wexford. Penelope Lively, who is regarded by many as among the very best of the British novelists, won the 1987 Booker Prize for *Moon Tiger* (Grove, in the United States), which recounts the life of Claudia Hampton, a war correspondent in World War II now writing a history of the world and dying of cancer.

In a class of its own is Doris Lessing's thirty-fifth book, *The Fifth Child* (Knopf). Written of and for our time, a time when, Lessing has said, "there is an ugly edge on events," *The Fifth Child* is set in pleasant English suburbia, from the 1960s until the present. Another variation in the theme of the threatened family, it brings to an almost perfect family, the Lovatts, nightmare and disaster in the form of their fifth child, "the fierce and unlovable Ben," who proves to be, inexplicably, a physical, mental, and moral monster with whom neither the Lovatts nor the larger society can cope. Lessing calls her fable simply "a horror story," but many critics have read into it national and international political implications and social messages. As Richard Eder wrote in the *Los Angeles Times Book Review:* "The monstrous Ben represents an underclass too numerous for closets to contain. He is the Third and Fourth Worlds, casting a growing and darkening shadow over the comforts of the First." Another writer who has long held the interest of discriminating American readers is Anglo-Irishman William Trevor, whose *The Silence in the Garden* (Viking) is his tenth novel and his first since *Fool of Fortune* (1983). It is the story of Carriglas, ancestral island home of the Rolleston family. It begins at the time of World War I and the Troubles, then moves forward years later to the building of a bridge to link the island to the mainland. Novelist Thomas Flanagan judged *The Silence in the Garden* to be "shamefully charming and in the end, as he wants it to be, heartbreaking."

The younger British writers, some of them more daring and innovative than most of our own, are continuing to make a strong, influential impression in America. William Boyd's *The New Confessions* (Morrow) was widely reviewed and argued over. It tells the life story, in his own words, of Scotsman John James Todd, born in 1879, who lives now in Mediterranean retirement following a career which involved trench warfare in World War I, filmmaking in the Weimar Republic, exile in Mexico, the Allied invasion of St. Tropez, and Hollywood in the McCarthy era. It is literary, allusive, and, in part, a deliberate pastiche, or as his publisher puts it, "equal parts Laurence Sterne, Charles Dickens, Robertson Davies and Saul Bellow, with a wry 1980's touch that is pure Boyd." The other side of the coin was stated by Susan Vigilante in the *Wall Street Journal:* "But all the fine writing in the world cannot invigorate a worthless wimp like John James Todd." In *Kansas in August* (Dutton) Patrick Gale gives us a complicated triangle story, set in contemporary London and involving an abandoned baby who is named Dan after a favorite pet guinea pig. Alan Hollinghurst, in *The Swimming Pool Library* (Random House), offers a tour of gay London in 1983, just before the onset of AIDS. Perhaps the most intricate and lively of the new British novelists is Peter Ackroyd; and his new novel *Chatterton* (Grove) is wonderfully complicated with a huge cast of English eccentrics from three different centuries, and several simultaneous plots, all involving forgery of one kind or another and centered around the poet Thomas Chatterton (1752-1770). Seldom has any foreign writer had such an instant and multiple impact on America of the type that British playwright, TV dramatist, and novelist Dennis Potter has demonstrated recently, and especially in 1988, which saw the publication of his second novel, *Blackeyes* (Random House), closely following the broadcast of his serial drama, *The Singing Detective.* In a major piece on Potter in *Time* (19 December), Richard Corliss described the story thus–"An aging British novelist pilfers the life of his beautiful niece for the plot of his new book"–and quoted novelist Julian Barnes's hard-nosed accounting of

Potter as a "Christian socialist with a running edge of apocalyptic disgust."

Although American publishers are willing to publish experimental fiction by foreign writers, it is not easy for any but a chosen few of American writers–authors such as Robert Coover, Thomas Pynchon, John Hawkes, and William Gass–to publish homegrown experimental fiction. By a kind of "trickle down" process some of the familiar devices and liberties of foreign writers are becoming acceptable in the context of our mainstream fiction. Thus it is all right when Clyde Edgerton, in *The Floatplane Notebooks,* at one point uses a wysteria vine as his narrator. Nevertheless, the technically experimental as well as fiction which is frankly experimental in subject and substance are quite rare. Among the former would have to be listed such 1988 achievements as poet Constance Urdang's *American Earthquakes* (Coffee House Press), which manages, in a series of fragments and very short vignettes mixing documentary fact and fiction, to tell a story of three generations of a St. Louis family. The boldly experimental punk rocker and minor cult figure Kathy Acker brought out two books in 1988. The first, early in the year, was *Literal Madness: Three Novels* (Grove). Later in the year Grove brought out *Empire of the Senseless,* which received prominent and favorable attention in the *New York Times Book Review* (16 October), where critic R. H. W. Dillard described Acker's method and purpose as "uniting radical form and forbidden language in a slashing and subversive literature that attempts at least to make it possible to live without a center in the empire of the senseless." Other noteworthy novels characterized by technical innovation include Maurice Roche's *Compact* (Dalkey Archive); Judy Grahn's *Mundane's World* (Crossing Press); Don Webb's *Uncle Ovid's Exercise Book* (Fiction Collective); and *Adele at the End of the Day* (Faber & Faber), by Canadian poet Tom Marshall, which alternates two consecutive stream-of-consciousness monologues.

Since subject matter, perhaps more than treatment, is what sells books, there are subjects which, at first glance, appear to be so oddly uncommercial as to be called experimental. A classic example of this is Nicholson Baker's well-received *The Mezzanine* (Weidenfeld & Nicolson), in which the entire outward action of the novel consists of a thirty-second escalator ride at the end of lunch hour. Equally, if differently, eccentric is *Krazy Kat: A Novel in Five Panels* (Knopf), in which author Jay Cantor uses Krazy Kat and

Ignatz Mouse and other George Herriman comic-strip characters to make new myths, funny and chic, for our age. In *Wyvern* (Ticknor & Fields), A. A. Attanasio has created an experimental historical novel, set in the years 1609-1630, a tale of pirates and the East Indies rendered most contemporary by its accounts of inner states of consciousness, a unique blending of kinds described by the publisher as "somewhere between the high-seas sagas of Robert Louis Stevenson and the spiritual sojourns of Carlos Castaneda." Joy Williams, one of our most highly regarded fiction writers, and quite possibly the blurb queen for 1988 (her new book appears with trumpets of praise by Ann Beattie, Mary Lee Settle, Harold Brodkey, Jim Harrison, and Thomas McGuane as well as story-writer James Salter, who declares her the peer of Céline, Flannery O'Connor, and Margaret Atwood), in *Breaking and Entering* (Vintage) tells the story of two thoroughly alienated drifters, Willie and Liberty, and their white dog, who break into vacation homes when the owners are away and live there for a while. Williams is a gifted, sometimes luminous writer, but what is unique about her work is a flatness of emotional affect, an utterly idiosyncratic point of view, and a language which, while credible and comprehensible, seems to be an excellent translation from an unknown tongue. Williams writes, as she seems to view our world, like a visitor from another planet. Just as oddly complex is the work of John Hawkes, whose latest adventure in eroticism and obfuscation, *Whistlejacket* (Weidenfeld & Nicolson), the story of, among lots of other things, the Van Fleet family and a memorial fox hunt, may or may not have been intended to be accessible, mainstream fiction. *Whistlejacket* earned mixed reviews, though longtime Hawkes fans loved it and critic-novelist Paul West said: "It is perhaps the finest of Hawkes's hymns to the flesh." Novelist Edmund White compared Hawkes to Picasso, Francis Bacon, and Hieronymous Bosch.

If this were an amazing year for the number and variety of short-story collections published, many of them first books, it was also a boom year for first novels. A surprising number were written by new writers of the apparently unquenchable southern renaissance. Among the best of these were John Ed Bradley's *Tupelo Nights* (Atlantic Monthly Press), the story of John Girlie in the little town of Old Field, much praised by Harry Crews; *Private Woods* (Harcourt Brace Jovanovich), by Sandra Crockett Moore, in which Sarah Lannom and her husband, Dick,

and former lover, Sonny, go deer hunting with bow and arrow in eastern Tennessee; Paula Sharp's *The Woman Who Was Not All There* (Harper & Row), praised in the *New Yorker*, and telling the story of Marjorie LeBlanc, nurse and a single mother of four, making a life near Durham, North Carolina; Stephen Stark's *The Outskirts* (Algonquin), a contemporary story set in middle Virginia, described by David Huddle as "a tough-minded exploration of alienated youth"; *Precious In His Sight* (Viking), by M. E. Hughes, set in 1960 in Belmont Parish and dealing with the history of the Patout family in a manner the publisher describes as "creole magic realism"; Peggy Payne's *Revelation* (Simon and Schuster), the contemporary story of a Chapel Hill minister, Swain Hammond, who apparently has a mystical experience (the book has been compared to a Frank Capra movie by some reviewers); and *Keeping Secrets* (Simon and Schuster), by Sarah Shankman, another tale set in rural Louisiana, which tells of the search of Emma Fine, who may be Jewish, for her history and identity. Two other first novels set in the South are of the highest literary quality and are outstanding works by any standards. Sarah Glasscock, in *Anna L.M. N.O.* (Random House), introduces the best hairstylist in west Texas, a marvelously rendered character. Well-plotted and written in a clear, clean style, just enough askew to be innovative, *Anna L.M.N.O.* is a fine, strong novel. Just as strong and very different is poet and story writer Cathryn Hankla's *A Blue Moon in Poorwater* (Ticknor & Fields). The precise accuracy and the gritty Appalachian authenticity of this remembered story of teenage Dorrie Parks and her family lightly disguise a dark subtext and a voice as original as it is clear and accessible. There is something of the best of Calvino there and of the art of William Goyen, who was Hankla's teacher; but the voice is her own and will be heard again. Another southern first novel, and one that received much critical attention, was Charlie Smith's *Shine Hawk* (Paris Review), which, with its contemporaneity, its free and easy sex, and its strong and obvious Faulknerian influence, gave it a high literary patina and invited critical response, not all of which was favorable.

It seems clear from the critical responses to this year's first novels that, other things (promotion, publicity, source, early reviews) being more or less equal, reviewers (perhaps, earlier, editors) are somewhat jaded and looking for something different enough to be interesting. There is no "line" on the first novelist, and there is too little time to read superficially conventional novels, like Glasscock's and Hankla's, carefully enough to discover the essential originality at the heart of their work. The good side of this condition is that, even though serious experimentation is not invited, imaginative innovation is encouraged. Sometimes it is a matter of special knowledge, as, for example, in the case of animal trainer Vicki Hearne, author of the highly praised extended essay *Adam's Task: Calling Animals by Name*. Her third book and first novel is *The White German Shepherd* (Atlantic Monthly Press), which follows Diane Brannigan in her search for a perfect white shepherd to play in a movie remake of *The Call of the Wild*. She finds one, Jouster, and learns a lot of new things from him. A long way from Lassie, but needless to say Jouster proves to be by far the most interesting character in the book. The subject matter of Jonathan Franzen's first book, *The Twenty-Seventh City* (Farrar, Straus & Giroux), surely raised eyebrows and attracted attention. Set in St. Louis in 1984, the story predicates the arrival of an Indian woman, thirty-five-year-old S. Jammu, from Bombay, together with her assistant Balwan Singh, to take over as police chief. Soon she and a wave of Indian immigrants are taking over the entire city. Only two people seem cognizant of the elaborate Jammu conspiracy and capable of resisting. One is the paranoid right-wing General Norris, CEO of General Synthetics; the other is a decent, honest man–Martin Probst, who must be co-opted or destroyed if Jammu is to succeed. A more obviously funny and satirical book was R. Howard Bloch's skewering of Berkeley, university and town, as "Beacon" in *Moses in the Promised Land* (Gibbs Smith). Crucial to uncovering the truth of these people is Moses Reed, the termite exterminator. The enemies of the united minds and souls of Beacon are described as "conservative people, housewives with dyed hair, people in American cars that are not energy efficient, cigarette smokers." The unrelenting, underclass bleakness of Mary McGarry Morris's *Vanished* (Viking) became the subject of many reviews and interviews. *Vanished* is the story of Aubrey Wallace, a slow-witted laborer in his late forties who falls in with Dotty Johnson, an abused and utterly ruthless teenager. Together they kidnap a baby, and the story covers five years of their "luckless, nomadic existence" as they wander up and down the East Coast. In a *New York Times* interview former social worker Morris said: "There are countless Aubrey

Wallaces in this world, little people, pale eyes, the briefest, simplest human creatures. They are the shadows in early morning doorways and the solitary late night climbing of wooden stairs. They wash dishes in restaurants and mop floors and pick up litter in the park, and they are always startled to be spoken to, because no one ever does." Matt Ruff's *Fool on the Hill* (Entrekin/Atlantic Monthly Press) was a Cornell campus novel with a mix of fantasy, published by the latest editorial *Wunderkind*, Morgan Entrekin, and was clearly supposed to be an attention grabber. In addition to cute and interesting students, the novel has ghosts from Greek myths, fairies, figures out of Tolkien, and a postmodern gimmick (it is supposedly written by a Mr. Sunshine, beginning with Cornell in 1866). Most critics found it to be deeply silly.

Among the other worthy first novels of the year were Michael Chabon's *The Mysteries of Pittsburgh* (Morrow); Brett Laidlaw's *Three Days in the Heart of the Earth* (Norton); Ellen Aikins's *Home Movies* (Simon and Schuster); Christopher Noel's *Hazard and the Five Delights* (Knopf); Linda Ashour's *Speaking in Tongues* (Simon and Schuster); Robert Olmstead's *Soft Water* (Vintage); and Eric Larsen's *American Memory* (Algonquin). Special mention should be made of *The Illustrator* (Summit), by James Robison, whose *Rumor and Other Stories* (1985) won him wide praise and, as well, a large award from the Whiting Foundation. *The Illustrator* was not generally as well received, though it is hard to understand exactly why since both its strengths and weaknesses are much the same–fragmentary, funny/sad, and, as Donald Barthelme has written, "affecting and profound, all at the same time." Perhaps the author's vision (Frederick Barthelme writes that in Robison's world "heartbreak turns on the choice of a verb") seemed just a little too special. Perhaps it was simply (again) that the characters are more interesting to themselves than to any real or imaginary reader.

The fiction of the world came to us in a wide variety of translations, some well-known and easily accessible by means of the large trade publishers, others from university presses and small presses. Latin America continued to engage the interests of publishers and readers. The much admired and influential Gabriel García Márquez was represented by *Love in the Time of Cholera* (Knopf), which tells a story, set in a country of Caribbean coastline, of the unrequited love (fifty years, nine months, and four days' worth) of Florentino Ariza for the beautiful Fermina Daza; and through that story García Márquez explores, among other magical things, the nature of love in all its guises. When, somehow, the lovers finally get together and make love, after (in fact) fifty-three years, seven months, eleven days and nights, what they experience is "the tranquil, wholesome love of experienced grandparents." As García Márquez writes: "It was as if they had leapt over the arduous calvary of conjugal life and gone straight to the heart of love." Richly symbolic and metaphorical, and often wonderfully funny, it is written in a style which Thomas Pynchon aptly labeled in the *New York Times Book Review* (10 April) as "maniacal serenity."

Other prominent Latin American writers whose works were attentively reviewed include the Chileans Isabel Allende, José Donoso, and Ariel Dorfman; the Argentines Adolfo Bioy Casares, Thomas Eloy Martínez, and Gerardo di Masso; Uruguayan Carlos Martínez Moreno; Brazilian Jorge Amado; and others. Allende's *Eva Luna* (Knopf), her third and most adventurous exploration of the wild literary territory of "magic realism," tells the story of Eva, a survivor and an irrepressible storyteller, interweaving an abundance of stories, factual and fabulous. Some reviewers found it a little rich in magic and thin on the side of realism, but, on the whole, it was respectfully received. Donoso, celebrated for his earlier gothic tales, especially *The Obscene Bird of Night* (1973) and *A House in the Country* (1984), here tells a more factual, if no less resonant story, an accounting of contemporary Chile during twenty-four hours of January 1985 when longtime exile, the singer Manungo Vera, and his young son return to Chile for the funeral of Pablo Neruda's widow, Matilde. In three sections–"Evening," "Night" (after curfew), and "Morning"–Vera rediscovers himself as he explores and rediscovers his native country, now tormented and confused. Against the documentary background is played a brief tragic love affair between Vera and the aristocratic political activist, Judit Torre. Ariel Dorfman's *Mascara* (Viking) is briefer, bleaker, and stranger than either of the others. It is the story, told by a narrator with no name, "of deception and betrayal," a story of faces and masks and cosmetics, featuring a plastic surgeon, one Dr. Maleverdi, who, in a world of shifty and shifting appearances, is constantly (and profitably) changing and rearranging his patients, who seem to have no life at all beneath the outward and visible. Gerardo di Masso's *The Shadow by the Door*

(Curbstone), which deals directly with Argentina during the days of the Dirty War, won that country's Cafe Iruna Prize. Thomas Eloy Martínez, in *The Peron Novel* (Pantheon), joins the fabulous tradition of the Latin writers with the more familiar North American documentary blending of "real" characters and events with fictional people and happenings. At once historical (it deals with the actual return of Juan Peron to Argentina) and self-reflexive (a journalist, among others, who is interviewed is Thomas Eloy Martínez), it creates an image of history as a hopelessly intermingled, inseparable anthology of fact and fiction, thus always more a matter of protean myth than recorded truths or rational patterns. Longtime friend of and sometime collaborator with the late Jorge Luis Borges, Adolfo Bioy Casares seems never to have doubted or questioned that the world we think we know, at least in literature, can only be an alchemical melding of the real and the fantastic. His *The Dream of Heroes* (Dutton), first published in Spanish in 1954, is set solidly in the suburbs of Buenos Aires in the late 1920s and deals chiefly with strange events during the Carnivals of 1927 and 1930. In her translator's preface Diana Thorold describes it as "among other things a meditation on the nature of courage and the macho ideal," adding, "It is social comment and moral allegory; it is a love story and a thriller; a mystery and a technical *tour de force*." Out of Uruguay comes the first fiction to treat the Tupemaro terrorists in any knowing detail, Carlos Martínez Moreno's *El Infierno* (Readers International). From Brazil we have Jorge Amado's *Showdown* (Bantam), an account of the founding of the Bahian frontier town Tocaia Grande. From Mexico we have *Notes of a Villager* (Plover) by José Ruben Romero (1890-1952), an autobiographical account, up to the age of twenty-three, of some of Mexico's most troubled years in this century.

By now, in a time of swift cultural mobility and interchange, both the form and content of the Latin American novels are familiar enough to North American writers and readers to have become seriously influential. Beyond the undeniable technical revolution and liberation are works being written by North Americans which have a similar content, not so much derivative as imaginatively explored. For example, Steven Dobyns's *The Two Deaths of Señora Puccini* (Viking) offers the story of four men at dinner, in a South American country torn by revolution, telling the story of their lives. (Dobyns, by the way, also published

Dust jacket for the American translation of Chilean Isabel Allende's third novel, in which the inventive Eva relates the picaresque tale of her life

his fifth novel about private detective Charlie Bradshaw–*Saratoga Bestiary,* Viking.) Similarly, gifted California novelist Kate Braverman focused on the Hispanic barrio of East Los Angeles and the lives of three very different women who live on Flores Street–Francisca Ramos, Gloria Hernandel, and Marta Ortega–in her large-scale novel *Palm Latitudes* (Linden/Simon and Schuster). Another American venture into Latin American culture, in this case both the matter and the manner thereof, is Lawrence Thornton's first novel, *Imagining Argentina* (Doubleday), a story of *Los Desaparecidos,* a novel at once political and visionary.

Thanks to the interest in Latin America, together with a pride in cultural diversity, we are witnessing the publication of interesting fiction by novelists writing out of the Hispanic experience in North America. Roberto G. Fernández brought out his first English-language novel, *Raining Backwards* (Arte Público), a satirical and at times surreal picture of the Cuban community in Miami. In *Rainbow's End* (Arte Público), Genaro González wrote of three generations of a Rio Grande family. Max Martínez told of Chicano life in rural Texas in *Schooland* (Arte Público), and in his first English work, *The Brick People* (Arte Público), Alejandro Morales dealt with California from the 1890s to the 1940s.

A variety of European works in translation appeared in 1988. From Germany came *Women in a River Landscape: A Novel in Dialogues and Soliloquies* (Knopf), by the late Heinrich Böll, set in and around Bonn in the affluent 1980s, its principal characters being (as accurately identified in *Publishers Weekly*): "the women–the transient wives and mistresses, imprisoned in imposing riverside villas, their bitterness and defeated hopes mocked by the apparent freedom of the Rhine flowing past their windows." Other than a sketchy outline of how they look and dress, all we know of the characters is their voices, what they tell us and unintentionally reveal. Just as dark and as satirical is *Woodcutters* (Knopf), by the Austrian writer Thomas Bernhard, who is considered a strong prospect for a Nobel Prize. Set at a midnight dinner party of *Culturati* in Vienna, it ridicules the art establishment and is haunted by the words of a disillusioned actor: "The forest, the virgin forest, the life of a woodcutter–that has always been my ideal." Elfriede Jelinek's bleak novel, *The Piano Teacher* (Weidenfeld & Nicolson), is also an attack on the artsy set in Vienna, exposed in a story of passion and perversion. In *Repetition* (Farrar, Straus & Giroux) Peter Handke follows the fortunes of one Filip Kobal, a Slovenian who tries to follow the traces and tracks of his dead brother, who was a resistance hero. In *The Pigeon* (Knopf) Patrick Suskind presents a simpler and leaner parable (a man's life and being are disrupted by the arrival of a pigeon on his windowsill) than his earlier *Perfume* and this time did not please his critics and reviewers as much. Two novels dealing with Jews in post-World War II Germany were Andre Kaminski's *Kith and Kin* (Fromm) and Jurek Becker's *Bronstein's Children* (Wolff/Harcourt Brace Jovanovich). Kaminski's novel features two very unusual and often comic Jewish families, the Rosenbachs and the Kaminskis, and, self-reflexively, stars a fictional character named Andre Kaminski. Polish-born Becker sets his novel in East Berlin in 1973 and through the story of his protagonist and narrator, Hans, his girlfriend, Martha, his insane sister, Elle, and above all his father, a survivor of the concentration camps, shows how the next generation has been shaped by the Holocaust. Perhaps the strangest and most interesting of the novels coming out of Germany this year is *Earth and Fire* (Atheneum), by Horst Bienek. Though able to stand on its own, this is the final novel in the tetralogy called the *Gleiwitz Suite,* all concerned with the town of Gleiwitz in Upper Silesia during World War II. Here the war is winding down as the Germans retreat and the Russians arrive and civilization collapses upon itself in ruins. The climactic event, witnessed by some of the characters, is the destruction of Dresden by firebombing on Ash Wednesday of 1945. Mainly the story follows the maturity to manhood of fifteen-year-old Kotik Ossadnik; but among the many other characters is the "real" Gerhart Hauptmann, the Silesian Nobel Prize winner who sees the end of Dresden in the distance from a country sanitarium. (The same historical event is crucial to the pseudonymous *Firestorm* [Morrow], by "William Coyle," half of whose double story is set on Shrove Tuesday and Ash Wednesday of 1945 and concerns Bernard Reardon, an Australian tail gunner in the RAF who participates in the Dresden raid.)

World War II is likewise the historical time for Stanislaw Lem's *Hospital of the Transfiguration* (Wolff/Harcourt Brace Jovanovich), Lem's first novel, produced before he began to explore the fantasy and science fiction genre. Here we follow the adventures of Stefan Trzyniecki, a doctor who seeks to flee the war and the Nazis by working in a provincial insane asylum, only to discover that there is no escape and all the world, inside and outside, is mad.

Several Scandinavian novels arrived on the scene: from Denmark, Hans Scherfig's *The Missing Bureaucrat* (Fjord); from Norway, Bibi Lee's *Music From a Blue Well* (University of Nebraska), the story of an adolescent girl before and during World War I; and *The Honeymoon* (St. Martin's Press), by Knut Faldbakken, a contemporary and erotic story of married love.

From the Netherlands, via Louisiana State University Press, came Cess Nooteboom's *Philips and the Others,* which was the productive author's first novel, written in the 1950s, a poetic story of obsessive love. From Spain came Eduardo Mendoza's *The City of Marvels* (Harcourt Brace Jovanovich), a picaresque story set in Barcelona and bracketed by two world's fairs, 1888 and 1929, detailing the rise to riches and power of Onofre Bouvila, a country boy possessed of na-

tive wit and the energy to match his appetites. Another novel from Spain, a homegrown example of "magic realism," is Joan Perucho's *Natural History* (Knopf), a nineteenth-century detective story to which have been added contemporary flourishes and problems such as vampires, huge spiders, giant fleas, and people who turn to stone.

France was the source of several of the year's notable novels. Emmanuel Carrere, in *The Mustache* (Collier/Macmillan), thoroughly explores the existential dilemma of a man who shaves off his mustache and nobody notices. In *Lazarus* (Wolff/Harcourt Brace Jovanovich) Alain Absire invents a life story for the man Christ raised from the dead. In *The Devil Laughs Again* (Lyle Stuart) Regine Deforges concludes a World War II trilogy, following the protagonist, Lea Delmas, through the confusion of liberation. Perhaps the most interesting French novel in translation this year was the posthumous *W, or the Memory of Childhood* (Godine), by Georges Perec (1936-1982). Author of some of the most complex experimental fictions of our era, Perec here is accessible enough for all, telling two apparently separate stories in alternating chapters, one an autobiographical account of Perec's childhood during the Nazi occupation, and the other about "W," an imaginary island nation which Perec says he invented and, in fact, wrote up in these self-same chapters when he was twelve or thirteen years old. Not any utopia, but instead a kind of deranged and irrational Sparta where everything is based on athletic competition, W is more like the real world in the ways in which all forms of deadly competition are brutally equalized. As Perec wrote: "It is necessary that even the best be uncertain of winning, it is necessary that even the feeblest be uncertain of losing. Both must take on equal risks and must entertain the same hope of winning, the same unspeakable terror of losing."

Another way of dealing with the experience of World War II is suggested by the Italian art historian and novelist Anna Banti in *Artemisia* (University of Nebraska), a self-reflexive re-creation of the life and times of the female artist Artemisia Gentileschi (1590-1642). Published in Italy in 1947, this intricate and experimental novel is haunted by the war which had just ended. Going back even more in time, *The Late Mattia Pascal* (Eridanos Press), written and published by Luigi Pirandello in 1904, tells the story of Mattia Pascal, a loser who hit it big at Monte Carlo. Also appearing for the first time in English is the surrealistic novel, first published in 1929, *Hebdomeros* (PAJ Publications), by the painter Giorgio de Chirico. Closer in time are the three novels of Ferdinando Camon depicting peasant life of the Veneto region as he remembers it–*Memorial, The Fifth Estate,* and *Life Everlasting* (Marlboro). *Memorial* is in honor of his mother. The other two are set in post-World War II Italy, ending in the 1960s as the peasant world, linked to the rest of the world at last by modern technology, ended. The author calls the autobiographical *Life Everlasting* "a sort of non-fiction novel."

Eastward, on the other side of the Adriatic, the now-celebrated Albanian novelist Ismaile Kadare produced *Doruntine* (New Amsterdam Press), a murder mystery complete with black magic and set in medieval Albania. The *Wall Street Journal* described its powerful ambience as "a world of dark, batlike terror." From Yugoslavia the Serbian Milorad Pavic, a poet and professor of literary history at the University of Belgrade, produced his first novel, *Dictionary of the Khazars: A Lexican Novel in 100,000 Words* (Knopf), in two separate editions–a "Male Edition" and a "Female Edition": "Be warned that ONE PARAGRAPH is crucially different." Adventurously published and promoted, it has received extensive, if mixed, coverage. Set loosely in the form of a dictionary, it adds up to the imagined story of a real first-millenium people who have disappeared off the face of the earth and from earth's history. In an interview in the *New York Times,* Pavic is cheerfully explicit about his novel's implications. "The Khazars are a metaphor for a small people surviving in between great powers and great religions," he says, adding that the aesthetic experience of it should be "something like a feast eaten in a dream."

In the Soviet Union Anatoli Rybakov saw the publication of his novel of the Stalinist era, written in the 1960s but long deferred and delayed. *Children of the Arbat* (Little, Brown), published in English, received extraordinary attention in the United States. It is a large novel which, as the poet Yevtushenko has written, aims to reveal "all the layers of society in the early 1930s in Moscow." But it has a tightly focused central story, dealing with two young students, Yuri Sharok and Sasha Pankratov, who live at 51 Arbat Street. The action takes place during late 1933 and 1934. Sasha, coming from a family of the Communist "nobility," is a dedicated member of the elite Young Communist League, but is swept up in the atmosphere of purge and certifi-

able paranoia and exiled to Siberia as a subversive. The story concludes with the news of the murder of Kirov, leader of the Leningrad party, and the prospect of darker times ahead. Perhaps Rybakov's most unusual accomplishment is his use of Stalin as a character in the novel, presenting his thoughts and feelings as well as his actions; and though his Stalin is not without some virtue, it is the most negative appraisal of that leader to appear from any Soviet writer with the notable exception of Solzhenitsyn. The other side of the coin, as it were, is to be found in two other foreign novels published in America in 1988, one by an Italian and the other by a Russian émigré. Roberto Pazzi's *Searching for the Emperor* (Knopf) explores the inner life, sometimes hallucinatory, of Czar Nicholas II when he and his family were held prisoner at Ekaterinburg. The story is told in counterpoint with the story of his young Prince Ypsilanti, lost, together with his regiment, the Preobrazhensky Guards, trying to find and rescue the royal family. A brief autobiographical novel by émigré Gaito Gazdanov, *An Evening with Claire* (Ardis), proves to be essentially, and at its best, the memoir of a teenage machine gunner for the White Army. Other adventures in the re-creation of modern Russian history include *The Kirov Affair* (Harcourt Brace Jovanovich), by Adam Ulam, director of Harvard University's Russian Research Center. This fictional account of the death of Sergei Kirov in 1934, including among its characters Stalin, Khrushchev, Beria, Brezhnev, and Molotov, comes armed with fulsome blurbs by John Kenneth Galbraith, Henry Kissinger, and Arthur Schlesinger, Jr. Another novel set in Soviet history and making full use of historical characters is British journalist Alan Brien's *Lenin* (Morrow), told in the form of Lenin's (imaginary) diary.

The struggles in the Middle East continue to produce fiction as well as news and sorrowful history. Yoram Kaniuk's *Confessions of a Good Arab* (Braziller) is the story of the life and loves of Yosef Sherara, who is also known as Yosef Rosenzweig. In *The Road to Ein Harod* (Grove) Amos Kenan, writing originally in French, creates a futuristic Israel which has become a military dictatorship. More widely reviewed was *Arabesques* (Harper & Row), by Anton Shammas, a novel written in Hebrew by a Palestinian Christian who studied with Paul Engle at the University of Iowa. Engle appears, in person, as a character, as do two different heroes named Anton Shammas. Not at all immune to the influence of the latest postmodernist devices and the ways and means of "magic realism," the story is, nevertheless, at heart, an accounting of the author's childhood in Fassuta, a village of Galilee. In a review in the *New Yorker* (17 October) John Updike praised the novel for its "crisp, luminous, and nervy mixture of fantasy and autobiography." *The Immortal Bartfuss* (Weidenfeld & Nicolson), by Aharon Appelfeld, was selected by the *New York Times Book Review* as one of the "Notable Books of the Year" and is described as "a spiritual portrait of a man who survived the Holocaust and now resides in Israel." Israeli novelist Amos Oz published *Black Box* (Wolff/Harcourt Brace Jovanovich), an epistolary novel. On the surface it is a family novel dealing with Alec Gideon, the descendant of early, old-time settlers, now living in the United States; his ex-wife Ilana, a Polish Jew; her present husband, Michel, an Eastern Jew; and Boaz, the troubled and troublesome son of Alec and Ilana. Just a family novel, but the family is representative of Israel as it has become, and their quarrels and problems have larger, symbolic implications. From the other side comes *Cities of Salt* (Random House), translated from the Arabic of Abdelrahman Munif. This novel is concerned not with the present but with the 1930s and, in particular, the discovery and development of oil fields by Americans who, perhaps inadvertently, become the actors and agents of Satan, destroying the ancient order and ritual of Bedouin and rural culture, replacing this with urbanization, the frantic and foolish culture of the city.

It is not surprising, when Japanese products of all kinds are found thriving in America, that Japanese fiction should be a growth market as well. One novel which received considerable notice was *The Ark Sakura* (Knopf), by Kobo Abe, a fantastic, futuristic tale of a rich fat man named Mole, living, in anticipation of the Apocalypse, in a subterranean, high-tech bunker he calls his "Ark." When a group of con artists join him there, bad things follow. Masako Togawa's *A Kiss of Fire* (Dodd, Mead) is a complex novel of suspense dealing with arson. More widely reviewed than either of the above was *Scandal* (Dodd, Mead), by the Japanese Catholic writer Shusaku Endo. Here, in a variation on the story of Dorian Gray, a Japanese writer, Suguro, of great distinction and moral rectitude, discovers that a lookalike, a double, perhaps himself, has been living a life of debauchery in the notorious Shinjuku quarter of the city. American writers are beginning to feel free to write of Japanese characters

in a Japanese setting. Witness *The Eight Corners of the World* (Chelsea Green), by Gordon Weaver, whose central character is Yoshinori Yamaguchi, a Japanese-style hustler and film producer.

China is beginning to add to our literary environment. Chinese novelist Jia Pingwa won the Mobil Pegasus Prize–which brings twenty-five hundred dollars in cash, a paid-for translation into English, and publication by LSU Press–for the novel *Turbulence*. Already on the scene, received with respect and interest, is Zhang Xianliang's *Half of Man Is Woman* (Norton), the story of a young man who finds love in his exile during the Cultural Revolution.

This year there are more African novels, coming from different parts of Africa, in the American bookstores. Best known is *Anthills of the Savannah* (Doubleday), by the distinguished Nigerian novelist Chinua Achebe. His bleak story, set in the imaginary African nation of Kangan two years after a coup, tells of three old school friends– Reginald Okong, now "His Excellency," the paranoid ruler of Kangan; Idem Osodi, poet and editor of the local paper; and centrally, Chris Oriko, commissioner of information. And, perhaps most important of all, is Chris's lover, Beatrice Okoh, a survivor who endures the conflicts and terrors of the times. A powerful novel of the grim life in contemporary Zaire is Sony Labou Tansi's *The Antipeople* (Marion Boyars), which won France's *Grand prix de L'Afrique Noire*. In the sad story of a rural schoolmaster, Dadou, it describes the collapse of a decent world. From profoundly troubled Sudan, translated out of Arabic, there is Tayeb Salih's *Season of the Migration to the North* (Kesend), telling of the narrator's return to his village in Sudan after years of study in England. *Publishers Weekly* praised the book for its "trance-like telling." Joseph Diescho is a Namibian studying at Columbia. In *Born of the Sun* (Friendship Press) he writes of a crucial year in the life of a Namibian peasant who becomes a committed activist. The struggling world of contemporary East Africa is evoked, through the story of fifteen-year-old Hassan Omar, in Tanzanian novelist Abkularazak Gurnah's *Memory of Departure* (Grove). Finally, Central Africa is the scene for British writer J. G. Ballard's visionary novel, *The Day of Creation* (Farrar, Straus & Giroux), a delicate fusion of fantasy (what Ballard calls "the speculative genre") and the realistic mode he used in his autobiographical and highly successful *Empire of the Sun* (1984). In a parched country torn by an ongoing war between the followers of General

Harare, a former dentist, and Captain Kagwa, a police chief, the protagonist and narrator, Dr. Mallory of the World Health Organization, almost miraculously uncovers and discovers a new, Nile-size river, which he names the Mallory. The bulk of the book is the journey by Mallory, aboard the *Salammbo*, together with the oddest company and crew this side of Conrad, or maybe Chaucer, to find the source of the river. Many disasters follow, and the river itself eventually disappears, leaving everything worse than before. Part fable and, judging by the work of contemporary African writers, more accurate and realistic than one might hope, *The Day of Creation*, like Achebe's *Anthills of the Savannah*, offers at least a hint of hope in the image of an indestructible African woman–"A strong-shouldered young woman, with a caustic eye, walking along the drained bed of the Mallory with a familiar jaunty stride."

As we steadily approach the end of the century, it is no wonder that there is an increasing effort to rediscover good books which have been lost in the shuffle of commerce and no surprise that the reprinting of classics in new or special editions is a serious business. The *Washington Post Book World* regularly runs a column, "Rediscoveries," in which guest writers are invited to try to salvage personal favorites from oblivion. The Book-of-the-Month Club has been bringing out its Classic Series, and among the 1988 titles are John O'Hara's *Appointment in Samarra*, A. B. Guthrie, Jr.'s *The Big Sky*, Richard Condon's *The Manchurian Candidate*, Edwin O'Connor's *The Last Hurrah*, and Vladimir Nabokov's *Lolita* (this last, strangely, with an introduction by Erica Jong). Meanwhile the University of Georgia Press continues to bring out new editions of black American fiction long out of print. Among the titles reprinted as Brown Thrasher Books in 1988 are *Rosiebelle Lee Wildcat Tennessee: a Muskhogean County Novel*, and *Baby Sweets*, by Raymond Andrews, and *The House Behind the Cedars*, by Charles W. Chesnutt. Special editions were published of Barnaby Conrad's *Matador* (Capra Press) and, designed and illustrated by Barry Moser, Eudora Welty's *The Robber Bridegroom* (Harcourt Brace Jovanovich). Dashiell Hammett's *Woman in the Dark: A Novel of Dangerous Romance*, published this year by Knopf, had previously appeared only in three installments in *Liberty* magazine and once, briefly, in the 1950s as a paperback. Novelist Berry Fleming, now in his eighties, has been given new literary life by Second Chance Press, which brought out new editions of three of his novels in 1988–*Colonel Effingham's Raid*, *Lucinderella*, and *The Make Believers*.

Stendhal's *The Pink and the Green* (New Directions), an unfinished novel first published in 1920, has now appeared for the first time in English. J. G. Ballard's first novel, *Hello America*, a fantasy in which North America is abandoned by its inhabitants, had never been published before in America until Carroll & Graf released it this year. *Tungsten*, a 1931 novel by the celebrated Latin American poet Cesar Vallejo, was republished by Syracuse University Press. Described by *Publishers Weekly* as an "agitprop novel," *Tungsten* tells the story of Servando Huanca, a pure Indian and a pure hero who battles against bad Americans and bad (mixed blood) native exploiters. Stephen Spender's recently rediscovered *The Temple* (Grove) has a historical as well as a literary interest; this account of two visits to Germany, in 1929 and 1932, shows the last days of the Weimar Republic and offers portraits of Spender's friends W. H. Auden and Christopher Isherwood in their lively youth. Unquestionably the most significant republication of 1988 is to be found in the Library of America edition of *Flannery O'Connor: Collected Works*, edited by Sally Fitzgerald, which brings together for that distinguished series and for the first time 2 novels, 28 short stories, 8 essays, and 259 letters by O'Connor.

The Year in Short Stories

David R. Slavitt

It isn't supposed to happen. The whole elaborate early-warning system of literature is designed to keep us posted about what talents may be slouching toward Madison Avenue to be born. But despite the labors of all those editors of magazines both little and big, there are still surprises, and out of the blue a couple of unknowns pop up, out of nowhere. Not a single one of the stories in Mary Gaitskill's *Bad Behavior* (Poseidon) or in Jonathan Schwartz's *The Man Who Knew Cary Grant* (Random House) ever appeared in any magazine anywhere. And it wasn't because they hadn't been submitted.

What we have is an altogether irrational market. The demise of the *Saturday Evening Post, Collier's*, and other such mass-audience outlets for short fiction was probably inevitable after the television stations began broadcasting programs that are more or less dramatic equivalents of short stories. The implication for literature was curiously healthy, however, for the form was freed of its commercial lures and turned into a high art. It became something like poetry—not worth doing except for its own sake. The persistence of a handful of outlets for short fiction in the *New Yorker, Esquire, Playboy*, the *Atlantic Monthly*, and one or two others was charming, almost quaint, but irrelevant. The basic situation was not changed. The short story was a highbrow, low-revenue enterprise.

In recent years, however, there is a new development in that there are more and more books of short fiction being published, and these books are getting more attention in the book pages of newspapers and magazines and doing better in the stores. Having had her stories widely rejected, Gaitskill hit it lucky at last, won an Avery Hopwood Award at the University of Michigan and, partly on the strength of that, found an editor in New York who liked her collection. Poseidon, an imprint of Simon and Schuster, published the collection. They are unquestionably accomplished, impressive stories, but their setting and their tone are also appealing—an opportunity to stake a claim in the field that Tama Janowitz, Jay McInerney, and Madison Smartt Bell had

been so profitably mining. And these previously unpublished pieces not only became a book here but were sold abroad, over and over, to more than a dozen foreign publishers. An indubitable success!

Gaitskill's stories are just fine and they deserve every good thing that luck or cunning can supply. But the quirkiness of the route by which they reached this happy outcome also has its spooky aspect. Imagine that at this very instant, tens of thousands of typewriters and word processors are banging or clicking away and reams upon reams of short stories are coming into being—and of this vast quantity, rather a lot of the work is good. Some of it is brilliant. But in the cubicles of magazine offices, or in living rooms and bedrooms of editors' apartments, piles of manuscripts accumulate, a distressing number of them unimpeachably excellent. At that point, the task of choosing among them becomes an exercise in whimsy, the sheer pickiness of a cuisine of surfeit.

But it doesn't matter. As Gaitskill and Schwartz demonstrate, one can garner rejection slips or even give up, figuring that there's no point to it, that one would do better to wait for a mailing from Ed McMahon announcing multi-million-dollar prizes that "You may already have won." And by some long-odds chance, one can come out with a book from a commercial publisher and make a mark as a writer of impressive gifts. That is surely the case with both of these collections. Gaitskill writes mostly about the distressing lives of fast-track urban waifs who are, with greater or less complicity on their own part, being abused, sometimes even physically—as in "Romantic Weekend" or "Secretary." There are intersections of misapprehensions that might be funny if their implications weren't so dark and if their settings weren't so seedy. What ought to be conversations turn out to be overlapping fantasies. There is, in a cumulative way, a philosophical suggestion about the human condition which takes these Gaitskill pieces beyond Janowitz's glitz and reaches territory Françoise Sagan used to explore.

 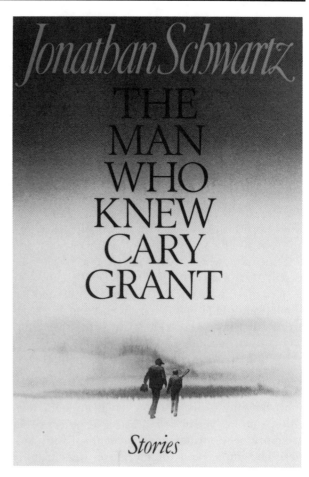

Dust jackets for two short-story collections that include only previously unpublished works

Jonathan Schwartz's collection almost certainly bears some relationship to the promptings of real life, for all these stories are about Jesse Savitt and his father, Norman Savitt, a songwriter. (Schwartz's father was songwriter Arthur Schwartz.) It is a familiar setting, a recognizable world, and the pieces have a ring of truth. They are—as a good many stories are, I suspect—objets trouvés with which the author may have fiddled a little but with a kernel of actuality. There is an unanswerable authority a writer can get when he allows God to be his collaborator and sticks close to a donnée. Whatever the provenance of the material, Schwartz's stories are full of heart, risking sentimentality but never going over the edge, secure in an honesty of vision that clings to details with the mercilessness of a child's vision, and puts that child's vision to good use as a characterization of the son.

Schwartz is not exactly a newcomer. He has a previous collection of stories, *Almost Home*, and a novel, *Distant Stations*, both published in 1979. He and his agent and his publisher wrangled around for a while with this book, trying to decide whether to call it a novel or a collection of stories—after all, the same characters persist throughout the book. As if J. D. Salinger had never published his stories, or Sherwood Anderson, for that matter, the publisher fretted and puzzled, suggesting at one point the title "The Man Who Knew Cary Grant: A Story" as a curious compromise, but Schwartz held out for truth in labeling and was right to do so. His sense of how life *is* involves the re-vision that is close to the heart of many stories, a changing of perception as either the character or sometimes just the reader learns to see more deeply and truly than before.

Norman Savitt is not a particularly good father, but he is wonderful—in the odd ways the odd title suggests. He is a figure who has obvious parental shortcomings for which the son, Jesse, more than compensates in hero worship. If their distances are agonizing their closenesses are even more heartbreaking, as in "Chloe Hummel of the Chicago White Sox," when Jesse flies out from New York to Los Angeles where his father has been working, has the cab pass by the house on Cañon Drive in which the father has been living, and then, on his way back home, calls his father from the Los Angeles airport, claiming to be at Ninety-sixth and Broadway. It is at the same time ludicrous and devastating, all the more devastating because of the ludicrousness. Indeed, throughout this wonderfully controlled and accomplished book, it is the counterbalance Schwartz maintains between the pathetic and the absurd that gives him the authority that, in the short story, is almost everything.

None of these stories was previously published, but they were submitted, at least tentatively–to the *New Yorker*, of course, and to the *Quarterly*–where editor Gordon Lish gave a response that the book's editor characterized as "Lish-like." What he said was something like "This isn't what we're into just now." What Lish is into is not without interest to observers of the literary scene. In addition to his duties at the *Quarterly*, he is an editor at Knopf and a prominent teacher of creative writing. He also writes on his own, novels and short stories as well. His second collection of stories, *Mourner At the Door* (Viking), was published this year, and it is an odd and interesting book, not at all amiable but at times admirable in the risks it takes and the occasional achievements it can claim.

Lish's stories are wrecks of stories as his language is a kind of assault on language. And yet, behind these technical tricks, what he is toying with is an aspect of the truth, a truth as wily and cantankerous as Lish's own tactics. The start of "Leopard in a Temple," for instance, is disarmingly blunt: "Look, let's make it short and sweet. Who anymore doesn't go crazy from overtures, from fanfares, from set-ups, from preambles, from preliminaries? So, okay, here is the thing–this is my Kafka story, fine and dandy. Actually, it is going to be my against-Kafka story. Because what I notice is you have to have a Kafka story one way or the other. So this is my Kafka story, only it is going to be one which is against Kafka. Which is different from being against Kafka's *stories*, although I would probably be against those, too, if I ever went back and really reread any of them."

Garrulous, gabby, annoying, and yet what he has already accomplished is the establishing of a voice, disagreeable but curiously trustworthy. "You see what I am saying to you? Because I am saying to you that nothing is out-of-bounds so far as I myself am personally concerned–unless it is

something which is so dead and buried that I have got nothing to gain from unearthing it. . . ."

What the narrator reveals in that story, his dark and dreadful secret, is that his mother used to say KLEE-YON-TELL, as in "they cater down here to the finest kleeyontell." It's dopey and bizarre, but it works somehow, gives substance and tone to the speaker's anguish, which we see in another aspect in his anti-Kafka turn:

> Listen, I also woke up in my room once, and guess what.
> Because the answer is I was still no different.
> From head to toe, I had to look at every inch of what I took to bed with me.
> Hey, you want to hear something?
> I was *un*metamorphosed.

A small piece of cleverness, but Lish gives it just a little amplitude and resonance–with things like that "kleeyontell" which may be the real subject of the story, its strenuous self-loathing that would be intolerable if it were more directly addressed.

Hugh Nissenson's new book, a collection of "stories and journals" oddly entitled *The Elephant and My Jewish Problem* (Harper & Row), is likable and engaging, as different from Lish's work as one could imagine, and yet there is a kind of peek-a-boo playfulness that is not, after all, so dissimilar. Nissenson is collecting stories from two old volumes, *A Pile of Stones* (1965) and *In the Reign of Peace* (1972), but by putting them with bits of journalism, essays, reportage, and what we generally think of as nonfiction, he is making, I rather suspect, a kind of claim for the persona behind both forms of expression, as well as for the "truth" of the "fiction" and for the fictionality, or at least the artifactual and composed quality of nonfiction. Our attention, therefore, is always slightly elsewhere, and this is, as any magician understands, the desirable circumstance in which to perform, and the necessary condition for some otherwise impossible feats.

But there is also a philosophical or even theological coherence to the book, with pieces of fiction and reportage about the Jewish Problem, which is to say the ongoing struggle with an incomprehensible and even demonic deity. The holocaust, or smaller but altogether consistent samples of evil–the rape and murder of a young girl, the death of a small boy, the sickness unto death of a wife and mother–try our faith. At the same time, there can be a socialist, an agnostic if not an atheist, condemned to hard labor in a Tsarist lead mine which it is most unlikely he will survive, and for him, in the darkness of his Warsaw cell, there can be moments of holy illumination. This is a difficult point to make for any writer. Nissenson is a master, an amazingly dexterous craftsman, who not only can convey this mystical experience but can approximate it in the minds and hearts and souls of his readers. And then, by juxtaposition with the adjacent journal articles, there is a further, almost rabbinical insistence that this is not merely tale-telling, that this is more than a short story and is as true and matter-of-fact as anything we can know of this world.

Nissenson has sometimes been compared to Isaac Bashevis Singer, which is not surprising, considering that both men write about Jews and a struggle with God that goes beyond the parochial but still draws its nourishing richness from ethnic specificity. Singer is sprightlier, more impish, often sexier than Nissenson, but their similarities are considerable—aside from the basic likeness of sheer excellence. Each of them seems to be struggling with God or, more specifically, faith in God. Singer himself had a new collection this year, entitled *The Death of Methuselah* (Farrar Straus & Giroux). In no way does it diminish these twenty new stories to discern in them a general pattern which is, after all, the pattern of most of Singer's work. He is the son and the grandson of rabbis, and he and his brother Israel Joshua Singer went secular, left the rabbinical study house and ventured out into what is generally called "the enlightenment." Isaac Bashevis Singer has never been entirely comfortable about his having abandoned the life and faith of his father, and his stories are defiantly profane, in the root sense of that word (what goes on before or outside of a temple). Having left the rabbinical study, he is inviting or daring or pleading with God to follow him out into the jostle and the shmutz of ordinary life. He describes the way people behave, the bizarre things they do when they are driven, often by some version or other of love. "If people knew the truth, the world would collapse like a house of cards," says the wife of a ritual slaughterer who is seducing the narrator of "The Peephole in the Gate" on shipboard, as they make their way to America. "We made love right then and there. I never knew that such a small woman could have such large desires. She tired me out, not I her. All the while, she kept on prattling about God. Sabbath Eve she put three candles into three potatoes, draped a shawl

over her head, covered her eyes with her fingers, and blessed the candles."

How can this be? It is not the infidelity that Singer seems to find remarkable, but the fidelity, the perfectly sincere and devout observance. From this odd angle of vision, Singer writes stories that in some ways recall some of the John O'Hara stories of the 1940s and 1950s. This is not so astonishing as it might first seem, for although the settings of their fictions are far removed, they are neighbors in a way, appearing next to one another in Peter Prescott's interesting anthology that came out late in the year, *American Short Stories* (Norton). O'Hara was born in 1905 and was only a year younger than Singer. There is, in the typical story of each of these writers, the sudden opening of an abyss into which we are invited—or dared—to look. What makes Singer different and rather more complicated than O'Hara is that he understands quite well the vertiginous thrill of looking down, and what he dares himself and his readers to do is then to look up again and not get dizzy. That heavenward glance was not something O'Hara felt much impelled to try.

The Prescott anthology was published late enough in the year so that it carries the sad news of Raymond Carver's death. Carver was one of the eminent practitioners of the short story, and he had a book out this year, *Where I'm Calling From* (Atlantic Monthly Press), the collected short stories of someone who was one of the major players in the game. I have had some problem with these stories, or, more specifically, with their success. The stories, which range from the respectably competent to the superb, ought to have had a certain success. But the attention they achieved was disproportionate even to their very real merits. What I always suspected was that there was a kind of romanticism, a Jacobin silliness in some of his readers' and editors' enthusiasm. This was hardly Carver's fault, but it was irksome, nonetheless, that stories about blue-collar types, drunks, and failures of one kind or another should be sandwiched in among the ads for Buccellati silver and Glenlivet Scotch in the *New Yorker*. It was condescending to the people who were Carver's subjects, and it was unfair to other writers who didn't have his (dis)advantages.

On the other hand, none of this was Carver's doing or responsibility. He wrote, apparently, out of his own experience, and he was very good indeed. That subtlety and acuity of observation are not limited to the upper-middle class

ought not be surprising. The usual tactic is that
of displacement, as in the title story, in which the
speaker is calling, literally, from an alcoholic
drying-out facility, or figuratively from whatever
spiritual *deserto* we fear or believe in. This narrator recounts a seizure suffered by a big, fat fellow named Tiny who "suddenly . . . wasn't there
anymore. He'd gone over in his chair with a big
clatter. He was on his back on the floor with his
eyes closed, his heels drumming the linoleum. . . .
A couple of guys got down on the floor beside
Tiny. One of the guys put his fingers inside
Tiny's mouth and tried to hold his tongue."

Tiny has almost nothing to do with the
story. He comes in so the narrator can say what
is really on his mind: "I'd like to ask him if he
had any signal just before it happened. I'd like to
know if he felt his ticker skip a beat, or else
begin to race. Did his eyelids twitch? But I'm not
about to say anything. He doesn't look like he's
hot to talk about it anyway. But what happened
to Tiny is something I won't ever forget. Old
Tiny, flat on the floor, kicking his heels. So every
time this little flitter starts up anywhere, I draw
some breath and wait to find myself on my back,
looking up, somebody's fingers in my mouth."

That doesn't happen. What does is less dramatic, less predictable, but likelier, and probably
worse. Whatever one fears is only a distraction.
The real peril is tamer, more familiar, and, as
often as not, the outcome of the character's own
weakness or choice. And if it seems that a man
might have extricated himself, might have exerted himself and made a difference, those moments are perhaps delusional also. There is a
gritty and admirable stoicism here, a hard-won
knowledge that gives the work an authority that
has nothing to do with caste or class. Carver's
death is a real loss.

Andre Dubus is a name often linked with
Carver's, and there are certain similarities between the two writers. Both of them describe
lives of a certain seediness which, cumulatively, becomes an emotional and even philosophical cli-
mate. There is also an excellence, a countervail-
ing subtlety and *légèreté* in the stories of both
these men, a craftsmanship that makes the im-
promptu lives they are examining all the more af-
fective. There is no condescension in either of
them but instead a quality of attention that all
but redeems the dismal hopelessness of their characters.

Dubus, who recently received a MacArthur
Fellowship, writes about the Merrimack Valley,

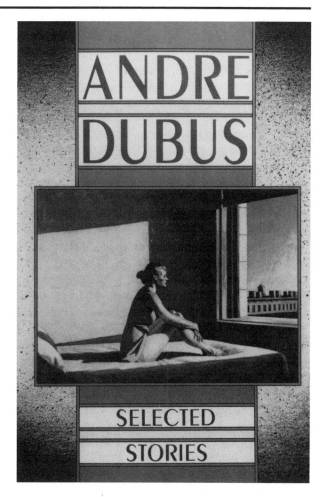

*Dust jacket for the collection that includes representative
pieces from Dubus's earlier volumes as well as two new stories*

those depressing mill towns north of Boston, and
his *Selected Stories* (Godine) offers representative
pieces from his earlier collections as well as two
new stories. The publication of such a collection
is not unremarkable–for although the quality of
the work is such that there ought to be such a
celebratory gesture, the actual prompting is at
least in part the sudden prominence of the writer
as a result of a dreadful accident in which he lost
one leg and much of the use of the other after having stopped on a highway to help some distressed
motorists.

It wasn't that the accident produced the
prominence or the MacArthur Fellowship, but it
did serve to call attention to work of indisputable
excellence. What is striking is Dubus's attention
to setting and landscape, which is not merely an
inert background but serves almost as a spiritual
surround, something the characters have earned,
or have imposed upon themselves in their passion and suffering. One can arrive at such a convic-

tion in a place like Haverill, I suppose, especially if one is of a religious bent, as Dubus's epigraphs suggest him to be. Thus, in "The Winter Father," which is about the painful weekend visits of a divorced father with his children, the mise-en-scène of restaurants and movie theaters and all those terrible trips in cars becomes the focus of the story, the punishment the father persuades himself is right and just. And the conclusion of the story, its turn, is a simple matter of an improvement in the weather which brings the possibility of trips to a beach. Amazingly simple, it is at the same time a bold and austere piece of storytelling, for no one can deny that many of the stories of our lives have to do with such mysteries as improvements in the weather, inner and outer. To manage such an elemental turn without any heavy-handedness or pomposity, entirely within the range of the perfectly matter-of-fact, is a feat of real dexterity. What he ends with is a Joycean epiphany in which the father and his two children are lying on the sand. Holding his daughter's hand, the father "reached over for David's, and closed his eyes against the sun. His legs touched theirs. After a while he heard them sleeping. Then he slept."

Harold Brodkey also had a collection of stories appear during the year, *Stories in an Almost Classical Mode* (Knopf), a volume of such extreme handsomeness as to suggest that the publishers believe their own flap copy about how this man is a "major twentieth-century American writer" whom "a small clutch of writers and critics not ordinarily given to breathless adoration has compared . . . to Freud, Wordsworth and Whitman." It is a bit vertiginous to imagine an overlapping of the Freudian, Wordsworthian, and Whitmanian categories, or what kind of beast would inhabit that tiny tropical glade. All I can think of is Big, and maybe something that has to do with childhood. This kind of nearly meaningless invocation of famous names is what second-rate academics do when they are trying to make themselves and their subjects seem important as they drone on to indifferent audiences at MLA meetings.

But what do I know? These MLA drones are the people who decide what literature is, what books will be assigned to freshmen and sophomores, what works will make it from mere books to the empyrean of assigned texts. And however literature works, Brodkey's achievement as a promoter is considerable. He has managed to get more mileage out of one unfinished and unpub-

lished novel that has been "in work" for years than a lot of other writers have contrived from the completion and publication of twenty.

On the other hand, one must also admit that these pieces are, for all their hyperbolic and brow-beating excess, impressive performances. There is a fervor that works more often than not, and while the risks are obvious–most of the lapses to which Brodkey is subject seem to me a consequence of his lack of any sense of humor–there is a way in which this grappling with the world can be commanding and persuasive. The subjects are consistently painful, the acute pains of childhood and displacement being the thistles that Brodkey grasps most tightly. Adoption and its woes, harridanlike women, and ineffective men whirl about in an inferno of suffering in which a young protagonist finds himself trapped, and to which he has been condemned quite arbitrarily. The second paragraph of his title story, "A Story in an Almost Classical Mode," tells us: "I was supposed to have a good mind–that supposition was a somewhat mysterious and even unlikely thing. I was physically tough, and active, troublesome to others, in mischief or near delinquency at times and conceit and one thing and another (often I was no trouble at all however); and I composed no symphonies, did not write poetry or perform feats of mathematical wizardry." The shapelessness of these indifferently disposed phrases and clauses, with the near-collapse of "and conceit and one thing and another," is not inadvertent. I suspect that the awkwardness is a deliberate gesture of good faith, as if Brodkey were saying he was too much occupied by the truth of these tales, their pain, their arbitrary knottiness to have patience with ordinary sentence making.

What is amazing is that he gets away with this as a general rule. One's patience frays–this is perhaps a response for which the author has calculated and upon which he relies. He is daring us to join "them," to align ourselves with the tormenting siblings and step-siblings, the preoccupied parents, or the biological parents for whom the adoptee yearns and against whom he also rages for having betrayed him or, as in the title story, for having sold him. Brodkey is testing our attention the way children test the love of those around them, seeing how much they can get people to tolerate. It's the kind of book that deserves a place on the shelf, but hardly the kind to which one is likely to return for pleasant browsing or to renew the pleasures one remembers less and less distinctly.

Dust jacket for Brodkey's second collection of stories. The first collection appeared in 1958.

One way of suggesting a little more clearly my difficulties with the Brodkey approach is to compare his work with that of some less well-known practitioners who are hunting in the same woods. Kermit Moyer's *Tumbling* (University of Illinois Press) is also concerned with childhood and its intimate outrages. Moyer's is a first collection but his work is hardly obscure, individual pieces having appeared in the *Sewanee, Hudson, Georgia,* and *Southern* reviews. He is, for that matter, rather Freudian in his angle–incest is the subject of one story, and in others there is the loss of innocence from the observation of some version of the primal scene. But Moyer assumes his readers to be shrewd enough to pick up on these gestures without his having to do very much in the way of lecturing. Indeed, the triumph of these pieces, which are very good, is their dexterity and their tact. "The Compass of the Heart" is one of those primal scene stories, and the adolescent boy who is in love with his father's mistress is a marvel of sweet candor without being tiresome or obvious. We watch him as he sneaks out of his tent to peep into his father's, to try to make out through the distortions (of course!) of mosquito netting, the coupling of his dad and Peggy Landis. "There was the Peggy Landis of exaggerated Southern gentility and then there was this other one in the tent groaning the name of our Savior while she rode my father's thrusting hips–and I was lost somewhere in the gulf between the two," the boy tells us. But what really happens is much more interesting even than that, for the next night he goes back for another glimpse and this time gets something he wasn't expecting, snatches of a conversation that he gets quite wrong but that, in its wrongness, is also right. A clumsier writer would make rather more of the conjunction between sex and the impending death that is the subject of this overheard and misunderstood exchange of sentences, but such a writer would achieve far less in terms of resonance and effect. The actual business of a short story is transacted, after all, not at the typewriter or word processor but in the minds and hearts of the readers. Moyer's tact and modesty are not accidents but calculated strategies of recruiting us as his aides and accomplices. And having conspired with him, the allegiance and commitment we feel to his characters and outcomes is all the greater.

Marianne Gingher's *Teen Angel And Other Stories of Young Love* (Atheneum) is obviously about youngsters, and one must suppose that the publishers would have no objection to a success in what is called the young-adult market. It may even be that this kind of audience is what Gingher also has at least partly in mind, having published pieces of the collection in *Seventeen* and *Redbook*. But she also publishes in the *North American Review*, and the stories don't seem in any way to condescend. Actually, my reason for mentioning them here is what I take to be a quite successful adaptation of the Theocritan strategy of pastoral reduction. The shepherds and farmers of Theocritus and Virgil (or the Shakespearean bumpkins in the comedies) can get away with basic truths we'd be warier about accepting from complicated people like ourselves. In "The Magic Circle" then, Gingher has her protagonist, Dobie Rinehart, thinking about his parents' troubled marriage–even while he is at the Midwinter Dance on the floor with his date: "Sixties music made Dobie think of his parents, of how whenever, say, an old Dionne Warwick song came on the radio, his mother sang right along. Sometimes his father would sidle right up to her and do the harmony, and they'd look so enraptured that Dobie had to turn away. It was as if the love between them only existed in fixes of memory. It seemed detached as an old wedding gift, an ornamental paperweight. . . . All the endless-seeming mush dried up in time; it turned to concrete. You could walk on it, stomp on it. Hearts were nothing but baby rocks." At that level of accomplishment, it doesn't much matter who the intended audience is, just so long as they're able to identify and delight in an unsentimental accuracy of observation and graceful, mimetic prose.

David Updike also writes about childhood and youth, and his first collection, *Out on the Marsh* (Godine), would be interesting and laudable even if he weren't John's son. That connection may be as much a burden as it is a help, for one reads the material with a different and more demanding attention–particularly when the son ventures upon ground his father has already staked out. The first piece, "First Impressions," is divided into sections, the first of which is "The Garden," in which he describes a garden and a house we already know from John Updike's work, a place the family moved out of and felt nostalgic about. The comparison is hard not to make, then, between the vision and the technical facility of the two writers. The son is not yet confident enough to risk some of the father's more daring moves. These are well-made, carefully crafted pieces and are worth anyone's attention, but it will be some time before David Updike grows older and maybe even starts to get a little bit bored by things he knows he can do. It is at that dangerous juncture that writers either push on to new inventions in fiction or they collapse back upon their known strengths and competences.

It is not unlikely that David Updike may one day find himself at that awesome crossroads. He has the necessary eye and ear and the intelligence. Now and then he gives us glimpses of what he may one day be pushing toward. There is a slight piece, little more than a vignette really, called "Agawam," in which the narrator talks about visiting the town where he grew up, how it feels to come home, and how he is surprised by and even resentful of changes that go on in the town during his absence. He builds himself a simple one-room house out in a wooded part of his mother's property, establishing his own claim to the place. And in a lovely explication of the paradox of a person's connection with a place that is in some way sacred he realizes, "All that time I was working alone in the woods, sawing boards and banging nails and wrestling with enormous

Dust jacket for Updike's first collection of stories, primarily about childhood and youth

beams, something was silently changing, and when I finished and looked up, it was only to discover that the earth had shifted beneath me, and the place to which I had always returned now pressed me gently away."

In different ways, both the son and the father can be proud of that. But even though my intention in the foregoing sentence was friendly and approving, there is also a danger I can see in that easy relationship between father and son. There have to be struggles between any older writer and one of a younger generation. Wouldn't it be better if David were writing jangly, odd, weirdo, or wacko things that his father didn't even understand, let alone like? What if the mise-en-scène were urban and ugly rather than comfortable and suburban?

What if the work were more like that of, just for example, Ehud Havazelet, whose *What is it then between us?* (Scribners) is also a debut volume? Havazelet's is a different sensibility, a different notion of how stories should be and of what writing and life are. The title piece, with its wonderful and terrible line from Walt Whitman, is the story of a confrontation between a young man and the young woman whose lover he used to be. The actual exposition of narrative gets managed only by the by in lulls in the speed-freak patter that makes up most of the text but is hardly irrelevant to the machinery of the tale. The encounter is one between inner and outer madnesses. The narrator spews out information, some of it real, some of it fanciful, some of it paranoid and bizarre, and the girl answers him: "You listen. I don't live in that world. I never heard of that city. I'm not acquainted with sports heroes, potentates, figures out of legend. In my world, it's a good day if the buses run on time, you come out of the subway without some stranger's fingerprints all over your body. In my world, drunks swerve across the median doing ninety, terrorists from a country you've never heard of carry machine guns into the restaurant where you're trying to have a quiet meal. . . ." One way of gauging the accomplishment of a collection of short stories is to flip through the book and note the places where one has left markers, improvised bookmarks that are like blazes in forest trails, to help one find the treasures again. There are a lot of these in Havazelet's collection. The opening of "Glass," for instance, is irresistible: "Every night they broke glass and Wright Bellamy wanted to hide. A woman on the fifth floor began it. Wright could see her, wild-haired, crazy, waving a coffee cup against the sky. 'Who do you think you are?' she screamed, every night, 'Who do you think you are?' and Wright had no idea whom she was calling to. By the time she had thrown the cup hard on the air-shaft pavement below, the others would have gathered in their windows, bottles in hand, plates, mirrors. A black man bit the end of light bulbs and lofted them like grenades; a woman in a baseball cap sailed plates like Frisbees that arced alarmingly close to Wright's building. . . ." And the story that follows this batty and wonderful opening is by no means a disappointment.

Havazelet's recourse to this kind of exaggeration is never arbitrary but a measured faithfulness to the bizarre quality of modern urban life to which other writers respond in similar ways. Cut loose entirely from their original promptings, these distortions can be tiresome or trendy, the by no means novel surrealism of certain graduate writing courses. What is more interesting is the kind of work that keeps the tension between the reality and its distortion, turning that tension into an occasion for drama. Havazelet keeps those lines taut and tight. And this same tension is what enlivens Albert Lebowitz's splendid collection of related stories, *A Matter of Days* (Louisiana State University Press). These tales are all about David Stein, a successful but rather rumpled lawyer; Phyllis, his nervous wife; Solon, her younger brother; and Aggie, her beautiful and somewhat louche friend and former college roommate. The distortions in the perceptions of these characters—David, for instance, can hardly see himself except as he is reflected in the eyes of others and can't begin to imagine what the syllables of his name conjure—suggests the kinds of pressures under which they have been living. They are like those gnarled and deformed trees on the California coast that bear, even on calm days, the evidence of storms. But there are few calm days in these stories where even gentle breezes can make for great turbulence. The opening piece in which Phyllis tries to poison a squirrel in her attic might have been written by Erma Bombeck but then edited by Dostoyevski. As she darts up to the attic and down to the cellar, and runs to the store and back home again, she is trapped as surely as the terrified rodent in her house, and at least as desperate. And it is by sheer stylistic virtuosity that Lebowitz keeps Phyllis's precarious balance so that she wobbles and lurches but never quite collapses. It is, finally, a rendition in which style and spirit are identical. These are nine finely wrought stories by a writer of real mastery.

Joyce Carol Oates's place in the pantheon is by now fairly secure, and she had a new collection of short fiction appear this year, *The Assignation* (Ecco), in which there is the same kind of dizzying unreliability in the sane surfaces of things as there is in Lebowitz's work. Indeed, Oates takes this unreliability as one of her primary subjects. The other subject, I think, is the way in which events or objects or visions are transformed by the very process of sentence-making. These are short, fugitive pieces, quick tales, and the choice of form in a writer so diversely gifted is surely a calculated one. Oates can write huge novels or narrative poems or short lyrics with astonishing facility (she is often blamed for the burden this facility puts on her audience). A prose piece, then, of six and a quarter lines is, like one of Marianne Moore's omissions, no accident. Here is that short piece, entitled "One Flesh," and it runs in its entirety: "They are sitting at opposite ends of the old horsehair sofa waiting for something to happen. A rainy summer night, or is it a rainy autumn night, smelling of wet leaves. A muffled reedy music permeates the room like remembered music in which rhythm is blurred. One by one enormous soft-winged insects fly toward them, or scuttle above their heads on the ceiling. Several clocks tick in unison, sounding like a single clock." The provisional description ("or is it a rainy autumn night, smelling of wet leaves") and the grotesque detail of the insects scuttling overhead are literary and self-conscious, and they frame the aperçu for which she has been aiming and with which she ends, as the several clocks sound like a single clock.

A slight but deft series of gestures, they amplify and resonate as Oates repeats or varies them through the course of a fascinatingly intelligent volume. These stories are, at the very basic level, moments of re-vision, which is what stories all aspire to be, either in technical ways or more conventionally, for there is a kind of wisdom that comes from the special dislocations of fiction. *Dislocations* (Louisiana State University Press) is actually the title of Janette Turner Hospital's collection of stories, a remarkable and wonderful book in which the discontinuities are geographical, which is as good a ground for metaphor as any. It is not an accident that most of the great religions have in their sacred texts an account of a journey. Hospital's journey has taken her from Australia to India, England, the United States, and Canada, and her characters are almost always thinking of what their lives were elsewhere. Partings and, occasionally, moments of communion are never quite what we might have expected, so that there is a suggestion of some mysterious, subterranean reality, even a unity, to what her characters do and suffer. What I especially admire about Hospital's book, though, is her gentle humor, which can be sharp but never cruel—and which is all the more remarkable considering that class and ethnicity are the occasions for many of her sallies. Conversely, when she is writing about painful and even heartbreaking incidents—such as the unexpected generosity of

the parents to the returning daughter in "After Long Absence"—that same sense of balance and, in the old-fashioned sense, humor, keeps her from taking that extra half-step into sentimentality. She is a splendid writer.

This is not an exhaustive account of the admirable work of 1988. I might easily have begun differently and charted an altogether different course through this abundance. Which is, I suppose, the final message—that the quantity and quality of the work in short fiction is better than it has ever been. *This* is almost certainly the Golden Age of the short story. (It's nice to know it's the Golden Age of anything at all.)

Inadequately and somewhat guiltily, I list more than a score of other volumes, the mere mention of which is in no way a suggestion of any inferiority to the foregoing collections: *Feeding the Eagles*, by Paulette Bates Alden (Graywolf Press); *Emperor of the Air*, by Ethan Canin (Houghton Mifflin); *Disco Frito*, by Richard Elman (Peregrine Smith Books); *House of Heroes*, by Mary La Chapelle (Crown); *Welcome to My Contri*, by Geoffrey Fox (Hudson View Press); *The Cathay Stories and Other Fictions*, by MacDonald Harris (Story Line Press); *By Land, By Sea*, by William Hoffman (Louisiana State University Press); *Greyhound for Breakfast*, by James Kelman (Farrar, Straus & Giroux); *The Consolation of Nature*, by Valerie Martin (Houghton Mifflin); *Great Wits*, by Alice Mattison (Morrow); *High Ground*, by John McGahern (Viking); *The Wrong Handed Man*, by Lawrence Millman (University of Missouri Press); *Whoever Finds This: I Love You*, by Fay Moskowitz (Godine); *Water Into Wine*, by Helen Norris (University of Illinois Press); *Cover Me*, by Lon Otto (Coffee House Press); *Spirit Seizures*, by Melissa Pritchard (University of Georgia Press); *Women and Children First*, by Francine Prose (Pantheon Books); *Think of England*, by Frederic Raphael (Scribners); *Believe Them*, by Mary Robison (Knopf); *Dusk*, by James Salter (North Point Press); *Jack of Diamonds*, by Elizabeth Spencer (Viking); *The Hat of My Mother*, by Max Steele (Algonquin Books of Chapel Hill); *These Things Happen*, by Marian Thurm (Poseidon Press); *Open Door*, by Luisa Valenzuela (North Point Press).

The Year in Poetry

R. S. Gwynn
Lamar University

"Voices & Visions," public television's ambitious series on modern American poetry, had its premiere in January of 1988. Funded by the Annenberg/CPB Project and grants from the National Endowment for the Humanities, the National Endowment for the Arts, and the Arthur Vining Davis Foundations, the thirteen episodes were skillfully produced and, for the most part, enlightening. Helen Vendler was the senior literary consultant for the series, and poets and critics such as Richard Wilbur, Anthony Hecht, Adrienne Rich, Harold Bloom, and Marjorie Perloff appeared in the episodes to comment on the influences of the poets on the course of modernism. The poets selected for the individual segments were Walt Whitman, Emily Dickinson, Robert Frost, Wallace Stevens, William Carlos Williams, Ezra Pound, Marianne Moore, T. S. Eliot, Hart Crane, Langston Hughes, Elizabeth Bishop, Robert Lowell, and Sylvia Plath. With the series' plan to run concurrently with the average fourteen-week semester, there should be little argument about these choices, although several other poets (Carl Sandburg, E. E. Cummings, and Anne Sexton come to mind) might have made more interesting subjects for televised presentations than several of the poets who were included.

Several criticisms can be raised about the series, however. The first concerns the order of the segments. One wonders why, when the accompanying anthology and collection of critical essays were chronologically arranged, the series opened with Frost, followed with Pound and Hughes, and then backed up to Whitman. Dickinson was not covered until the series' seventh episode. One suspects that the PBS executives were troubled by opening with Whitman, given the episode's emphasis on the poet's homoeroticism, and were equally dismayed at the prospect of presenting the reclusive Dickinson to an audience largely composed of high-school and college students taking the course for credit. Public television is, after all, show business, and any series must lead from strength. Thus, a genial and be-

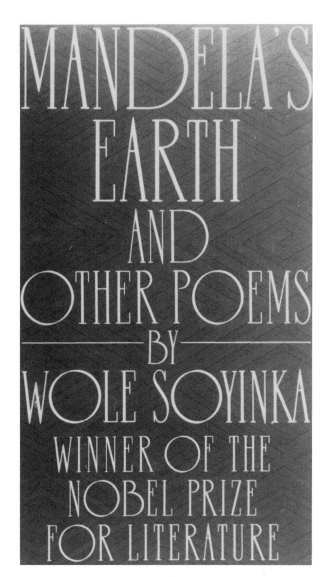

Dust jacket for the collection that includes Soyinka's satiric poem "Like Rudolph Hess, the Man Said," a protest against the imprisonment of Nelson Mandela

nign Robert Frost, presented as a public poet far removed from the complicated and often tortured private personality depicted in Lawrance Thompson's official biography, appeared first to give the impression that modern poetry and sanity could indeed walk hand in hand.

49

The other episodes, however, seemed to find little common ground as to how the poets' personal lives might be presented. Nothing was said about Elizabeth Bishop's unconventional private life, but in one episode an actor impersonating Hart Crane wistfully eyed a couple of sailors across a crowded barroom. As might be expected, the emotional troubles of Robert Lowell and Sylvia Plath were scrupulously explored, but there was little mention of Frost's tragic family life or of Eliot's chaotic first marriage. The episode on Marianne Moore lamented the poet's attainment of celebrity status in her later years but still presented her as a sort of Glenda the Good Witch of American poetry, including film clips of her at Ebbetts Field and retelling the famous anecdotes about Moore's experience with the Ford Motor Company in her failed attempt to come up with a name for the new automobile that eventually became the Edsel. Pound's admiration of Italian fascism was explored in detail, but little mention was made of the controversy surrounding the poet's receipt of the Bollingen Prize in 1949 for *The Pisan Cantos*. In an attempt to find some middle ground that might appeal to scholar, student, and general viewer, the series suffered from the lack of any type of consistent critical approach to the poets and their work. One wonders what most viewers made of Prof. Harold Bloom's airy invocation of Stevens as "the poet of the American sublime" or of Adrienne Rich's attempts to portray Dickinson as a proto-feminist. Indeed, if the series demonstrated anything it showed how fragmented the critical establishment is in its bizarre attempts to "deconstruct" modern poetry according to the tenets of currently fashionable theory.

The accompanying collection of critical essays and the anthology, both apparently designed for classroom use, suffer from a similar lack of consistent direction. Helen Vendler edited *Voices & Visions: The Poet in America* (Random House) and contributed her own essay on Stevens, the one poet of the thirteen who seems to have dominated critical inquiry in recent years, possibly because his often enigmatic poems lend themselves to all sorts of schools of interpretation. Vendler is as lively as ever but fails, for the most part, to explain how recent readings of Stevens, who was accepted and praised for his colorful exoticism during his life, have come to extol him, particularly the windy philosopher of *Opus Posthumous* (1957), as *the* key figure of American modernism. The other essays vary in quality. Calvin Bedient is

good on Whitman; and Hugh Kenner, as expected, and Vereen Bell are excellent on Pound and Lowell, respectively. Arnold Rampersad, who completed work on his biography of Hughes this year, makes a strong case for the poet, who is probably the weakest of the thirteen, as a central figure in the history of black culture, echoes of whose poems can be found in the speeches of Martin Luther King, Jr. However, other essays are of little or no use to either the scholar or student. John M. Slatin's analysis of Marianne Moore's idyllic "The Steeple-Jack" results in some bizarre leaps in which Slatin attempts to show that "Moore's representation of the steeple-jack was inspired, in part, by a sixteenth-century account of how, on a summer day in 1533, while the priest was celebrating mass, the devil climbed the steeple of the church in Shrewsbury, England, causing a great tempest and destroying both the town clock and the church bell." Readers are referred to the text of Moore's poem and invited to determine the relevance of this information.

Robert DiYanni's *Modern American Poets: Their Voices and Visions* (Random House) takes the prize as the worst-edited anthology in recent memory. Often the selections fail to match the contents of the television programs and critical volume. Moore's "The Steeple-Jack," to cite but one example, is not included in the anthology; neither is "An Octopus," which is dealt with at length in the program episode. Even worse, however, is the slipshod proofreading of the poems. Here are some famous lines as they appear in the anthology: "Sorrow is my own yard/were [*sic*] the new grass/flames as it has flamed/often before but not/with the cold fire/that closes round me this year." "None may teach it–Any [*sic*]–/ 'Tis the Sea [*sic*] Despair." Using anthologies such as this, students who complain about the obscurity of modern poetry have my sympathy.

After viewing the series and reading the material, one is left with the sobering impression that there were indeed giants in the not so distant past and that contemporary poetry labors in the obscurity of their long shadows. Only thirty years ago, I suspect that the average man or woman on the street could name at least one or two living American poets. Frost, after all, was a public figure, and Sandburg, in his sheepskin coat, graced the pages of *Life* toasting a glass of champagne with Marilyn Monroe. Asking the same question today, even to a classroom full of English majors, will in most cases result in a profound silence. It may well be that Robert Lowell was the last American poet to make a dent in his country's consciousness, even if he owed much of his celebrity to his refusal to accept an award from a president and to his appearance in one of Norman Mailer's best-sellers. Indeed, there is something unsettling in the thought that the two living American poets who have won the Nobel Prize are Polish-born Czeslaw Milosz and Russian exile Joseph Brodsky. Judson Jerome's useful *1989 Poet's Market* (Writer's Digest Books) lists over seventeen hundred literary magazines in the United States that publish poetry, and there is no shortage of poets to fill their largely unread pages. But where are the major figures? And what are they writing that will be read and discussed in classrooms fifty years from now?

The title essay of Donald Hall's *Poetry and Ambition: Essays 1982-88* (University of Michigan Press) begins with this assertion: "I see no reason to spend your life writing poems unless your goal is to write great poems." Hall, as savvy an observer of the contemporary scene as anyone could wish, goes on to observe that most contemporary poems, while "*readable*, charming, funny, touching, sometimes even intelligent" are also "usually brief, . . . resemble each other, . . . are anecdotal, . . . do not extend themselves, . . . make no great claims, . . . connect small things to other small things." To account for this contemporary phenomenon, Hall is forced to invent a new poetic genre: "We write and publish the McPoem—ten billion served—which becomes our contribution to the history of literature as the Model T is our contribution to a history which runs from bare feet past elephant and rickshaw to the vehicles of space. Pull in any time day or night, park by the busload, and the McPoem waits on the steam shelf for us, wrapped and protected, indistinguishable, undistinguished, and reliable—the good old McPoem identical from coast to coast and in all the little towns between, subject to the quality control of the least common denominator." The analogy is well taken, and its extension seems true enough: "And every year, Ronald McDonald takes the Pulitzer." Hall goes on to blame the creative writing programs ("the workshops of Hamburger University") for the situation and cites an ever-increasing surplus of creative writing teacher-poets, whose sole function seems to be to turn out even more of the same, as the norm. The ambition of today's poet may urge him to write poems for the *New Yorker*, poems for tenure, and poems for the NEA, but

it somehow fails to inspire him to attempt poems that will retain their freshness when removed from "the steam shelf" and left sitting for several chilly decades on the table of Time.

With Hall's disquieting remarks in mind, it is instructive to turn to *Mandela's Earth and Other Poems* (Random House) by the Nigerian writer Wole Soyinka, winner of the 1986 Nobel Prize for Literature. No one, I think, would argue that Soyinka is a great poet. He has divided his literary activities among a number of genres–the novel, criticism, autobiography, plays–and his poetry has a hasty quality that verges at times on incoherence. Nevertheless, these poems reveal a largeness of scope and a moral force that have become increasingly rare in American poetry. Since the Nobel Prize has perhaps too often been awarded to the kind of high-minded humanitarian who is not likely to merit serious discussion solely on his or her literary merits, it comes as something of a surprise to discover that Soyinka, even when expressing his outrage over the continued imprisonment of South African political leader Nelson Mandela, turns instinctively to satire. "Like Rudolph Hess, the Man Said," takes a quote from Pik Botha, South African foreign minister, for its epigraph: "We keep him (Mandela) for the same reason the Allied Powers are holding Rudolf Hess." With devastating sarcasm, Soyinka explores a repressive regime's absurd rationalizations: "Mandela? Mandel . . . Mendel . . . Mengel . . . Mengele!/It's he! Nazi superman in sneaky black face!" Stating the obvious fact that the free world's tolerance of the South African regime has been abetted by that country's abundant resources of precious metals, Soyinka concludes with a peroration that is both moving and funny:

> *Gold*! Ah yes, Mandela-Hess,
> You got us in this mess. The Allied Powers
> Rightly hold you pacing wall to wall
> Treading out your grand designs
> In commie jackboots. Mandela-Mengele,
> You are *ours*! We'll keep you close.
> Your *Doppelganger* haunts us to the vaults.
> Yes, "thars gold in them thar mountains"
>   –would *you*
> Let Mandela loose?

Some years ago Soyinka was criticized for not fully supporting a cultural and literary movement known as Negritude, a third-world position roughly parallel to the American Black Power movement of the 1960s. "A tiger," mildly replied

Soyinka, "does not need to proclaim his tigritude."

In contrast, the American winners of major prizes announced this year suffer by comparison. The Pulitzer Prize for Poetry was awarded to William Meredith for *Partial Accounts: New & Selected Poems* (Knopf), which was reviewed in these pages last year. Meredith is certainly what passes for a distinguished poet in this country: he began his career as a Yale Younger Poet; he is a member of the Academy of American Poets; he has taught at universities from Princeton to Hawaii; and he has been poetry consultant at the Library of Congress. In the collection's title poem Meredith describes his own open-heart surgery with admirable modesty that says much about his estimate of his own abilities and much more perhaps about the inconsequential status of poets in this Republic:

> When they needed a foreign part,
> a valve which was not to be found
> or spared elsewhere in his ample,
> useful body, they chose a pig's valve.
> This will be compatible, they reasoned,
> with such pig-headed machinery
> as has maintained a minor poet
> for sixty-three years in America.

Last year I commented on Meredith's self-characterization as "a mild-spoken citizen," quoting a poem about Aleksandr Solzhenitsyn and the Soviet concentration camps that concluded with a reference to "that terrible archipelago/ conceived and made by men like ourselves." The point I made then seems worth reiterating: to equate "men like ourselves" with Stalin, Hitler, or other such subhuman aberrations of the species seems so simplistic and banal as to become meaningless. Have American poets grown so morally pusillanimous that they cannot call evil by its proper name without feeling themselves guilty of self-incrimination?

The National Book Critics Circle Award for Poetry was presented to C. K. Williams for *Flesh and Blood* (Farrar, Straus & Giroux), which was also briefly mentioned in this essay last year. Born in 1936 and thus of a younger generation than Meredith, Williams began his career in the tumultuous late 1960s. He has slowed down somewhat since those days. He currently works in ten-line stanzas with flabby neo-Whitmanesque lines, and his subject matter has grown middle-aged and suburban. Here are some lines from "Some of Us," a poem typical of those in the collection:

Dust jacket for the 1988 gathering of poems that Simpson "would like to be remembered by"

> How nearly unfeasible they make it for the rest of
> us, those who, with exactly our credentials,
> attain, if that's how it happens, the world of the pub-
> licly glamorous, the very chic, the "in."
> It isn't so much being omitted, left home from the
> party, as knowing that we'll never get there,
> never participate in those heady proximities our insa-
> tiable narrations ever tremble toward.
> What would be there, we ask ourselves. Better bos-
> oms? Better living rooms?

The language here does not rise above the level of competent expository prose, though I fail to see how anyone can "attain" a world or "participate in heady proximities." As far as form is concerned, Williams's choice of the ten-line stanza seems about as arbitrary as the "ghazals" that Adrienne Rich and Jim Harrison churned out twenty years ago or, for that matter, the unwieldy unrhymed sonnets of Robert Lowell's *His-*

tory (1973). Now that Williams has won the Pulitzer, he can perhaps tell the rest of us how it feels to be among the "in." Williams's *Selected Poems* appeared this year from the same publisher.

One honor awarded to an American poet did seem appropriate and justified. In March Howard Nemerov was named the third United States Poet Laureate, succeeding Richard Wilbur. With characteristic wit, Nemerov referred the reporters who converged on him following the announcement to a poem he had written thirty years earlier, "From the Desk of the Laureate: For Immediate Release." *The Collected Poems of Howard Nemerov* appeared over a decade ago, but the poet has continued to produce excellent work, including last year's *War Stories*. Of the three poets thus far selected for the position, Nemerov comes closest to fulfilling the public role that the office's lofty title implies. Like Karl Shapiro and the late John Ciardi, he is at his best as an observer of contemporary American life, at times with a detached skepticism and at others with pointed barbs. Nemerov's "Boom!," a satirical look at the religion "industry" during the Eisenhower years, seems almost prophetic in its depiction of a swank resort called "the Vespation-Carlton" filled with shameless hucksters of the cloth. In another mode he can be metaphysical and profound. In the much-anthologized "The Goose Fish" two lovers encounter, on a moonlit shore, the remains of a monstrous fish, a grinning memento mori:

> There in the china light he lay,
> Most ancient and corrupt and gray.
> They hesitated at his smile,
> Wondering what it seemed to say
> To lovers who a little while
> Before had thought to understand,
> By violence upon the sand,
> The only way that could be known
>   To make a world their own.

When asked by reporters about his poetic style, Nemerov related an anecdote about a brand of cigar he used to smoke while playing poker: "The cigar I smoked was called a Vermont Factory Smoker. On the band was written, 'All Quality, No Style.' I think that should take care of your question about my style."

To have written "The Fury of Aerial Bombardment" and "The Groundhog," two of the finest poems of the century, is an enviable accomplishment, to say the least. Richard Eberhart's *Collected Poems: 1930 to 1986* (Oxford University

Press) is a much-needed compendium of the work of American poetry's elder statesman, a poet whose best work is so familiar that one is likely to forget that Eberhart is still writing well in his ninth decade. Is it possible that Eberhart was Robert Lowell's teacher at St. Mark's School or that he was born three years earlier than W. H. Auden? The poet is brief in his introductory comments to this volume, repeating a few lines he spoke in 1983 on his induction into the American Academy of Arts and Letters: "Poetry goes down into the darkness of the subconscious and comes up with a morning glory out of the enriched mud and schist of the world. The morning glory could be a lily, or a rose, Chartres Cathedral, or the Parthenon, or John Keats, a quality of perfection dreamed of by mankind." For many reasons, the citation of Keats is just, for Eberhart represents the continuation of the Romantic tradition; many of his early poems could be faulted in that they are expressions of emotion that often fail to find Eliot's "objective correlative" to evoke the same response from the reader. He is also, among poets of this century, something of an exception in his fondness for abstraction. Eberhart would be the last to deny this; in "Mystery of the Abstract" he refers to a distinguished partisan of the other camp:

> No reality but things said William Carlos
> Williams. A tag. Make it abstract, ideal.
> Soon we will be abstracted from life, be nothing,
>
> Time Space, live, hope, death are overlays of life.
> These masterful ideas make us human as we are,
> No one escapes them, we have to believe in them.

Many of the recent poems in this collection seem to be final assessments of other poets: Samuel Taylor Coleridge, Ralph Waldo Emerson, Federico García Lorca, Auden, and many others. In another sense, these poems could be taken as eloquent farewells to other practitioners of the art that has sustained the poet so well for so many years.

Last year it was a pleasure to note the appointment of Howard Nemerov's predecessor, Richard Wilbur, to the laureateship. This year it is equally satisfying to welcome Wilbur's *New and Collected Poems* (Harcourt Brace Jovanovich), which will replace the dog-eared copies of *The Poems of Richard Wilbur* that many of us have been carrying around for over twenty years. The new edition retains most of the earlier collection and adds work from *Walking to Sleep* (1969), *The*

Mind-Reader and Other Poems (1976), and *The Whale and Other Uncollected Translations* (1982), as well as the contents of *Lying and Other Poems*, a chapbook issued in 1987 by Cummington Press. Wilbur's work is a national treasure, and any attempt to praise it further becomes a futile exercise in trying to find new adjectives; nevertheless, it should be noted that the labels that have too often been applied to him in the past–elegant, witty, graceful, and so on–have become, with some critics, no more than reflex actions by which his work may politely be dismissed. Wilbur, more than any poet of his generation, has resisted the vagaries of fashion: he does not "confess"; he does not practice "open form"; and he does not write topical poetry that becomes little more than a historical relic a few years after its composition. His work is of a piece, even though he has experimented widely with poetic forms and approaches to subject matter. Many of his early poems are remarkable for the sheer pleasure of watching a young man in love with what Wallace Stevens called "the gaeity of language." The later work is more restrained in this respect but has deepened in its understanding of the "things of this world" to which Wilbur always returns for his subjects. The poems that he has written in the last twenty years are among his best, even if they have not found equal billing in the anthologies with such earlier ones as "Mind" or "Death of a Toad." Among them I would single out "Cottage Street, 1953," a memory of a meeting with the young Sylvia Plath shortly after her first suicide attempt; "The Writer," a narrative about the poet's daughter, the excellent short-story writer Ellen Wilbur; and "The Catch," a witty love poem which I quoted at length last year. Here, in its entirety, is a short historical meditation, "To the Etruscan Poets":

> Dream fluently, still brothers, who when young
> Took with your mothers' milk the mother tongue,
>
> In which pure matrix, joining world and mind,
> You strove to leave some line of verse behind
>
> Like a fresh track across a field of snow,
> Not reckoning that all could melt and go.

We are indeed lucky that the present collection will keep Wilbur's tracks fresh.

Louis Simpson's *Collected Poems* (Paragon House) is another worthy addition to any library, putting under one cover forty years' work by the Pulitzer Prize-winning poet. In 1983 Simpson pub-

lished *People Live Here*, a selected edition that might have remained adequate had the poet not published *The Best Hour of the Night*, one of his finest individual collections, the same year. In comparison with Wilbur's career, Simpson's is one of diverging courses. After coming to this country from his native Jamaica and serving in Europe during World War II, he began as a formalist, writing tightly constructed pieces such as "My Father in the Night Commanding No" and "Early in the Morning," poems that caused him to be lumped in with the Academics, to use the terminology of the time, and editing, with Donald Hall and Robert Pack, *New Poets of England and America*, the quintessential 1950s anthology. In the early 1960s, however, Simpson loosened his idiom and forms, experimenting for several years with surrealism and the "deep image" type of poetry championed by Robert Bly. In the 1970s the poet settled into his present manner, writing elliptical, ironic narratives of suburban life like those in his latest four collections. A short poem from the early 1960s, "In the Suburbs," foreshadows the direction of Simpson's most recent work:

> There's no way out.
> You were born to waste your life.
> You were born to this middleclass life
>
> As others before you
> Were born to walk in procession
> To the temple, singing.

Many readers and critics have mistakenly called Simpson a satirist, failing to understand that the poet's "You" here is an inclusive one; he might as well have said "I." Simpson has his sardonic side, to be sure, as a poem such as "The Beaded Pear," with its all-too-accurate depiction of American family life ("The children are home at six,/and they sit down to eat. Mom insists/on their eating together at least once/every week. It keeps the family together."), makes clear, but his stance is more often than not compassionate as he attempts to assign some value to the lives of those in a culture that has replaced the temple with the shopping mall. This collection is also essential for many reasons, not the least being its reminder that Simpson has written some of the best poetry of World War II. *On Louis Simpson: Depths Beyond Happiness* (University of Michigan Press), edited by Hank Lazer, is a comprehensive collection of reviews and essays that should prove a useful reader's companion.

Like Simpson and Allen Ginsberg, Daniel Hoffman was one of that remarkable group of poets who studied with Mark Van Doren at Columbia University in the late 1940s. In "Crossing Walt Whitman Bridge" Hoffman wittily alludes to his illustrious peers:

> Walt, my old classmates who write poems
> Have written poems to you.
> They find you, old fruit,
>
> In the supermarket, California;
> They hear you speaking from the brazen mouth
> Of your statue on Bear Mountain. . . .

Hoffman has had his share of recognition over the years, but it is a shame that his portion has not been larger. He can seemingly do anything, claiming, "I can still cobble rime royale by hand." *Hang-Gliding from Helicon: New and Selected Poems 1948-1988* (Louisiana State University Press) is a satisfying collection that could only be faulted by its omission of any portions of *Brotherly Love* (1981), Hoffman's remarkable long poem about William Penn and the founding of Pennsylvania. There are so many sides to Hoffman's work that it is impossible to mention them all. However, it is interesting to note that he was writing ecological poems such as "On the Extinction of a Species" in his first book, which won the Yale Younger Poets Award in 1954, long before the issue became fashionable, and continues to do so in one of the most recent poems in the collection, "The Last Lynx." Hoffman is a fine poet who continues to produce work of high quality.

The world of poetry readers can probably be divided roughly between those who can abide Charles Bukowski and those who can't. No matter how one feels, Bukowski's recent autobiographical movie, *Barfly*, is one more indication that the poet is now an international figure. *The Boardinghouse Madrigals: Early Selected Poems 1946-1966* (Black Sparrow Press) contains poems that, in the poet's words, are "taken from the first few books; others were not in books but have been taken from obscure magazines of long ago." A bibliography might have told a fascinating tale of the strangest poetic career in recent memory, but the book does not include one. Crushed beer cans, stubbed-out cigarettes, aging women with varicose veins, and a bruised heart worn on the sleeve are Bukowski's stock-in-trade, and, like someone cornered in a seedy bar by a garrulous and slightly intimidating drunk, the reader has little choice but to hear him out. Bukowski says

that "the early poems are more lyrical than where I am at now." The last poem in the book, "Destroying Beauty," is a fair example:

> a rose
> red sunlight;
> I take it apart
> in the garage
> like a puzzle:
> the petals are as greasy
> as old bacon
> and fall
> like the maidens of the world
> backs to the floor
> and I look
> at the old calendar
> and touch
> my wrinkled face
> and smile
> because
> the secret
> is beyond me.

Taken in small doses, Bukowski can be refreshing in his candor; unfortunately, Bukowski does not come in small doses.

Another poet one can either love or hate but never quite ignore is Diane Wakoski. Wakoski raises self-absorption to an art form, railing on endlessly about the inadequacies of her face and figure, the men who have betrayed her, her troubles getting anything to come out right in the kitchen, and on and on. After a while, her marathon complaining starts to grate on the nerves:

> I have always been poor, and never managed well.
> I took taxis when I was tired and thus had no
>   money for food
> halfway through
> the week. The mediocre wines on my table cost as
>   much as
> emerald necklaces,
> and I always look like I live on welfare.

Emerald Ice: Selected Poems 1967-82 (Black Sparrow Press) runs over three hundred pages, a fair indication of Wakoski's refusal to compress the details of her emotional life. On rare occasions she is capable of venturing into subjects. In "Silver" she begins, "How much I want to sit down/at my table and pick up a heavy silver spoon to eat my soup." The poem concludes, "What I want/is to hold it and to somehow transform the ritual of eating/into something non-organic/ . . . /I want beautiful silver so that I can pretend I will never have to die."

Dust jacket for the collection that includes poems about the author's experiences as an Air Force pilot in the Vietnam War

For contrast, one turns to May Sarton's *As Does New Hampshire* (Bauhan), a slim volume of regional poems culled from the poet's earlier collections, including the *Selected Poems of May Sarton* (1978). Classical and classy, graceful and always a bit aloof, Sarton always seems to be overlooked when lists of the century's best women poets are compiled. The opening couplets of "A Guest" are testimony to her careful style:

My woods belong to woodcock and to deer;
For them, it is an accident that I'm here.

If, for the plump raccoon, I represent
An ash can that was surely heaven-sent,

The bright-eyed mask, the clever little paws
Obey not mine, but someone else's laws.

The young buck takes me in with a long glance
That says that I, not he, am here by chance.

And they all go their ways, as I must do,
Up through the green and down again to snow,

Not one of us responsible or near,
But each himself and in the singular.

After listening to the angst of a poet like Wakoski, I find this fine poet's cool control as bracing as the landscape she depicts.

There are always poets one is vaguely aware of, but often they remain not much more than names seen in some anthology's table of contents. John Wieners and Robert Bagg are two such poets. Wieners's *Cultural Affairs in Boston: Poetry & Prose 1956-1985* (Black Sparrow) contains a great deal of gossip about the Black Mountain group, some campy chatter about dead starlets, unapologetic accounts of the gay life, and a body of writing that is distinguished for nothing except its irresponsibility. I quote the last lines of "Memories of You":

inwardly I scream and dream of the day
when I will be free
to marry
and breed more children
so I can seduce them
and they be seduced by
saintly motorcyclists in the dawn.

Bagg's *Body Blows: Poems New and Selected* (University of Massachusetts Press) is sometimes heavy with name-dropping ("Old Buddies;/Amabile and Garrett, Starbuck and Scully:/Maderna's fountains, which Wilbur raised to their Christian heights. . . ."), but as often Bagg's work is affecting, particularly in several poems about divorce. "Muscongus Bay Sloop," an account of a recently separated man who undertakes a therapeutic repair job, is a fine narrative:

He'd built two kitchens for his wife,
made her a giant bed morticed to the floor–
"Odysseus' bed" she had called it.
He panelled the raw insides of their summer
    A-frame;
to pot her flowers he shaped hexagons of drift-
    wood.
So it wasn't surprising to find him
building again. But what he chose
to revive was a sloop launched on Muscongus Bay
in the eighteen-eighties, which for years
he'd let moulder under torn canvas in a boatyard.

There is nothing flashy about either form or idiom here; the poem is simply a good story, compassionately told.

No matter how hard one tries to keep abreast of the poetry scene, there always seem to be poets one has never heard of who have managed to publish enough work to merit selected editions–such as David Bromige and Felix Pollak. Bromige's *Desire: Selected Poems 1963-1987* (Black Sparrow Press) is the winner of the 1988 Western States Book Award and contains work from almost twenty earlier collections. Born in England in 1933, Bromige is professor of English at Sonoma State University. He is occasionally witty, even more often tedious, and at times reveals large lapses of taste, as in "What Counts":

I say the wrong thing
because I want to be desirable to you
because you show me signs
that say I am. I want to win you by quick-
    thinkingness
& so I can, just name a time & place
meanwhile, keep talking, while you tell me this.

Pollak's *Benefits of Doubt* (Spoon River Poetry Press) contains work by an Austrian native who fled Hitler to become curator of special collections in the library at Northwestern University. Pollak, who died in 1987 after suffering increasing visual impairment for fifteen years, was remarkably unsentimental about his blindness. Here is a short poem on the subject, "The Request":

"This," said the kindly old volunteer
who installed my Talking Books machine,
"is a life-time loan by the government.
Please return it, when you no longer
    need it."

There is a great deal of variety in Pollak's collection, but these last poems are remarkable for their evocation of a familiar world rendered strange and fearsome:

        Is the skin of my face growing
over my eyes? I resist the impulse to look into
the mirror of a store window. I know there would
    be
no reply.

The year was not notable for new anthologies. Only two were received for this review, and both were highly limited in their contents. The problem with any anthology that tries to restrict its contents–regionally, ethnically, thematically, or otherwise–is that all too often poems appear in it that may be representative of the criteria for inclusion but of little intrinsic value. Such is the case with *Gay & Lesbian Poetry in Our Time* (St. Mar-

tin's Press), edited by Carl Morse and Joan Larkin. No one would deny the validity of or need for such a collection, especially when the ongoing tragedy of the AIDS epidemic fills the pages of every newspaper and magazine. On the other hand, an anthology that forces poets of the highest caliber to appear next to rank amateurs who seem to know nothing about the elements of writing is inexcusable. One wonders if poets like James Merrill, Frank Bidart, Olga Broumas, and Alfred Corn, to mention only a few, had any idea of the editors' lack of discrimination and taste. The editors report that one writer would not allow his work to be included for fear of being "ghettoized"–a wise move considering some of the lesser inhabitants of this particular ghetto. Indeed, Morse and Larkin are incredibly self-indulgent in the space they give themselves, with Morse awarding himself more pages of poetry than W. H. Auden and both editors participating in an eleven-page self-interview in lieu of an introduction. One is hardly reassured by Larkin's ingenuous remarks: "Thom Gunn is another poet whose work I simply didn't know." Is it possible to trust an editor who hasn't heard of Thom Gunn, certainly one of the most distinguished British-American poets of his generation? In his own poetry Morse likewise does not acquit himself well. In "Dream of the Artfairy" he envisions "all the art ever made by fairies/[becoming] invisible to straights," including the following fill-in-the-blank lines:

–I taste a liquor never brewed
    from tankards ———— ——— ————,

–The mass of men lead lives ——— ————
    ————.

–Call me ————.

One will grant that other quotes from Walt Whitman, Oscar Wilde, and Gertrude Stein are appropriate, but Dickinson, Thoreau, and Melville might be surprised at the company they are forced to keep here.

The exclusion of certain poets from the anthology is, again, a remarkable show of editorial ignorance. Where is the estimable May Sarton? Where is Elizabeth Bishop? And why, when Larkin and Morse include Robert Peters's *The Great American Poetry Bake-off* in their bibliography of critical works on gay and lesbian poetry, do they not include any of his fine poetry, particularly sequences from the powerful *What Dillinger*

Meant to Me? (1983). On the other hand, certain inclusions are just as odd. Auden, to cite one example, wrote some very explicit poetry about his sexual orientation in his last years. Instead, the editors choose to include "Lay Your Sleeping Head, My Love," "A Lullaby," and an excerpt from "In Time of War." One selection, however, seems an invasion of a dead poet's privacy that should have been stopped by his literary executor. No poet was more discreet in his private life than Langston Hughes; even Arnold Rampersad, Hughes's thorough biographer, can come to no sure conclusions about the poet's sexual life, citing the rumors that followed Hughes all of his career but ultimately admitting that no proof of his sexual preference is ever likely to surface. Including a poem like the famous "Harlem" is pointless, particularly in the case of a dead poet powerless to control reprint rights for his work. Exploitation is the word that comes most readily to mind.

There are nevertheless some good poems in *Gay & Lesbian Poetry in Our Time*, particularly work by May Swenson, Marilyn Hacker, and James Schuyler; certainly Edward Field's "World War II," a simple yet harrowing narrative account of a B-17 raid and tragic ditching in the English Channel, must rank among the finest of modern war poems. Here are some lines about a fellow flyer who gives up his place in the life raft to save the narrator:

> That boy who took my place in the water
> Who died instead of me
> I don't remember his name even.
> I was like those who survived the death camps
> by letting others go into the ovens in their place.
> It was him or me, and I made up my mind to live.

This poem and several others notwithstanding, this anthology does no one much credit.

Another anthology, this one limited by genre (light verse), is *Sometime the Cow Kick Your Head: Light Year '88/9* (Bits Press), editor Robert Wallace's fifth entry in this diverting series. According to Wallace, "There are corny poems John Hollander will probably hate, and sophisticated poems readers who don't know who John Hollander is will probably hate. . . . So there isn't a logical way to read this book. Do skip and browse. Find what you like." Doing so is usually rewarding. I open the book at random to "Song of Granny Smith" by Mary McArthur:

> Stay me with Winesap,

> Comfort me with Gravenstein,
> For I am sick of love
> For apples, applesauce, and apple pie.
> Baldwin, Pippin, Tolman Sweet,
> Keswick, Cortland, Northern Spy,
> Russet, Ribston, Normandy,
> Snow, Melrose, Spy Gold, Lodi.
> My beloved's a ruddy McIntosh.
> Jonathan's the apple of my eye.

In his thoughtful introduction, Wallace laments the long shadow of Matthew Arnold, whose critical views reach into the present century: "Never more than now has poetry needed all of its voices, especially the light, or needed to resist the strangling blandishments of critical high–higher, and highest–seriousness. In a time when so much so-called 'serious' poetry seems designed to alienate the all-but-forgotten general reader, light verse offers 'a natural bridge into more serious and important kinds.' " A quick perusal of the table of contents reveals such distinguished contributors as X. J. Kennedy, William Stafford, Marge Piercy, Daniel Hoffman, May Swenson, and Donald Hall. The book's final section of parodies will elicit smiles from partisans of that increasingly rare genre. Here are the opening lines of John Shea's "Baby":

> You do doo-doo, you do doo-doo
> All the time, it's true,
> Making my life and home your own,
> Mein Kommandant, my stink-bomb man,
> Choking the room with the smell of you.

Wallace's anthologies provide a much-needed corrective to the long face and furrowed brow that too many deem the only appropriate mask for the contemporary poet.

Lying on the desk like a thick slab of white marble, the second edition of *The Norton Anthology of Modern Poetry* (Norton), edited by the late Richard Ellmann and Robert O'Clair, presents an inviting target for all sorts of potshots. It has been fifteen years since the first edition appeared, and a revision is obviously long overdue. The new version is over four hundred pages longer and makes an effort to update the selections of the poets who were first included and also to add some new names who have emerged since 1973. As it now stands, the anthology stretches from Walt Whitman (b. 1819) to Cathy Song (b. 1955), making modernism the longest single period in the history of English literature. To its credit, the new edition adds a number of Com-

Dust jacket for Adcock's third and most highly praised poetry volume

monwealth poets (among them the wonderful Australian, Judith Wright), a few new British poets (Tony Harrison and Craig Raine are two worth mentioning), and the requisite quantity of minority writers such as Alberto Ríos, Leslie Marmon Silko, and Rita Dove. A quick perusal of the table of contents gives a fair idea of who's who in the pantheon, according to Ellmann and O'Clair, and who's not. Thus, Adrienne Rich (eighteen pages) outranks Emily Dickinson (eleven pages), and A. R. Ammons (sixteen pages) stands higher on Parnassus than Edwin Arlington Robinson (fifteen pages). Richard Hugo outranks John Berryman by three pages; Audre Lorde, Amy Clampitt by the same number. It should come as no surprise that Rich, Ammons, Hugo, and Lorde are all published by Norton. Some of the omissions are startling: May Sarton, May Swenson, Weldon Kees, X. J. Kennedy, and Donald Hall are only a few whose names do not lead all the rest. In a val-

iant effort to be *au courant* the editors have outdone themselves, it seems, in compiling notable examples of that contemporary phenomenon, the women's same-sex love poem, including examples by Marilyn Hacker, Adrienne Rich, Carolyn Forché, and Audre Lorde. After the umpteenth variation on lines like Forché's "our clits beat like/ twins to the loons rising up" one starts looking for his copy of *The Home Book of Verse*. Nevertheless, this is the standard anthology of modern verse for classroom use, and one can take comfort from the fact that 1,865 pages allows a great deal of latitude for picking and choosing.

The anthology poets, those one expects to encounter upon opening any collection of contemporary poetry, were prominent in 1988, led by W. S. Merwin, whose *The Rain in the Trees* (Knopf) is his first collection in five years. Merwin's *Selected Poems* (Atheneum), also published in 1988, offers a retrospective look at a career that began in 1952, when W. H. Auden chose *A Mask for Janus* for the Yale Younger Poets Award. The early work, especially "The Drunk in the Furnace" and poems from *The Lice* (1967) such as "For the Anniversary of My Death," remain compelling and valuable. Nevertheless, over the years Merwin's poetry has grown so vaporous that even a relatively straightforward poem like "Liberty," from *The Rain in the Trees*, takes on a mythic cast:

> and the guides tell the names
> of the sculptor and the donor
> and explain why it is ours
>
> also how much it weighs
> and how many come to see it
> in a year
>
> and the name of the island
> from which the foreigners
> used to watch it

The last stanza, with its paradoxical twist (think about it for a minute), is typical of Merwin's manner—full of portent but never quite signifying what the poet is getting at. In the present collection, several things seem clear enough, the most obvious being Merwin's conviction that we are living in the last days:

> I want to tell what the forests
> were like
>
> I will have to speak

in a forgotten language

The title of the book, apparently referring to the rapid exhaustion of the world's tropical rain forests, sets an ecological theme that runs throughout the work. Consequently, the tone is one of unrelieved grimness, and, like one of those street corner doomsayers who has made a career of proclaiming that "the End is Near," Merwin quickly grows tiresome. Two decades ago he was saying the same thing, only more memorably, in vivid poems such as "The Last One." These days a poem such as "Airport" offers only a few pat observations:

> the building is not inhabited it is not
> home except to roaches
> it is not loved it is serviced
>
> it is not a place
> but a container with signs
> directing a process

When a poet can come up with nothing more original than complaints about the soullessness of an airline terminal, it's abundantly clear that he has nothing new to say.

James Merrill, on the other hand, is still capable of a few surprises. Here is a short poem from *The Inner Room* (Knopf), entitled "Laser Majesty":

> Light show at the Planetarium.
> Shlock music. Seven colors put through drum
> Majorette paces. "We saw God tonight,"
> Breathes Wendy. Yes, and He was chewing gum.

There are, to be sure, several distinct James Merrills—the poor little rich boy of the autobiographical poems, the learned globe-trotter (present here in "Prose of Departure," a sequence about Japan), the savant of the Ouija board from that interminable epic, *The Changing Light at Sandover* (1982)—one or two of which are fairly unbearable; but as a satirist or, more recently, as an elegist, he has few peers, as witness these closing lines from "Losing the Marbles," a meditation on, among other things, aging and loss of memory:

> What are the Seven Wonders now? A pile
> Of wave-washed pebbles. Topless women smile,
> Picking the smoothest, rose-flawed white or black,
> Which taste of sunlight on moon-rusted swords,
> To use as men upon their checkerboards.

Merrill is as adept as ever at fitting form to subject; this versatile collection contains interesting examples of haiku, sapphics, and the villanelle.

Speaking of versatility, I should mention another collection from Alfred A. Knopf, John Hollander's *Harp Lake*. Anyone who has read Hollander's delightful guide to English versification, *Rhyme's Reason* (1981), will know that he is a master of verse forms, in particular the witty "shaped" or spatial poem (represented here by "Kitty and Bug"). It would be equally pleasant to praise other aspects of Hollander's poetry, but with this poet content is seemingly a secondary concern. Although no less an authority than Harold Bloom says that *Harp Lake* (a reference to the Sea of Galilee) "confirms his authentic eminence, comparable in my judgement to that of Merrill, Ashbery, Ammons and only a few others in his own generation of American poets," Hollander's poems have a way of evaporating the second the reader turns the page. "Ballade for Richard Wilbur," a twist on Wilbur's own "Ballade for the Duke of Orleans," is certainly witty enough ("Dick [au lieu du Duc] I have never vied/With you for any prize; yet we're tied, for when/You 'die of thirst, here at the fountain-side,'/Je meurs de soif aupres de la fontaine.") but after the inventiveness is praised there is nothing more to be said. Similarly, in what must be the most obscure literary allusion of the year, the opening and closing lines of "The Widener Burying-Ground" ("In spite of all the learned have said,/We hear the voices of the dead. . . ./And Reason's self must bend the ear/To echoes and allusions here.") parody Philip Freneau, but to what purpose I have no clue. Hollander's poetry so successfully begs the question of any serious purpose that the reader is compelled to dismiss it.

From the other side of the form/content argument comes Robert Creeley, formulator of the most widely quoted variation on that theme ("form is never more than an extension of content"). One could argue that *The Company* (Burning Deck) contains precious little of either. Here is a representative Creeley *reductio*, "Not Much":

> Not much you ever
> said you were thinking
> of, not much to
> say in answer.

Another? Try "Just in Time":

> Over the unwritten
> and under the written

and under and over
and in back and in front of
or up or down or in
or in place of, of not,
of this and this, of
all that is, of it.

Creeley's book is "in part supported by a grant from the National Endowment for the Arts in Washington, D.C., a federal agency." The ten-dollar, fifty-page paperback (twenty dollars signed) is hand-painted with two colors on every page.

Imagine, if you can, a contemporary poet who includes an acknowledgement to reprint a poem that appeared in a high-school literary magazine! That is Dave Etter, whose *Selected Poems* I mentioned last year. He is regional, folksy, conversational, formless, and so utterly without affectation that it's hard to believe that he, Hollander, and Creeley are practitioners of the same art form. *Electric Avenue* and *Midlanders* (Spoon River Poetry Press), both issued this year, are companion volumes, consisting of short, expert soliloquies after the manner of Edgar Lee Masters. This one is entitled "Janice Nelson: Community Hospital":

"If Kimberly dies,
I'll kill myself," Pa said.
"If Kimberly dies
and you kill yourself,
I'll kill myself," Ma said.
"Please, please, please, please, please
stop that kind of talk at once
or I'll kill both of you,"
Sister Kimberly said,
rising from her pillow,
her face drained of color.
And the doctor came
into the noisy room
and said to Pa and Ma,
"Out, out, out, out, out.
Get out before I kill you."

Etter has staked out an undisputed claim to this rich Illinois territory, and he continues to mine it profitably.

Another poet one would have identified heretofore as a regionalist is James Applewhite, whose earlier books were published by university presses at Virginia, Georgia, and Louisiana State. With *River Writing: An Eno Journal* (Princeton University Press) he moves north, picking up an equivocal endorsement from the omnipresent Professor Bloom ("a stance and style wholly adequate

to the philosophical and spiritual reach of his poignant concerns") and carrying with him the heavy baggage of epigraphs from Jacques Derrida and Paul de Man. When a poet discovers deconstructivist theory and Wallace Stevens simultaneously his readers are in for some heavy going:

I use *foam, stream,* and *tongue*
For their sound. So language refers to itself.
Milliped with tail in its mouth, it circles
In these woods and every word is a leg touching
Water of tree. The cliff shows an intrusion of
    quartz,
Crystalline vein continuing even where
Softer stone has rotted to loam. Word is not
Object but both exist and align. This poem
I am writing is not precisely the one in my head
As I was running. This presence is an illusion.

Except for one brief excursion to the Grand Tetons, the book consists of meditations on the poet's solitary walks on the banks of the Eno River, near his home in North Carolina. His descriptions are accurate, but he rarely encounters much of dramatic interest; by the fourth or fifth poem the reader knows what to expect and starts thumbing on rapidly in search of narrative or at least the sight of another human being.

Traveling in an opposite direction is Jay Wright, whose selected poems appeared last year from Princeton. *Elaine's Book* (University Press of Virginia) is the seventh in the Callaloo Poetry Series, which has published impressive black poets such as Gerald Barrax. Publicity releases can usually provide perfect examples of double-talk, and the one accompanying Wright's book is no exception: "diverse technologies, crafts, imaginative arts and cosmologies lead toward a harmony integral to the poetic geographies Wright traverses in his exploration of otherness and difference." The poetry isn't much clearer, a series of obscure poems with titles such as "Guadalupe-Tonantzin" and "Zapata and the Egúngún Mask" interspersed with untitled prose passages such as the following: "And the triumph of empiricism is jeopardized by the surprising truth that *our sense data are primarily symbols*"; or "Sister, he was so good that I wanted to turn him over on his flipside and see what they was like." It's hard to imagine what sort of reader Wright's work would appeal to.

Walter McDonald has published three full-length books since 1985, with two more promised, from Harper and Row and the University of North Texas Press, respectively, for 1989. This year's collection is *After the Noise of Saigon* (University of Massachusetts Press), winner of the Juniper Prize. McDonald has produced so much poetry in the last few years that he seems to have trouble keeping up with it. Here are some lines from "Rigging the Windmill," which appeared in *Witching on Hardscrabble* (1985):

> The last pipe mated, I twist this wrench
> as if the water of the world depended on it.

Here are some lines from "Rig-Sitting," a poem in the present collection:

> On the derrick, I twist this wrench tight
> as if the oil pipes of the world depended
> on it.

Perhaps the substitution of "oil" for "water" here is an indication of the direction the Texas economy has taken in the intervening years. In his best work McDonald draws effectively on the west Texas landscape, his knowledge of hunting and fishing, and his experiences as an Air Force pilot. This last area I find most original, particularly in such a powerful piece as "The Food Pickers of Saigon," in which he turns from a memory of Vietnamese going through the trash outside a wartime base to an admonition to his own children not to leave food on their plates:

>   I call them back
> and growl, I can't help it. It's like hearing
> my father's voice again. I never tell them
> why they have to eat it. I never say
> they're like two beautiful children
>
> I found staring at me one night
> through the screen of my window,
> at Tan Son Nhut, bone-faced. Or that
> when I crawled out of my stifling monsoon
> dream to feed them, they were gone.

It is true that McDonald often repeats himself, but what he repeats is usually more compelling than what most poets never say once.

Stanley Moss has been writing poetry for over a quarter of a century, but his work retains its charm and variety. His new book, *The Intelligence of Clouds* (Harcourt Brace Jovanovich), contains a touching elegy to James Wright, a clever meditation on Giuseppe Garibaldi and Abraham Lincoln, and some excellent travel poems about China. These lines close "In Defense of a

Dust jacket for a series of dramatic monologues told in the voice of a "fictional" Sidney Lanier

Friend," a character sketch of an "old revolutionary":

> Owning his home makes him uncomfortable,
> and it's true he slept in a fruit crate with his sisters,
> that he believes the working class sees a different sunset.
> No one will deny his life of wild love
> has left him caring, with a sweet intimacy
> few others have. When I took him fishing,
> he wouldn't put a worm on his hook.

One of the strongest collections of the year comes unexpectedly from Betty Adcock, whose *Beholdings* (Louisiana State University Press) is her third book. I say "unexpectedly" by design, for, while Adcock has always been a competent poet, her earlier work, marked to a large degree by autobiographical narratives of childhood and family, never quite set itself apart from that of others who use the same resources. With the present volume, however, she soars on the wings of surprise. When I open a book by a woman and find a poem entitled "Plath" I automatically expect the worst, another sappy paean to St. Sylvia. Adcock's poem, though, is about *Aurelia* Plath, the late poet's mother:

> Ambitious as metal or jewels,
> that fury reflects, refracts
> beyond the reach of academic necrophiliacs,
> the puffing of suicide buffs,
> the industry and swagger of sexual
> politicians male and female.
> Such poetry cannot be unfaithful.
> It stands like one of those reptiles
> dead for millennia,
> skeletal track of a tranced
> imperative engine—
> bone-castle so massive and glittery
> no future could ever have lived in it,
> neither art's nor woman's.

This is fine, energetic writing, saying what I suspect many have felt but lacked the courage to put on paper. Another remarkable poem begins by describing a type of African termite colony that builds twin mounds that miraculously meet in midair: "Who was it said/the perfect arch will always separate/the civilized from the not?" At the end of the poem's first section, Adcock completes a stunning analogy:

> I've got this far and don't know what
> termites can be made to mean. Or this poem:
> a joke, a play on arrogance, nothing
> but language? Untranslated, the world gets on
> with dark, flawless constructions rising,
> rising even where we think we are. And think
> how we must hope convergences will fail this time,
> that whatever it is we're working on won't work.

The poem is entitled "Digression on the Nuclear Age."

Paul Monette's *Love Alone: Eighteen Elegies for Rog* (St. Martin's Press) would seem inevitable, a series of poems on the death of Monette's longtime lover, Roger Horwitz, from AIDS. Many, I suspect, will come to this book seeking the poetic counterpart of Randy Shilts's excellent *And the Band Played On: Politics, People, and the Aids Epidemic*, which remained on the nonfiction bestseller list during 1988. A personal memoir might have added another dimension to Shilts's straightforward reporting, but Monette is simply not equal to the demands of the subject. While his

unpunctuated free associations are emotional enough, the lack of structure so obscures any literal information about Roger Horwitz that he never quite emerges as a character who achieves some sort of tragic status. The dying man remains only a victim, and the blame for his disease is never pinpointed. The medical details can be ponderous:

> how are my lymph nodes
> how are they not a mere three-quarters
> centimeter at the neck in the vampire spot
> cm and a half in the armpit not suggestive
> unless they harden or start to throb taking
> four hundred milligrams *ribavirin* b.i.d.
> the magic dose if results released 1/9
> prove to be long-term of course when you cry
> all day an afternoon can be frightfully
> long-term but we mustn't muss the curve with
> personal agendas equal dose *acyclovir*
> ditto twice a day this part purest guesswork

Citing but apparently misunderstanding Wilfred Owen's famous remark about his own work, that "the poetry is in the pity," Monette makes the mistake of assuming that any attempt at employing poetic techniques would somehow be at odds with the sincerity of his voice: "I would rather have this volume filed under AIDS than under Poetry, because if these words speak to anyone they are for those who are mad with loss, to let them know they are not alone." The contradiction here, which Monette fails to recognize, is that his and Horwitz's story needs precisely to reach those who are *not* "mad with loss," those for whom the AIDS epidemic is still the occasion for black humor or a shrug of unconcern.

Among younger poets who published collections in 1988, Andrew Hudgins shows the most promise of eventually finding a readership that is not limited to the Academy. Hudgins was a runner-up for the Pulitzer Prize for his first book, *Saints and Strangers* (1985), and the new collection, *After the Lost War* (Houghton Mifflin), further displays his strength with the dramatic monologue. Hudgins's subject and persona here is Sidney Lanier, a poet still memorialized in the names of many southern school buildings but little-read in the South and elsewhere. Lanier is a fascinating subject in many ways. He enlisted to fight in the Civil War, was captured, returned to Georgia already dying of tuberculosis, and went on to pursue successful, if brief, twin careers as musician and poet until his death in 1881 at the age of thirty-nine. Between Edgar Allan Poe and the

Fugitives, he is the only southern poet of note, and his reputation far exceeds his poetic output. Today only a few of his poems are readable, and even such a standard anthology piece as "The Marshes of Glynn" has to be offered apologetically as a relic of one of the most dismal eras in the history of our poetry. Hudgins makes it clear that his Lanier is not to be confused with the figure in the history books: "the voice of these poems will be unfamiliar to anyone who knows the writings of this historical figure." "After the Lost War: *In Montgomery–August 1866*," is my favorite in a collection of memorable work. In this poem the fictional Lanier describes the banality of day-to-day living under Father Ryan's "Conquered Banner":

> Our weekday streets are much like Sunday's,
> so business, as you might expect,
> sets no one's heart to fluttering.
> I don't believe a man in town
> could be induced to go into
> his neighbor's store and ask, "How's trade?"
> He'd have to make amends
> for such an insult all his life.

There is nothing romantic in this description of defeat; at the end of the poem the poet apprehends an appropriate *symboliste* emblem for the ruined South, buzzards who are doused with kerosene and set aflame by drunken sailors:

> For them it must be hideous,
> but from the ground it's beautiful–
> in some odd way an easement of
> the savage tedium of days.
> But more than that: perhaps you know,
> with the younger generation of the South
> after the lost war, pretty much
> the whole of life has been not dying.
> And that is why, I think, for me
> it is a comfort just to see
> the deathbird fly so prettily.

Reading Hudgins's poems, one is struck most by what poetry Lanier *might* have written, given his wartime experiences alone, if only the taste and tradition of the time had moved him toward the type of realism used in Hudgins's monologues.

The Lamont Poetry Prize is awarded annually by the Academy of American Poets to a distinguished second book of poems. A list of past winners might reveal more about the art of literary politics than about the craft of poetry. Garrett Hongo's *The River of Heaven* (Knopf) was the winner for 1987, and the book's list of dedicatees–

there are poems "for" Gerald Stern, Edward Hirsch, Mark Jarman, Philip Levine, and Charles Wright–sounds like a roll call of the current power structure. A Japanese-American born in Hawaii and raised there and in Los Angeles, Hongo writes the sort of narrative memoir that could more efficiently be rendered in prose. Here are some representative lines on pro-basketball fandom from "The Cadence of Silk":

> Now I watch
> the Lakers, having returned to Los Angeles
> some years ago, love them even more than
> the Seattle team, long since broken up and aging.
> The Lakers are incomparable, numerous
> options for any situation, their players
> the league's quickest, most intelligent,
> and, it is my opinion, frankly, the most *cool*.

The River of Heaven is innocuous, placid, and about as memorable as a late-season sleeper between the Pacers and the Bucks.

Kelly Cherry has four novels and two books of poetry to her credit. Her new collection, *Natural Theology* (Louisiana State University Press), is often too true to its title, containing such lines as "Study from beginning to end. / Alpha and omega–these are the cirrus alphabet, / the Gnostics' cloudy 'so–and yet.' " The book literally starts from Alpha with a poem entitled "Phylogenesis," and its first section contains two poems about primitive hunters. Cherry has command of a versatile technique and is able to step across eons to compose "A Scientific Expedition in Siberia, 1913," a re-creation of the logbook of an exploratory party that discovers a glacier containing a perfectly preserved mammoth:

> A vast block of the past–
> An ice cube for a drink in hell
> (If anything cools that thirst).
>
> Inside, preserved like a foetus
> In formaldehyde, like
> Life itself, staring back at us
> The mammoth creature struck
>
> Poses for our cameras. . . .

The poem goes on to describe the team's dogs devouring the uncovered carcass, but from that point on the narrative becomes somewhat muddled. Cherry's mixture of anthropological, theological, and autobiographical materials is exciting and highly original, but her poems occasionally fall short of the high marks for which she aims.

Nevertheless, she is a poet with no shortage of ideas, something of a precious commodity among her contemporaries.

The renewed interest in the Vietnam War, primarily stimulated by recent films, has also shown up in contemporary poetry. John Balaban, Yusef Komunyakaa, R. L. Barth, and Bruce Weigl have written perhaps the best poetry about that conflict. Weigl's *Song of Napalm* (Atlantic Monthly Press) contains a thoughtful introduction by novelist Robert Stone which says that the book represents "a refusal to forget. It is an angry assertion of the youth and life that was spent in Vietnam with such vast prodigality, as though youth and life were infinite." This refusal, or perhaps impossibility, to forget is clearly seen in lines like "With sleep that is barely under the surface / it begins, a twisting sleep as if a wire / were inside you and tried at night / to straighten your body." There has been a certain amount of similarity in the work of the Vietnam War soldier-poets; the prostitutes of Saigon, the drugs, the suffering civilian populace, the battlefield narrative, and the flashbacks of veterans have been the standard subjects of much of this poetry. Possibly because the setting was so remote and the danger so inescapable, few of the war poets have managed to go beyond the literal surface of events, as if the very situation of this war somehow obviated the need for metaphor. Weigl cannot avoid the expected vignettes either, but he can occasionally reach beyond them to create a memorable narrative. "Snowy Egret," an account of a neighbor's son who senselessly kills a bird, is one of the best poems in the collection. It concludes with this powerful stanza:

> I want to grab his shoulders,
> shake the lies loose from his lips but he hurts
>   enough,
> he burns with shame for what he's done,
> with fear for his hard father's
> fists I've seen crash down on him for so much less.
> I don't know what to do but hold him.
> If I let go he'll fly to pieces before me.
> What a time we share, that can make a good boy
>   steal away,
> wiping out from the blue face of the pond
> what he hadn't even known he loved, blasting
> such beauty into nothing.

In this case, an indirect method of relating the effects of war on its survivors yields the greatest returns.

Dan Jaffe's *Round for One Voice* (University of Arkansas Press) contains some interesting work about a Jew's search for identity in a Christian world. Jaffe breaks no new ground in his autobiographical poems, but "The Tragedy of Shylock," a retelling of Shakespeare's *The Merchant of Venice*, is notable for its originality and metrical control:

> They ask for Christian mercy from a Jew,
> As if I cared for their philosophy.
> If I just pulled his beard and then withdrew,
> What would be gained? They'd not let Shy- lock be.
> But when was mercy ever sired by hate?
> When were mad dogs caressed? Let them learn this:
> Good begets good; evil begets justice.

David Romtvedt's second collection, *How Many Horses* (Ion Books), turns on the poet's experiences raising horses in northern Wyoming, a region and subject matter that will inevitably link his work to that of Gretel Ehlich, who, sounding rather like a spokesperson for Busch beer, calls Romtvedt's poetry "resonant as mountain meltwater." However, Romtvedt's lines are far removed from the pastoral idylls of the television commercials; life on the ranch can be unrelentingly brutal. "Something Inside" is a shocking narrative about a mare named Marthe that keeps straying into a neighbor's pasture, despite repeated warnings:

> One day Cyprien comes walking up leading Marthe.
> Her eyelids are shut kind of crumpled
> and there's blood on her face. Cyprien
> walks straight up to the house and he throws
> two eyeballs down in front of me–Marthe's eyes.
>
> You can't believe, Belem, how big
> a horse's eyes are. Cyprien shows me
> his knife and how he took the pointed end
> of the blade, slipped it gently in the corner
> of both sockets and popped her eyes out.
> Like that. And he walks away. "She never
> gonna find her way into my field again,"
> Cyprien says over his shoulder.

It is to Romtvedt's credit that he can return again and again to the subject of his horses without becoming redundant or pretentious. As he says, "I won't try to deceive you / with talk of animals as metaphors / for universal human values. / The simple truth is I have come to care / for the horses and maybe I do believe / they are as important as we are."

Dust jacket for a book of poems that novelist Robert Stone, in his introduction, characterizes as "an angry assertion of the youth and life that was spent in Vietnam with such vast prodigality, as though youth and life were infinite"

In a recent book review Greg Kuzma, who seems of late to be trying to out-Jarrell Jarrell in the acerbity of his judgments, did score one point; he referred to the Knopf poetry series as being "dedicated to the preservation and dissemination of the poetry of gentility." As much as I generally disagree with Mr. Kuzma, I must agree that he was on target here. When one runs down the list, which now extends to twenty-eight books, one encounters the names of Brad Leithauser, Mary Jo Salter (Mrs. Leithauser), Amy Clampitt, and others who write the sort of poems in which words such as "mild" become the ensigns of a genre. Such a poet is Stephen Sandy, whose *Man in the Open Air* (Knopf) contains many lines such as these from "After a City Shower":

> The traffic brays, but the stalled horses
> Calmly stare, exhaust in their nostrils,
> As if they were hearing the wind's bel canto

In tall grass. Out of the horns of plenty
Banter drifts near *A La Vielle*

Russie: "move out," she tells him, "so don't
Go back." Her voice turns liquid, "allow me
To send you some." The silver parcels
And the practiced tintinnabula of hungers
Surround me. . . .

Another series that seems to have no discernible direction comes from the University of Georgia Press, both of whose books for the year arrived adorned with the recommendation of John Ashbery. Arthur Vogelsang's *Twentieth Century Women* is praised for depicting a world which "is three-fifths reality and two-fifths dream, but the resulting surface is so artfully camouflaged that it's impossible to know which is which." Change the proportions slightly, and you end up with a good description of Ashbery's own work. Here are the opening lines of Vogelsang's "Hollywood Presbyterian":

> It was a dark wet day, relief and rest for the palms.
> Illness has called to health, where the Virgin
> Mary is not lusted after in these rooms,
> And when the Gray Poet has nursed sensitive amputations
> 117
> Years ago, a Famous One instead is stuck with a Critic,
>   a Lover,
> The voice of This, sour grapes cartoons of the Living Voices,
> *Le Figaro* (Dimanche), and a Bug that's been
> Long, hard, and black, or long, hard, and white—
> Its mysterious heat down, the plane home only days away.

Of Donald Revell's *The Gaza of Winter* Ashbery says that he was surprised "by the calm ease of his effortlessly propelled lines which always took me to the unexpected places even when they sounded most reassuring and familiar." Revell's titles alone ("For Borges," "Eumenides," "Fauviste") are enough to intimidate most readers. The poems themselves are somewhat less obscure; this is from the title poem:

> A marriage is Gaza. Ours is blind at a mill
> now, every turn of which seems meant to instruct
>
> the dark in darkening, hearts in how to instruct
> themselves in spite. There will be blanks instead of words
> from now on, a grist of silence for the mill.
> But why is it I still think of going blind

with you as my life's work? In our first winter,
I followed you up the steps to where your body
slipped out of grey ice and lit the mean

rooms wonderfully. What would happen if those
    mean
rooms turned up again, a few steps from the mill
we turn?

Nothing else in the collection quite rises to this
level of metaphoric control, though. Revell is too
often unable to resist the siren lure of hollow
lines like "Interregnum / always is every door
staggering // into the aimless circles of night
couples / and of their small radios inside the Common."

Another poetry list that has been around
for a long time is the Breakthrough Series from
the University of Missouri Press, for which an established poet (in this case Deborah Digges) se-
lects the annual winner of the Devins Award. *Waiting for a Hero* by Penelope Wilkinson Austin was
the 1988 winner; *These Modern Nights* by Richard
Lyons was selected for the 1989 prize. Both
books were published in 1988. Austin is well traveled and verbally precise, sounding at times like
a rather more personal version of Elizabeth
Bishop. Many of the book's poems are about serious illness, presumably the poet's own:

   "You don't choose/u, u chooses you,"
the doctor tells me. But I don't tell him
how many time I've heard such words before.
   The therapists begin their ritual chant:
"Couch angle six." "Open to fourteen wide."
"She has a ten line." There, see, a ten line.

A small red cut-out casts the laser beams
   across my body's pyramids and dunes.
   They align lead pieces above me. Chanting
   stops,
and I am left alone, lying in light.

Lyons's work–rootless, culturally knowledgable,
melancholy–defies easy categorization, though
his favorite mode is narrative. These lines are
from "The Doctor & the Young Groom," a vignette from Anton Chekhov's medical career:

If a voice goes out only to disperse, a sip for the
   ears,
a cat's ghostly cry,
then the doctor is revising a sentence: *the cattails
are broken & scattered on the road like the legs
of dead herons,* like he scoffs
the pens stabbed into a blotter

beneath a ring of light from a lamp.

Today, he thinks, I lanced a Custom Officer's boil.
I had to laugh, blood dribbling down the buttocks
like the vile borscht the Tartars stew in pots
under the wet black trunks of winter trees.

   Too much sophistication can be the down-
fall of a poet, unless he tempers it with an equal
measure of irony. Paul Violi does so in *Likewise*
(Hanging Loose Press). Much of his work is high-
spirited silliness like "At a Bank near the Metro":

Let's have the money or else.
Just do what I say
and nobody will get hurt.

There's nothing quite like a poet who enjoys his
own jokes. Somewhat later in the book one encounters "Haiku":

Don't just look at my face.
No change, just large bills.
One wrong move will be your last.

The book contains parodies of, among others, Williams and Villon and a cute spatial poem called
"Marina," which consists of nothing more than a
catalog of the boats' names arranged to show
their positions in the slips. Violi may lack the
high seriousness that some would demand of contemporary poetry, but it's hard to resist opening
lines like these:

I listen to the crickets and hear
the machinery at the bottom of the night.

They are all made in Hong Kong
out of interchangeable parts.

   Lisa Zeidner is another poet whose high spir-
its can be infectious. *Pocket Sundial* (University of
Wisconsin Press) is full of work that keeps one
turning the pages, quite an accomplishment in
view of the fact that several of Zeidner's poems
seem to go on forever. Garrulousness like hers
has its pitfalls, and many of the poems run out
of steam midway through. One that doesn't is
"Gypsy Moths," in which the poet manages to
make something both poignant and funny out of
memories of being beaten by her father as a
child while her mother stood by without intervening.

I could still cry discussing this,
as if motherlove were a wash of sunlight

and I the frail, stunted houseplant.
If the Freudians are right, then everything
can be traced to that primal neglect.
"You can feel that," my companion said,

"but in your more grown-up head
you must realize it's not so simple;
if you were your child, you'd beat you too."

After reading yet another poem in which a poet blames his or her unhappiness on some failing of the parents, I am ready to applaud Zeidner's hard-earned sanity: "It could have been worse: / I was always fed, never molested; / I was not raised in an orphanage / by angry nuns with rulers. . . ." Zeidner has a way of cutting through the sentimentality that surrounds many tired subjects. Here are some speculations on Anne Frank:

And we do love a dead artist,
especially one who dies poor
and is not too prolific.
What if Anne had kept a diary
until her death at eighty in Silver Springs?
What if eighty such diaries were found,
common as the arrowheads and vases
we walk by in museums.

This is poetry with bite and wit, one that is unafraid to be outrageous.

Compared with Zeidner, the earnestness of Maura Stanton's voice in *Tales of the Supernatural* (Godine) seems very quiet, but that sense of calm has been the hallmark of this underrated poet's style. At a supermarket checkout, she contemplates the appeal of the lurid tabloids that have become a staple of the American mental diet: "Every week the garish headlines/Insist there is another world/That ordinary people see–/ Spaceships land in backyards;/A baby cures a multitude;/ An angry ghost destroys the china/To the amazement of a waitress. . . ." The conclusion is appropriate:

Everyone reads the shocking news,
Silently, or to a friend,
Eyebrows moving in irony
Or lips in private wonder,
And on every stranger's face
I see a flash of agony:
Why not? Why not a miracle?

Stanton is at her best in autobiographical poems like "Polio Epidemic, 1953" or the fine "Sorrow and Rapture," where she remembers sitting in an empty theater, "Glad to be out of Civics and His-

tory," watching a film of *La Traviata*. After the movie ends, she returns to the quotidian:

Then the bus stopped on top of the hill.
I looked over the roof tops of Peoria
Shaken with rapture. What town was this?
I saw the brewery, my high school, a steeple,
Slate-colored shingles, the glimmer of river,
And beyond, smokestacks of Caterpillar
Where the wire mesh gates had just opened
    on thousands
Of laborers with their metal lunch pails.
Still dazzled, I got off at my stop.

Among her other merits, Stanton has as fine a sense of rhythm as any American poet I can think of; though not a rigid metricist, she handles the loose blank verse line with rare skill.

Another poet with a good feel for the poetic line is Jeffrey Skinner, whose *A Guide to Forgetting* (Graywolf Press) was selected by Tess Gallagher for inclusion in the National Poetry Series. "A Grace" opens with some perceptive words about the state of contemporary poetry:

Let's have no more *I remember*
poems, at least not until the self thaws out
and we can move easily in more than one direction.
So much lunatic pruning in a dead garden,

so much pretty blue smoke and mirrors . . .
And let's have no more kneeling
for good reasons, dropping God's name
like a cast-iron doorstop,

forcing Him into the shape of a tree,
say, which would much rather go on treeing.

Skinner is vigorous but sometimes careless; there are some verbal infelicities that a judicious editor should have caught, like the mangled pronoun in this line: "Between my father and I, a vast language." The book concludes with a skillful sequence entitled "Sonnets to My Daughters Twenty Years in the Future." Here is an apt passage detailing what happens to the poet when the responsibilities of parenthood sink in:

                    So long,
languid mornings of fresh coffee and the *Times*!
So long forties flicks, prize fights in the after-noon!
    My beer, my cheese and crackers! Goodbye
solitary walks, slow lovemaking with your
    mother. . . .
Hello, vast disorder with small hands and eyes–
Narcissus is dead, your first, most merciful crime.

Elton Glaser's *Tropical Depressions* (University of Iowa Press) is a mixed bag, poems on such standard subjects as students, middle age, and marriage that seem to have been run through the contemporary poetry assembly line. The book's final section, however, is quite good, a series of poems on the poet's hometown, New Orleans, which he describes as a town "full of Tabasco/and clarinet players named Sidney,/grasshopper ethics with a catfish smile." Although in a couple of seascape poems ("Wading the Gulf," "Bay St. Louis") the poet is distracted into rhapsodies about his companion's breasts, he can occasionally keep to the matter at hand, as in "Cottonmouth," a narrative about a close encounter with a poisonous snake. Here is its conclusion:

> He would not strike; I could not stir–
> Until, like a comic scene relieving
> The heartstop of tragedy, a vagrant turtle
>
> Picked its slow way out of the marsh
> To gawk at the standoff, its old man's neck
> Telescoping from the shell for a better look.
>
> And in that stretched second
> Of the snake's distraction,
> I pulled free from the treeroot,
>
> Leaving one life behind me
> On the beach, and another
> Walking backwards into the future.

A number of poets seem to be discovering the sonnet form, among them Debra Bruce, whose *Sudden Hunger* (University of Arkansas Press) also contains work in heroic couplets and terza rima. Bruce is a good observer, but her meters often strike me as rather forced. Here is a representative sestet, from "Mother and Daughter," a sonnet which recounts a dress-shop psychodrama:

> Her mother is watching in the mirror
> under the bright bulb. When she leaves, the girl
> is alone, so close to me I can hear her
> still breathing hard. So many dresses swirl
> under her hand as she pushes them, hits
> the empty hangers. Nothing. Nothing fits.

I particularly notice the repetitious "so" in the fourth line, a word apparently added to pad the meter. Nevertheless, this is intense versifying, even if the poet might be advised not to be so self-conscious in her avoidance of regularity.

Elizabeth Seydell Morgan's *Parties* (Louisiana State University Press) also contains some nicely turned sonnets. Here are the opening lines of "Safeway":

> This world is category. Raw meat
> In slick clear film does not insinuate
> Its bloody flesh into meringue-topped sweet
> Potato pie. Dark beer and milk don't mate
> In this geometry. The Safeway's grid
> Defines my need; aisle B the bread, white wine
> On C, detergent stacked to pyramid.

It is interesting to note that many contemporary poets, in an attempt to avoid the sonnet's traditional romantic associations, are using it as a vehicle for realistic descriptive poetry.

Another time-honored genre that is undergoing a renaissance is the dramatic monologue. I have already mentioned Andrew Hudgins's work; another interesting though not entirely successful example is Margaret Lally's *Juliana's Room* (Bit Press), a series of poems spoken by Juliana Pastrana (1832-1860), who toured the globe as "The Ugliest Woman in the World," and by those who knew her. According to Lally's introduction, offstage she was "brilliant, kind, soft-spoken, and spiritually elegant," a counterpart to her contemporary, the celebrated Elephant Man. Pastrana married her unscrupulous manager and died giving birth to a son; after her death and that of the infant, her widowed husband exhibited their mummified remains. Here are some lines of Juliana's during her brief period of married contentment:

> Ah, the peace.
> Evenings, he comes through the door –
> We read Shakespeare.
> The fire sings. I cover my brow
> With my hands as I read, and, in a moment,
>   I'm Juliet.
> Or, for love of me, the Moor stays at the bed-side,
> Poised between lips and the tomb.
> For me. Macduff can show them only little
>   rags of grief.
> I spend my time undoing the Creation:
> I pray, "Let there be Darkness."

Oddly, there are only eighteen total pages of poetry in this sixty-four-page book; the rest is given over to commentary or blank pages. Pastrana's story is certainly intriguing enough to have inspired more than the few brief glimpses Lally gives us.

David Dooley's *The Volcano Inside* (Story Line Press) is a far more ambitious attempt to get inside the minds of personae. Dooley takes on vari-

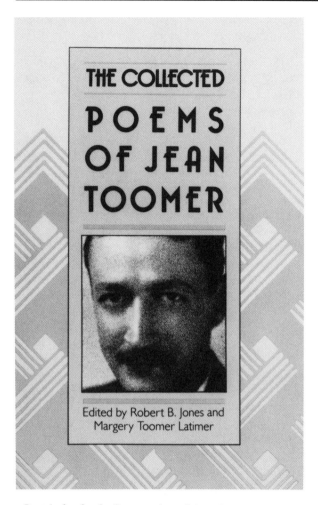

Dust jacket for the first complete edition of Toomer's poetry

a wild look, surely on some kind of drug.
  "Ray?"
Weeping. Stains on the shirt. He made himself enter the room.
Precious Jesus, the blood. The little girl, her
  body
broken on the bed. The electric blanket,
  soaked through.
What money he had, fifty dollars, and the key
  to the Olds,
he couldn't not give him that. The boy gunned
  out of the driveway
and knocked down the mailbox. He sank by
  the window,
trying to name all the authorities who must be
  notified.

To the Place of Trumpets (Yale University Press) by Brigit Pegeen Kelly is this year's winner of the Yale Series of Younger Poets competition, judged by James Merrill. In his introduction to Kelly's poems Merrill praises the way she "retains the wild, transforming eye of childhood," particularly as it relates to her Catholic background. These lines are from "Imagining Their Own Hymns":

And these angels that the women turn to
are not good either. They are sick of Jesus,
who never stops dying, hanging there white
and large, his shadow blue as pitch, and blue
the bruise on his chest, with spread petals,
like the hydrangea blooms I tear from
Mrs. Macht's bush and smash on the sidewalk.

Kelly's poetry will probably not generate the excitement of some of the previous winners of the series, but she is a rewarding poet, sure of her craft.

Alberto Ríos is generally recognized as one of the best of the younger generation of Hispanic poets. *The Lime Orchard Woman* (Sheep Meadow Press) is a collection that focuses, for the most part, on other lives, occasionally using a surrealistic technique that is reminiscent of the "magic realism" of the contemporary South American novel. Ríos employs the idiom of the cartoon in "Mr. Disney's Animation":

My cousin Eddie didn't like his food
Managing daily to hide it
Securely under his unstylishly wide collar
But then one day
His mother in a fit shook him.
The night's meal, and then others—

Whole dinners came down

ous guises—a fortune-teller, a bored housewife remembering her first husband, a Jewish country musician stranded in Austin, Texas—and he manages to make his characters live through their streams-of-unselfconsciousness. Dooley also handles the narrative expertly, particularly in the unsettling "Revelation," an account of a minister who, to prove that "the greater the love,/the greater the burden," takes into his home and heart an abused teenager from the streets. The poem's conclusion provides a lesson on the perils of charity that is worthy of Flannery O'Connor:

         After the session meeting one afternoon,
he drove up and opened the garage door.
   The radio
loud inside. "Ray?" Not on the first floor.
A whimpering from below. He descended the
   stairs.
Still some smell of the damp. The boy
   crouched near the furnace,

That hadn't come out in the wash,
liver, mushrooms, a tongue.

Ríos is generally entertaining, even if his poems seem to suffer from lack of any ambition to get beneath the surface of his characters and events.

Several other books received for review deserve brief mention. David Rivard's *Torque* (University of Pittsburgh Press) was the 1987 winner of the Agnes Lynch Starrett Poetry Prize. The book contains some good narrative poetry, but Rivard often outstays his welcome by letting his poems run on needlessly. John Daniel's *Common Ground* (Confluence Press) reveals the poet's environmentalist concerns in a number of places; he is particularly adept at describing landscapes. Julia Wendell's *An Otherwise Perfect History* (Ithaca House) has an interesting long poem, "A Two-Spoked Wheel: Lyrics to the Deaf Composer," about the tortured life of Bedřich Smetana, the great Czech musician. Donna Brook's *What Being Responsible Means to Me* (Hanging Loose Press) is a collection of short poems, many marked by the poet's incisive wit. The first poem in the book is entitled "Vanquishing Our Enemies": "I will put X into a big brown paper bag/and set the bag afire in Y's hallway./When she tries to stamp out the blaze, Y will get her feet/covered with X." Charles Behlen's *Dreaming at the Wheel* (Corona Press) is strong in evoking the sense of the west Texas landscape and also in revealing the poet's sense of the absurd, especially in "Tornado," a hyperbolically comic narrative of a storm demolishing a shack-up motel.

Another book from the same publisher, Tim Seibles's *Body Moves*, also demonstrates a wry sense of humor. Seibles has an amusing love-fantasy poem addressed to, of all unlikely candidates, Martina Navratilova. *Ridge Music* (University of Arkansas Press) is the second collection by Harry Humes, whose first book won the 1984 Devins Award from the University of Missouri Press. The subjects of the poems are rural, showing the poet's love of the Pennsylvania hill country. Fleda Brown Jackson's *Fishing with Blood* (Purdue University Press) contains some informed poetry about the outdoors, in particular the title poem and a sequence entitled "Central Lake." Sonia Gernes's *Women at Forty* (Notre Dame University Press) stands out on the strength of "Different Stars," a series of poems in the form of a journal detailing a visit to New Zealand. Vonna Adrian's *A Gaggle of Voices* (Bits Press) is a charming collection of light verse, mostly on academic

subjects. A title such as "Phrases Toward a Sentence Defining Henry James's Preferences in Female Companionship" is a fairly apt summary of the book's appeal. The second half of the volume contains more serious work that displays Adrian's sense of formal structure. John Burt's *The Way Down* (Princeton University Press) focuses on historical subjects. One very fine poem is "Plains of Peace," a sympathetic account of the last days of President Woodrow Wilson.

William Logan's *Sullen Weedy Lakes* (Godine) also shows a historical slant, though many of Logan's subjects will be remote for most readers. One that will not be is Lewis Carroll, persona of "Christ Church, Oxford/26 October 1881," a witty letter-poem addressed to one of the author-scholar's "dear little girls." True to its title, Judith Skillman's *Worship of the Visible Spectrum* (Breitenbush) is replete with meditations on natural history with such titles as "Northwest Tillicums," "The Trout Farm as Metaphor for Guilt," and "Bard Rock Dinosaurs." There is an interesting example of the sestina entitled "The Hatchery After Dark." Robert Long is an art critic as well as a poet. Some of Long's Manhattan meditations in *What Happens* (Galileo Press) seem indebted to Frank O'Hara and James Schuyler: "It's 3 a.m., and I'm thinking/About how, lately, I've been on the phone too much." Long is another poet who can be superficially amusing without displaying much depth. Jane Flanders's *Timepiece* (University of Pittsburgh Press) contains one brilliant moment of spoofery, a poem entitled "Other Lives of the Romantics," which begins with "1808 Wordsworth dies from fall while hiking in Scotland" and concludes with "1883 Byron dies in sleep at age 95; posthumous publication of his 'Ecclesiastical Sonnets.'" In between, Keats marries Fanny Brawne, discovers anesthesia, and dies of a drug overdose. Forrest Gander's *Rush to the Lake* (alicejamesbooks) also has a few original moments, particularly in "Sumō," a poem about the life of a 370-pound Japanese wrestler. Richard Martin's *Dream of Long Headdresses: Poems from a Thousand Hospitals* (Signpost Press) draws on the poet's experiences as a hospital orderly for some graphically descriptive poems about cancer that are not for the squeamish.

On the Way (Paper Moon Press) is a first book by Minerva Heller Neiditz. Many of the poems show the poet's humanitarian concerns: "But in my dreams the IRS gives money away to my/favorite philanthropic causes." Michael Pettit's *Cardinal Points* (University of Iowa Press) has several poems based on Eadweard Muybridge's famous photographic studies of the human body in motion; unfortunately, the poems are rendered pointless by the book's failure to reproduce the photography on which they are based. Philip Fried's *Mutual Trespasses* (Ion Books/Raccoon) comes with strong recommendations from such diverse poets as A. R. Ammons, Marvin Bell, and Judson Jerome. The book might best be described as a sequence of deistic/agnostic meditations (or what the poet calls a "heretical testament") in which God is the principal player. Fried's deity is one "who suffer[s] all of matter-energy/and whose dreams expand with the thrust of a fireball/but who cannot lift a pinky to mend the sheath/of a single neutron torn from its groove in muscle." *Life-list* (Ohio State University Press) is by Robert Corder, who won the narrative poetry competition sponsored by the *New England Review* for "Shelley's Death." It is a fine poem, as is "Jean-Henri Fabre: The Sleep of Caterpillars," a short sequence on the work of the noted entomologist.

Lack of space prevents me from giving more than brief mention to a number of works of literary translation that seem notable. Vicente Huidobro's *Altazor: or A Voyage in a Parachute* (Graywolf Press) was translated by Eliot Weinberger. First published in 1931, the poem is a surrealistic fantasy on flight which seems indebted to the Futurist movement. Federico García Lorca is present in two collections, Carlos Bauer's translation of *Ode to Walt Whitman & Other Poems* (City Lights Books) and Greg Simon and Steven F. White's version of *Poet in New York* (Farrar, Straus & Giroux). Antonio Porta's *Kisses from Another Dream* (City Lights Books), translated by Anthony Molino, introduces a poet who seems to be an Italian counterpart of the American Beats. *Vegetation* (Red Dust) by Francis Ponge, translated by Lee Fahnestock, presents work by a noteworthy poet who has also appeared in collections of Richard Wilbur's translations. Harriet Zinnes's rendering of *Blood and Feather: Selected Poems of Jacques Prévert* (Schocken Books) is a valuable assortment of work by one of the seminal surrealists. *Twenty Prose Poems* (City Lights Books) by Charles Baudelaire was translated by Michael Hamburger, one of the leading contemporary masters of this difficult literary form. *The Early Poems of Yehuda Amichai* (Sheep Meadow Press) contains work by Israel's greatest poet, translated by Harold Schimmel, Assia Gutmann, and Ted Hughes. With the exception of the Ponge and Amichai col-

lections, all of these books are bilingual editions. *Weathering: Poems & Translations* (University of Georgia Press) is by Alistair Reid, longtime writer for the *New Yorker*. Reid is not remarkable as a poet, but this volume does contain some excellent translations, most notably of Jorge Luis Borges and Pablo Neruda.

In closing, I should mention five other books published during the year which will be of interest to readers. *The Collected Poems of Jean Toomer* (University of North Carolina Press), edited by Robert B. Jones and Margery Toomer Latimer, brings together fifty-five long-out-of-print poems by one of the major figures in Afro-American writing. Many will be surprised by what they encounter here, especially if they know Toomer only from his 1923 narrative *Cane*. Many of the early poems are clearly experimental, like "Poem in C":

Go and see Carlowitz the Carthusian,
Then pary bring the cartouche and place it
On this cashmere, while I tell a story.
The steaming casserole passed my way
While I reclined beneath Castalay,
Dreaming, ye Gods, of castor oil.

In later life Toomer devoted himself to the mystical teachings of G. I. Gurdjieff, the poet's so-called Objective Consciousness period. The collection is scrupulously edited and contains an introduction which places the poet in the context of his times.

Another poet who is experiencing something of a revival of interest is Weldon Kees, who committed suicide in 1955. Kees—musician, photographer, painter, critic, and poet—was one of the most brilliant contemporaries of Randall Jarrell, Theodore Roethke, and Lowell; even though his *Collected Poems*, edited by Donald Justice some years ago for the University of Nebraska Press, has stayed in print, only in the last several years have his letters, short stories, and now his miscellaneous essays and reviews been collected. *Reviews and Essays, 1936-55* (University of Michigan Press), edited by James Reidel, is thus an invaluable addition to the library of those who have long been fascinated by this poet's work. The book contains an introduction by Howard Nemerov, who knew Kees in the late 1940s.

Jeffrey Meyers's edition of *Robert Lowell: Interviews and Memoirs* (University of Michigan Press) gives a fairly complete overview of the poet's career and should prove a useful complement to Ian Hamilton's biography and the collection of prose pieces that was published last year. Since so much of Lowell's poetry is given over to autobiographical scrutiny, books such as this often seem more useful in reading his poetry than any of the scholarly studies of his work. Meyers's collection includes the famous *Paris Review* interview with Frederick Siedel and a number of reminiscences by poets, neighbors, and students.

Delbert Spain's *Shakespeare Sounded Soundly: The Verse Structure & the Language* (Capra Press), despite its fearsome title, is one of the finest books I have read on English versification. Prosody is a topic that many fear and, judging by many of the books I see, few have mastered. Spain draws on his theatrical experience, providing a book which looks at Shakespeare's poetry as *spoken* expression. He is excellent in describing the changes in English pronunciation over the centuries, providing an appendix of words which demonstrate the accentual shifts that make Shakespeare's meters difficult for the modern reader to follow. Spain calls his book "a handbook for students, actors, and directors"; those who would write poetry should be added to the list.

Finally, let me recommend Judson Jerome's *1989 Poet's Market* (Writer's Digest Books), both for its practical guidelines for aspiring poets and for its thorough listing of markets for poetry. Even if one agrees with Diane Wakoski's view that "the idea that people would thumb through a book or magazine and look at the names of publications where they could sell their poems without ever having read the magazine is, to me, not only stupid but it's immoral," this reference book can provide some wonderful moments just by browsing its contents. One finds publishers like Before the Rapture Press and magazines like *Superintendent's Profile & Pocket Equipment Directory*, which publishes "only poetry that pertains to highway superintendents and DPW directors and their activities." Wakoski aside, I think I'd be more troubled if someone told me he *had* read some of these publications before submitting work to them. I am also reasonably sure, writing this in anticipation of the forthcoming year's diverse crop of books, that somewhere in this country a hopeful poet is at this moment applying a stamp to an S.A.S.E. and enclosing a neatly typed copy of his "Ode to a Four-lane Overpass." More power to him!

The Year in Drama

Howard Kissel
New York Daily News

It has been remarked that dramatic literature consists of texts, but that theater consists of everything that goes into a production–the contributions of the actors, the director, the designers–that is not in the text. In New York we have less and less that can qualify legitimately as dramatic literature, more and more in which what matters is the nontextual contributions, which have become increasingly self-conscious, brittlely theatrical.

At times this deliberate two-dimensionality seems a kind of philosophical statement, carrying the 1960s commitment to "honesty" to new extremes, as if by asking the audience to suspend its disbelief, the writer, director, and actors were involving innocent spectators in a hideous deception. More often than not, however, the artificiality of the current theater stems simply from spurious writing. The knowledge of how people act toward one another, one senses, is regarded as secondary by many young playwrights. Their primary concern is effects, rather like those young filmmakers whose interest in character is far below their understanding of what the camera does.

One of the most critically acclaimed plays of the year was Craig Lucas's *Reckless*, which begins on Christmas Eve as a young woman, lying in bed with her husband, reminisces about Christmases past. Her tender reverie is broken when her husband tells her she must climb out the window and escape. He explains that he has hired a contract killer to murder her. The hit man will break into the house. There will be a scuffle with guns, in the course of which the gunman will "accidentally" kill her. The husband wishes he could stop the man, but there isn't enough time. He expresses a kind of perfunctory regret and urges her on her way. As she begins climbing out the window we hear the sound of glass shattered elsewhere in the house.

Happily the woman is picked up on the highway by a man who brings her home to live with his deaf-mute, paraplegic wife, who, we soon discover, is not a deaf-mute at all. But she fears that

Cover of the program for Craig Lucas's play that was praised by many critics as an allegory of the dislocations of contemporary life

if she exhibits too much independence her husband, who met her while caring for her in the hospital, might fall out of love with her.

All this takes no more than about fifteen minutes, and the play continues in similar fashion for about two hours, with constant "surprises," constant situations that strain credulity, situations whose metaphoric potential seems severely limited. Nevertheless much was made of the fact that the characters frequently use fictitious names or assume disguises, that they frequently abandon one another: *Reckless* was seen as an allegory of the dislocations of contemporary life.

It seems more accurate to call it second- or third-generation Absurdism. Though the term was applied almost indiscriminately to writers as diverse as Samuel Beckett, Harold Pinter, Edward Albee, and Arthur Kopit, one thing the Absurdists did have in common was a rebellion against the conventions of realist theater. They were in revolt against the tendency to orient a play toward the revelation of some unhappy deed far in the past that has exerted a powerful influence over all succeeding events.

In retrospect what these writers may have been rejecting was the specter of Freud, whose therapeutic technique was generally perceived as a kind of relentless reductivism, intent on locating some trauma that has had a lingering, remorseless impact on all that has subsequently transpired. In the Absurdist works the random, the fanciful, and the unexpected were all counterpoised against this harsh determinism.

Reckless has a series of psychotherapist characters, almost all of whom are deceptive or incompetent. The randomness, the fancifulness, and the unexpectedness of *Reckless* have none of the underpinnings of 1950s Absurdism. Lucas's conceits seem merely random, merely fanciful, merely unexpected, as if the playwright's task were largely to avoid fulfilling any of the audience's expectations. He may deploy any tactics he wishes with no particular regard to human resonance.

Even the admirers of *Reckless* conceded that its low point was two feeble attempts to parody TV game shows. For those who did not find *Reckless* worthwhile, these lame parodies were of the same cloth as the rest. That the play had so many proponents was due in part to an enormously talented cast, particularly the gifted young actress Robin Bartlett in the leading role. (She had given similar credibility to an even more ludicrous piece of neo-Absurdism, David Stephen Rappaport's *Cave Life*, which was about a contemporary woman who falls in love with a caveman in a diorama at the Museum of Natural History.) The other major strength of *Reckless* was its set, an elegant backdrop of soft, fluffy clouds against a light blue sky, a suitable wallpaper for a sophisticated child's nursery. The archness of the set reinforced the tongue-in-cheek tone in the writing.

In the Absurdism of the 1950s overt theatricality was used to mock the very idea of standard psychological motivation. In the new Absurdism theatricality is an end in itself, as if the need to jolt and divert the audience takes precedence over the old-fashioned concern for internal logic or plausibility.

Thus, in *M. Butterfly*, by David Henry Hwang, which won the Tony for best play, even the basic premise strains credulity. The only thing that made the plot believable was the audience's knowledge that the events actually took place. A French diplomat stationed in Communist China during the early 1960s initiated an affair with a star of the Peking Opera, was made to believe he had a child by her, and maintained the relationship even after returning to the West, discovering only twenty years later that the woman he had loved was in fact a man. (A high-level diplomat might have suspected this, if not from the physical evidence, at least from his knowledge of the country to which he had been posted: it is not a secret that stars of the Chinese opera, following long-standing traditions, are men.)

More curious, it seems not to have occurred to the diplomat that at the height of the Red Guards' xenophobia it was rather irregular that he, as a foreigner, was able to rent an apartment in which to conduct the affair. It came as a surprise to him that his lover was engaged in espionage as well as deception. The play never manages to probe the subtle human reasons behind these almost preposterous events. Instead it reduces the affair to an illustration of Western sexism, racism, and imperialism.

Hwang's play is not without provocative wit. What made the play chic, apart from its reliance on these highly modish "-isms" to give it the appearance of a play of ideas, was that it was staged by the great English director John Dexter with a flamboyant theatricality that has become scarce in New York. The set and costumes were designed by the brilliant Japanese designer Eiko Ishioka. Only the two major characters are examined with any semblance of depth. The rest are presented as caricatures, as if to say that events like this are bound to happen in a world that is no more substantial than a cartoon.

Another eagerly received piece of Nouvelle Synthetique was Richard Greenberg's *Eastern Standard*. The promising first act is a *Rashomon*-like examination of the same scene from several points of view. In a midtown Manhattan restaurant that serves Grouper Tortellini we first see a table with two young men, an architect and an artist, who are staring at a man and a woman at a nearby table. The architect is attracted to the woman, the artist to the man. Their conversation is spirited, though from the beginning their efforts at wit and cleverness are strained, as when one says, "I'm thirty and I still have parents. If that's not an admission of failure —."

After a blackout these two converse in pantomime, and our attention becomes fixed on the table with the man and woman, who are in fact brother and sister. She is a high-powered albeit disenchanted financier. He is gay and has chosen this lunch to inform his sister he has AIDS, though he begs her to tell no one. After another blackout these two mime conversation, and we focus on a third table where a homeless woman, whose ravings we have heard at a distance during the first two scenes, is arguing with a waitress. The two have an altercation, and the bag lady flings a bottle–a Perrier bottle–at the waitress, which brings the occupants of the two previous tables together.

In the second act the financier and her admirer have been paired. So have her brother and his, though somehow their relationship has remained chaste and the fatal secret has not been divulged. They are all spending the summer together in the Hamptons. Incredibly they have invited the bag lady and the waitress (who is, of course, an actress) to stay with them. The playwright himself has one of his characters call this situation "preposterous," as if to forestall our own objections.

During her stay the bag lady is surprisingly decorous. She cooks for the group and gives every evidence of being gentrified. As soon as she leaves, however, her benefactors discover she has stolen many of their valuables. (Perhaps in this Greenberg has been obeying the principles of French classicism, in which nothing untoward is allowed to happen in view of the audience, though he violated these principles in the throwing of the Perrier bottle in the first act.)

Midway through the second act, after the artist has grown impatient with the lover he so desires, declaring that "Telling the truth is just a new trend in deviousness; it doesn't make you any less guilty," the brother finally admits he has AIDS. The artist agrees to care for him. After much anxiety the architect and the financier agree to marry, and the play ends with the architect's grandiloquent toast: "To all the disappointments, which are inevitable, and compromises, which are legion, and lies, which are our daily bread . . . and to the sadly infrequent–accidental–

happinesses of all the rest of our lives." Like the above speech, the play fairly yearned for eloquence and too often seemed just hollow.

Artifice, however, is not necessarily irredeemable. In A. R. Gurney's *The Cocktail Hour*, the chronicler of WASP life has fashioned a potentially old-fashioned play about an upper-class family whose son, a playwright, asks permission of his parents to use them as "material." The tongue-in-cheek autobiographical tone, the unabashed self-consciousness make the play very "modern." The deftness with which Gurney moves between the actual family drama and the theatrical underscoring of that drama is quite dazzling. Only an experienced writer could, dramaturgically speaking, have his cake and eat it too.

The play has a strong element of nostalgia not just for the seeming certainties of WASP life in earlier decades but also for the conventions of WASP theater, which, ridiculed during the Absurdist era, now have the charm of distance. The playwright's mother speaks wistfully of all those plays she saw starring Ina Claire. She and her husband both remember fondly the Lunts' technique of overlapping dialogue, and Gurney gives them a delicious parody of it.

The Cocktail Hour, which examines in great and witty detail the institution from which it takes its title, is inevitably an elegy for a way of life, a style of theater past retrieving. Even in its heyday the drawing-room comedy was seldom as astute about its characters and its milieu as Gurney's loving evocation.

Gurney also wrote *Another Antigone*, a topical play about an uncompromising classics professor in a university beset by trendies. One of the students in his class on Greek tragedy, instead of writing a term paper, wants to submit her own version of *Antigone*, in which Jane Fonda battles Ronald Reagan over nuclear proliferation. He points out that this is not at all what Greek tragedy is about.

Gurney's play also parallels Sophocles', though, unlike *The Cocktail Hour*, the artifice seems strained. So does a subplot in which the professor's intransigence is attributed to his supposed anti-Semitism. The injection of this issue into the play adds too much reality for it to sustain. But it is full of wise humor, and its satire of the plight of academia, where, as a dean laments, there is a huge enrollment for "that course in Comedy where all they do is study 'Annie Hall,' " strikes home beautifully.

Michael Weller, who captured the mood of young people in the 1960s so forcefully in *Moonchildren* (1971), attempted to convey the concerns of their parents in *Spoils of War*, which was first presented Off-Off-Broadway, then in a weaker version on Broadway.

The plot concerns a young man in his last year of boarding school who is determined to reconcile his bitterly estranged parents, who had separated when he was barely old enough to remember them together. None of the details of the domestic story makes sense. It is hard to see why the sensitive son would care about bringing his flamboyant mother and his earnest father, clearly incompatible, together. Late in the play we discover that the boy never mailed a letter that might have effected their reconciliation at a time when it was still feasible. Lingering guilt over his betrayal may be the reason for his belated attempt to unite his parents.

Though the skeleton seems flimsy, the way Weller has fleshed it out is full of interest. The parents' relationship flowered during the Depression, when they were radicals committed to a better future. Their marriage was short-circuited by World War II. The boy's attempt to bring them together occurs in the wake of McCarthyism, when the frustrations of those earlier, cataclysmic events created a national mood of self-doubt, recrimination, and hysteria.

The hollowness of the 1950s causes the mother to say, "Let's live for something bigger than rent and the price of hamburger . . . I want the pain, I want that terrible closeness we had once." Her closest friend retorts, "Wasn't that a housing problem?"

The character of the mother, a woman given to self-dramatization and self-indulgence, is a wonderful creation, brought to life with enormous zest by Kate Nelligan. But in neither version did the play itself jell.

August Wilson, whose *Fences* took all the awards last year, continued his cycle of plays examining the lives of American blacks decade by decade. The first to be produced in New York, *Ma Rainey's Black Bottom*, was set in the 1920s, *Fences* in the 1950s. The latest, *Joe Turner's Come and Gone*, is set in 1911. The title comes from a blues song about a Tennessee governor's brother who lured black men into crap games, kidnapped them, and forced them to work for him.

What Wilson seems to be doing is locating the social and economic antecedents of the chronic dislocations of American blacks. The play is set in a boardinghouse in Pittsburgh. With few exceptions, the characters seem to be in transit. People pass through seeking kin, seeking new lives. Against their immediate concerns there is a fascinating subplot in which Wilson tries to demonstrate the impact of the transcendent, either the adopted Christian religion or the folk traditions still remembered from the African past, on these unsettled lives. His most arresting character is a haunted giant of a man trying to exorcise personal demons, moving through the play as if carrying the mark of Cain. He terrifies the boarders, but they see him in a different light when he breaks down trembling in a parlor revival meeting.

Although there was poetry in much of the play and certainly in the performances, *Joe Turner's Come and Gone* seems highly schematized, more a work of classification and analysis than imagination. Even the reconciliations the characters effect seem "willed" by the playwright, lacking conviction. Wilson's eagerness to salve the wounds of his characters, of his people, deprives the play of forcefulness and vitality.

Turning his attention to black problems several decades earlier, Charles Fuller, the author of the Pulitzer Prize-winning *A Soldier's Play* (1981), presented the first two parts of an envisioned five-part work entitled *WE*, which is about blacks during and after the Civil War.

The first of the plays, *Sally*, though named after a stormy female character, was notable for its depiction of a young southern black named Prince who escaped slavery and joined the Union army, where his bravery earned him the rank of sergeant. As the play progresses he is put in the torturous position of having to quell an insurrection among his men, all of whom are black and infuriated that they receive three dollars a month less than their white counterparts. His white superiors explain that until the Union cause is won these injustices cannot be dealt with. Forced to choose between his cantankerous men and the abstraction of the Union, Prince chooses the abstraction. As a result several of his men are executed, leaving the others demoralized and Prince a broken man.

This depiction of an early lesson in the meaning of "freedom" for a former slave is weakened by the aimlessness and sketchiness of the play around it, which consists of little more than vignettes more suited to a miniseries than the stage.

Cover of the program for David Mamet's savage comedy about Hollywood

Prince, the second play in the series, tells a little about Prince's ongoing difficulties but focuses on a man named Burner who finds himself in a predicament as unpleasant as Prince's. He is the foreman of a group of blacks working on an experimental farm run by Union do-gooders. When the former slaves ask why picking cotton for Yankees is less demeaning than picking it for slaveowners, they are told they will be paid. But the money is not forthcoming, and Burner must represent his angry workers as Prince did his aggrieved soldiers. Fuller's strength is in depicting the agony of men caught between loyalty to their own and some higher principle. But the situation is less involving than the earlier play and left one unsure why three more plays are necessary when the first two are already variations on the same theme.

One of the freshest plays of the year was Lee Blessing's *A Walk in the Woods*, about secondary-level Soviet and American negotiators who decide to supplement their official meetings in Geneva by unofficial walks in the nearby woods. If they have stronger personal rapport, perhaps they can move their respective nations closer to peace. The two men are aware of the difficulties of their positions. As the Soviet puts it, neither of their nations can afford to be "second in the quest for peace," which he amends to "second in the appearance of the quest for peace."

The play is not without weaknesses, particularly the way it favors the Soviet, giving him the lion's share of the wit and charm. But it manages to bring political issues within the ken of human encounters (unlike, for example, *M. Butterfly*, which drains the human element out of its extreme situation, leaving it a series of "statements"). Blessing's play ends on a bittersweet note, as the men recognize their own frailty and the quixotic nature of their ambitions.

The South African playwright Athol Fugard was represented this year by *The Road to Mecca*, a lovely, atypical play about an elderly lady who, when her husband dies, decides to take up sculpting. (Apparently the play is based on an actual South African folk artist.) The strange shapes she builds in her garden and the eccentric way she redecorates her cottage fill the other people in her village with insecurity and fear.

The play takes place the evening the local minister wants her to sign papers that will remove her to a home for the elderly. A young woman who has befriended her helps her summon up the courage to fend off his seemingly well-meaning effort. The play ends with a beautiful image in which her courageous decision to defend her own integrity illumines not only her little house but the fearful world around it. Unlike many of Fugard's plays, which address the problems of South Africa directly and often unsubtly, *The Road to Mecca* has the tender quality of a piece of folk art itself.

Wendy Wasserstein, a chronicler of the generation that came of age in the 1960s, has caught beautifully the comic, somewhat depressing drift of her colleagues over the last twenty years in *The Heidi Chronicles*. Unlike many of her contemporaries, whose senses of balance and humor were utterly destroyed by that tumultuous decade, Wasserstein's alter ego, Heidi Holland, an art historian, describes her profession—and herself—as "slightly removed . . . neither the painter nor the subject, but a highly informed spectator."

Wasserstein has a shrewd eye and a perfect ear for the inanities and glibness of her contemporaries as, ever in search of freedom and power, they embrace a succession of collective passions (feminism, careerism) that effectively constitute forms of self-delusion. She remains aloof from the herd, but that does not mean she does not experience her own disappointments. Wasserstein is at her best describing the foibles of Heidi's friends. The male population of the play consists of two old friends from Heidi's adolescence, an intellectual, flippant womanizer and a witty, gay pediatrician. Neither of them can sustain a relationship with her, which limits the emotional potential of the play, but as a clearheaded, compassionate portrait of a generation, it has no rivals.

David Mamet's offering this year was a savage comedy about Hollywood, *Speed-the-Plow*, which gained notoriety for the novelty of its casting. The lone female role was played by the rock star Madonna, whose histrionic abilities are minimal but whose publicity value is peerless. Since the play itself is about three hustlers, the casting seemed to reflect the cynicism of the subject. Fortunately the cast also included the Mamet veteran Joe Mantegna and the dazzling comic actor Ron Silver. Mantegna played Bobby Gould, a former producer suddenly elevated to head of production in a studio. Silver was his former partner, Charlie Fox, now his subordinate, trying to persuade him to have the studio produce a film they both know is garbage but which stars the hot property of the month. (As the apprentice mogul puts it, "That's what we're in business to do–make the things they made last year.") Madonna played a temp, who tries to persuade the production head to produce a film based on a highbrow book about the fate of the earth. (The grandiloquence of what she reads from the book suggests Mamet may be parodying Jonathan Schell.)

It is clear that neither property has much substance. What matters in Hollywood is not what gets done but who does it, who has the power. The temp at first appears to represent something loftier, but as the exasperated Fox asks: "She's out with Albert Schweitzer in the jungle? No, she's here."

Mantegna and Silver understood the particular rhythms of Mamet's dialogue brilliantly. They threw the inanities back and forth like crack vaudevillians. Madonna missed the musicality of the language. She lacked even stage presence. But none

Cover of the program for the 1988 revival of Samuel Beckett's Waiting for Godot, *which starred Robin Williams and Steve Martin as Vladimir and Estragon*

of Mamet's earlier or better works received this much attention.

Two extremely promising new voices were heard in 1988. One belonged to Howard Korder, who had in fact studied acting with Mamet. His play, *Boys' Life*, is a largely comic, somewhat disturbing look at the generation a few years behind Wasserstein's, the yuppies, whose outlook is summed up by one of Korder's characters: "We drift into record shops, we eat Cajun food, wear nice clothes. I don't want to help other people. I say I do, but I wish they'd all go away." She articulates the selfishness all the characters in the ironically titled play exemplify. Only as the play ends does their lack of fiber take on a certain poignancy.

An especially impressive debut was *The Film Society*, by Jon Robin Baitz. The play is set in an English enclave in South Africa, a boys' school in Durban run on nineteenth-century English models. The calmness of school life is threatened by a few teachers with original, independent ideas. In the course of the play, the miscreants are dealt with and the school's ability to pursue its irrelevant existence is assured. Baitz shows with wit and passion how outmoded, meaningless institutions perpetuate themselves, a much more interesting, more universal comment on South Africa than the host of plays that assault audiences with the obvious.

In closing, perhaps a word should be said about one of the great box office successes of the season, Samuel Beckett's *Waiting for Godot*. The eagerness of New Yorkers to get tickets did not represent a new understanding of or enthusiasm for Beckett. The revival starred Robin Williams and Steve Martin and was directed by Mike Nichols. Since Beckett's own fondness for vaudeville humor and the slapstick comedy of Laurel and Hardy is well known, at first sight it did not seem a bad idea to cast two comics as Vladimir and Estragon. Martin, it turned out, had a suitably light touch for the stage business. Williams found it almost impossible to resist doing his own shtick. There is, interestingly enough, a line in the play in which Pozzo says, "But I am liberal." Since the word itself was in the text, Williams later used it as an expletive, flinging it at Martin in a way that echoed the dismal presidential campaign. Also, when Williams delivered the line "Nothing happens, nobody comes, nobody goes, it's awful," he did it as if he shared the audience's presumed exasperation with the play rather than as the statement about Existence Beckett intended.

Neither was able to suggest the fragility or delicacy of two old men struggling to make it through each gnawing day. Unlike many productions, which go for somber, existential pauses, this one concentrated on gags. If someone did not know the play–and many in the audience seemed too young even to have studied it in school–they might imagine it was a precursor of *Saturday Night Live*, though not as funny. It had too little weight to be either baffling or boring. Only when F. Murray Abraham and Bill Irwin, as Pozzo and Lucky, were onstage were you likely to remember that this was a seminal play of the twentieth century.

Beckett did not come to New York but was amply informed about the production, which, he confided in a letter to a friend, he "deplored." This, of course, was shortsighted of him. The whole tone of the evening was so uncannily American that one couldn't help thinking if the opening nighters in Miami, where the American premiere was held thirty-two years ago, had seen this production, Beckett might have been a box office writer from the start.

As it happened, earlier in the year a Dublin actor, Barry McGovern, presented a one-man show based on various Beckett works, entitled *I'll Go On*. McGovern, a tall, angular, gaunt man who radiates so much nervous energy he suggests a Giacometti illustration for some limited edition of Beckett's work, captured pungently the grotesqueness, the pathos, the austerity, and the savage humor of Beckett. If there were any doubts about the intense theatricality of Beckett's work, McGovern laid them to rest. But the skills of McGovern and the depth of his commitment to the writer bore no comparison to the celebrity production, which underscored the shallowness of even the theatricality that, in much of New York these days, has replaced any concern for texts.

The Year in Literary Biography

Mark Heberle
University of Hawaii at Manoa

Life writing in 1988 includes that ultimate audacity, a new life of Shakespeare, as well as the completed two-volume biography of a quasi-Shakespearean figure among American black poets and the beginning of a three-volume life of a transplanted Irish writer who claimed to write better plays than Shakespeare. One year after Richard Ellmann's magisterial *Oscar Wilde*, new biographies of Bernard Shaw, Nora Joyce, and Sean O'Casey remind us of Ireland's disproportionate role as the birthplace of great writers. One year after studies of William Faulkner, Ernest Hemingway, Ezra Pound, and Sylvia Plath, the lives of John Cheever, Jean Stafford, and Truman Capote remind us once again of the personal agony and self-destructiveness that seem to run in American writers. Two important subjects reappear in many of these works and emphasize the importance of simple environmental realities in the fashioning of literary works, which would seem to be composed in order to transcend such phenomena: the primal importance of parents and their awesome influence upon the lives and the works of their offspring; and the need to write in order to pay the bills.

In *Young Shakespeare* (Columbia), the distinguished Shakespearean scholar and critic Russell Fraser guides us through the first thirty years of the most important life in English literature–and the most elusive. The work tries to steer a middle course between the purely documentary encyclopedia of Samuel Schoenbaum's *William Shakespeare: A Documentary Life* (1975) and the purely fictional narrative of Anthony Burgess's *Nothing Like the Sun* (1964), the two best current substitutes for a successful and satisfying biography. Fraser outlines the sixteenth-century context in seven chapters that cover rural and urban Stratford, sixteenth-century education, London, the public theater, Shakespeare's playwright contemporaries, the bubonic plague, and the system of noble patronage of the theater and poetry. Woven into this panorama of Shakespeare's world is a hypothetical reconstruction of the life, roughly chronological, that provides a richly suggestive tapestry of possible sources–experiential, social, and literary–for the works themselves, which begin with the Henry VI trilogy and end with the Ovidian narratives *Venus and Adonis* and *The Rape of Lucrece*, presumably written during the plague years of 1592 and 1593 when the theaters were closed. This natural hiatus in Shakespeare's dramatic career is an apt conclusion for Fraser's life, marking off the brilliant early works from the greater plays that followed, with the nondramatic poetry an impressive transition between early and middle Shakespeare.

Fraser is most powerful, interesting, and controversial in his interpretation of Shakespeare the artist. Discarding traditional views of Shakespeare as a natural prodigy like Mozart on the one hand or as a theatrical apprentice who bloomed relatively late as a playwright on the other, he sees him as carefully and ambitiously acquiring his preeminence as a dramatist much as he was to acquire material and social success: "not a born poet, he made himself a poet." Shakespeare was fluent and productive from the beginning, Fraser argues, completing the first ten plays already by 1592 and achieving popularity and fame in all three genres–history, comedy, and tragedy. Verbally and structurally artful from the beginning, with a natural genius for comedy, he had yet to make his art his own. Initially a lesser artist than Christopher Marlowe in history, tragedy, and Ovidian narrative, Shakespeare imitated his master in *Richard III*, *King John*, and *Venus and Adonis*, works that attempt more than Marlowe was capable of but are less successful. Although Shakespeare's plays are more naturalistic than Marlowe's, they are fundamentally mimetic, transcending the limited particularity of narrow realism and the truths of any ideological viewpoint in order to create worlds of their own. Fraser presents a Shakespeare who is nondidactic and even nonmoral, a legitimate enemy of the Puritans who wished to close down the theaters.

Ultimately, however, this life is curiously antibiographical. Fraser presents possible analogies between what we find in the works themselves and what we might be able to say about Shakespeare's life experiences; yet most of the discussion denies that we can understand the historical Shakespeare by interpreting the works any more than we can understand the historical Mark Antony by reading *Julius Caesar*. He suggests much but concludes very little about the man himself, leaving the reader to infer that Shakespeare was probably unhappily married, uncommitted to any religious or ideological standard, and extraordinarily ambitious for success. Above all, Fraser's Shakespeare is an impersonal artist whose personal identity and experience, transformed and transmuted into something rich and strange in the works themselves, can never be recovered: "Cold-blooded and provident, Shakespeare made capital of his friends and acquaintance. He dispersed them, however, standard practice for this credentialed writer who understood how art and life aren't the same." This is a fairly traditional view of Shakespeare's identity, combining scholarly prudence with Romantic exaltation of the playwright's negative capability.

Only roughly chronological, Fraser's account uses juxtaposition and analogy rather than a developing life history to represent Shakespeare. The resulting stream of associations is sometimes startling: in the year that Shakespeare died, Pochahontas stayed at the Bel Savage Inn, where Marlowe's *Dr. Faustus* was later staged; in the 1530s, Henry VIII staged Catherine of Aragon's divorce trial in the great hall of the former Blackfriars priory, where Shakespeare's company staged *Henry VIII* four generations later, including the playwright's own version of the proceedings; "scaffold" meant stage and place of execution for the Elizabethans, who loved public exhibitions of all kinds, and Shakespearean tragedy is predicated on this etymological hint. The fourth chapter of the book opens by transporting us imaginatively from sixteenth-century Stratford through London county by county and street by street, following the route that Shakespeare must have traced when he arrived in town in the 1580s. Unfortunately, however, Fraser's travelogue is a bit too detailed and allusive for the map of London and environs on the inside cover to be helpful, and the book in general is not easy to follow. The constant crosscutting makes for a rather incoherent narrative, and Fraser's maddeningly elliptical and indirect style bewilders as much as it enlightens. Although the book is dedicated to his students and is intended for a general audience, it attempts to compress too many

Dust jacket for the biography of the Restoration poet and dramatist that also offers a detailed treatment of the period's political and social history

professional conclusions and conjectures into too little space; the resulting scholarly impressionism presents little that Shakespeare specialists do not already know but far too much that will elude nonspecialists. The title itself is somewhat misleading, since much of the discussion deals with works and historical events after 1594, Fraser's terminus. But "young Shakespeare" is not distinguished as a biographical subject from the later man, although the title implies as much–perhaps a sequel is intended, but it could provide little additional material about the life itself. In sum, a biography of Shakespeare that would be readable, scholarly, and satisfying for all of Shakespeare's admirers (and, as Fraser points out, we are *all* bardolaters) has yet to be written.

Shakespeare dominated the stage in his age, but John Dryden dominated poetry as well as drama during the Restoration period, although he recognized with characteristic sound judgment that the work of himself and his contemporaries was silver to the Elizabethans' gold: "the second temple was not like the first," he noted. While

Shakespeare was not of an age but all time, Dryden's works were intimately tied to the distinctive political, social, and literary milieu of the later seventeenth century, a world that is exhaustively brought back to life in James Anderson Winn's *John Dryden and His World* (Yale, 1987). This is probably the most important work yet published on Dryden: Professor Winn is intimately familiar with everything published by and about the poet, all the documentary records, the details of Restoration political, social, and court history, and the minutiae of the Restoration stage. Fortunately, much of this material is relegated to the 114 pages of small-type appendices and notes that follow and support the 500-page text. Like Fraser's, Winn's literary biography is the product of years of scholarship, but it is far more direct, straightforward, and readable; the author's intention is to help the general reader understand and enjoy Dryden. For readers who find themselves interested in Winn's detailed treatment of the Restoration court, politics, and stage as well as Dryden's work, this book will be enjoyable indeed.

Winn argues that Dryden marched with Milton at Cromwell's funeral in 1658 and wrote "Heroique Stanzas" to commemorate the Lord Protector; he was also present at Charles II's coronation in 1661 and wrote *Astraea Redux* to welcome back Cromwell's mortal enemy. Frequently accused of such apparent political opportunism during his life and after his death, Dryden was in any event intimately involved in public affairs: he was appointed poet laureate by Charles in 1668, losing his official position in 1688 when the Glorious Revolution replaced James II and his official poet, now a Catholic like his exiled sovereign. A public poet whose own viewpoint was always clear but never merely personal, Dryden characteristically addresses his readers as "we" or "you," encouraging them to define with him a community or relationship marked by shared values and attitudes. Winn's generous descriptions and commentaries dealing with every one of the works—panegyrics, epics, satires, meditative poems, odes, songs, plays, dramatic prologues and epilogues, dedicatory letters and other literary criticism, translations and metaphrases, histories—remind us of Dryden's astounding versatility and the degree to which virtually all of his work is occasional, topical, and rhetorical, intended to engage directly and persuade its various audiences ethically, aesthetically, and politically. Even the adaptations of *Oedipus* and Shakespeare's *Troilus and Cressida*, both produced during the Exclusion Crisis of 1678-1679 when the Parliamentary party sought to use the alleged Popish Plot against Charles to remove his brother James from the succession, are of some immediate political interest, as Winn points out. The scheming Creon resembles the Whig leader Anthony Ashley Cooper, first earl of Shaftesbury, in demagoguery and physical deformity, while the debate between Hector and Troilus in the latter play may reflect some contemporary criticism of Charles's own sexual irresponsibility. Winn finds the post-1688 translations pregnant with criticism of the Williamite regime that replaced James's, criticism that would have been apparent to Jacobite readers if not to the royal censors. Important original works like *Annus Mirabilis* (1667), *Absalom and Achitophel* (1681), and *The Hind and the Panther* (1687) more directly comment upon critical contemporary political, royal, and religious events and issues.

Winn is particularly illuminating in showing how most Restoration literature tends to be intimately circumstantial, including plays; writers and their audience seem to be virtually members of one family, sharing a common frame of references that played themselves out in the literary marketplace. He argues convincingly that public issues themselves were more personal and less theoretical than we might have supposed, and political ideology more flexible. During Dryden's lifetime, after all, one king was executed, another exiled, a third restored from the continent, a fourth imported from the Netherlands; a republic and a dictatorship were established and abolished, a monarchy overthrown, restored, and modified; Anglicanism, Puritanism, and Catholicism were variously established or disestablished as the government religion; and the first Western political parties, the Whigs and the Tories, were founded. Dryden himself was raised in a mildly Puritan family which had him educated under the staunchly Royalist Richard Busby at Westminster School; he married into the Howard family, several of whose members were prominent Catholics. By Restoration standards, Dryden was not overly inconsistent ideologically, and his willingness to change and modify his literary principles and practices, acknowledging his own failures as well as his successes, is one of the marks of his genius.

Winn's enthusiasm for Dryden and his world is not always contagious, however. Not many of the plays seem worth the attention paid to them, nor all of the dedications. The author's circumstantial interpretations of the contemporary context and references of these works rely upon our sharing his interest in Restoration ephemera. Dryden's own purposes in each work are always well defined, but there is little critical discrimination between good works, bad works, and justly forgotten works. Attempts to show Dryden's positive development as a writer are sometimes convincing but largely irrelevant for an author whose ouevre is so occasional: *Religio Laici* (1688) is a better religious poem than the more ambitious and more original *Hind and the Panther,* largely because Dryden had no audience for the later poem, and the mature poet could still churn out embarrassing propaganda like *Britannia Rediviva* (1687) when circumstances called for him to do so. The author never questions Dryden's political allegiances, implicitly supporting his post-1688 Jacobitism and seeing him as a courageous spokesman for the principle of legitimate succession rather than as a self-interested adherent to a widely feared and distrusted monarch.

While Winn uncritically accepts Dryden's enthusiasm for the Stuarts, his study painstakingly details Dryden's dependence as a professional writer upon royal grants to himself and his wife, all of which are recorded in an appendix. Dryden's concern to make a living for himself is the subject of many of his dedications and a major objective of nearly all the works, and Winn constantly reminds us of the writer's material circumstances and Dryden's most important identity, that of a professional writer. Otherwise, however, Dryden seldom comes to life as a private person. Like Fraser, Winn scrupulously avoids conjectures about Dryden's intimate life, about which we know almost nothing–his lengthy affair with Anne Reeves, one of his company's actresses, is merely referred to in a documentary appendix of "facts" that are known about her. Altogether, his biography is a splendidly informative appreciation of John Dryden's works that unquestioningly accepts Dryden's own best view of himself, his writings, and the world for which he wrote.

Fred Kaplan's *Dickens: A Biography* treats another giant of English literature, one who dominated the early- and mid-Victorian novel much as Shakespeare dominated the Elizabethan stage and Dryden the whole of Restoration literature. Kaplan's work is inferior to Edgar Johnson's *Charles Dickens: His Tragedy and Triumph* (1952) in

Dust jacket for the most recent biography of the Victorian novelist. The author draws much of his information from Dickens's own letters and those of his friends.

treating the earlier works, and it overuses autobiographical displacement in criticizing the works, but it provides a more well-focused, energetic narrative of the writer's turbulent life that relies heavily upon Dickens's own letters and those of his friends, many of them previously unpublished. Dickens's Faustian energy and restlessness are evident throughout, and the works and life blend into one another authentically; using letters and other documentary sources, Kaplan interweaves the words and feelings of Dickens and his friends seamlessly into the biography without losing continuity or authorial control of the narrative.

Kaplan shows how Dickens's male friends provided professional and personal encouragement, and how his nine children produced material responsibilities and happiness, but just as much dissatisfaction; however, the relationships most important for his works involved his parents. Previous biographers and critics have found the key to much of Dickens's art and life in childhood trauma: the twelve-year-old boy, forced to work labeling bottles at Warren's Blacking Warehouse while his father was thrown into the Marshalsea debtors' prison, felt abandoned and disgraced by his own parents; the mother moved the entire family into the Marshalsea with John Dickens to save lodging expenses; and Elizabeth insisted that the boy return to child labor even after her husband's release, though she was successfully resisted by the financially improvident father, who sent the boy to school instead. Kaplan argues that Dickens never forgave his pretty but irresponsible mother, who died senile and spiritually abandoned by her famous son, supported financially until her death in 1863 but otherwise largely ignored. John Dickens continued to hover unsuccessfully and irritatingly on the edges of his son's fame, borrowing money from Dickens's publishers, but he was not totally rejected: Charles even provided him with a job at the *Daily News* when the novelist became its general editor briefly in 1845. After his initial success as a court reporter, Dickens spent the rest of his life successfully escaping the imprisoning confinement and poverty burnt into his soul by these childhood experiences, and much of his adult life as an author, journalist, actor, reader, public speaker, and philanthropist was intended to reform the social, educational, and economic conditions that were indirectly responsible for the hopelessness that he had experienced as a child. By contrast with his London childhood, however, his early years at Rochester and Chatham in Kent had been idyllic, and his father had encouraged him to feel that through hard work he could some day hope to own the eighteenth-century mansion at Gad's Hill Place on the Gravesend Road. All these childhood experiences were the stuff dreams and nightmares are built on, and Dickens reimagined and transmuted them over and over again in his works from *The Pickwick Papers* (1836-1837) through *Bleak House* (1852-1853) and *The Mystery of Edwin Drood* (1870), let alone the more directly autobiographical works: *Oliver Twist* (1838), *David Copperfield* (1849-1850), *Little Dorrit* (1855-1857), and *Great Expectations* (1861). Kaplan's criticism of childhood motifs and displacements throughout Dickens's works is impressive, but he also reminds us how the life also came to repeat yet change the conditions of childhood. Dickens seems to have been unable to keep from fathering even more children than John,

but he provided for them generously though begrudging his sons' failure to become distinguished, a resentment wholly alien to his careless father. He began to attribute qualities of his mother to his wife, Catherine Dickens, which helped to justify separating from her in 1858, something his father would never have been self-willed or cruel enough to do. He provided for Catherine generously–and complained about his generosity petulantly in his will–but like Elizabeth Dickens, his wife was banished from the Dickens household forever, nor did he ever visit her. Finally, he bought Gad's Hill Place in 1856 and lived there with his family when not traveling through England, Europe, or America. Returning like Pip at the end of *Great Expectations* to the idealized setting of his boyhood, Dickens could also revel in the Shakespearean associations of this place–being able to own and enjoy Gad's Hill fulfilled his own childish great expectations and confirmed his own identity as the Shakespeare of his age.

While the irresponsible, selfish, or loveless mother reappears frequently as Dickens's female villain throughout the novels, his heroines are angelic sister figures–Kate Nickleby, Little Nell, Florence Dombey, and their successors. Their original was his wife's sister, Mary Hogarth, who died in Dickens's arms when she was seventeen and was later replaced by Catherine's other sister, Georgina, who joined the Dickens household in 1842, remained with her brother-in-law after the separation, and ministered to him and his children until his death. Somewhere between the unloving mother and beneficent sister-in-law lay Dickens's numerous objects of flirtation, all of them theatrical performances, Kaplan notes, combining gallantry and chaste passion but symptomatic of Dickens's dissatisfaction with his marriage. When he took the actress Ellen Ternan as his mistress and separated from Catherine, the resulting accommodation established a relative happiness for Dickens in his relations with women that lasted for the rest of his life, but it was incomplete: Georgina was his sister-in-law, Ellen his lover, and Catherine his wife, but only Georgina lived in the household and none could appear with him publicly.

It seems perversely right that Dickens should have given up Catherine for an actress, even a mediocre one like Ternan, who abandoned her career after Dickens began to support her. Dickens's most important relationship was with his audience, and he was constantly on stage himself, literally as well as figuratively. Vigorously engaged in directing, producing, and acting in amateur theatricals within his own family and among his numerous friends, who came to include the legendary early Victorian Shakespearean actor William Charles Macready, Dickens found the applause of an audience even more exhilarating and satisfying than the praise of his readers. Theater also provided an outlet for ministering to society, both through the charity funds that they generated and through increasing the prestige of the literary profession in Victorian England, a cause to which Dickens contributed tirelessly, not least because it justified himself. In the 1850s Dickens began to perform public readings of his novels as a source of personal income. A substitute for the exhilaration of acting now that the novelist had attained middle age and become a well-respected public figure, the readings were directly generated by Dickens's failing marriage: not only did they provide additional income to maintain the three households he would support for the last twelve years of his life, but they also provided a personal happiness not often enjoyed within his own family. In the 1860s the readings became an end in themselves, an escape from the unhappiness attendant upon the death of so many friends, but they contributed to the novelist's demise, particularly the lucrative but exhausting tour of America in 1867 and 1868. Dickens's scheduled "farewell tour" of England in 1868-1869 had to be cut short when he collapsed near the end in Chester, but at the end of the year he not only made out his will but also rescheduled the remainder of the readings for early 1870. Characteristically, he had completed the tour, had just directed his two daughters in a local play, and had only just finished a chapter of *The Mystery of Edwin Drood*, a final novel set in the Kentish landscape of his childhood, when he collapsed for the last time, in Georgina's arms, and died at Gad's Hill on 5 June 1870.

Everywhere, Kaplan vividly captures the almost ceaseless activity of the man, from walking thirty miles after a quarrel with Catherine, to establishing and overseeing a home for former prostitutes, to his assiduous editing and proofing of his journal *Household Words*. But he never romanticizes or idealizes Dickens's nearly manic energy, seeing it as an element of the novelist's sometimes desperate will to empower himself. One of the many fine features of Kaplan's life is its revealing portraits of Dickens's many distinguished friends and his own ability to attract such friends

to him, but it also reveals the splendid egocentricity that drew others but could cast them aside when Dickens felt his own interests or sense of his own integrity threatened: "Generous when unchallenged, his notion of compromise was total victory. His aggressiveness, stubbornness, and inflexibility seemed tyranny to some, the power of genius to others."

In *From Copyright to Copperfield: The Identity of Dickens* (Harvard), Alexander Welsh briefly examines Dickens's disillusioning tour of America in 1842 and then presents fresh interpretations of the three novels that followed it, *Martin Chuzzlewit* (1842-1844), *Dombey and Son* (1846-1848), and *David Copperfield* (1849-1850). Although not a literary biography, Welsh's book provides a suggestive picture of Dickens at mid career, a somewhat less confidently self-directed figure than Kaplan's human dynamo, although his argument extends rather than questions the biographer's view of Dickens. Welsh notes that Dickens's primary motive for his American venture combined literary idealism with financial self-interest: he hoped to convince his American hosts to join with English writers in establishing an international copyright so that authorized editions of American and English literary works could be published freely in both countries. Establishing his right in the pirated editions of his works published in America would benefit Dickens's pocket, of course, and Americans were quick not only to turn him into a public celebrity and leave him no privacy but also to question his own selfish interests in the proposal, which drew almost no support in America. Stung by his reception, Dickens satirized the venality and vulgarity of American society in *Martin Chuzzlewit* but also self-critically registered these attacks on himself comically in that novel and tragically in *Dombey and Son*, according to Welsh, before presenting a reasonably direct and positive self-portrait of his progress from an unhappy childhood to a career as a novelist in *David Copperfield*.

Welsh argues that Dickens was undergoing a mid-life vocational crisis in the 1840s, and the relatively long hiatus between *Martin Chuzzlewit* and *Dombey and Son*, his most carefully constructed, serious, and successful novel to date, marks the crisis and its resolution, while *David Copperfield* signals his rededication to the career that he would pursue for the rest of his life. Aspects of Dickens's life during this period cited by Welsh and more largely developed by Kaplan support this view: the decision to write an autobiographi-

BERNARD SHAW

1

The Search for Love

A BIOGRAPHY BY
MICHAEL HOLROYD

Dust jacket for the first in a projected three-volume biography of the noted Irish playwright

cal fragment at this time, transmitted to his friend and eventual biographer John Forster, as well as his quickly abandoned attempt to be the full-time editor of the *Daily News* and his interest in becoming a police superintendent, both possible alternative careers.

The most satisfying biography of the year is only one-third completed. Michael Holroyd's *Bernard Shaw: The Search for Love, 1856-1898* (Random House) covers its subject's life through his marriage to Charlotte Payne-Townsend. The title itself is provoking, for one scarcely associates Shaw's personality with eros, but Holroyd makes good on his title in often surprising ways. Shaw's father was born into the upper-class Irish Protestant aristocracy, but his grandfather Bernard died penniless after being embezzled by his business partner and left his widow with eleven children. Not only poor himself but a hopeless alcoholic, like two of his brothers, Shaw's father

married Lucinda Elizabeth Gurly ("Bessie") for her inheritance, but his wife's family objected and managed to cut the couple off. Holroyd's view of the marriage reflects Shaw's own and is conveyed with the archness that makes this biography such a delight to read and so true to its subject's own voice: "George Carr Shaw had gained a wife and lost a fortune. There was nothing to be done—it was enough to make one weep with laughter. When they drove off after the wedding, George Carr Shaw turned to kiss his bride. She felt so disgusted that she was still protesting more than thirty years later."

Brought up in genteel poverty in Dublin, Shaw was not forced into manual labor like Dickens but suffered the indignity of attending the lower-class Catholic-administered Central Model Boys' School. More significantly, his family was peculiarly loveless: Bessie despised her drunken husband and provided no affection for her only son but instead transferred all her emotional loyalty and personal ambitions to the musical impresario George Vanderleur Lee, who not only established his Amateur Musical Society two doors from the Shaw household but also leased a cottage for himself *and* the Shaws south of Dublin in 1866. When Shaw was seventeen Lee moved his musical empire to London and established the New Philharmonic Society, and Bessie and her two daughters followed; after several years of drudgery as a Dublin clerk Shaw left his father behind and followed to London, moving in with Lee and Bessie in 1876. The almost unmentionable horrors of this childhood and adolescence fueled Shaw's hatred of his first name (hence the creation of "GBS" as his professional signature); his teetotalism (and other gestures to avoid contamination, including vegetarianism, wearing all-wool Jaeger suits, and an antivaccination mania); his contempt for Ireland; his tendency to defuse and distance direct emotional reactions to injustice, frustration, and desire with intellectual irony; and his drive to validate and empower his genius through solitary effort: "Work became his mistress. He kept no other company." During his first two decades in London, Shaw made the British Museum his first real home, and work became an end in itself, whether or not it could provide a living. Of Shaw's three major literary activities during these years, only the dramatic and musical criticism was commercially and professionally successful. The four novels went unpublished, and of the plays that followed, only *Arms and the Man* (1894), written for the popular

West End theaters, was fully successful; three plays went unstaged, *Widower's Houses* (1892) had two performances, productions of *The Man of Destiny* (1897) and *Candida* (1897) were long delayed and unsuccessful, and while *The Devil's Disciple* (1897) proved a great financial, artistic, and popular success, it was only seen in America. Nonetheless, Shaw brilliantly wrote on, establishing himself as London's leading critic, one of its most public men of letters about town, and its most celebrated unproduced playwright. In 1898 he collected seven of his plays in *Plays: Pleasant and Unpleasant* (two volumes) together with the famous prefaces that combined witty social commentary with overstated literary criticism and self-promotion: "Why should I get another man to praise me when I can praise myself?" he wrote in a later volume with the deliciously paradoxical title *Three Plays for Puritans* (1901). In addition to all his literary activity, Shaw found time to help organize the Fabian Society with Sidney and Beatrice Webb, help them establish the London School of Economics, write political pamphlets and articles, and serve as an elected borough councilor for St. Pancras's vestry, involving himself energetically in the minutiae of local municipal government and pressing to cleanse the local council of political corruption and the borough itself of threats to public health.

Work was *not* Shaw's only mistress, however, and the heart of Holroyd's biography is his fascinating reconstruction of Shaw's grand flirtations and loves. Holroyd details eleven separate affairs from Shaw's love for Alice Lockett from 1881 to 1885 to his marriage with the wealthy and aristocratic Charlotte Payne-Townsend in 1898. Gallant but cautious, Shaw was attempting in all of these relationships to gain the happiness that his mother had denied him, but they typically took the form of a romantic and intimate intellectual partnership. Shaw loved to play the mentor and adviser, and curiously re-created the primal ménage à trois that had characterized his mother's relationship with Lee and her husband; adopting the Lee role, Shaw became a stimulating but sometimes maddening presence in the households of Ida Beatty, Edith Bland, Eleanor Marx (Karl's daughter and the mistress of George Aveling), and Janet Achurch, whose acting career he assiduously promoted. An infatuation with Geraldine Spencer left her hoping for a proposal but never receiving one, but once she married the philosopher Herbert Carr, Shaw tried to infiltrate their household without success. With two ex-

ceptions, these liaisons were technically chaste and sometimes completely nonphysical, but Shaw composed his passion in letters that were answered as romantically. His affair with Jenny Patterson, which nearly overwhelmed his identity at times, was the great sexual experience of his life–and profoundly Oedipal. Jenny was a friend of his mother's and fifteen years older than Shaw himself. Marriage was out of the question for both of them; and after she became jealous of his more intellectual infatuations, she broke off from him bitterly. The actress Florence Farr was Shaw's other sexual partner, and although he persuaded her to divorce her husband (from whom she was separated), Shaw failed to come through after all, and she turned her attention to William Butler Yeats. Initially, Charlotte herself proposed unsuccessfully to Shaw but then forced him to pursue her by refusing to allow him the satisfaction of continued intellectual intimacy without marrying her, and, finding he could not be happy without her, Shaw found himself surprisingly and happily married at forty-two.

Holroyd admires Shaw and allows Shaw's view of himself full scope, but he also properly corrects him at many points. Shaw's denial of his mother's disinterest in love helped him deny the sexual component of her partnership with Lee (a relationship that clearly affected his own matter-of-fact depreciation of sex). He claimed that his famous beard grew by chance, but the young Shaw grew it soon after his arrival in London to cover a smallpox scar. Holroyd treats the life of Shaw with an irony and crisp wit that his subject practiced and would have admired, as in his description of the end of the marriage between Charlotte's own mismatched parents: "The volume of domestic unhappiness rose, submerging her humdrum husband. Early in February 1885 he decided to die. There was nothing much wrong with him—a little rheumatism perhaps—and he was comparatively young. But his patience had given out, and for a polite man there was nothing else to do." This volume ends with Shaw's wedding and his work on *Caesar and Cleopatra* (1906) and *The Perfect Wagnerite* (1898).

Like Shaw, James Joyce left Ireland to immortalize himself as a writer, but his Irish Catholic origins placed him far below the Shaws socially, and he even married below his own social class, taking Nora Barnacle of Galway and Finn's Hotel with him when he went off to Europe in 1904. Nora has often been regarded as far below her husband in other ways as well, a chamber-

Dust jacket for the biography of Nora Barnacle Joyce that not only details her emotional support for her husband, James Joyce, but also attempts to reveal her presence and influence in his works

maid who became his mistress and a quaint source for his creations of quotidian humanity and the female psyche, rewarded for her loyalty and devotion to his genius with a civil marriage ceremony in 1931. When Brenda Maddox approached Joyce's biographer Richard Ellmann with a proposal to write a life of Nora, he felt it was unneeded and unrealizable. But Ellmann later altered his judgment. *Nora: The Real Life of Molly Bloom* (Houghton Mifflin) tells the other side of the story with strong enthusiasm for both Nora and her Jim, and presents one of the most impressive and absolutely authentic love stories in English literature.

Nora did not ask Joyce to marry her nor did she need to doubt his complete devotion and nearly sole dependence upon her for his emo-

tional needs. In almost every way, she was the stronger person as well as the less selfish—only Joyce was sexually jealous, only Nora threatened to leave, and with both of the children. She put up with his almost comical drunkenness, his frequent fecklessness as a provider, and his increasingly exclusive interest in the fictional worlds of *Ulysses* (1922) and *Finnegans Wake* (1939), but without her companionship it is unlikely that Joyce could have written either. Beyond providing emotional support, Nora provided much of the detail for Joyce's work, and this biography reveals her presence and influence throughout Joyce's writings and should prove good hunting grounds for Joyce explicators. As Maddox points out, for example, Nora's surname derives from the "glorious name of Irish goose," as Joyce exclaimed in his notebooks for *Finnegans Wake,* and the many references to seabirds in the works are deliberate tributes to Nora herself. At the end of the fourth section of *A Portrait of the Artist as a Young Man* (1916), Stephen Dedalus ecstatically observes a girl along the seashore whom his imagination begins to metamorphose into a bird, and this epiphanic vision summons him to assume his vocation of poet-priest; Maddox's book allows to identify this girl with Nora, whom Joyce defined briefly in an alphabetic notebook entry: "Wherever thou art shall be Erin to me." Maddox emphasizes the similarities that drew them to each other, not just the differences—both were birds of flight, eager exiles from the narrowness and unhappiness of difficult family situations and the degrading oppressiveness of Irish poverty. Curiously enough, Nora came to reject Ireland even more strongly than Joyce, and she enjoyed Europe more.

Maddox has been resourceful and comprehensive in personally visiting all the numerous "Joyce countries" in Ireland, France, Switzerland, Italy, and England, in interviewing all available friends and relations of Nora and Joyce, in researching documents in the numerous Joyce archives, and in examining every written record to and from Nora (her missing letters may be part of a collection of Joyceiana sealed until 1991 in the National Library of Ireland). She has enormously expanded Padraic O'Laoi's earlier biography, *Nora Barnacle Joyce: A Portrait* (1982), focused on her life in Ireland. The disappointing life of the Joyces' indolent and alcoholic son Giorgio—Nora's favorite—and the tragedy of their schizophrenic daughter Lucia—Joyce's pet—enrich and deepen what becomes a family narrative by its end. The terrible odyssey of the family across Europe during the catastrophe of 1939-1941 is particularly gripping. Maddox also corrects previous portraits of Nora, including Ellmann's, in numerous details and answers most of the important questions that have led her to write the life–those connected with the civil marriage of Nora and Joyce in 1931 in London, for example. Joyce agreed to this unnecessary affirmation of their life together in order to satisfy his American daughter-in-law's insistence that any of her children by Giorgio must be legitimate but also to encourage his own prospective brother-in-law's successful help in obtaining a financially lucrative copyright of the American edition of *Ulysses*. She corrects Maria Jolas's mistaken recollection that Nora was declared "a great sinner" at her funeral–a legendary detail that has spoiled Nora's final reputation to the present. The Swiss priest was merely reciting Gretchen's prayer to the Blessed Virgin from *Faust,* a common last benediction in German-speaking countries but an allusion that would have delighted both Joyce and his wife, who had become culturally cosmopolitan like him by the end of her life. Maddox manages to celebrate Nora's story without denigrating Joyce, although occasionally tendentious feminist clichés startle without illuminating, and her enthusiasm for Nora's ability to provide Joyce with the notorious pornographic letters that matched his own during his trip to England in 1909 seems witless: Nora's skill in fulfilling Joyce's masturbatory fantasies in order to dampen his violent sexual jealousy may be admired, but it neither helps Nora nor feminism to claim that she was a good pornographer, particularly considering Joyce's taste in such matters. His need for the letters do show how helpless and lost he was without Nora's presence, one of the most important revelations of this fine book. Nora often denied that she resembled Molly Bloom, and she disliked *Ulysses* in general, only reading the first twenty-seven pages; she claimed a curious preference for *Finnegans Wake,* and Maddox uses part of Anna Livia Plurabelle's final monologue to memorialize her: "I done me best when I was let. Thinking always if I go all goes. A hundred cases, a tithe of troubles and is there one who understands me?" Maddox's book often achieves such understanding.

It has been said that the three most important women in Joyce's life were Nora, his London publisher Harriet Shaw Weaver, and his Paris publisher Sylvia Beach, the American expatriate who established Shakespeare and Company as an avant-garde bookseller during the golden age of high modernism in the 1920s and brought out the first edition of *Ulysses*. If so, the publication of *James Joyce's Letters to Sylvia Beach, 1921-1940* (Indiana University Press, 1987) overwhelmingly confirms Nora's preeminence in Joyce's life. This is a superbly definitive edition of this correspondence, which Prof. Oscar A. Silverman began to assemble before his death in 1977; the executive editor is Melissa Banta, curator of the SUNY Buffalo Poetry/Rare Book Collection, a major Joyce repository. The volume includes a foreword by A. Walton Litz, a preface by Banta, excellent biographical introductions to each of the five chronologically sequential sections of letters, a brief epilogue dealing with Sylvia Beach's life after Joyce's death and the closing of the bookshop during the German occupation of Paris (she refused to sell her last copy of *Finnegans Wake* to a German officer), and superbly detailed explanatory notes to all the letters.

Most of this material is more interesting than the letters themselves, which largely consist of requests for money or books from Joyce to his publisher and directions for correcting proofs of portions of Joyce's *Work in Progress* (ultimately entitled *Finnegans Wake*) being submitted to various periodicals and for which Shakespeare and Company served as Joyce's agent. Only two important personal subjects intrude, and they are tied to the almost exclusively professional concerns of these letters: Joyce's terrible eye problems, which provide an implicit explanation or justification of his difficulties in responding to proofs; and the wretched financial state of the Joyce family, which justifies the requests to forward checks to Joyce's various addresses. The most interesting letter, printed in an appendix, is the only one written by Sylvia Beach; on 12 April 1927 she reasserted her admiration and affection for Joyce's work but complained about his overwhelming demands upon her: "When you are absent, every word I receive from you is an order. The reward for my unceasing labour on your behalf is to see you tie yourself into a bowknot and hear you complain." The letter was never sent, however, but one can appreciate its sentiments after reading through twelve years of pleasantly impersonal requests for help (Joyce ended his professional connection with Shakespeare and Company in 1932 shortly after forcing Beach to surrender the rights to *Ulysses*). Scholars interested in *Finnegans Wake* may wish to examine many of the letters and Joyceans generally will want to look at this correspondence, which reemphasizes Joyce's overwhelming dedication to seeing his work in print, but otherwise provides little self-revelation.

A more substantial and important collection of correspondence is *The Letters of T. S. Eliot: Volume I, 1898-1922* (Harcourt Brace Jovanovich), edited by Valerie Eliot, the poet's widow. Published on the centenary of Eliot's birth, the edition as a whole is intended to provide an indirect biography of the writer. Volume 1 was originally to have covered the years from 1898 to 1926, so this collection will be appended by a second volume next year covering 1923 to 1926. The 1922 termination is appropriate, however, taking Eliot's life to the October publication of *The Waste Land* in the first issue of his new literary journal the *Criterion* and the American publication of the poem in December.

Just after the English publication of *The Waste Land,* the "Bel Esprit" project to fund Eliot's release from his job in Lloyds Bank so that he could devote full time to poetry had been vetoed unless his supporters could guarantee him some financial security. The poet was concerned about his wife Vivien's precarious physical and emotional health and his responsibility for her material and physical welfare should he give up the bank position, as he argues in a November letter to Pound. Three days later the project was misrepresented and attacked in the *Liverpool Post,* prompting an angry protest from Eliot and a subsequent apology from the newspaper. A letter on 27 December to the American literary philanthropist John Quinn expresses Eliot's gratitude for certification of the U.S. copyright of *The Waste Land,* an inquiry about Quinn's opinion of additional poems previously forwarded for possible publication, and Eliot's gratitude and satisfaction over Quinn's enjoyment of the *Criterion* together with a plan to have it published by Boni and Liveright, who had published *The Waste Land* in America. At the end of the year a letter to his brother Henry reviews how receiving the *Dial* prize for poetry might advance Eliot's literary career, his work on the *Criterion,* and the state of Vivien's health. Eliot is on the verge of international fame, his wife is teetering on the edge of another nervous collapse, and the poet seems to be anticipating both eventualities. At times like this the Eliot letters do seem to recapture the life of a writer who refused to allow a biography of himself. However, even in his often delightful letters to younger siblings, his dutiful, heartfelt, and fre-

quent letters to his mother, and the early, mildly improper letters to Conrad Aiken and other Harvard comrades, Eliot always seems to be as formally dressed in his correspondence as in his personal life. Most of the letters are professional in the widest sense—concerned primarily with the status of his career, whether or not he is satisfied with it, and how he may improve it—or they are attempts to advance himself directly. The bulk of them seems remarkably purposive and probably reflects the essence of the man himself, an upper-middle-class American to the core in his drive to achieve fame and fortune, even as his marriage was collapsing about him. Of course, he was even able to capitalize on Vivien's collapse and his own in writing the great poem that would immortalize him and define the essence of high modernism. Truly upset by his father's sudden death in January 1919, Eliot impressed upon John Quinn his desire to have a book published in America—it would be too late to show his father that he had made the right career decision to go off to England and become a writer, but "my mother is still alive." Eliot's buttoned-down ambition seethes through the formality of these rather mundane and unmemorable testaments of himself, and it will be interesting to see whether he began to adopt a more meditative persona once his greatness became established.

That the letters have been published at all is a tribute to the determination of Valerie Eliot, whose superb 1971 facsimile edition of *The Waste Land* manuscripts revealed how much Pound had contributed to helping Eliot shape his poem. To allow others access to such communications seems to have been an offense against what was expected among the Eliots: his mother assumed that she ought to destroy Eliot's letters to her in 1924 (and apparently did so), and he burned much of his correspondence to his mother and brother Henry after their deaths in 1929 and 1947 as well as having a friend incinerate his letters from Emily Hale in 1957. After marrying Eliot in the same year, Mrs. Eliot discovered that he had forbidden publication of his letters but agreed to let her do the job on the condition of selecting and editing them. The project now nearing completion has taken her over twenty years and promises a fuller revelation of the self-concealing poet than has yet been possible; yet Eliot's proviso remains troubling to scholars; it is not clear what letters have been selected or why or how they have been edited. A fuller explanation by Mrs. Eliot in the next volume would help

Dust jacket for the concluding volume of the most extensive biography of the leading figure of the Harlem Renaissance

to allay fears that this memorial to her husband is not also a whitewash. In any case this first installment is a handsome book that will be essential for all students of Eliot and modernist literature: besides an extremely detailed and helpful chronological summary of Eliot's first thirty-four years, the over six-hundred letters are finely annotated, with biographical notes on each correspondent, and a generous collection of photographs and illustrations. Letters *from* Eliot's family members, his wife, and his friends to Eliot as well as to others are also included, helping to fulfill the larger biographical intentions of the volume.

Garry O'Connor's *Sean O'Casey: A Life* (Atheneum) deals with another expatriate, like Eliot, and a member of that distinguished class of Irish exiles who have contributed so much to modern English literature. O'Casey fairly worshipped Shaw and enlisted his support in his continual guerrilla warfare against his critics once he had re-

moved himself to England, but he remained more fundamentally Irish in temperament and soul than either Shaw or Joyce, his character shaped by the stern and self-defensive righteousness of middle-class Irish Protestantism. O'Connor rightly points out that the more he imitated Shaw the less he fulfilled his own genius for creating unique comic tragedies that superbly combined a powerfully emotional naturalism with irony and satire. O'Connor draws his nineteen chapter titles from icons of Irish nationalism, references to O'Casey's own works, and haunting phrases from his great friend and enemy William Butler Yeats ("Two Eternities," "They Dreamed and Are Dead," "Slouching Towards Bethlehem") and divides the life into three sections. "Swords of Light" (1880-1921) covers the years in Dublin when O'Casey moved from Gaelic nationalism through socialism while working as a laborer on the Great Northern Railway and wrote songs, journalistic pieces, and the first rejected plays. "On the Run" (1921-1927) covers the national and soon international success of the Dublin trilogy (*The Shadow of a Gunman, Juno and the Paycock, The Plough and the Stars*), the initially temporary move to London, the quarrel with Yeats and Lady Gregory over the Abbey Theatre's rejection of *The Silver Tassie*—which encouraged him to make his exile permanent—and his marriage to the beautiful Irish actress Eileen Carey, twenty-three years his junior, who was to have younger lovers yet never be truly unfaithful to her husband during their long and happy life together. "The Shape of a New World" (1927-1964) deals with O'Casey's years in England, the experimental plays, the continual polemics against literary and political enemies (like Shaw, O'Casey became a public scold and an improbable Stalinist), the birth of his three children, and the writing of the massive six-volume autobiographies. Ultimately, O'Casey became famous and celebrated in England and, especially, America, while he and Ireland carried on a family quarrel for the rest of his life.

O'Connor's biography tellingly reveals the pervasive distortions of the autobiographies, written over sixteen years (1938-1954), which began in the wonderful impressionistic sketches-cum-narrative of his childhood and youth in *I Knock at the Door* and *Pictures in the Hallway* and ended in the always lively but monomaniacal self-defenses and lashings of his critics in the last two volumes. Like Jean-Jacques Rousseau in his *Confessions*, O'Casey grows somewhat wearisome as he becomes famous. O'Connor demonstrates that not only are O'Casey's recollections historically inaccurate but they also chronologically rearrange and reinterpret the events of his own life in order to exaggerate the hardships and disappointments of his early family history as well as his working-class credentials, and they shape his life narrative to more dramatically detail his progressive triumphs over adversity. For example, he placed the death of his miserably widowed sister Bella ten years before the actual event in 1918 so as not to interfere with the greatest trauma of his early manhood, the death of his mother, Susan. Unfortunately, the crosscutting from O'Casey's narrative to O'Connor's renders the first section of the work rather confusing and shapeless even though it deals with the most exciting events of O'Casey's life, including the early years of the Abbey Theatre, the great labor strike of 1913, the formation of the Irish Citizens Army (for which O'Casey was secretary and official historian), the Easter Rebellion of 1916, the civil war against the Blacks and Tans at the end of World War I, and the formation of the Irish Free State.

O'Casey might be regarded as an enfant terrible of Irish literature, but only with strange qualifications: his first play was produced after he was forty years old, and he became more and more childishly self-justifying as he grew older. The most important person in his life was his beloved mother, with whom he lived at home for his first thirty-eight years, until her death in 1918. She put up with her son's failure to make much of a living for himself and indulged him in the long years of his literary apprenticeship at home. Eileen provided a wonderful substitute during the almost four decades of life in England. In between lay the early 1920s, the years of O'Casey's great and controversial triumphs at the Abbey Theatre, which made him both the supreme celebrant and critic of his countrymen: the first-night audience of *The Plough and the Stars* found it a wonderful evocation of Irish character, but it was attacked within the same week and nearly driven from the stage as a betrayal of the martyrs of 1916. O'Connor shows how O'Casey's initial willingness to accept criticism and rejection of his plays and then go on to improve them hardened into a defiant resolution to go his own way after *The Silver Tassie*, his expressionistic and nihilistic condemnation of World War I, was tentatively sent back for revision by Lady Gregory. (The play was first produced in London in 1929.) Thereafter, O'Casey's plays written in England,

written to please himself, were often courageously experimental but seldom achieved the ironic humanity or the implicit self-criticism of his greatest work.

The most absorbing section of O'Connor's book is the final third. Here the author presents O'Casey's exile with a blend of compassion and criticism that resembles the writer's own best qualities. Although O'Casey often seems an almost impossible person in many ways, he was admired by many and loved by those who knew him best. His close friendship with Harold Macmillan, his publisher and later prime minister of England, illustrates the strong loyalties and affection that O'Casey could summon even in those who didn't share his manias and recognized that O'Casey's lifelong eye problems could be extended to his political blindness: "He wasn't much of a thinker," Macmillan noted in characterizing O'Casey's stupid advocacy of Soviet Communism, "he thought everyone ought to be equal out of kindness." The last twenty years are movingly detailed, O'Casey progressively withdrawing from the London literary world into reclusive writing, the O'Caseys living off the royalties from new editions and film adaptations of earlier work and Eileen's acting career, and giving up their own home in London to become tenants in the countryside (a dependent status that satisfied O'Casey's image of himself as a laborer), the aged husband accepting his wife's need to have a sex life outside the marriage yet cherishing her undiminished love for him. O'Casey never got over the death by leukemia of his twenty-one-year-old son Niall just after he had quarreled with his father's justification of the Soviet invasion of Hungary in 1956; he was still mourning him during his eightieth birthday party in outpourings that are reminiscent of his plays at their best—"Niall you went wearing a tiny nosegay of but 21 . . . Oh, God to think of it; I buried a Father when I was a little boy, and a Son when I was an old, old man." The title of O'Connor's epilogue, "Saint or Gunman," exaggerates the extremes of O'Casey's persona, but O'Connor's fine critical biography allows an appreciation of both.

Two 1987 works may be mentioned briefly in introducing significant biographies of American writers published in 1988. Arthur Miller's autobiography *Timebends* (Grove) begins with the infant gazing up through his mother's skirts—and Miller's attraction to the feminine is revealed as the primal energy of his art—but after some initial childhood impressions the author's meditations and brief narratives swing forward and backward through the seven decades of his turbulent and exciting life as one of America's most important moralists of the theater. That time *bends* in such ways is not only a major theme of the book but also another source of his literary creations and a daily experience of the writer throughout his life. Thus, Miller finds himself reviewing his own plays, recovering their sources, revisiting their locations, and only now recognizing their significance, and the narrative as a whole takes the form of re-creating and reimagining a life in all of its contexts; an alternative title might be "Remembrance of Things Past." The blending of past and present, narrative and commentary, and literature and politics, although sometimes confusing, provides a rich personal and social history of the fading American century by one of its most perceptive critical observers and participants. Miller is at his most passionate in defending his plays against their critics and in arguing that the American theater has abandoned significant ideas and social relevance. Miller is best at narrating anecdotes, recording his own direct experiences, and providing character sketches of others (although he treats his marriage to Marilyn Monroe with understandable but disappointing indirectness); he is less successful in making large political and social generalizations and in analyzing his inner life, where he tends to sometimes overwrite.

Long before he became an incarnated Norman Rockwell figure, Carl Sandburg shared some of Miller's socialist passions, but one would scarcely imagine this from North Callahan's account in *Carl Sandburg: His Life and Works* (Penn State University Press). This biography is unique among those I have read in the past two years: it is an old-fashioned panegyric, nominating Sandburg for national laureate. Unfortunately, this book actually performs a disservice to Sandburg's reputation through its simpleminded and superficial eulogizing, which evades every possibility of actually understanding rather than simply praising his life and work. The biographer was a friend of the family and has interviewed Sandburg's relatives, but otherwise his research seems to be minimal, and it ends in 1978. The book is also poorly written and never goes beyond cheery and unexamined clichés in narrating the life or interpreting the works. One example, which follows Sandburg's first meeting with his future wife Paula, will be enough: "How fortunate Carl was in meeting this young woman only the next sixty years could tell. She was to be truly a guiding light, a helpmate, and inspiring companion throughout his illustrious career, choosing voluntarily to stay in the background." The book almost never goes beyond such vacuous description to analyze the life or interpret the works.

Sandburg was an early idol for Langston Hughes, whose life story has now been completed in Arnold Rampersad's *The Life of Langston Hughes. Volume II, 1941-1967: I Dream a World* (Oxford). Like the first volume (reviewed in the 1986 *DLB Yearbook*), this is a minutely detailed, exhaustive, and precise narrative account of Hughes's friends and fellow writers. Here again Rampersad lets Hughes and those who knew him speak for themselves as much as possible, and his comprehensive analysis and evaluation of Hughes's life and work is judicious and careful even as it establishes Hughes's lasting importance. On the whole, however, this is a less interesting story, largely because the writer's life itself was more settled, and much of his most important work was behind him. Instead of the professional and personal traumas of the young, dynamic poet who made himself into a vital new voice for black America, embraced Marxism, and traveled through Africa, Paris, the Soviet Union, and Republican Spain, we discover here a more cautious and increasingly prominent spokesman: first black editor of *Common Ground;* first black writer invited to the Yaddo Writers' Colony; first black American member of P.E.N.; only black writer on the World War II Writers' Board; and so on. During this period Hughes's identity as the leading black writer of the moment yielded variously to Richard Wright, James Baldwin, Ralph Ellison, and LeRoi Jones (Amiri Baraka). Hughes was finally able to buy a house of his own in Harlem, his spiritual resting place, and lived there from 1948 until his death in 1967.

Nonetheless, this volume opens with the writer at the lowest ebb of his life, evicted from his Harlem apartment, recovering from gonorrhea, being attacked savagely by blacks and whites alike as an atheist and Communist for his pro-Soviet poem "Goodbye Christ," and forced to sell his rights in his five books previously published by Knopf in order to raise four hundred dollars. The story told here is the account of a powerful professional and personal recovery, a not always heroic but deeply authentic success story. Hughes found that he had to temper or repudiate his socialist convictions in order to make a living as a writer, and he went so far as to de-

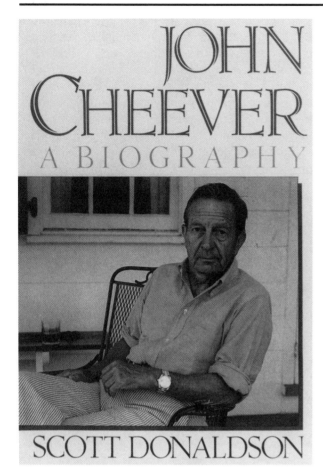

Dust jacket for the first full-length critical biography of the novelist and short-story writer best known for his chronicles of suburbia

nounce them to the HUAC witch-hunters (by contrast, Miller freely admitted his past associations and was convicted though never imprisoned). But his objective was always racial justice whatever the ideological matrix, and if Marxist dogma crippled his ability to further the dreams of blacks, he could happily cast it off. More problematical was the likelihood of making a living as a writer, difficult even for the greatest of white American authors, and doubly hard for a black poet. Rampersad shows how Hughes was forced constantly to churn out anything he could in order to survive—poetry, stories, songs, libretti, newspaper columns, plays, anthologies. He spent months on the road lecturing both to black and white audiences; indeed, he was the first black client of the leading American speakers' bureau. Ralph Ellison and other less prolific, less demotic black writers, later remarked that Hughes had wasted too much of his time on work that was unworthy of him and had therefore never produced the important work that he should have

been doing. Indeed, even much of the poetry cited and analyzed by Rampersad bears the marks of a facility that was only too easy for Hughes to manage but not distinguished enough to be of lasting value. Hughes's feverish attempts to succeed monetarily in the 1940s sometimes seem almost pathetic parodies of the American dream. For example, he kept writing World War II songs, certain that if he could produce the "Over There" of this conflict the royalties would end his money problems; once his gospel musical *Tambourines to Glory* had been successfully produced in 1963, he began turning it into a novel in order to double his profits. Income from lectures, stories, and the Jesse B. Semple columns in the *Chicago Defender*–probably Hughes's most important work in dramatizing and validating the black American perspective–allowed him a bank balance of $1,010.26 in 1944, which Rampersad notes was the most money Hughes had ever possessed in his life after twenty-three years as a successful writer. Only in the mid 1950s, as a result of a post-1941 body of work that is simply staggering in its quantity and variety but uneven in its quality and significance, was he financially comfortable, but the pattern of producing too much too soon continued.

The subtitle of volume 1, *I, Too, Sing America*, implied that Hughes's work provided words for a people that the rest of America had failed to hear; the subtitle of volume 2, with its echoes of the vision of Martin Luther King, Jr., that had been inspired by the work of Hughes himself, reflects the writer's distance from the more radical and separatist black consciousness of the 1960s as well as those whom he felt had lost all dreams of a just America and substituted nihilistic and violent nightmares instead, Wright and Baldwin in particular. Rampersad's treatment of Hughes's relationship to the civil rights movement cautiously reproduces the puzzling ambivalence evident in his attitude, which was indicated by alternating activism and withdrawal from commitments. Such behavior may reflect the desire of a now-prominent national figure to enjoy the rewards of his years of exhausting activity, the relative conservatism that had begun with the turn away from socialism, uncertainty, old age, or other possibilities, but it is one of the many secrets of this fascinating public figure who kept his private self elusive. Rampersad discusses Hughes's suspected homosexuality at length and comes to no certain conclusion, just as, in volume 1, the source of his gonorrhea remained a mystery. Although the external detail of this biography is presented with extraordinary clarity and comprehensiveness, I never felt that I knew Hughes very intimately–but it may be that no one ever has, neither his closest friends nor his biographer. Perhaps we will have to wait for a revelation that transcends what even good life writing is capable of: at his wonderfully offbeat jazz and blues funeral, orchestrated by Hughes before his death, the last number played was Duke Ellington's "Do Nothing Till You Hear From Me."

While Miller was willing to risk jail while exercising his first amendment rights during the McCarthyite hysteria and Hughes censured himself, Lillian Hellman both preempted the HUAC questioners with a fuzzy letter neither denying nor admitting her earlier membership in the Communist party *and* pleaded the fifth amendment. This is just one of many charges brought against her by former friends and acquaintances and the biographer Carl Rollyson in *Lillian Hellman: Her Legend and Her Legacy* (St. Martin's Press). Although the title suggests that this life is a tribute to her enduring significance, it would be more accurate to define this book as a brief against Lillian Hellman. Rollyson's preface, "A Legend in Her Own Time," establishes the three principal charges against his subject: her aggressive self-aggrandizement and intolerance of others not fully supportive of her own viewpoints; her untruthfulness about herself, most evident in the self-embroidery of the later autobiographies, especially *Scoundrel Time* (1976), her narrative of the HUAC years; and her irresponsible and disingenuous political viewpoint, which included a deplorable infatuation with communism. These three complementary attributes are combined in the most famous single line of her self-created legend, part of her 1952 statement to the HUAC chairman: "I cannot and will not cut my conscience to fit this year's fashions." But Rollyson's own epigraph for her life, taken from *The Little Foxes* (1939), is less exalted and more genuine: "God helps those who invent what they need." Indeed, the biography is organized to characterize her life as a performance: a useful, detailed "cast of characters" (important friends and enemies, the witnesses interviewed by Rollyson) is followed by a narrative of thirty chapters, each headed by the successive themes, works, and settings of her life history, from Alabama to Hollywood, New York, Spain, Moscow, Long Island, and places in between. The narratives themselves, in Rollyson's words, "reflect the melodramatic rhythm of her

existence as she plays, by turns, the villain and the heroine." The book reproduces or paraphrases at length the testimony concerning Hellman of both friends and enemies. Ostensibly fair-minded and factual, frequently attesting to her extraordinary impact on everyone who met her, these revelations tend to expose rather than honor Hellman. And Rollyson's always interesting and often penetrating analyses of her character are almost invariably critical, as in his description of her 1980 lawsuit against Mary McCarthy: "Hellman, herself a caustic critic of others, was blatantly trying to intimidate those who would exercise the same privilege. Never was it clearer that she had put herself in another category altogether–freedom of speech for everyone, except those who had attacked Lillian Hellman." In his introductory chapter, Rollyson even cites gratuitously two unnamed enemies who hated her ("She was a *viper*") and expressly declined to be interviewed for the book.

Rollyson is the most detached and harshly judgmental of this year's biographers, but although his attitude toward Hellman as a person is unsympathetic, his thorough treatment of her works reclaims a significant literary reputation for her after the attacks of the 1980s on both her person and her writings. She is "America's finest radical playwright" as well as its most unsentimental, and Rollyson provides excellent analyses and evaluations of all the works, including detailed treatment of Hellman's sources, her revisions, the initial productions and reviews of them, as well as later scholarly criticism. He shows how painstaking a writer she was, researching the social and historical context of all her plays (spending a month traveling in Ohio to capture the atmosphere of small-town life for *Days to Come*, 1936, and compiling a hundred-thousand-word background notebook for *Watch on the Rhine*, 1941), and carefully revising her work until it was ready for production (she wrote eight full versions of *The Little Foxes*). Rollyson notes how carefully she revised stage directions, structure, and speeches in the *Collected Plays* of 1972. He also takes movie scripts more seriously than she claimed to, and his fine criticism of the films demonstrates how effectively Hellman not only adapted *The Children's Hour* (1934), *The Little Foxes* (1939), and *Watch on the Rhine* but actually improved her own work. Besides giving attention to the Hollywood work, he reevaluates the adaptations, another important subgenre of Hellman's career, arguing that *The Lark* (1956) is not only one of her best works but curiously autobiographical, and here as in his criticism of all the plays Rollyson reveals Hellman's displacement of her own life in the works.

Despite its bias against Hellman herself, this is a comprehensive and valuable life of the writer. Although Hellman's will made her editor William Abrahams her "one and only authorized biographer" and restricted the collection of her papers at Texas to his exclusive use, Rollyson has been a formidable researcher. He has not only interviewed about eighty of Hellman's intimate acquaintances and incorporated their judgments extensively into his narrative but has also investigated and incorporated important unpublished sources, including the papers of her former husband Arthur Krober, the forthcoming book on her affair with the American foreign service officer John Melby, and even notes taken during her college lectures. He shows that Hellman was hardworking but frequently both dictatorial and incompetent as a director, unable to regard actors as more than lowly mouthpieces for her scripts; no less hardworking and dictatorial as a teacher, she was eminently pragmatic and dedicated, and her students found her inspiring. The biography provides new and authoritative accounts of her numerous love affairs, her relationship with Dashiell Hammett–the most important man in her life–and the figure of Julia, Hellman's heroic Nazi-fighting friend, who was probably an invention of the writer's own imagination.

Rollyson's study largely reflects the portrait of Hellman's self-contradictions presented in William Wright's earlier biography (1986), though it covers the works more fully. Similarly, Scott Donaldson's *John Cheever: A Biography* (Random House) presents little about Cheever's darker side–problems with alcohol, depression, his marriage and his sexuality–that was not already revealed in Susan Cheever's 1984 memoir of her father, but it provides a close analysis of the works. Unlike Rollyson, Donaldson is a sympathetic biographer and attempts to understand Cheever from the writer's own point of view. Donaldson edited last year's Conversations with Writers volume on Cheever, and this biography has been long awaited. He has outdone even Rollyson in obtaining interviews (170 altogether) and integrating them into his account, and he has also had the complete cooperation of the author's literary executor, his widow Mary, as well as free access to private papers and letters, resources not fully available to Hellman's biographer. This is the

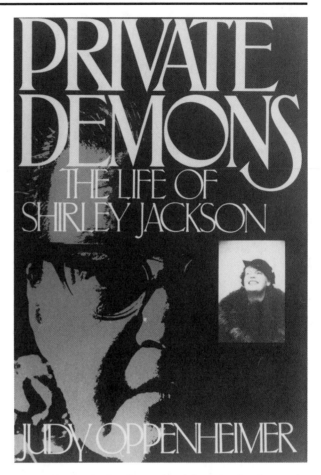

Dust jacket for the first biography of the writer best known for her short story "The Lottery"

first full-length critical biography of Cheever, a detailed, meticulous, and objective survey of the life, works, and circumstances.

The eleven-year-old boy who announced to his parents that he wanted to be a writer spent the rest of his life fulfilling his early ambition and raising a successful middle-class family, realizing his own belief that "genius did not need to be rootless, disenfranchised, or alienated.... A writer could have a family, a job, and even live in a suburb." His need to provide material security for his growing family without abandoning his integrity as a serious writer partly accounts for Cheever's need to produce short stories in the first two decades of his career and then, having established his reputation, to turn to the greater profits of novel writing in the late 1950s and thereafter. Despite his outward professional and personal success, however, Cheever's life and art reflect the influences of his father's failure in business and his mother's role as the family's chief provider; his feeling of disappointing the former and being neglected by the latter; and his quasi-incestuous love for his older brother Frederick, Jr., the father's favorite. Donaldson notes that all three are reimagined in the various dissatisfied husbands, domineering and unloving women, and "dark brother" figures that populate Cheever's fictional worlds, which, like his own marriage and family, both transcended and recapitulated the primal relationships of his childhood. Cheever remained something of an insecure child throughout his life, which helps account for the fundamental gentleness of his character and fiction as well as his search for love, female and male, outside the marriage. Love is the great theme of all his work, Donaldson points out.

Cheever and his brother also inherited their father's alcoholism, and it nearly destroyed the writer's life and work in the late 1960s and early 1970s *after* the golden era of 1957-1964, when he seemed to achieve all his professional and personal goals. Encouraged and fertilized by his summers at the Yaddo Writers' Workshop, the young Cheever diligently perfected the art of the short story as the consummate *New Yorker* author (he published eleven stories in the magazine in one year, 1940), gained membership in the National Institute of Arts and Letters for his short fiction, won national awards for the *Wapshot* novels, and settled into a comfortable suburban home in Ossining, New York, that personally validated his public recognition as America's great chronicler of suburbia. The years of depression and constant drinking that followed were accompanied by reduced productivity as a writer, resentment of his wife's career as well as emotional and sexual estrangement from her, and a nearly fatal personal collapse that culminated in Cheever's year at Boston University in 1974-1975, when he was both a college professor and a drunken street bum.

Up to 1975 Cheever's life follows a pattern of success followed by disintegration all too familiar in American letters, but he gave up alcohol and broke that cycle thereafter, and his "rebirth" produces Donaldson's best writing, including an interesting comparison with F. Scott Fitzgerald, the only writer Cheever ever wrote criticism about. Donaldson notes that *Falconer* (1977), Cheever's darkest yet most affirmative novel, is also the best, and that the *Collected Stories* of 1978 won a Pulitzer Prize and reclaimed Cheever's preeminence in short fiction. Despite the cancer that blighted his last two years, Cheever came to accept unapologetically and acknowledge publicly the troublesome sides of his own identity, including his bisexuality, though he remained lonely to the end.

Although Donaldson seems fairer to his subject than Rollyson, this is a less interesting biography. The narrative is comprehensive but spare, with details sometimes linked only by chronological sequence. Much new information is revealed about Cheever (such as his affair with Hope Lange), but Donaldson provides less reflection or analysis than he might; and though he admires Cheever, he doesn't capture his personality very vividly. Clearly but colorlessly written, the book tends to employ clichés when it extends its scope beyond Cheever's life, and too many generalizations about the writer are left unexplained or undeveloped: Cheever's inveterate, almost automatic tendency to tell stories, asserted but scarcely exemplified; his awe of E. E. Cummings and close friendship with Ralph Ellison and other writers; the unmistakable (but unexplained) difference between Cheever's style and John Updike's. Donaldson's commentary on the works is generally good, though he fails to identify some of the later works being alluded to in chapter 1 that reflect Cheever's view of his parents. The index is quirky and inadequate, covering all biographical and title references but nothing else, and the endnotes are vaguely organized, lack page numbers to Donaldson's text, and are virtually impossible to collate with it.

The looseness of Donaldson's narrative may derive from his overreliance on the testimony of interviews, which tends to encourage organization by anecdote. On the other hand, Donaldson's bland paraphrases of such anecdotes provide the most lively glimpses of the writer's character in the biography: Cheever in a business suit entering the elevator of his New York apartment every morning in the 1940s and riding down with all the similarly dressed male residents, but then descending into the basement, where he would strip down to his shorts and spend the working day in an overheated, unused storeroom composing his fiction on a typewriter; Scarborough's most famous writer being arrested for vagrancy one day in the 1950s as he walked about town in his worn-out writing clothes, the only male resident who stayed home to work in a community of Manhattan-bound commuters; Cheever, recognized in a McDonald's restaurant in Chicago, graciously signing his name on his admirers' napkins. Perhaps most striking of all was the tribute paid him by his fellow residents of suburbia after the writer's death in 1982 and his burial in his native Massachusetts: "Back in Ossining, Cheever's adopted hometown mourned his passing. By administrative fiat, flags flew at half-mast for ten days. (Ben and Janet Cheever lowered the flag at the Highland Diner themselves.) It was 'as if the heart of Ossining were gone. . . . Cheever was as closely associated with Ossining as Emerson with Concord or Tolstoy with Yasnaya Polyana,' the local newspaper proudly pointed out."

Like Cheever, Shirley Jackson was an important (though less frequent) contributor to the *New Yorker* in the 1940s and thereafter and a long-time resident of a small town (although hers, North Bennington, Vermont, was an appendage of Bennington College, not Manhattan). In *Private Demons: The Life of Shirley Jackson* (Putnam), Judy Oppenheimer has written the first biography of this gifted fabulist, whose works include one of the best American Gothic novels (*The Haunting of Hill House*, 1959), a masterpiece of claustrophobia and psychic entombment (*We Have Always Lived in the Castle*, 1962), and a pathbreaking fictional study of multiple personality (*The Bird's Nest*, 1954), as well as two collections of autobiographical vignettes about raising children (*Life Among the Savages*, 1953, and *Raising Demons*, 1957). But above all, she is known as the author of "The Lottery," detailing a small New England village's annual stoning of one of its inhabitants, which achieved an unparalleled notoriety when it appeared in the *New Yorker* in 1948. The nearly hysterical outrage of many readers of "The Lottery" demonstrated that she had hit her target, the darker and murderous impulses that coexist within conventional small-town mores and enforce conformity—forces which Jackson and her husband, the noted scholar-critic Stanley Edgar Hyman, sometimes found directed against them and the other outsiders associated with the experimental college on the hill that overlooked North Bennington, which included Howard Nemerov, Ralph Ellison, Bernard Malamud, and Hyman among its faculty.

Judy Oppenheimer's title suggests that the writer's real enemies were internal, however, and her biography uncovers them and shows how they also penetrated the works themselves. In the event, perhaps, she makes a bit too much of Jackson's eccentricities. Jackson was a fundamentally private writer, drawing her stories from her direct experience, who claimed to have parapsychological powers and good-naturedly advertised herself as America's only witch who was also

a practicing writer. But she was also very successful throughout her career and managed to raise four children without much help from her husband. Stanley was constitutionally unfaithful, and his wife grew resentful of the Bennington coeds in his classes, but they were deeply devoted to each other and enjoyed entertaining literati from the college and New York at frequent parties in their huge North Bennington residences. The increasing agoraphobia that overtook Jackson in the late 1950s and early 1960s had many sources: her heavy drinking and use of amphetamines and barbiturates to get her through her overloaded personal and professional responsibilities; overeating, which swelled her grotesquely to well over two hundred pounds and probably was both cause and effect of Stanley's philandering; and her alienation from the town itself, which they both brought upon themselves not only by living within it (unlike most Bennington faculty) but also by flaunting their unconventionality and intellectual and social superiority to its inhabitants. Between 1962 and 1964 Jackson found it nearly impossible to leave her bedroom, a condition chillingly forecast and effected by the writing of *We Have Always Lived in the Castle*, but psychotherapy and the support of her family seem to have led to a recovery by 1965, when the forty-eight-year-old author died of a cardiac arrest, probably a result of the many years of physical indulgence.

Numerous contradictions and anomalies abounded in Jackson's life, as Oppenheimer shows throughout, and most were not simply painful or frustrating but also energizing both personally and professionally, like the curious relationship with the local community. The marriage itself productively linked an archetypal New York Jewish intellectual and a well-off WASP princess, both relatively ugly and egocentric. Both witch and housewife, Shirley Jackson wrote fiction that satisfied both impulses. A more troubling and destructive contradiction was her relationship with her mother, a conventionally mindless social climber. Her daughter seemed to reject the mother's life and its values, yet she wrote lengthy letters extolling her own success as a writer, mother, and wife in order to gain an approval that her mother never allowed her. Geraldine Jackson's reaction to a very flattering review of *We Have Always Lived in the Castle* was typical: she couldn't tell whether the review was good or not, she claimed, but she complained about the accompanying photo and blamed her daughter for allowing herself to become so bad looking. Shirley Jackson composed a bitter reply but thought better of it, substituting an airy, unconcerned response, thus outwardly ignoring her mother's continuing disapproval, but it was one of the factors that led to her subsequent breakdown.

Judy Oppenheimer has interviewed all four of Jackson's children, and their testimony, reproduced verbatim, takes up much of the narrative. The accounts of Jackson's high-school and college classmates as well as close personal and professional friends like Ralph Ellison and Roger Straus have also been used to produce a biography that is often mundane in its details but authentically revealing. Like Rollyson and Donaldson, however, Oppenheimer overuses direct testimony, and she provides less analysis or interpretation than either. The idea that Jackson could see hidden "evil" everywhere and revealed it in her works needs more explanation than it receives, for example. The author's generalizations and interpretations are rather vague where they do occur, and they are sometimes weakened by her writing, which is often mawkish in tone and awkward in expression, filled with clichés and unsettling metaphors: for example, "Her eyes [Jackson's] unerringly picked up the dark edges lurking behind the suburban gauze . . . right into the nutty core of reality itself." The works are well described, but evaluated or analyzed only cursorily.

A more successful study, indeed the most absorbing narrative of an American writer this year, is David Roberts's *Jean Stafford: A Biography* (Little, Brown). While Shirley Jackson's life was grotesque in many ways, Stafford's seems a catastrophe, and Roberts skillfully and movingly details the painfully slow disintegration of health, character, and art that characterized it. A notable *New Yorker* contributor like Cheever and Jackson, Stafford achieved phenomenal overnight fame and financial success with her first published novel, *Boston Adventure* (1944), which was the third highest-selling book published in America that year. With the small fortune earned from the novel, she was able to buy a house of her own in Damariscotta Mills, Maine, and she and her soon-to-be-famous husband Robert Lowell moved there in 1945. A second and better novel, *The Mountain Lion*, a reminiscence of her childhood days in Colorado, like several of her best short stories, followed in 1946 to glowing critical reviews though much lower sales, and in the summer of that year the Lowells were hosts at their home in Maine to a galaxy of literary stars that in-

cluded Peter Taylor, Delmore Schwartz, R. P. Blackmur, John Berryman, Eileen Simpson, Richard Eberhart, Philip Rahv, and the editor Robert Giroux. At the age of thirty Stafford seemed to be at the center of postwar American literature with infinite possibilities ahead of her.

In fact, however, the summer of 1946 marked the beginning of an initially slow and later precipitous personal and professional decline. The six-year-old marriage was already troubled and apparently sexless, and Lowell had an affair that summer with one of the last houseguests, Gertrude Buckman, who briefly became the second Mrs. Lowell in 1948. Stafford suffered a complete breakdown and was hospitalized during much of 1946-1947. A novel dealing with her childhood and youth, "In the Snowfall," was begun in 1947 but abandoned in 1950, and her third and last published novel, *The Catherine Wheel,* was published in 1952. Stafford had written all or parts of *four* other novels even before *Boston Adventure,* but her final novel under contract, ultimately entitled "The Parliament of Women," was transferred from Random House to Farrar, Straus & Giroux. Twenty-two years after she had committed herself legally to writing it, Stafford told a friend in 1975 that its completion was "miles and miles in the future," and at her death it was a pastiche of passages, scenes, and outlines that seem to combine an extension of *Boston Adventure* with an incoherent collection of autobiographical fragments covering stages of her own life and her father's. Giroux assembled the portions dealing with the fateful summer in Maine and published them whole in the *New Yorker* in 1978 as "An Influx of Poets," one of Stafford's best short stories.

Unable or unwilling to continue as a novelist, Stafford became a master of shorter fiction in the 1940s and 1950s, but her icily polished and ironic realism seemed slightly outdated in the 1960s and 1970s, and she turned increasingly to reviews, journalism, and puff pieces for high bourgeois magazines to make a living. Though her *Collected Stories* won a Pulitzer Prize in 1970, they seemed testaments to an earlier career, and among the most powerful and integral writing of her final decade were her artfully caustic and cynical letters. By the end of her life she had virtually been forgotten.

David Roberts pays tribute to Stafford's artistry with straightforward descriptions and evaluations of the major works, but he also shows where and how she increasingly fell short of herself. As Roberts shows, however, the narrowing and eventual decline of her writing was largely influenced by the misery of her personal life. The two final uncompleted novels deal with a life that had probably become too chaotic and deplorably painful to re-create even in fiction. Stafford was probably truly content only as a young child in California before her father's bankruptcy made him move the family to Colorado, the beginning of their slide into poverty and vagabondage, and later during her short marriage to the *New Yorker* writer A. J. Liebling in 1959-1963. Her first date with Lowell in 1938 ended when her demon lover managed to crash his car into a wall, smashing her nose and cheekbone and permanently disfiguring her. This should have been a portent of his later more deliberate brutalities, and she married with enormous misgivings, virtually begging a kinder, gentler, but less dominating beau named Robert Hightower to form a menáge à trois with them. The experience of surgery after the accident produced her excruciating short-story masterpiece "The Interior Castle," but she had already suffered gonorrhea and possibly syphilis during her year in Germany and would be plagued with chronic emphysema, a heart attack, strokes, and assorted other ailments that led to over thirty major hospitalizations during her life. She was responsible for much of her misery, of course. She divorced her second husband, a magazine editor who truly loved her, partly because she was still in love with Lowell. She alienated family members, friends, and professional associates with acerbic criticism and cruelty and then suffered from loneliness. Her health problems were exacerbated by her manic smoking, and all the conditions of her unhappiness were both cause and effect of her frightful drinking. She was already an incipient alcoholic in the last years with Lowell; she was embarrassingly drunk at her induction into the National Institute of Arts and Letters in 1970, and even after a stroke in 1976 rendered her speechless for the last three years of her life, she continued to drink herself into unconsciousness. From 1964 onward Stafford lived in the Long Island home left to her by Liebling and became a local eccentric, but not a very pleasant one. Virtually friendless and alone at the end, she gave the world her last *figo* by leaving virtually all her property to her cleaning lady and making her the literary executor as well.

David Roberts began his research in 1983, infatuated with Jean Stafford, whom he had never met and first read in 1975. His account draws heavily on important witnesses, including Stafford's early beau Robert Hightower, her second husband, Oliver Jensen, and the writer Peter Taylor, all of whose loyal admiration of her validates her biographer's. Roberts's hypotheses about her childhood experiences, a tragic ménage à trois that she probably participated in at the University of Colorado, and the likelihood of her having contracted syphilis in Germany and its chilling effect on her sex life are first-rate detective work, well-argued and documented, that suggestively illuminate some of the darkness that lies at the heart of her works and life. His examination of the earlier unpublished novels and especially the autobiographical details of "In the Snowfall" are particularly revelatory. Ultimately, the most important dark figure in Stafford's troubled life may have been her father. She fled from his failure into literature; yet the last novel that she could not complete was supposed to be about John Stafford. Her father spent the last forty years of his life working absurdly and fruitlessly on a vast treatise that he was sure would restore his fortunes and reform the American economy, and Roberts notes the uncanny parallel with his daughter's unfinished work, a futile twenty-five-year project. Just before his death at the age of ninety-two, Jean Stafford wrote of him to her sister, "That so preposterous a life should be so endlessly prolonged is an unfathomable mystery." Ironically, the same could be said of Stafford's final few years, spent in a bitter alcoholic haze, speechless, her wonderful mind crippled by aphasia. The father's life may have been farce, but his daughter's was certainly a tragedy, and David Roberts has been faithful to Jean Stafford by revealing it with such clarity and understanding.

While Stafford's self-destruction played itself out privately in the suburbs of Long Island, Gerald Clarke in *Capote: A Life* (Simon and Schuster) relates a more public professional and personal suicide in excruciating detail, skewering not only the Tiny Terror of New York gossip but Capote's rich and famous targets as well. Norman Mailer declared Capote the most perfect stylist of America in 1958, and he gained genuine popular acclaim from both coasts through Nebraska with his self-described nonfiction novel *In Cold Blood* in 1966. Increasingly thereafter, however, he gave up writing for being written and talked about and for television talk-show appearances, and his abandonment by the celebrities that he had titillated and enraged with character assassinations and revelations accelerated the alcoholism that he inherited from his mother and the drug addiction that he chose for himself. He died wasted, friendless, and alone, in 1984.

In *Literary Outlaw: The Life and Times of William S. Burroughs* (Henry Holt), Ted Morgan, no less exhaustive than Clarke, takes us on a tour of hell as he chronicles the career of the most literally destructive of the Beat generation idols. Burroughs has gone through bouts of depression, homosexual promiscuity, ingestion of every drug that was available, his accidental murder of his common-law wife–the central event of his subsequent literary career–and partial responsibility for the death of his alcoholic son through his parental neglect. The book is based on one hundred hours of interviews of the subject that called forth his photographic and phonographic memory, and the result is a nonjudgmental, linear narrative that simply reproduces the facts without analysis.

The Beats fled from the alleged horrors of modern American bourgeoisiedom, and so did William Everson, who entered a Dominican monastery in 1951, became Brother Antoninus, and has written some of the best American religious poetry of the past three decades. Like Morgan's biography, Lee Bartlett's *William Everson: The Life of Brother Antoninus* (New Directions) is based on extensive interviews with the poet and his wife, and although Burroughs and Everson seem to be members of different species and to have lived on separate planets, Everson's life is just as unusual. Raised as a Christian Scientist, a conscientious objector whose wife deserted him during World War II, probably the only janitor to have received a Guggenheim fellowship to write poetry, a master printer who founded the Lime Kiln Press at UC Santa Cruz and produced books that have won national awards for artistry and beauty, Everson startled the California literary world by entering a religious order and startled the Catholic church by pulling off his robes after a public poetry reading eighteen years later in 1969, where he announced his need to leave the monastery as well as his imminent marriage to a woman thirty-five years younger than himself. Happily married to Susan Rickson Everson for twenty years, Everson has composed a diminishing body of poetry that makes the profane sacred. Afflicted with Parkinson's disease since 1977, his reading of his poetry was a highlight of the 1986 MLA Convention in Chicago. Lee Bartlett's short biography presents his life in close detail and with implicit admiration.

Kathryn W. Crabbe's *Evelyn Waugh* (Continuum) is the latest in the fine series from Frederick Ungar, Literature and Life: British Writers, which now numbers well over twenty-five titles from Shakespeare to Tom Stoppard. A chronology and twenty-page biography are followed by chapters on all the novels and a final epilogue on Waugh's style in his writings and life. This 170-plus-page volume glances at the other nonfictional work and provides a handy guide to the major fiction, but of course a complete life of Waugh awaits the completion of Martin Stannard's two-volume biography (volume 1 was reviewed in the 1987 *DLB Yearbook*). We should also note revisions of two classic biographies in the Lives and Letters series that have been brought out recently by the Hogarth Press. Norman and Jean MacKenzie's superb 1973 biography *The Life of H. G. Wells: The Time Traveller* has been updated with the most recent revelations about Wells's love affairs and an epilogue on his relationships with Rebecca and Anthony West, Moura Budberg, and Odette Keun. And Anthony Powell's fascinating story of the first important English biographer, *John Aubrey and his Friends*, revised in 1963, has been republished in paperback.

Finally, three superb collections of letters appeared in 1988. In *What years I have spent!*, the third volume of the *Letters of Mary Wollstonecroft Shelley* (Johns Hopkins University Press), Betty T. Bennett completes her edition, providing the letters written by this great Romantic survivor between July 1840 and November 1850. Separate appendices include letters written by others in response to the writer's death and texts of all the letters discovered since 1980, when volume 1 was published. *The Letters of Jack London* (Stanford University Press) have been compiled by Earle Labor, Robert C. Leitz, and I. Milo Shepard in a three-volume edition that provides over fifteen hundred of the more than four thousand surviving letters written by London between 1896 and his death in 1916. A more selective edition is *The Letters of Edith Wharton* (Scribners), edited by R. W. B. and Nancy Lewis, which includes four hundred of the most characteristic and biographically important letters of this prolific and eloquent correspondent.

Eugene O'Neill's Letters: A Review

John Henry Raleigh
University of California, Berkeley

This year marked the centenary of the birth of Eugene O'Neill, the only American dramatist to be awarded the Nobel Prize in Literature as well as four Pulitzer prizes. Because of O'Neill's importance, not only to American drama but to world literature, the event was commemorated with seminars, revivals of his plays, and readings by well-known actors and actresses. Several scholarly publications devoted to O'Neill's life and work also appeared during the year, most notably The Selected Letters of Eugene O'Neill *(Yale University Press), edited by Travis Bogard and Jackson R. Bryer.*

The Selected Letters of Eugene O'Neill contains 560 items out of some 3,000 extant O'Neill letters, some of which are telegrams and other brief messages that are held in great part by the Beinecke Library at Yale. The editors have done an excellent job with annotations that are as brief as possible but clear and with informative introductions for each of the eight sections into which O'Neill's life is divided, from "Beginnings, 1901-1916" to "Ending, 1945-1952." The editors have made several types of silent connections, sacrificing "absolute editorial and bibliographical purity . . . for readability in numerous instances."

For anyone interested in O'Neill the published letters have two centers of gravity: the life of the man and the ideas, opinions, theories, and practices of the playwright. In the autobiographical realm no great surprises or revelations are displayed. In large part, as the editors say: "The great majority of the letters reflect the daily concerns of an ordinary human being talking to the inhabitants of his personal world." Furthermore, in the two biographies that already exist, Arthur and Barbara Gelb's (1962) and Louis Sheaffer's (1968, 1973), we already have detailed scrutinies of every aspect of O'Neill's life, and in both biographies there are quotations of important parts of some of the letters, now published for the first time, that the biographers had examined in manuscript. Nevertheless, there is now available the full text of important letters, and the letters in toto constitute an abbreviated outline of O'Neill's life in his own hand.

Dust jacket for the edition of O'Neill's correspondence selected from more than three thousand surviving letters

I have said that there are no major revelations about O'Neill's life, but there are qualifications about key persons and events in that life. For instance, the man who was to write *Long Day's Journey Into Night* (1956) wrote in 1909 from Honduras a long letter to his father and mother which closed as follows: "Cannot tell how I miss you both. I never realized how much home and Father & Mother meant until I got so far away from them. Lots of love to you both. Your loving son Eugene." On the other hand, whenever in his later life he spent some time with a happy or contented or noncontentious family, he invariably remarked on how wonderful it was. Of the Rippin family in New London, with whom he stayed in 1913, he said in a letter to a Rippin daughter in 1919: "Your family gave me the most real touch of a home life I had up till then–quite a happy, new experience for an actor's son. I've never forgotten to be grateful to all of you for it–above all to your mother." These same sentiments are repeated in letters to the Sheridans, of New London, the Quinns, friends of Agnes Boulton O'Neill, and the Comminses, Saxe Commins being his future editor. It was such feelings as these, plus remembrances of other happy families in the New London days, that finally led to *Ah, Wilderness!* (1933).

The letters show O'Neill in a variety of moods, from somber to ecstatic. There are quite a few love letters, principally to Beatrice Ashe, Agnes Boulton O'Neill, and Carlotta Monterey O'Neill (those to Maibelle Scott did not survive, unfortunately). O'Neill's love letters are often filled with a hyperbole that suggests, to me anyway, a straining for effect rather than a genuine sincerity (this, of course, might only consist of living up to the conventions of what a love letter should be in the times at which he wrote). This suspicion of mine is enhanced by the fact that in 1927, having begun his romance with Carlotta but still married to Agnes, he was assuring *both* of them how much he loved *each* of them. Thus, "Own, own wife: God how I miss you!" but also, and using a favorite nickname for Carlotta, "Dearest Shadow Eyes (which cannot go out!): God, how I long for you! There is little else to write you, Heart's Desire!" As in so many of his dramas, the exclamation point (!) was supposed to indicate emotional intensity.

The single most powerful and somber letter in the whole collection is the one he wrote to Agnes on 29 July 1920 from the hospital where his father lay slowly dying, much too slowly, in excruciating pain from cancer of the intestines. The stench of human corruption pervaded the room as the seventy-six-year-old man, thin and shrunken, no longer articulate, tortured with pain, mumbled for God to take him and release him, while his wife and son looked on:

he seems to me a *good* man–in the best sense of the word–and about the only one I have ever known.

Then why should he suffer so–when murderers are granted the blessing of electric chairs?

O'Neill's own last years were somber enough as well, as the Gelbs and Sheaffer have abundantly documented. His own ill health appears to have been virtually lifelong; at least from the 1920s on there are constant complaints of bouts of illnesses of various kinds, often, as might be expected, of a respiratory nature. By the Tao House days the illnesses multiplied, as the Parkinson's, or whatever it was, steadily worsened, as did his health generally, to which can be added Carlotta's considerable list of illnesses. As his body fell apart, so did his patriarchal relations. The letters to his three children, Eugene, Jr., Shane, and Oona, are all in their earlier years kind and "fatherly": encouragement, advice, money. While it is true that his relations with Eugene, Jr. remained pleasant enough up to the latter's unfortunate end as a suicide, the letters to Shane and Oona undergo a devolution: Shane's fecklessness and inability to settle on any occupation increasingly exasperated his father; while Oona's emergence as a minor New York celebrity, chosen by the Stork Club as debutante of the year, infuriated him (his fuse for his only daughter was extremely short). Before she met and married Charles Chaplin, O'Neill had written her off because she had gone to Hollywood. To his lawyer Harry Weinberger, who handled the alimony and child support he gave to Agnes, he wrote: "If ever you see the lady [Oona], make this clear–and strong. If Hollywood is in, then I'm out–*forever*!" By the same token his hatred of Agnes deepens and deepens, as, short of ready money in the 1930s and 1940s, he has to keep paying her; more important, he blamed her, both genetically and environmentally, for what he regarded as the wayward fates of Oona and Shane. Thus to Weinberger on 27 February 1929: "The whole point is that Shane is a Boulton and just naturally dumb and shiftless, like all the rest of them, where education and books are concerned. . . . I am through–until such time as he proves himself not to be a parasitic slob of a Boulton. . . . All best, Harry. Enclosed the dole to the inveterate trollop." His own last years were as terrible as any he inflicted on his tragic dramatic characters: "fastened to a dying animal," increasingly cut off from old friends, and totally dependent on his love-hate relationship with Carlotta. From 1949 on the written communications keep dwindling both in number and in size. Epistolarily speaking, it all ends not with a bang but with a whimper, usually a declaration of his love for Carlotta, sometimes estranged from him.

But they always made up; in fact, Carlotta was the only genuinely stable thing in his life.

As a playwright, O'Neill had many revealing things to say about his craft. One of the most interesting was said early on, on 14 February 1915 in a letter to Beatrice Ashe from Harvard, where O'Neill was taking George Pierce Baker's famous course in play writing. Although O'Neill is here talking of letter writing, the distinction that he makes between effortless and effortful modes of writing will hold for his whole career as a dramatist. "I didn't 'compose' that letter either. It just trailed from the end of my pen, in one of those moments so satisfying to a writer when his feelings and thoughts come out of his brain all properly attired in words, not naked as is their usual wont. And what a task it is to fit words on to a naked, and beautiful idea! There are times when one cannot find a dress of words becoming to the thought. No matter what one picks out, it looks dowdy." Many years later, in 1945, in answering the letter of an aspiring playwright, he clarified his own methods, and speed or slowness of composition, into four types or classes. First, there were the ones that just "happened," *Desire Under the Elms* (1924) and *Ah, Wilderness!* He had had no previous thoughts or notes about them: "I simply awakened with those plays in mind." And they were both written rather rapidly. Second, there were what he called the "easy" plays, built up from a previously conceived but brief idea and written with great rapidity. His examples were *The Emperor Jones* (1920) and *The Hairy Ape* (1922), each of which was written, according to O'Neill's memory, in about ten days. Third, there were the plays that finally developed out of a short note, among the many that he kept in his notebook, for ideas for plays. Two such notes, no more than a line, germinated both *All God's Chillun Got Wings* (1924) and *The Great God Brown* (1926). Since many of his notes never did grow into plays, O'Neill speculated that his unconscious had selected and developed these two works. Fourth, and the case with most of his plays—he gives *Strange Interlude* (1928) and *Mourning Becomes Electra* (1931) as his examples of this type—there is a slow germination period and extensive preparations: one note becomes many notes; then a detailed scenario; then a first draft of the play; then a second draft; and then the final cutting. Furthermore, although he does not say this in the letters, the play was further reduced for production on the stage. Elsewhere, in the letters, he

says that the published version of any of his plays is superior to the shortened text for the stage.

I should not wish to elaborate a full-scale theory about O'Neill's plays based on his own statements about composition in 1915 and 1945. But surely, it is irresistible not to say that celerity and ease of composition (*Ah, Wilderness!, Desire Under the Elms, The Hairy Ape, The Emperor Jones*) make plays that have both a coherence and spontaneity that are lacking in the more laboriously constructed ones, such as *Strange Interlude* and *Mourning Becomes Electra*—"No matter what one picks out, it looks dowdy"—all this added to the fact that *Desire Under the Elms, The Emperor Jones*, and *The Hairy Ape* have distinctively stylized, unrealistic dialogue, while *Strange Interlude* and *Mourning Becomes Electra* attempt normative, middle-class American speech. Yet O'Neill felt too that the use of dialect, at which he was rather skillful, was an evasion. This dilemma he put in a letter to Joseph Wood Krutch in 1929: "Oh for a language to write drama in! For a speech that is dramatic and isn't just conversation! I'm so strait-jacketed by writing in terms of talk. I'm so fed up with the dodge-question of dialect! But where to find that language!" At the same time, any such theorizing as the above is compromised in some part by his last two crowning accomplishments, *The Iceman Cometh* (1946) and *Long Day's Journey Into Night*, although at first glance they seem to embody once more the dilemma between ease and effort posed in 1915. *The Iceman Cometh* just flowed out spontaneously and was composed rapidly, while *Long Day's Journey Into Night* was slow and laborious in composition. Yet in each case the play was undeniably a great one, as O'Neill himself always insisted. He was often throughout his career saying that his current play, sometimes a very bad one, was a great one, but at the end of his career he was indubitably right. And, as for dialect, *The Iceman Cometh* is in great part a dialect play, and even, in a small way, *Long Day's Journey Into Night* is a dialect play also, what with the faint brogue of James Tyrone and the Broadway lingo of Jamie. And, of course, *Hughie* (1958) is a consummate dialect play, a masterly evocation of the argot of a small-time New York gambler in the 1920s. Most of his best plays, whether easily or laboriously composed, benefit from the use of racial, cultural, or social dialect.

About his theatrical heritage, the legacy of his early immersion in *The Count of Monte Cristo*, he was of two minds. On the one hand, he thought that nothing of his could fail *as theater:*

"The real truth is I was practically born in the theatre and I couldn't do anything that wasn't practical in the theatre if I tried. I'm too wrapped up in the theatre as a medium. I've simply made it a bit broader and deeper than usual show-shop but what I write always *can* be done." On the other hand, he also thought that at times that same theatrical heritage overpowered the playwright in him: "my medium has at times taken the upper hand and become an end in itself and the slumbering director in me (son of the Count of Monte Cristo) has swamped the author. *Dynamo* was a good example of this." I believe he was right in both cases. The theatrical heritage was both his great ally and his fatal tempter. On still another occasion he put the dichotomy in another fashion; his "production" ideas came so thick and fast that they outpaced his actual writing of plays: "You see, all these ideas of mine are being incorporated into my own plays bit by bit as they fit in but I can't write plays fast enough to keep up with the production-imagination section of my 'bean.'" This sentiment was uttered, of course, in the 1920s when O'Neill was turning out a seemingly unending stream of plays, many of which depended for much of their impact on stunning theatrical effects, as in *The Emperor Jones* or *The Hairy Ape;* or were overpowered by these effects, as with *Dynamo* (1929).

His "ugly duckling" that never turned into a swan, *Lazarus Laughed* (1928), remained unshakably in his memory as one of his most imaginative efforts. Of *Dynamo* or *Days Without End* (1934) he would finally admit that they were failures, but he never gave up on *Lazarus Laughed.* More imaginative than the play itself were some of the ideas he concocted for its possible production: Feodor Ivanovich Chaliapin as Lazarus speaking the lines in Russian, or Paul Robeson doing it in "white-face." The wildest one was Spencer Tracy. In 1943 Lawrence Langner wrote O'Neill saying that Tracy would like to meet him and, evidently, Tracy was considering doing an O'Neill play (whether on stage or film is not said). O'Neill was too ill to have Tracy come to Tao House, but in his reply to Langner, O'Neill ran over some likely roles for Tracy in O'Neill plays: *The Great God Brown* would be a good bet; *Strange Interlude* and *Marco Millions* (1928) would not. Then: "My best bet for Tracy would be *Lazarus Laughed*." Then follows a long description of

a scaled-down version of the play, taking it out of the "colossal overhead class" and concluding that Tracy should read the play with the revised version in mind. As late as 1945 O'Neill still had hopes for *Lazarus Laughed* since he had requests for its translation in France and Italy that might conceivably lead to a production. The Moscow Art Theatre, so he was told, had been forbidden to do so because the play was "Too mystic." If there is an afterworld and O'Neill is in it, he's still concocting ways in which *Lazarus Laughed* could be produced.

On the vexed question of autobiography in his plays O'Neill himself liked to think that he had kept himself, and any real person or persons, out of his plays, the directly autobiographical ones excepted. In 1939 he wrote to Grace Rippin: "And I make it a point never to put real people I have known into my plays. All my characters are my own fabrication. They may have certain points about them which resemble, at times, certain traits in persons I have known, but the whole character is never true to that of any actual character." I believe that he is probably correct in this assertion, and that many of his critics, in their indefatigable search to find O'Neill-Tyrone archetypes appearing in the plays written before *Long Day's Journey Into Night*, have overdone things and have oversimplified things as well by doing just what O'Neill warned against: taking one or two traits to establish a resemblance between two characters but neglecting to consider both characters as unique totalities.

In this review I have purposely concentrated on what I think were key experiences in O'Neill's personal life and key ideas of his dramatic existence. In so doing I have left out a number of aspects of his life that are revealed in these letters. To indicate that range of experience I can do no better than to quote the editors' succinct summation: "the reader may be surprised by O'Neill's day-to-day appearance as an ordinary man, avowing friendships, showing concern for his children, warring with the IRS, raging now with love, now hatred, swearing at Establishments, tolerating most personal contacts except from swindlers, watching over his health, going to ball games, spoiling his pets, and trying, sometimes not very successfully, to bring his diurnal existence into a reasonably coherent fiscal, personal, and spiritual order."

T. S. Eliot Centennial: The Return of Old Possum

Edited by Jewel Spears Brooker
Eckerd College

In 1935 T. S. Eliot responded to a Harvard University request for biographical updates from alumni. This brief and whimsical autobiography is a perfect example of that charming evasiveness which led Ezra Pound to dub Eliot "Old Possum." To steal a phrase from Emily Dickinson, he tells the truth, but tells it slant. This shy American expatriate, by now considered a major English poet, chronicles his life since graduation from Harvard. He tells of having written a doctoral dissertation, which "was accepted, I suppose, because it was unreadable." He tells of his brief career in teaching, of his journalism, of how he got into banking "under the false pretence of being a linguist," and then of his move to the publishing house of Faber & Gwyer. He tells of an "ordinary day's work"–"talking to authors whose work I do not want to print" and "giving lectures to institutions which can't afford to pay for them." And then, warmed to his assignment, he writes about himself as a person with modest pleasures and fears. "I prefer sherry (light dry) to cocktails. I ... like such games as poker, rummy and slippery Ann for low stakes. I like certain very simple and humane kinds of practical joke ... I never bet, because I never win ... I like detective stories ... and tend to fall asleep in armchairs." And "I am afraid of high places and cows."

No wonder he became "Old Possum" to his friends and their children; no wonder he was called "the invisible poet" by one of his first critics. The simultaneous impulse to reveal and to conceal, to court intimacy and maintain distance, this perpetual protective game playing is an essential part of Eliot's personality and also of his work as a writer. The curious Mr. Eliot charmed London and for a quarter of a century most of the Western literary world, receiving the Nobel Prize for Literature, the Order of Merit, a host of honorary doctorates, and numerous other awards. But then, as was perhaps inevitable, the personality lost its charm, the work came under hostile eyes, and for a couple of decades after his death, a favorite academic parlor game became the baiting

Dust jacket for the American edition of the collection that includes many of Eliot's letters written up to the publication of The Waste Land

of Old Possum. In 1988, a century after his birth on the banks of the Mississippi River in the heart of America, the world turned back to Possum, and in general, was impressed anew with his wit and with his power as a critic and a poet.

The centennial evaluations and reevaluations have affirmed Eliot's position in the Western literary tradition. He remains at the center of modern letters with *The Waste Land* universally recognized as the century's most influential poem, and *Four Quartets* widely considered as this century's equivalent of *Paradise Lost* or *Essay on Man.* Eliot also stands as the most important literary critic of the century, the intellectual journalist who, when the century was young, outlined the issues of tradition, influence, and language which remain at the center of our concern as critics at the end of the century. In the early 1920s, with one collection of essays, *The Sacred Wood,* and a handful of poems, notably *The Waste Land* but also shorter pieces like "The Love Song of J. Alfred Prufrock," his centrality was established. In 1939 Eliot's great older contemporary W. B. Yeats died, and the mantle passed. Eliot was invited to give the first Yeats Memorial Lecture, a gesture that even at the time was seen as especially appropriate. Eliot became the elder statesman of international letters in part because of the scope of his work as critic, poet, dramatist, and publisher; in part, because of his grasp of how literature works as an institution; in part, because of the dazzling nature of the poetry. Although extremely difficult, his poetry resonated in unique ways in the modern world of war, urban decay, religious crisis, and cultural fragmentation.

One of the most significant events of 1988 was the long-awaited appearance of the first volume of Eliot's letters. The poet at first opposed publication of his letters but then agreed that if they were to be published, his wife should edit them. Mrs. Valerie Eliot has been working on the project for decades, and in September 1988 she brought out the first of four volumes. Meticulously edited and beautifully produced, it covers the years 1898-1922, the crucial formative years and those leading up to *The Waste Land.* The letters were serialized in newspapers, including the London *Times,* and were spoofed in *Private Eye,* an English satiric magazine. The second volume is planned for publication within the next two years.

Mrs. Eliot took part in various centennial activities, including a dinner party at L'Ecu de France, her husband's favorite French restaurant, and a reception at Lloyd's Bank, in which he once worked as a clerk. The Bishop of London presided at a memorial "Mass of Thanksgiving" (Mozart's *Coronation Mass*) for Eliot's life at St. Stephen's Church in Gloucester Road, where he long served as a churchwarden. There were memorial services at Westminster Abbey, where he is perpetually remembered with a large tablet in Poet's Corner, at St. Michael's Church in East Coker, where his ashes are entombed, at Little Gidding, at St. Edmundsbury Cathedral, and other churches in England. There were also numerous tributes to Eliot on the London stage and on television and radio stations throughout Britain.

There were many Eliot centennial celebrations in the United States as well. The T. S. Eliot Society, with headquarters in his native city of St. Louis, sponsored a four-day celebration which included performances of *Murder in the Cathedral* and *The Elder Statesman,* numerous musical and reader's theater renderings of his poetry, and a symposium with participants from the United States, Canada, England, Ireland, Germany, South Africa, and Japan. Visitors attended this conference from as far away as China and as close by as across the street. Participants included Cleanth Brooks, Russell Kirk, A. D. Moody, David Perkins, Ronald Schuchard, Carol H. Smith, George T. Wright, and Michael and Gráinne Yeats. The Eliot Society, which was founded in 1980 by the Hungarian poet Leslie Konnyu and has grown in the last three years from a living-room discussion group to an international fellowship, meets annually in St. Louis for an Eliot memorial program. Jewel Spears Brooker, president 1985-1988, presided over the expansion of the society to its present level, and Grover Smith, president 1989-1991, will lead the society into the poet's second hundred years.

A second international celebration of note was held at Washington University in St. Louis, an institution founded by Eliot's grandfather. The high points of this program included affectionate memorial remarks by Eliot's old friend Robert Giroux and "The Poets Read Eliot," a program in which poets read and commented on Eliot's poems. James Merrill read "The Love Song of J. Alfred Prufrock"; Amy Clampitt and Anthony Hecht read from *The Waste Land;* Howard Nemerov read "Animula"; and Richard Wilbur read *Ash-Wednesday.* There were many smaller celebrations in the city, including one at St. Louis University and several intimate readings organized by the St. Louis Humanities Forum.

The American tributes began early in 1988, with Harvard University sponsoring a series of centenary lectures running from mid February to early April. William Alfred, Seamus Heaney, William Arrowsmith, Blanford Parker, Helen Vendler, David Perkins, and W. J. Bate participated. Other centenary conferences were held at the University of Arkansas at Little Rock (home of the *Yeats-Eliot Review*), the University of New Hampshire at Durham, Miami University of Ohio, the California Institute of Technology, the University of South Florida at St. Petersburg, and at various larger professional meetings such as that of the Modern Language Association, at which there were six different Eliot sessions. Two other North American conferences should be mentioned. The University of Western Ontario in Canada, in cooperation with the Stratford Theatre, sponsored a lecture by Lyndall Gordon, as well as other lectures and entertainments; and the National Poetry Foundation (University of Maine) had a late summer conference featuring many distinguished scholars of Eliot and his age. Cleanth Brooks, Hugh Kenner, A. D. Moody, and Grover Smith were featured speakers in this varied program. Many of the NPF lectures will be published in 1989 in *T. S. Eliot: Man and Poet*, edited by Laura Cowan.

Some of the most sparkling events in what must be called the "Year of the Possum" were theatrical productions in New York and Boston. In April the Manhattan Theatre Club presented an evening of readings arranged and directed by Bill Wadsworth. "T. S. Eliot at 100" began with Robert Giroux sharing some of his memories (Giroux appeared over and over during this centennial year) and then Kate Burton, Blythe Danner, Edward Herrmann, and Sam Waterston read from the poetry. Another glittering evening was presented in October by Symphony Space, also in New York. This program, "In Different Voices: T. S. Eliot at 100," consisted of major artists reading from Eliot's poetry. Edward Albee, Anthony Hecht, John Ashbery, John Hollander, Donald Barthelme, Richard Howard, Thomas Disch, and Susan Sontag were the readers. In early October, an elegant program, "The Word in the Desert," consisting of readings by Jill Balcon and Gabriel Woolf, was held at the Hirshhorn Museum in Washington. Finally, in this brief review of the Year of the Possum, the program presented in December at Sanders Theatre, Harvard University, should be mentioned. The evening, arranged by Andreas Teuber, director of the famous Poets' Theatre, featured readings from Eliot's poetry and plays by distinguished actors, a staged reading of *Sweeney Agonistes*, poems in musical settings, and more. Participants included Robert Giroux, Anthony Hecht, Christopher Ricks, Irene Worth, Donald Hall, and many others.

The essays that follow are themselves a centennial event. They were all especially commissioned for this yearbook tribute and represent a wide range of views and topics. It is hoped that they will remain useful for years to come.

Growing Up With T. S. Eliot

M. C. Bradbrook
Cambridge University

When eighteen, I went up to Cambridge University in the autumn of 1927, where the dynamo of literary discussion was the work of T. S. Eliot. In my northern home I had never heard his name, though I had been eagerly reading Shakespeare, the Metaphysicals, and French classical literature, which gave me a good lead-in. For me the most modern poet was W. B. Yeats, chiefly the Celtic twilight of *The Land of Heart's Desire* and *The Wind Among the Reeds*, which I had copied and colored by hand. Eliot stung like a strong electric shock, but also switched on a brilliant roving light over the bewildering, always changing scene of the late 1920s.

We undergraduates found ourselves not in a brave new world but a kind of new Inferno. Dante was the controlling force of *The Waste Land* (1922): Conrad Aiken witnessed that Eliot constantly carried the little volumes of the Temple Classics around with him. Not by chance, Dante and Baudelaire were part of our required reading for the new Cambridge tripos, reformed only in 1926. A young lecturer named Ivor Richards had become a friend of the poet, who in 1926 had given the Clark Lectures, our most prestigious set of public lectures in English. Eliot became an honorary fellow of Richards's college, Magdalene, where his portrait by Wyndham Lewis now hangs in the hall. At Oxford, where Eliot had resided but where the English course stopped at 1832, he was officially without any attention, although undergraduate clubs like the Martlets received him. I still preserve a note by an eminent Oxford don, to whom I had lent the *Collected Poems* in 1935: "I am ashamed to find that I have kept this so long–but I have very much enjoyed looking through it. Besides–it has been very useful in deciding me not to buy it!"

In Cambridge, Eliot's poetry was an example of his own dictum that poetry can communicate before it is understood. If hard to grasp, his poems were overwhelming when read aloud. We gathered in our rooms to read him to each other in the evening. With all a Welshman's power of oratory, Richards read him in lectures. A young and unknown member of Emmanuel College, Frank Leavis, who gave Girtonians a weekly hour on modern poetry, read with narrower intensity; I can still hear his voice in "Burbank with a Baedeker" and "Gerontion." Leavis was as magnetized as we were, though not everyone joined our little society. F. L. Lucas of King's College and others of conservative and classical taste joined the Oxford dons. But our young poets, Empson, and in those days, Brunowski, grew upon him. Kathleen Raine has recorded her encounter with Eliot's poetry in "Waste Land, Holy Land" (collected in *The Inner Journey of the Poet*, 1982): "I first read a poem by T. S. Eliot in a magazine I picked up by chance, *The Criterion*. I was at the time (1926) so ignorant as never to have heard his name and I therefore had, as a first-year undergraduate, the pleasure of discovering him for myself; for the impact was instantaneous and tremendous." Empson and Brunowski had read mathematics, and Raine had read botany; so the influence of Eliot was by no means confined to the English faculty. Richards, who had taken his degree in philosophy, describes his own first meeting with *Ara Vos Prec* (1920): "I came away with it–unable NOT to read it in the Market Place after happening on it in Galloway and Porter's bookshop–spreading the resplendent thing open: lost in wonder and strangeness and delight." Richards was seized "almost at once with the idea that he would be *the one hope* for the then brand-new English Tripos. I was just beginning to lecture for it" ("On TSE," in *T. S. Eliot, The Man and His Work*, edited by Allen Tate, 1966). Eliot became the basis in 1926 of the shape given to our tripos course.

Richards tried to persuade Eliot to come to Cambridge; but I think his poetry–and his criticism, which we equally absorbed–worked more potently on us, became more a part of each one's interior quest, than if they had been attached to a person. It was imprinted, as it is said early habits are imprinted on infants before they learn to distinguish clearly at all. Baby ducklings, fostered by a man, will develop all the habits they normally develop toward a parent of their own species, following him line astern, in the disconcerting way of baby ducklings. We appropriated Eliot's lines, they became part of our identity, without our perceiving that he did not entirely share

our world. That made no difference to us. That strong electric shock, that brilliant flash of light, "What the Thunder Said," came inwardly, the godlike inscrutable message of some order beyond the chaos we encountered in philosophy, in society, and in our personal lives.

Even those of us who were not scientists felt the repercussions of relativity and quantum theory. We learned that it was possible to believe the wave theory on Mondays and Thursdays and the particle theory on Tuesdays and Fridays; Empson made poetry out of exhilarating skepticism and paradox. But for many, the effects were largely destructive, since verification became the sole criterion of credibility. I myself went through a period of agnosticism for fifteen years.

Socially, the revolutions that had followed World War I left us shaken in political beliefs; many became Communists or fellow travelers. We were not old enough to have known the horrors of the war itself. My own memories were of men in hospital blue, of gray "camouflaged" ships in the Mersey and the Clyde, of one air raid at Whitley Bay, of my father moving from one port to another, taking us in his wake; but we saw him very little, and what he was doing we never knew.

We sang "Tipperary" and other songs round the piano. Only in 1929, with the publication of *All Quiet on the Western Front*, and in reading Wilfred Owen, did the experience of war become available. But Eliot's poems had already recorded the seismograph inwardly; we got the meaning before we got the message.

Our world was precarious, religious faith was at its lowest ebb. Eliot transmitted the feeling of emptiness, of loss. The notorious statement in which Richards attributed to him "a complete severance between his poetry and *all* beliefs" (*Science and Poetry*, 1926) was later repudiated by Richards himself. What Keats had termed "the feel of not to feel it" is not the absence of all belief but rather an act of mourning, an anguished memory.

> April is the cruellest month, breeding
> Lilacs out of the dead land, mixing
> Memory and desire. . . .

The dry land, the waste land, constantly evokes such memories, not only in terms of human love, but of the sacred, a dimension banished by logical positivism and dialectical materialism. In the life of the "unreal City" of the dead, at once London and Dante's Inferno, we did not think how strange it was that Dante should supply Eliot– and Owen–with the desolate vision. Leavis read us "Strange Meeting" by Owen, and we listened.

Naturally, "Eliot and the problem of belief " was something we debated; but as Kathleen Raine says, "that first impact is irrecoverable. . . . We did not read his poems in any perspective at all; rather, we were in them, ourselves figures in that sad procession of Eliot's London, that 'Unreal City' in whose unreality lay its terrible reality. We knew that city by participation. . . . Indeed we may often have misunderstood the poet whose words we borrowed as a kind of magical incantation to help us to bring under control the situation of our own lives." It was inevitable that for us personal and sexual images should reverberate with the deepest tones. Half-understood psychology, reductive and crudely assimilated, added to the natural vulnerability of adolescence. "What fun, all the Freudian stuff!" cried Empson, analyzing George Herbert. Yet Eliot imparted a radiance in the strictness of his technique, his exactness of evocation. His total commitment to what could never be exactly defined left open chinks for some infiltration of the sacred, though we could not then recognize it. The strictness of his technique was reinforced by his critical essays, his concentration, his ironies; the history and theory of literary criticism was one of our options, and with Eliot's example we rid ourselves of much that passed under those titles. Here of course Richards led the way, followed by Leavis's *Scrutiny* group–the first number appeared in May 1932, and before the year was out, Eliot was there being discussed. Empson and I wrote for early numbers but both, for different reasons, discontinued.

The early 1920s had set up a neurotically disturbed way of life for the war's survivors: a generation of emancipated women, the million "superfluous" ones whose men had been slaughtered, and who cut their hair like men (the "Eton crop"), lived in bachelor flats, or the bed-sitting-rooms of typists, like Eliot's woman in "The Fire Sermon." There were men who felt guilty because they had survived, a feeling that was generally understood only after World War II, when it afflicted survivors of the concentration camps. Eliot suffered acutely after his rejection by the U.S. Navy, but in 1917 Herbert Read, home from the front, had been made a pacifist by his experiences and only wanted to get back to "Civvy Street"; therefore, he quite failed to understand Eliot's self-

defensive explanations. Richards, who had also been rejected, collapsed mentally about the same time as Eliot, and so did another friend of Richards, Mansfield Forbes. Eliot's poetry gave us the transmuted pain of his own experience made explicitly in the dedication of *The Waste Land* and in its opening section.

In this time of a new permissiveness and unexplained collapse, Eliot gave a name to "a conflict of sensations without name," and the relief was the greater because his poetry combined precision in the chiseling of phrases (the objective correlative) with the structural freedom offered by his "mythical method"–lack of a narrative structure, juxtaposition of past and present, recall of poetic power from other poets in a new context which seemed to negate what it invoked, as in "A Game at Chess." Words of sensuous keenness combined with semantic gaps in a language sophisticated yet in some ways primitive, telegraphic.

Anthropology was powerfully present at Cambridge with Sir James Frazer still walking in the courts of Trinity, and Jane Harrison at Newnham, which helped us in the understanding of the mythical method. We made that connection readily, and by this participation were educated; our meager experience was enlarged by the imaginative absorption of what we could not directly know. This is the old definition of poetic education.

Eliot had learned from Laforgue and Mallarmé; and their influences, more directly perceptible in the earlier poems, in "Whispers of Immortality" and the Sweeney poems, were fed into *The Waste Land*, as in the seduction of the typist ("Well now that's done; and I'm glad it's over") or the briefer recollections of the river nymphs ("The broken fingernails of dirty hands") to issue in the positive commands of "What the Thunder Said":

The awful daring of a moment's surrender
Which an age of prudence can never retract
By this, and this only, we have existed.

Although "give, sympathize, control" breaks down into madness and dream where social, religious, and sexual elements are fragmented–

London Bridge is falling down falling down falling
    down
Poi s'ascose nel foco che gli affina
Quando fiam uti chelidon–O swallow swallow

–and resolved in "Shantih shantih shantih."

The effect of *The Waste Land* was not gloomy but exhilarating and intensely stimulating. Our confusion was understood, our time had found a voice. No other encounter can have the effect of great contemporary poetry met in youth, which not only interprets experience but is itself experience. It grew within my privileged generation, became part of ourselves, and has ever since remained so.

Eliot himself described being possessed in this way by Laforgue, "to whom I owe more than to any one poet in any language," as he confessed in "To Criticize the Critic" (1961). He encountered Laforgue in 1908–"Conversation Galante," the earliest poem he retained in later collections (written 1909), is based on Laforgue's "Autre Complainte du Lord Pierrot." The general effect was indirectly described in *The Use of Poetry and the Use of Criticism* (1933). "At this period (adolescence) the poem or the poetry of a single poet, invades the youthful consciousness and assumes complete possession for a time. We do not really see it as something with an existence outside ourselves; much as in our youthful experience of love. . . . It is not a deliberate choice of a poet to mimic, but writing under a kind of demonic possession by one poet." The effect of Eliot upon my generation was exactly the same as the effect of Laforgue upon Eliot twenty years before.

Small wonder that faced with such varieties of claims as Richards's on the nature of Eliot's belief and the imitations of all the younger poets, Eliot at first repudiated the idea that he had expressed the disillusion of a generation and maintained that in *The Waste Land* he had merely expressed a personal grouse against life. He was a private person and a poet of the inner life; this did not invalidate the celebrated assertion in "Tradition and the Individual Talent," one of the earliest essays, "The more perfect the artist, the more completely separate in him will be the man who suffers and the mind which creates." But the obverse view emerged in the introduction to *The Use of Poetry and the Use of Criticism:* "If poetry is a form of 'communication,' yet that which is to be communicated is the poem itself, and only incidentally the thought and experience which have gone into it. The poem's existence is somewhere between the writer and the reader." Nine years later, in 1942, in "The Music of Poetry," he was affirming that the reader's interpretation may be better than the author's, that there may be more in the poem than the author was aware of; and

by 1951, broadcasting on the poetry of Virgil, he conceded (*Listener*, 13 September): "A poet may believe that he is expressing only his own private experience; his lines may be for him only a way of talking about himself without giving himself away; yet for his readers what he has written may come to be the expression both of their own secret feelings and of the exultation or despair of a generation." Eliot himself had been shifting his reading of his own poems. Though I now feel *Four Quartets* (1936-1942) to be the crown of his work, it did not come to me at all in the same way as *The Waste Land*. I was living through the scenes of which Eliot wrote; indeed from 1943 to 1945, I maintained my air-raid duties in Kensington, within a short distance west of his own patrol. So I too had heard at the ending of interminable night the blowing of the horn, that sustained "All Clear." (I was shocked when a young reader thought it was a motor horn.)

The negation of negation grows more obvious to me with the years, as I continue to grow up with Eliot. The affirmation, the fine repudiation of unbelief in "The bone's prayer to Death its God" is transformed to "only the hardly, barely prayable/Prayer of the one Annunciation" ("The Dry Salvages"). That prayer must be internally present to create the full effect of the *sestinas* in "The Dry Salvages." Leavis, who turned against Eliot in 1932–rumor said he rejected Leavis's offering for *The Criterion Miscellany*–was at the end troubled by *Four Quartets*, which he was too responsive not to find very disturbing; but he could not understand the nature of Eliot's hope.

Eliot set his father's motto at the front of his first critical work: *Tacuit et fecit*. The motto might be his own. The power of implication, of engaging the reader, was closely linked to his powers of elimination. Forty years ago, in a collection of pieces made to celebrate his sixtieth year, I wrote in a rather Leavisy tone which particularly enraged Leavis: "Mr. Eliot's style works by reservations and implications–in his own phrase it has tentacular roots. . . . Its safeguard and perhaps its intention is to involve the lively working cooperation of the reader. He does not supply statement however subtle or communicate feelings however just and pertinent. He starts off a process" ("Eliot's Critical Method," in *T. S. Eliot: A Study of His Writings By Several Hands*, edited by Balachandra Rajan, 1947). In 1930 one of the effects of his criticism was that after reading his "Four Elizabethan Dramatists," I embarked on a doctoral thesis which was published as *Themes and Conventions of Elizabethan Tragedy* (1935). This permanently shaped what was to be for the rest of my life my main critical interest. So growing up with Eliot–a process which still continues–shaped both my inner stability and my daily work.

T. S. Eliot's Urban Imagination

Robert Crawford
University of Glasgow

At age sixteen T. S. Eliot left St. Louis; St. Louis never left T. S. Eliot. That city is, as he pointed out, the basis of his urban imagery, and the urban is one of the most important elements in Eliot's verse. Revisiting St. Louis later in life, Eliot spoke of his satisfaction at being born there rather than in Boston, New York, or London. Significantly, he did not even imagine himself being born in a rural setting; significantly, too, his adopted Englishness was also accompanied by a strong attachment to particular American roots. Eliot once described his urban habits as prenatal; St. Louis was the city of his gestation.

Some of the features of that city which had impressed Walt Whitman when he visited it in 1879 also left clear marks on Eliot, who was born there nine years later. Whitman noted its "solid riches, probably a higher average thereof than any city," but these were counterpointed by "reminders of old, even decay'd civilization." St. Louis was cosmopolitan in its combination of "native and foreign" qualities. Whitman noted great factory chimneys belching smoke; most of all, he noted the presence of "earth's most important stream," the Mississippi.

Eliot's family was fairly well off (his father was president of a St. Louis brick company), but to allow Eliot's grandmother to remain in the house which her husband had built, the family lived in what Eliot remembered as a rather drab, slummy area of the city. Eliot felt that to spend childhood beside the Mississippi was an experience deeply ingrained in those who had known it. His boyhood St. Louis was to him perched at "the beginning of the Wild West." He was aware there of remains of a very different, native American society, and, like most of his coevals, he liked to read adventure stories set in that Wild West. From contemporary St. Louis, he stole names

and ideas for his poetry–Prufrock and Sweeney have their origins there, as does the famous "yellow fog" which Eliot recalled as the smoke of St. Louis factory chimneys. His early poetry would be set in drab slummy districts, such as those which he had known in his St. Louis childhood and in the Boston of his student days. These real cities contributed to the imagined zones of "Preludes" or "Rhapsody on a Windy Night," or else to the elaborate town-house interiors, like that in "Portrait of a Lady." As a poet Eliot was fascinated by the slummy as well as the sophisticatedly urban, and he was interested in juxtaposing the modern city with more primitive ways of life. The city in *The Waste Land* (1922), *Sweeney Agonistes* (1932), and *The Cocktail Party* (1950) is most clearly London; the primitive in these works is not the Wild West, it is the jungle and desert of turn-of-the-century anthropology with its rites of fertility and violence. But that powerful urge to combine the city with the savage harks back to Eliot's St. Louis boyhood. The other cities that he knew best–Boston, Paris, and London– contributed much to his writing, but all were mapped onto St. Louis.

Long before he went there, Eliot knew London well. Young and old he read Sherlock Holmes stories eagerly; he admired Charles Dickens, in whose work the city was so often a prison. But in poetry the work of two Scottish poets was particularly important in offering nourishment to his developing urban imagination. The poetry of James Thomson and John Davidson meant much to Eliot in adolescence and underlay his subsequent reading both of Baudelaire and of Dante. Thomson, most famous for *The City of Dreadful Night* (1874), had come from Clydeside to London where (like Eliot later) he worked as a city clerk and developed a poetic vision which presented the city, often using Dante's language, as a phantasmal hell, an urban desert of despair. Thomson's poetry used landscapes of gloomy canal banks and human wreckage; its atmosphere was brooding, though sometimes lacking in concrete details. Such details were mustered impressively in the best work of Davidson, who wrote most memorably about the life of a low-paid London clerk in "Thirty Bob a Week," a poem which Eliot regarded as eternally great. In that monologue, which uses a sharp modern diction, the punishing routine of the clerk, traveling daily on the subway to and from the suburbs, is juxtaposed with the violent horror of his inner life: "So p'r'aps we are in Hell for all that I can tell/

And lost and damn'd and served up hot to God." Another Davidson poem describes a host of city clerks crossing London Bridge; elsewhere Davidson showed Eliot how to make poetry out of run-down London areas such as the Isle of Dogs. Davidson's work prepared Eliot to respond (when a student at Harvard) to certain passages of Baudelaire.

Much later Eliot described himself as one who had *lived* Baudelaire's lines "Fourmillante cité, cité pleine de rêves,/Où le spectre en plein jour raccroche le passant ..." (Swarming city, city full of dreams/Where the ghost in broad daylight accosts the passerby). In Eliot's first major poem, a thin dreamer called J. Alfred Prufrock accosts the reader and brings with him a dingy urban landscape that seems to dog him everywhere he tries to go:

> through certain half-deserted streets,
> The muttering retreats
> Of restless nights in one-night cheap hotels
> And sawdust restaurants with oyster-shells:
> Streets that follow like a tedious argument
> Of insidious intent ...

The poem's epigraph (from Dante) seems to place Prufrock in hell, but Eliot's real vision of the city as hellish had to wait until the writing of *The Waste Land*. The would-be lover Prufrock is more an inhabitant of Limbo, too impotent to get to the desired, but feared goal of those well-appointed, female-dominated town-house interiors protected by "the eternal Footman." Such an interior is to the fore in "Portrait of a Lady" where the preciosity of its pseudosophisticated "bric-a-brac" is set against the much less grand, much less pretentious street life of reading "the comics and the sporting page" in the park, or being stirred "when a street-piano, mechanical and tired/Reiterates some worn-out common song." The contrasts of a St. Louis childhood became the contrasts of Eliot's verse.

In 1910-1911 Eliot was in Paris, enjoying the streets, the atmosphere of intellectual ferment, and modern low-life urban writing like that of Charles-Louis Philippe's *Bubu de Montparnasse* (1901). All these elements fuse in the sense of throbbing excitement and urban hallucination of "Rhapsody on a Windy Night" where "Every street lamp that I pass/Beats like a fatalistic drum."

The drably urban, the conventionally "unpoetic" continued to excite Eliot, who was bringing English-language poetry further into the urban landscape explored by Thomson and Davidson. Eliot was also aware of drab horrors, torpors, and vacancies. Against those he set, ironically, the inanities and listlessness of urban over-refinement. At Harvard he enjoyed studying philosophy and made trips to the Boston music halls; he even experimented with that most urban of popular forms—vaudeville. But he also incisively caricatured polite Boston, which he once described as being refined beyond the point of civilization:

> When evening quickens faintly in the street,
> Wakening the appetites of life in some
> And to others bringing the *Boston Evening Transcript*. . . .

Eliot's attitude toward Boston was similar to his attitude toward Oxford, where he spent the academic year 1914-1915; he thought it very pretty, but deadening. It was London that excited, drew, and horrified his imagination.

In London Eliot met Ezra Pound, who appreciated and encouraged his writing; there he moved with Vivienne, the English woman who had become his wife and with whom he would have an increasingly anxious marriage. Eliot settled in London against his parents' wishes, took a job in a bank, and did large amounts of literary work in his evenings. The strain of a punishing schedule and of marital and religious worries began to tell on him. T. S. Eliot the London banker was also in search of religious peace. For a time he considered becoming a Buddhist (he had studied Buddhism and Sanskrit at Harvard). He walked the London streets, fascinated by Sir Christopher Wren's church architecture (in his Baedeker guide to London he marked Wren churches he had visited). But he also carried Dante's *Inferno* in his pocket.

All these aspects of Eliot's London life fueled *The Waste Land*. It is wrong to think of *The Waste Land* simply as an urban poem, but without its city it would be as unthinkable as Joyce's *Ulysses* without Dublin. During the later stages of writing the poem which, with Ezra Pound's help, would be crafted into *The Waste Land*, Eliot had been reading Joyce's great urban novel with strong admiration. Like *Ulysses*, *The Waste Land* bonds the modern city on to ancient myth; it sets demotic urban pub talk against the language of high culture; it attaches the whole of world history to an often unprepossessing urban landscape. Eliot's principal city in the poem is London, but it is a London whose river, sweating oil and tar, encrusted with memories of litter and grandeur, and ironically juxtaposed with the water of primitive fertility rites, is closely related to "the brown god . . . almost forgotten/By the dwellers in cities" of *The Dry Salvages* (1941)–the Mississippi flowing under the Eads Bridge at St. Louis. The memory of standing on that bridge in flood time was one of Eliot's most vivid early recollections.

When London explicitly enters *The Waste Land*, the reader stands on London Bridge in the "Unreal City" of Thomson and Davidson while a crowd of workers heads for their work "on the final stroke of nine." The language used of them is Dante's, but in an abrupt interruption one of the modern urban pedestrians is addressed as a man who has fought in an ancient Greek sea battle. All of history seems present on London Bridge. Eliot took this device of seeing the modern urban worker as an ancient seaman from a story by Rudyard Kipling called "The Finest Story in the World." Kipling was another of Eliot's lifelong enthusiasms, and this story about a modern London bank clerk who is the reincarnation of various historical characters lent much to *The Waste Land*, forming another ingredient to nourish Eliot's urban imagination. Eliot's clerkly world was also inhabited by Joseph Conrad's Marlow, narrator of *Heart of Darkness*, where London confronts the jungle. Both Conrad and Eliot could see London as "one of the dark places of the earth."

Eliot worked on what would become *The Waste Land* over a period of about ten years, and it develops themes from his earlier city poetry. The rich town-house interior of "Portrait of a Lady" becomes the overelaborate artifice of the room which houses the later poem's Cleopatra figure. The dingy landscape of littered streets and vacant lots in the early poetry becomes the dull canal bank and the gashouse-scape of *The Waste Land*. But it is not only the lower-class cityscape that features in the poem; it also uses lower-class demotic speech ("It's them pills I took, to bring it off, she said"). Eliot has been attacked for manifesting snobbery and scorn in such diction, but the women discussing contraceptives in a London pub are no more or less admirable than the Cleopatra figure whose room's decor masks with high art a scene of violent rape, or than the homosexual Mr. Eugenides (his name, ironically, means "Good Breeding") proposing a "weekend at the Metropole." "Breeding" not in the sense of aristo-

cratic pedigree but in the sense of sexual fertility is central to *The Waste Land;* sexuality is seen as a trapping cage; there passes before the reader a succession of London lovers ranging from the automatic and banal modern house agent's clerk and bed-sit typist to the illusory splendor of Queen Elizabeth's sordid flirtation with one of her courtiers. These urban lovers' inanity is set against the exploded and now apparently useless if fascinating rituals of primitive fertility cults. London is seen as banal, empty, but maybe no less so than the rest of the desert of life. The poem is bleak, but not without flickering moments of hope, the most positive of which also take place in the city and link the demotic to the exalted in a moment of respite when friendly noise in a fishmarket workers' bar is juxtaposed with the splendid comfort offered by the interior of a Wren church near London's financial district.

> O City city, I can sometimes hear
> Beside a public bar in Lower Thames Street,
> The pleasant whining of a mandoline
> And a clatter and a chatter from within
> Where fishmen lounge at noon: where the walls
> Of Magnus Martyr hold
> Inexplicable splendour of Ionian white and gold.

But the succeeding parts of *The Waste Land* banish any lasting sense of tranquillity. The "peace" held out by the poem's last line is never reached; rather it is like the exhausted collapse at the end of "Gerontion" and "The Hollow Men." Eventually, what *The Waste Land* does to London is to destroy it, and the last mention of the city takes us back to a London Bridge seen daringly in terms of a child's nursery rhyme ("London Bridge is falling down falling down falling down"). With it fall poetic fragments of Eastern and Western civilization.

Sweeney Agonistes operates in similar urban territory, and Eliot was working on it soon after the publication of *The Waste Land*. This play, set in London, is closely patterned on Aristophanic comedy as explained by F. M. Cornford, who saw such comedy as deriving from fertility rites. Eliot sets tormented but banal life in a London flat against an apparently appealing but in reality equally empty life dreamed of in the "Gauguin shades" of the stereotypical South Seas. The play draws on Eliot's love of music hall and vaudeville and is closely related to his appreciation of Marie Lloyd, a music-hall star who was the subject of one of a series of "London Letters" which Eliot wrote for the American magazine, the *Dial*.

Eliot's enjoyment of London music hall is a reminder that though the city in his major poetry tends to be seen as unattractive or ambiguous, Eliot did greatly enjoy aspects of urban life.

Because of marital, religious, and other personal crises, the 1920s were probably Eliot's unhappiest decade. But in 1927 he decided to become a British citizen, joined the Church of England, and, though his marital problems worsened, he seems to have found at least a measure of stability. When he returns to the theme of the city in the *The Rock* (1934), he deals with the building of a Christian London which represents Christian society in general. *The Rock* is uneven, but this reengagement in verse with the theme of the city looks forward to the great poetry of the *Four Quartets*, Eliot's late masterpiece.

In *Four Quartets* Eliot's urban imagination combines with an imaginative encounter with rural landscape which had increased throughout his work and is manifest in poems such as *Ash-Wednesday* and *Marina* (both 1930). In the first of the quartets, *Burnt Norton* (1936), London features with its "gloomy hills," representing a "twittering world," and the Davidson territory of the subway is treated, being seen less as a hell and more as a representative of an empty darkness through which one may pass to eventual light. The subway is back in *East Coker* (1940), the second quartet

> when an underground train, in the tube, stops
> too long between stations
> And the conversation rises and slowly fades into
> silence
> And you see behind every face the mental empti-
> ness deepen
> Leaving only the growing terror of nothing to think
> about. . . .

But this emptiness in the city now carries with it another possibility, since for the Christian Eliot "the faith and the hope and the love are all in the waiting." Eliot, by the time the quartets were written, was separated from his wife, was playing an active life in his church and society, serving on various committees, and was working as a director of the publishing house of Faber & Faber. Yet *East Coker* overturns ideas of conventional success.

The poet implicates himself among those "eminent men of letters" and the "Distinguished civil servants, chairmen of many committees, industrial lords and petty contractors" who simply "all go into the dark." If anything, in the quartets, this London world of apparent success is seen as less noble than the grueling, thankless task of the fishermen endlessly putting out onto the drift of the sea and its drifting wreckage in *The Dry Salvages* (1941), where Eliot in this third quartet recalls the scenes of his childhood summers at Gloucester, Massachusetts, and connects these with the riverscape of the Mississippi at St. Louis (though these places are not named). It is in *Little Gidding* (1942), the last quartet, that Eliot finally locates salvation in the city when his apocalyptic urban imagination, which had already destroyed London in *The Waste Land*, sees in the wartime destruction of London during the blitz a manifestation of pentecostal fire. Drawing on his experiences as a rooftop firewatcher during bombing raids, when he had noticed houses turned to "Dust in the air suspended," Eliot links the destruction of the blitz to the Christian idea that salvation may entail a total sacrifice of all held dear. In a remarkable passage modeled again on Dante, Eliot meets a "familiar compound ghost" on the asphalt city street after an enemy raid. Though this figure pours scorn on what might be regarded as Eliot's "lifetime's effort," he nonetheless makes possible the difficult and challenging perception of how the enemy war plane ("the dark dove with the flickering tongue") may be a token of savage pentecost when it "breaks the air/ With flame of incandescent terror." This wartime poetry presents again the city as a locus of destruction, yet finds in it a difficult hope, a purgative fire leading to "A condition of complete simplicity/ (Costing not less than everything)." With such a sacrifice and difficult reconciliation Eliot's poetry ends, moving past "the longest river" and other childhood images toward "the crowned knot of fire" and eventual unity and silence. Fittingly, the powerfully urban imagination nurtured in Eliot from his earliest St. Louis childhood concludes by imaging the key to salvation located in the peculiarly urban terrors of the London blitz.

Eliot's Works and Days: Poetry and the Possibility of Political Discourse

Joseph Bentley
University of South Florida

T. S. Eliot's complete body of poetry, from "The Love Song of J. Alfred Prufrock" (1911) through *Four Quartets* (1936-1942), is a display of radical transformations in technique and subject matter. In the early poems Eliot's stylistic signature is the mundane or quotidian image. "I have measured out my life with coffee spoons," is the paradigmatic early Eliot line. In these poems unimportance is transmuted into its opposite: a center of focus. Later, in *The Waste Land* (1922), most imagery of this kind is relegated to backgrounds of concern. The stylistic foreground is taken over by form, by the reader's necessary uncertainty about the relations of episodes to each other and the relations between pattern and detail. Neither the quotidian image nor the problematics of form take focus in *Four Quartets*. There the concern is primarily with meaning. Form and image are important, of course; but the poems seldom permit us to forget that we are being challenged to understand and, if possible, believe. Taken together, these phases reveal Eliot's search for the possibility of a poetry that can enter history as political discourse.

Eliot's "progress" is from images through structures to ideas. Nothing is ever so simple, especially in a major poet, but the progression has heuristic value as a way of bracketing Eliot's career as a unitive work of art. If we are to have some chance of seeing the epic dimensions of this unitive work that Eliot called *The Complete Poems and Plays, 1909-1950* (1952), we need a theory of verbal behavior broad enough to place the quotidian image into a clear relation with form building and contemplation. Such a theory is to be found in Hannah Arendt's 1959 book *The Human Condition*, a neo-Marxist reconstruction of the classical taxonomy of human activity. When we understand her classes of activity, we will understand the traditions of defining the human condition Eliot's phases evoke. The classical world, Arendt shows, divided the whole of human activity into two classes, the *Vita Activa* and the *Vita*

Contemplativa. The second was the highest activity a person could aspire to perform. Its task was to understand the inner nature of the universe, the realm of eternity beyond the mandates of practical life. Only a gifted few–those touched by *thaumazein* or the experience of wonder before mystery–could devote their lives to the way of contemplation, the attempt at using reason to seek out, recapture, and explain the original moment of *thaumazein*. Ordinary mortals must devote their lives to some form of the *Vita Activa*, the generic term for those activities we perform to optimize our personal and collective lives.

The *Vita Activa*, Arendt explains, was subdivided into labor, work, and action. All of the European languages preserve some version of these terms, though the original distinctions have been blurred for at least fifteen hundred years. Labor, the class of activity most relevant to Eliot's use of the quotidian image in his early poems, was understood to refer only to activity necessary to survival in nature. Food gathering, cooking, cleaning, daily maintenance, and tending children are examples of labor. Such activities are necessary, but they are also temporary: they must be repeated at the regular intervals, daily, seasonal, or generational, dictated by nature. Though tools and techniques vary from one period to another, labor is always mandated by the same needs. Labor, to summarize, is natural, must use physical force, is cyclical, and is not subject to historical change. Finally, we share it with all animals.

Work, by contrast, is the manufacture of durable objects, like houses, furniture, ships, and tools. It is an attempt to build an artificial environment to satisfy the desires of a population increasingly aware that they must complete a development that nature did not finish. Aristotle, in his *Physics*, argues that nature strives for completeness and usually achieves it–trees, for example, or fish–but has failed with humans. It is thus our task to correct nature's mistakes and build an extension of our bodies through an ever improving methodology of being alive, an evolving *techne tou biou*. The most important implication of work is that it is part of an ongoing process moving toward perfection. It is, to summarize, corrective of nature, must use physical force, is on a straight time line, and is immersed in history through its quest for improvements in technique. We share it with only a few animals.

Action, finally, is nothing more than political speech. Its concern is the art of structuring human groups into increasingly secure and efficient organizations. This can be accomplished through the skills of the speaker projecting his concepts of policy into an arena of contending ideas. Only the most convincing practitioner will prevail. He will imprint his private personality on the community in ways that will continue long after his death. He will thus have a kind of immortality. Action is unique to humans, uses no physical force, is unrepeatable, and is the very material of history itself.

Before considering Eliot's poetic embodiment of these distinctions, several points must be emphasized. The *Vita Activa* is rigidly hierarchical. Only the *aristoi* or best men engage in action; work is the province of technicians, a respected but lower class of human being; and labor is to be performed only by women, slaves, and animals. Further, these distinctions draw a clear line between private and public realms. Labor is done by people who are confined to the household, work bridges the two, and action can only be carried out in the public realm. Beyond action, however, lies the highest activity of all, contemplation of both a religious and a philosophical kind. Arendt shows that the "event" that ushered in the Renaissance is the reversal of these activities, with contemplation reduced to a level below action, work, and even labor. Later, the "event" that accompanied the arrival of modernity is the reduction of action and work to labor, the quotidian, daily, always to be consumed and redone entity that announces its temporariness by being isolated from history. When we assent in advance to the prescheduled obsolescence of products, policies, and ideas, we erase the distinctions between them. We turn all activity into labor, exit from history, and allegorize it as an autonomous process.

To see how the classical *Vita Activa* operates in Eliot's early poems, consider the brief "Morning at the Window."

> They are rattling breakfast plates in basement kitchens
> And along the trampled edges of the street
> I am aware of the damp souls of housemaids
> Sprouting despondently at area gates.

The daily labor of cooking and cleaning is not shown. It is confined to the lower floor within a household. Women do this labor, live underground, and remain hidden from the public street. Only sounds reach the speaker's point of view. The sounds of labor engender a fantasy of housemaids' souls emerging from area gates as despondent plants–mushrooms or some other sort

of fungus. As plant life, the souls are quotidian, like the labor their owners perform. Damp, sprouting souls will grow, decline, die, and be replaced too rapidly for anyone to notice a turnover in personnel.

The word "soul" is the most affecting aspect of this metaphor. We can hardly escape the experience of watching a metaphysical essence, a principle of individuation, an immortal soul become covered with damp matter and be annihilated by routine. In the rest of the poem fog tosses "twisted faces from the bottom of the street" and tears the smile from a woman's face. The smile hovers and vanishes along the roofs. We know that smiles do not become detached from faces–except in the tale of a certain Cheshire cat by Lewis Carroll. But in this context of fog-beshrouded motion, the detachment seems to be the speaker's counterfantasy to the despondently sprouting souls of housemaids. Smile equals form; face equals matter. The form is released from its entrapment within matter and allowed to escape. In an Aristotelian view souls are forms, so the fantastic final event releases a soul from labor, sends it over the rooftops to freedom.

"Morning at the Window" is typical of Eliot's early work. Irony, metaphysical wit, and surrealistic play dominate the experience we have of the poetry. But there is no denying the inescapable lament for the diminished lives of those condemned by circumstance to quotidian labor. The sense of endless, Sisyphean repetition of drudgery applies to women in the poems more than to men. At the end of "Preludes" the worlds move "like ancient women/Gathering fuel in vacant lots." In the same poem a woman watches "the night revealing the thousand sordid images/Of which your soul was constituted."

Eliot is careful to show, however, that quotidian labor afflicts not only the proletariat, but also oppresses the middle class. "The Love Song of J. Alfred Prufrock" is, among other things, an extended meditation on the endless repetition of all forms of activity. Decisions will be made over and over again, Prufrock muses, so there seems to be no urgent need to make any at all. Michelangelo is discussed by women who "come and go," thus reducing art to a cycle of commentaries. Novels are read, tea is drunk, overwhelming questions are avoided, and the language of intimacy is lost in the bourgeois salon only to be faced again and again forever.

Among the most suggestive statements of the quotidian in the poem is the reference to "all the works and days of hands/That lift and drop a question on your plate." Prufrock refers earlier to an overwhelming question that he prefers not to specify. Such questions suggest contemplation, philosophy, some encounter with *thaumazein*, the awesome wonder of existence. Later, he will suggest another kind of question, social speech that has a chance of leading to intimacy. That question is also unaskable. Further, the *Works and Days* is a Greek epic about agriculture and its attendant problems. If questions are lifted from and dropped on plates, with the allusively generated presence of ancient farmers certifying the cyclical nature of everything, then contemplation, love, thought, friendship, and wonder are all reduced to quotidian labor. All activity is confined to the household and its basement kitchens. Prufrock derides his own attention to changing fashion and goes in search of mermaids.

An extremely useful point about the quotidian is supplied by Erich Auerbach in *Mimesis: The Representation of Reality in Western Literature* (1946). It is the defining characteristic of Petronius. The Trimalchio section of *The Satyricon* is dominated by this kind of image. The practical, mundane, trivial events, functions, and objects which continue to occupy a former slave's view of the world impose a feeling of decentered and scattered randomness on the scene and its characters. Auerbach's point is that the quotidian image isolates us and the figures in the work from the flow of history. The quotidian merely recurs endlessly, from day to day. Any immersion in it is a loss of history, a fall into that private realm where public events are irrelevant, where no free action to shape the past policies into a potential future can be practiced. In Auerbach's word, the quotidian is "intrahistorical," locked within history rather than on its edge, oscillating between inner and outer positions, ready to push it in a chosen direction.

Eliot, we know, admired Petronius and learned much from him. One of the insights he might have developed there is that the quotidian image is the very opposite of an ideological or revolutionary device. If the flow of modern history has reduced both the *Vita Contemplativa* and the *Vita Activa* to labor, the lowest place in the hierarchy, making a cardinal virtue of instant obsolescence, it would seem that the message is a call for something drastic to be done. Quite the reverse, however, is the inevitable message. Revolu-

tion is in itself quotidian, a violent rupture which must be endlessly repeated. Further, revolution is idle gossip in Petronius and absent from Eliot's early work. The reason for its absence is the Petronian implication that the quotidian is by nature intrahistorical, cut off from radical politics of all kinds. It is defined, also, by routine revolutions, the cycles of nature. The authority of natural needs is so overwhelming that it makes politics inconceivable. In some situations the need for revolutions makes revolution impossible. Neither gluttons nor those who starve can enter the realm of political speech, the region of history. Their attention must be directed toward their own needs in a direct way.

What conclusion must we make about Eliot's later poetry, now that we are seeing the reduction of a hierarchy of behavior to its lowest term as the dominant motif in the first phase of the complete poetry? Nothing in the later work suggests a reestablishment of the idea that political speech can be useful. In "Gerontion" history is presented as a house in which we are all confined. As a result, the public realm where politics can be valid is no longer real. There is no common place where history can be debated and generated into structure through the force of mind. All places and times are confined to Gerontion's house, the place where a woman labors in a kitchen. *The Waste Land* focuses on seasonal cycles, the problematics of structure, and the gratuitous nature of interpretation. However thunder is understood, it provides no recommendations to the public on how to reenter history. Past works are called in to be recycled as devices to shore up ruins. The ending is apolitical in showing the fisher king turning his back to the land and, like Candide, setting his own lands in order. Policy for all is unthinkable.

The Waste Land does, however, contain an explicit message on the subject of the importance of transcending the quotidian. The message is placed at one of the poem's positions of maximum emphasis. After a speaker interprets the first thunder word as *Datta*, give, he goes on to assert the primary importance of acts that are so charged with implication that their consequences can never be reversed. "By this and this only we have existed" summarizes the importance of acting in irreversible ways. However we interpret this part of the poem, we must see it as a statement of the importance of going beyond the endless repetitions dictated by nature. Rectilinear time must somehow be entered, even though personal history seems to require an abandonment of membership in a community debating its future.

Four Quartets provides an explicit commentary on these issues. The coexistence of time and timelessness at the still point of the turning world announces a redemption of the quotidian that no political theory can promise. If every cycle of works and days, labors and generations, confined within the basement kitchens of history, is also interpenetrated by the timeless and dimensionless, then all behaviors in the *Vita Activa* and the *Vita Contemplativa* are freed from hierarchical arrangement. In simple terms, the Christian narrative concerns the incarnation of the eternal in a worker, Jesus the carpenter, and the crucial importance of laborers–women and fishermen–in spreading the apolitical news that the reduction of a hierarchy to flatness is not a signal for despair but an announcement that all are equal in the points at which they recognize their intersection with timelessness.

Many passages in the quartets illustrate this point. Eliot finally comes to terms with the quotidian, with cycles, with the total impossibility of doing anything once and once only. In *The Dry Salvages*, for example, he lists a sequence of amazing events from communication with Mars to the definitive exploration of dreams as a prelude to reminding us of the obvious: that they are merely "pastimes and drugs, and features of the press/ And always will be." The press is in itself an example of the rapid superannuation of all news. The most direct statement in the quartets on this subject comes near the end of *East Coker*. After observing that each new start is a "raid on the inarticulate," an example of what Claude Lévi-Strauss has taught us to call "bricolage"–work with tools known to be inadequate and wrong, "shabby equipment always deteriorating"–Eliot nevertheless affirms the importance of proceeding with the quest.

> And what there is to conquer
> By strength and submission, has already been
>   discovered
> Once or twice, or several times, by men whom one
>   cannot hope
> To emulate–but there is no competition–
> There is only the fight to recover what has been
>   lost
> And found and lost again and again.

Here and in many passages in his late work Eliot recognizes the reduction of ideas to the repetitive

and quotidian but does not feel any sense of negation in that reduction. When time is inconceivable without its opposite, and all thought is bricolage, labor finds its redemption in the valorization of process over product, routine over conclusion, and experience over knowledge.

As assembled for publication in 1950, Eliot's complete poems form a single epic. It is the account of a journey through a maze where every route leads back to labor, the tyranny of confinement. The epic journey through the labyrinth ends with the discovery that ends and beginnings are always the same place. That conclusion tells us that a philosopher's contemplation of eternity has led to a discovery that action, work, and labor are equally involved, as sources of *thaumazein*, in the experience beyond words that is paradoxically captured in the poet's final words. *The Complete Poems and Plays, 1909-1950* is a far more extensive book than Hesiod's *Works and Days*, to a large extent because it does not forget to include it at the center of concern.

T. S. Eliot the Classicist: His Ideas in Historical Context

Grover Smith
Duke University

The following brief account has a specific and twofold purpose. This is, namely, to trace the historical associations of the terms "classicist" and "classical" employed by T. S. Eliot, and to suggest that as developed by him the terms hold a particular place in the history of ideas. The meanings attached by Eliot to these words continued a semantic process. The fact that, with reference to himself, he applied the term "classicist" in a manner divergent from traditional senses has indeed been noted, at least in the form of doubts as to its correctness. Otherwise, his use of it has often been accepted without historical surprise. For my part I have no wish to question its correctness, but I intend if possible to define what Eliot meant by it against the broad background of earlier history.

"Classicist," like "classical," depends for its meaning at any time upon the parent concept of "classicism." This has connotations both of Greco-Roman antiquity and of the seventeenth and eighteenth centuries, and in the latter context it stands opposed to ideas of the "modern" and eventually to various senses of "romanticism." The term "classic" follows its lead but can also denote with approbation any achievement, especially in art, having a distinction recalling the values of classicism. The connotations of all these terms are generally favorable except in the heat of romantic counterclaims. As for "neoclassicism," this word has no necessary use except with reference to imitations in a later period of the classicism shown by an earlier, and I shall avoid it here.

The negative critique of Eliot as a classicist takes a form represented in René Wellek's 1956 *Sewanee Review* article, "The Criticism of T. S. Eliot," after three decades still the standard compact survey of its subject. Wellek, without any censoriousness whatever, simply observes that "Eliot's taste is neither classical nor neoclassical"; that "Eliot's classicism is a matter of cultural politics rather than of literary criticism." Whether one reads these comments in the sense "No, Eliot is barely a classicist" or in the sense "As a description of Eliot 'classicist' is correct only in a certain aspect" makes little difference; in effect it is assumed that a "normal" classicism can be identified from which Eliot more or less deviated. On the other hand, in *Notes on Some Figures Behind T. S. Eliot* (1964), Herbert Howarth, pointing to origins of Eliot's classicism in the antiromanticism of Irving Babbitt, who was clearly one kind of traditional classicist, notices nothing irregular in Eliot's Christian revision of the idea. But I think that Wellek was right to adopt a historical test. I would only go beyond his assumptions about its usefulness and in fact accept Eliot's innovative senses for "classicism" by treating them as evolutionary stages in a series going back centuries. It is a paradox that "classicism," the name of a philosophy of fixed principles, is subject like other human ideas to a law of change in historical process. So classicism is unstable—a fact less in harmony with "classic" classicism than with Eliot's view of tradition—as Eliot doubtless realized when he labored to renew classicism for himself. The importance of his mind and art rubs off onto the transformation.

Eliot regarded several concepts more highly than classicism, and some of them—*discipline, tradition, order,* and *authority*—entered into his definition of it and indeed became its determinants; another, *orthodoxy,* emerging at a later stage, transcended it and, as a condition of his Christian humanism in the late 1920s and subsequently, superseded it in most senses except the lit-

erary. For, as Wellek says, Eliot's classicism was involved with cultural politics. It had been so with Babbitt also; but Eliot, like Babbitt, maintained an essentially ethical ground, both personal and cultural, upon which all of his classical doctrines were based. As is common knowledge, Eliot as a Harvard undergraduate in 1909-1910 had enrolled in Babbitt's course in modern French literary criticism and had become saturated in Babbitt's hostility to the influence of Rousseau and in his devotion to classical order. Babbitt blamed Rousseau for the self-glorifying tendency in nineteenth-century art and life, for the romantic cult of personal originality; these resulted from Rousseau's replacement of reason with feeling as the criterion of social good. Feeling answered to the deepest needs of human nature. Feeling, for Rousseau therefore, justified no less the self-expression of the artist than the social aspiration of the revolutionary; both were dedicated to liberation from the chains of opinion and custom. Babbitt set for Eliot the contrary example of demanding from art and for life the values of "restraint and discipline," perceived as emanating from "the classical spirit" because of its consecration to "a high, impersonal reason." Babbitt was culturally rather than politically anti-democratic; to counter the leveling effects of mass culture, he envisioned aristocratic intellectual discipline, not authoritarianism. He and Eliot would at length fall out over the sanctions of this discipline. Babbitt always held that the inherent reasonableness of human nature was enough; Eliot, even before his conversion to Anglo-Catholicism in 1927, held that external authority must exist to compel the individual.

The influence of Babbitt on Eliot over the years was prodigious, and it was to Babbitt the classicist that Eliot primarily owed his critical loyalties and, eventually more enduring, his technical commitment as a poet. Howarth has vividly demonstrated the indebtedness of Eliot's "Tradition and the Individual Talent" (1919) to what Babbitt called "the balance between the forces of tradition and the claims of originality," a balance he believed intrinsic to Greek literature. But the constant wrestling, not only with feelings but with tradition, that Eliot there saw as occupying the artist is foreign to Babbitt's mind, secure in classical epistemology. The half-idealist system adapted by Eliot from F. H. Bradley permits only an impersonal art by definition, for art is distanced from the immediate experience of the artist; but in order to give it significance the artist must pass ma-

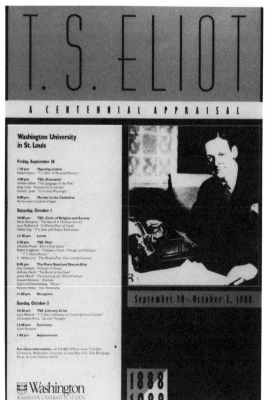

Posters for six of the events commemorating Eliot's centennial

Courtesy of the Salvador Dali Museum, St. Petersburg, Florida

terials other than his feelings, significant materials from tradition, through his individual, original, point of view. Complementing authority, tradition established itself by 1919 in Eliot's canons of classicism; authority in the sense of an arbiter of conduct conflicts with the teachings of Babbitt. Rather it came into Eliot's synthesis from a Continental source, Charles Maurras, who nominally associated classicism with two authoritative institutions–Catholicism and monarchism. Babbitt, to what extent no one seems to have gauged, must surely have influenced Eliot to extinguish residual faith in Unitarian Christianity, and also to resist Catholic Christianity in the years before 1927 when other modes of authority were proving persuasive. Several voices spoke.

Of those voices, that of Maurras reached Eliot's ear for the longest time and with the most attractive message. Maurras, a French political activist and journalist associated with the paper *L'Action française*, interested Eliot with his literary essays. But between roughly 1913 and the mid 1920s Maurras's classicism (French classicism, oriented toward the seventeenth century) weighed in Eliot's estimation no more heavily than the doctrines of Catholic and monarchist authoritarianism that Maurras packaged with it. He enunciated a gospel of the threefold tradition by which he said modern man might be saved from the anarchism of materialist democracy. This tradition, *classique, catholique, monarchique*–in the words of a 1913 commentary in the *Nouvelle Revue Française*, to which Eliot was a subscriber–provided social sanctions to enforce with the hand of authority the discipline requisite for classicism. Unlike the power-hungry Maurras, Eliot envisioned in these gifts of tradition a potential sane wholeness for the life of man. Maurras was appealing to tradition in the cause of restoring political authoritarianism through monarchy; he was not a Catholic, nor even a believer, and used Catholicism as a "front." In 1926 the Vatican condemned his movement and put *L'Action française* on the Index. But his rhetoric came over to Eliot in the interim as a message of hope for a world become irresponsibly at war within itself. Society, splintered into a diversity of factions and sects, that is to say foci of untruth, had faith only in the causes of its disease–Rousseau-like individualism, pluralism, democracy. Eliot saw that Babbitt's classic optimism, his trust in reason, yielded no cure for a moral disorder afflicting all of mankind, because it ignored the real nature of man–his fatal inheritance of Original Sin. Ronald Schuchard, in a 1973 article

in *PMLA*, set forth an abundance of circumstantial evidence suggesting Eliot's familiarity, as early as 1915-1916, with the classicism of T. E. Hulme, which evangelizes a secular version of this Christian dogma. Hulme, like Babbitt, found romanticism at fault and called for a new absolutism which should impose order upon society as upon literature and heroically sweep away the false freedoms of romantic individualism. Eliot gave a series of Oxford extension lectures in the fall of 1916 on modern French literature and probably incorporated in them, as Schuchard argues, ideas from Hulme as well as very obvious ideas from Maurras and Babbitt. Schuchard quotes a key passage from one lecture in which Eliot speaks of the twentieth-century return to classicism in France. There he characterizes the "ideals of classicism" as *"form* and *restraint* in art, *discipline* and *authority* in religion, *centralization* in government"; and he adds: "A classicist in art and literature will be likely to adhere to a monarchical form of government, and to the Catholic Church." This of France.

Eliot's references to Catholicism in the period go back to Maurras, not of course to Hulme, who recalls Thomas Hobbes. Eliot's attraction to Catholicism was abstract and for other people, in a country such as France with a current Catholic tradition; it was moreover only a cultural interest, just as the interest of Maurras and Hulme was. Like classicism, but more than classicism for him, Catholicism was part of cultural politics. Had he entertained any spiritual interest in it, that would have eclipsed this political interest; and this interest precluded spiritual interest. Having once lost his faith as a young man, he never regained it until his conversion to Anglo-Catholicism. Writers who do not believe in Eliot's conversion tend to become confused by his remarks about Catholicism at an earlier date. Especially there is *no* convincing indication that he was racked with religious perplexities in youth; he sought certitude in philosophy, was hindered by pessimism and skepticism from finding it there, and at the beginning of the 1920s looked speculatively at Buddhism (which had fueled his pessimism), but the evidence points to no serious engagement with the possibilities of Christian mysticism or of Christianity as a personal faith.

It was Babbitt, Eliot pointed out in *To Criticize the Critic* (1965), who in 1927 advised him to "come out into the open" about his recent conversion. He did so in 1928 in the preface to his essay collection *For Lancelot Andrewes:* "The general point of view [of the essays] may be described as classicist in literature, royalist in politics, and anglo-catholic in religion. I am quite aware that the first term is completely vague, and easily lends itself to clap-trap; I am aware that the second term is at present without definition, and easily lends itself to what is almost worse than clap-trap, I mean temperate conservatism; the third term does not rest with me to define." The consternation of many readers at this announcement is not quite done with; the phrase "royalist in politics" (which, after sixty years, it may be presumptuous to suggest is only an oxymoron) still strikes some as displaying ignorance of twentieth-century British politics, despite the clarifying and scarifying remark about "temperate conservatism." It was a momentous announcement, not (except obliquely) a tribute to Charles Maurras and his threefold tradition but still perhaps an acknowledgment to him. Some months before, in the *Criterion*, Eliot had said in print that though he did not suppose "that the study of the work of Maurras or of the files of the *Action Française* could by itself make a Christian of anybody," nevertheless, "where genuine religious influences are at work also, or where there is any religious potency in the individual soul, they will be powerfully advanced." If Maurras helped convert him to Anglo-Catholicism, the timing was almost as strange as the event. Eliot's royalism, as Bernard Bergonzi pointed out in his 1972 study *T. S. Eliot*, casts an eye back to the seventeenth century. It is very different in reference therefore from Maurras's monarchism; and Eliot's Anglo-Catholicism, standing at the climactic position in the sentence, has attained the place of honor that Maurras would have accorded to monarchism. It had that place for Eliot. To the writer on Eliot's classicism, the preface to *For Lancelot Andrewes* brings a differently momentous announcement: that, not in the theoretical way in which the threefold tradition of Maurras could be viewed but in the intimacy of the spiritual life, Eliot was prepared to accommodate classicism and Christianity.

The alliance was not easy, and though it never really collapsed, the cogency of classicism for Eliot was diminished as time went on. The same principles of order and discipline held good as before; but tradition and authority in their religious aspect came to dominate their literary context. With religious faith as a positive standard, it ceased to be important whether in the arts Jean-Jacques Rousseau exerted a baneful in-

fluence. As early as June 1928, before issuing *For Lancelot Andrewes*, Eliot commented on Julien Benda's criticism that Maurras's neoclassicism was "itself a phase of romanticism": "I think [Benda] is right, though the charge does not seem to me to be nearly as deadly as he seems to suppose" (quoted by Howarth). Here was a long foreshadowing of the obiter dictum in *What is a Classic?* (1945) that "classic" and "romantic" were "a pair of terms belonging to literary politics"–something always known but not readily admitted when classicism flew from the masthead. In Eliot's *After Strange Gods* (1934) the downgrading of the conflict between classic and romantic, in view of the (temporarily) looming importance of literary orthodoxy, brought out a sense of tradition as a "largely" unconscious complement to the conscious maintenance of orthodoxy, and a sense of the concepts "romantic" and "classic" as "both more limited in scope and less definite in meaning." Even with his virtual abandonment of the idea of literary orthodoxy, Eliot never recovered for the concept of classicism in his prose the former vitality that had made it an article of literary faith. In the upshot, he came very close to losing interest in the classics of Greece and Rome, even in Virgil, the classical poet he best appreciated, except in so far as they presaged the Christian dispensation.

A promise to define Eliot's idea of classicism against a broad historical background obliges me to look beyond the crowded foreground of textual citations and identifiable direct models. Happily for this purpose a recognized source of data on eighteenth- and nineteenth-century classicism exists in the scholarship of Arthur O. Lovejoy, whose work moreover parallels Eliot's classicism in time and so requires no interpretative adjustments for possible changes in knowledge or opinion since the 1920s and 1930s. It provides for the period a "state of the art" philosophical summary of what classicism, and also romanticism, had come to mean prior to the present century. Lovejoy's papers on aspects of this large topic, as collected in *Essays in the History of Ideas* (1948), range in date from as early as 1916 to 1940; and the two papers most useful to the present inquiry, "On the Discrimination of Romanticisms" (1923) and "The Parallel of Deism and Classicism" (1930), may be seen to straddle the completion of two stages in Eliot's thinking on classicism, the one before conversion and the other after. Had Eliot followed academic scholarship, he might have found in Lovejoy certain guidelines for his use of terms such as "romantic" and "tradition." That unquestionably he knew nothing of Lovejoy's writings when they first appeared ensures the independence of their authority.

Now there is a principle widely regarded as basic to the history of ideas and adopted in the work of Lovejoy, that at any period prevailing philosophies of art are closely related to the contemporary philosophies of nature and to religion. In other words, attitudes toward various cultural enterprises tend to form a cluster and to become assimilated. This idea, as Jewel Spears Brooker reveals in her *Dictionary of Literary Biography* entry on T. E. Hulme (*British Poets, 1880-1914*, edited by Donald E. Stanford), is exemplified in Hulme's philosophy. An obvious corollary to the idea is that whatever enterprises dominate the mind of an epoch will tend to extend their domination philosophically, so that minor enterprises conform. Medieval religion (a dominant enterprise) and medieval art (a minor one) illustrate this point. In the history of ideas revolutions and counterrevolutions occur, and also the clusters may change their composition–as when a philosophy of art leaves religion and attaches itself to science. Something like this process may be seen in the formation of Maurras's threefold tradition of classicism, Catholicism, and monarchism. By seventeenth-century standards classicism was compatible with the French monarchy and its self-image and enjoyed an accommodation with the Catholic religion; but by eighteenth-century standards, those of the Enlightenment, a "purer" classicism insisted on disengagement from both. Much of the strangeness of Maurras's classicism and of Eliot's in turn results from thinking a cluster incongruous when really it manifests a possible throwback.

Certainly the more familiar version of classicism, that which stems from the Enlightenment, is one to make Eliot's version startle the conventionally educated. What one is likely to think of, especially if conversant with eighteenth-century English literature, is a classicism allied to deism or at least clustered with it, such as that detailed by Lovejoy in the second of the two papers cited. That the philosophers led the poets, rather than the other way about, seems evident enough; but the common alliance against religion, though desultory, and against authority, though ambiguous, had ancient bonds. Lovejoy itemizes nine distinguishable elements in deism which he finds replicated in classical theory. They are worth repeating, even though some of them have no great relevance to the classicism professed by Eliot; for in principle they contradict everything about it that touches on religion or any kind of superior authority. Partly because of their severely theoretical nature, they also contradict some of the practical precepts of Babbitt. In Lovejoy's terminology or as paraphrased they come down to the following: (1) *Uniformitarianism*–in aesthetics the quality of being comprehended and appreciated universally. (2) *Rationalistic individualism*–in aesthetics the equal value, for judging, of the unprejudiced feelings of all. (3) *The appeal to the "consensus gentium"*–in aesthetics the acceptance and imitation of what pleases everyone, i.e. the classics. (4) *Cosmopolitanism*–in aesthetics the rejection of national peculiarities. (5) *Antipathy to "enthusiasm" and originality*–in aesthetics the same antipathy (elite criticisms by the "connoisseur" being inconsistent). (6) *Intellectual equalitarianism*–in aesthetics the determination of artistic merit by democratic common sense. (7) *Rationalistic anti-intellectualism*–in aesthetics the avoidance of complex design and abstruseness. (8) *Rationalistic primitivism*–in aesthetics the view of the most ancient literary models as most "natural" and worthy of imitation. (9) *A negative philosophy of history*–in aesthetics the rejection of all supposed improvements in the arts. According to Lovejoy, this final element corresponded to the deist's rejection of revealed religion, as a false advance upon natural religion. The common denominator of all these elements was antitraditionalism, because tradition muddies nature, the clear spring of common sense; and antiauthoritarianism (in the arts as in philosophy), because no authority exists but common sense. That no artist or critic ever lived up to these rules goes without saying; and great allowances have to be made for the twentieth-century writer's awareness that equalitarian "universal suffrage" simply does not work for either. But the twentieth-century classicist, freed no doubt from the assumptions of deism, tailors his doctrine to the enterprise–be it monarchism or supernatural religion–that he believes rightly dominant, and his classicism takes that form.

The antiromanticism of Babbitt, a reaction against the "originality" licensed by Rousseau, relates to only one of the romanticisms distinguished by Lovejoy in the other paper cited. A different romanticism, German romanticism as it issued from Friedrich von Schiller and Friedrich Schlegel, took for its norm not the "nature" of Rousseau's faith in the feelings, "wild" nature, but rather an ideal of complex imaginative artificiality, anti-primitivistic and avid for "perpetual self-transcendence." From this was born the nineteenth century's incessant preoccupation with art form, the twentieth century's metamorphoses into art of the aberrations of the psyche. The chapter has yet to be written that will trace Eliot's development back to its origins in this enormous labyrinth, or reconcile it with a classicism that held rigorously to an "impersonal" art. And by what standard of classicism any art is to be judged, this essay does not pretend to decide. For Eliot to have dodged the perfervid primitivism of a D. H. Lawrence and to have immersed himself for example in the socio-scientific primitivism of Sir James Frazer and Sigmund Freud, Lovejoy's "rationalistic primitivism," speaks for a classical orientation in his own terms not to be denied by the casual bandying of such a term as "romanticism." Semantically of course this fact is unimportant; his classicism grappled to itself both tradition and Christianity, and not in the mode of cultural politics alone, in some measure thus "to purify the dialect of the tribe."

T. S. Eliot the Religious Poet

Ann P. Brady
Gustavus Adophus College

The hint half guessed, the gift half understood . . .

T. S. Eliot is a great religious poet. His stature rests both in the splendid quality of his verse and the surpassing elevation and sincerity of the religious experience it expresses. Writing on poetic drama for *Adam International* in November 1949, Eliot commented on human experience: "Beyond the verge of the nameable, classifiable emotions and motives of our usual conscious life, there is a fringe of indefinite extent, of feelings and emotions, which we can only see, so to speak, out of the corner of the eye, or in moments of accidental detachment from action." These elusive moments are glimpsed in *Burnt Norton* (1936) and their absence lamented: "Quick now, here, now, always–/Ridiculous the waste sad time/Stretching before and after." This transcendent experience is to Eliot the highest form of reality. For humankind, to move into the acceptance of reality is to attain its fulfillment–"the still

point," the state of "concentration without elimination," the condition of greatest intensity of experience. The meaning of these timeless moments breaking into time is pondered and explored in the whole of *Four Quartets* (1936-1942), one of the great poetic achievements of the century, a work the poet himself, in a 1959 interview for *Paris Review* (Spring/Summer 1959), considered his best, the one on which his reputation would stand or fall. Indeed, the whole body of T. S. Eliot's poetry from *Ara Vos Prec* (1920) moves inexorably toward the refining Dantean fire that crowns *Four Quartets*, to become one with the rose of celestial love.

Religious poetry had always interested Eliot, and he has had much to say on the subject. His most illuminating observations, however, are not to be found in his more overt and exclusive pronouncements on religion and literature. Like so many of his critical nuggets, some of his most engaging insights on religious poetry are scattered throughout his literary essays. Though his comments are numerous, Eliot's theory is consistent and his expectations persistent, so that a judicious sampling can suffice to represent his concerns. While analyzing, praising, and censuring poets who interest him, Eliot formulates his criteria for expressing religious sensibility. The foundation for all religious poetry, he says, must be sincerity (*sine*, "without"; *cera*, "wax"–from the custom of using wax to mask the flaws in shoddy sculpture). Writing about George Herbert for the 12 March 1932 *Spectator*, Eliot, in his most definitive and nuanced statement, notes the pitfalls involved in writing religious verse, into which Herbert never falls:

All poetry is difficult, almost impossible to write: and one of the great permanent causes of error in writing poetry is the difficulty of distinguishing between what one really feels and what one would like to feel, and between the moments of genuine feelings and the moments of falsity. This is a danger in all poetry: but it is a particularly grave danger in the writing of devotional verse. Above that level of attainment of the spiritual life, below which there is no desire to write religious verse, it becomes extremely difficult not to confuse, accomplishment with intention, a condition at which one merely aims with the condition in which one actually lives, what one would be with what one is: and verse which represents only good intentions is worthless—on that plane, indeed, a betrayal. The greater the elevation, the finer becomes the difference between sincerity and insincerity, between reality and unattained aspiration.

Thirty years later, in a pamphlet, *George Herbert* (1962), Eliot still praises this poet for never being guilty of "pious insincerity."

To avoid confusion, Eliot, in *For Lancelot Andrewes* (1928), calls attention to his use of the word "devotional" to describe certain poets because the word "religious" is so abused, and he goes on to define: "Devotional poetry is religious poetry which falls within an exact faith and has precise objects for contemplation." Eliot's own religious poetry falls under such definition, for he is a Christian poet with strong faith and strong religious sensibility. Christianity is an incarnational religion, viewing the material universe as created by and through God's Word (John 1: 1-5) and mediating that Word to humankind—what Eliot comes to define as "grace dissolved in place." Though it calls for asceticism to empty out the selfish to receive the divine Word, it is a discipline of affirmation, a purification of self, never a denial of the value of God's creation. In an essay entitled "The Beatrician Vision" in *The Poetry of Search and the Poetry of Statement* (1963), Dorothy Sayers succinctly points out: "Where Christianity is concerned, a total retreat from the material world is not merely heretical but impossible; for the central Christian doctrine is precisely that of God incarnate in matter, its central act of worship the bodily receiving of God's substance in the sacrament of bread and wine, and its unique eschatological expectation the Resurrection of the Flesh." Its chief commandment is to unselfish love (*caritas, agape*) manifested and exemplified in the life of Jesus Christ, whose ministry was one of material mercy leading to spiritual liberation, whose respect for and celebration of life are manifest in his definition of his own mission: "I am come that they may have life, and that they might have it more abundantly" (John 10: 10).

One of the great universal qualities of Eliot as a Christian poet, moreover, is his ability to accommodate the lessons of the great literature of Asia to his own faith. Not that Eliot makes a gummy amalgam of East and West. His absorption of the values of detachment, disinterested action, from the *Bhagavad-Gita* are familiar principles of Christian asceticism leading to unselfish love so powerfully articulated by the great poet-mystic St. John of the Cross, whom Eliot celebrates in *Ash-Wednesday* (1930) and *Four Quartets*. Like Dante and John of the Cross, Eliot, as poet,

does not follow the dualism of the Negative Way. As Helen Gardner points out in *The Composition of Four Quartets* (1978), what is unique in Eliot is not a blind assimilation of the Eastern tradition, but a selection of transformation of ideas compatible with the sacramental materialism of Christianity. Thus his poetry is enormously enriched and universalized by his knowledge and use of Eastern literature. In the mature Christianity of Eliot, East and West coalesce. But the seeds are already there in *The Waste Land* (1922), long before the poet's conversion to Christianity, and these seeds serve to nourish the authenticity of the religious poetry.

The "Ariel Poems," which began to appear in 1927, mark the poet's spiritual "sea-change," culminating in the poignantly resplendent dream-vision of *Ash-Wednesday*, and spilling over into the heart-piercing beauty of *Marina* (1930), where one sees a world transformed. These poems diffuse an experience of restoration resulting in a surpassing gratuitous joy channeled through intercession whereby one learns that love, fortunately, can never be earned. Words of *The Elder Statesman* three decades later (1959) attempt to summarize the feeling: "In spite of everything, in defiance of reason,/I have been brushed by the wing of happiness." These poems of conversion embody a tone of serene joy and homely comfort never again to be absent from Eliot's poetry, and which will fructify in his masterpiece, *Four Quartets*.

The incarnational idea of "grace dissolved in place" reaches its most transcendent, because most immanent, expression in *Four Quartets*. All four are sacramental, each poem celebrating its particular place as a channel of divine revelation, and its moments of time as vehicles of eternal life. In speaking of what his own craft owes to Dante in *To Criticize the Critic* (1965), Eliot notes that *The Divine Comedy*, by expressing every emotion that humankind is capable of experiencing, is "A constant reminder to the poet, of the obligation to explore, to find words for the inarticulate, to capture those feelings which people can hardly even feel, because they have no words for them; and at the same time, a reminder that the explorer beyond the frontiers of ordinary consciousness will only be able to return and report to his fellow citizens, if he has all the time a firm grasp on the realities with which they are already acquainted." Certainly this formulation of the poet's obligation is borne out in the composition of *Four Quartets*, where Eliot expresses feelings "hardly, barely" expressible in human language, yet does so through a firm hold on the realities of ordinary time and place.

Such polar qualities fit Eliot as a poet of incarnation and as a poet nonpareil of *the* Incarnation. Among modern poets he is unsurpassed. Only Gerard Manley Hopkins's sprung coils of vibrating awe in "The Wreck of the Deutchland" or "The Windhover" express so powerfully the height and depth of the central Christian mystery. And Eliot's quiet, serene, humble contemplation in *Four Quartets* gives another perspective entirely. In the excitement of religious conversion the poet of *Ash-Wednesday* asks, in a half-articulated prayer to Mary at the end of part IV, to be shown the fruit of her womb, and is answered by the wonderful tour de force reflection on the Word which opens part V, spinning, punning, gyrating, almost inebriated in the joy of the Dantean revelation: "Against the Word the unstilled world still whirled/About the centre of the silent Word." In *Burnt Norton* the Incarnation persists as the still and everlasting light at "the still point of the turning world." In *The Dry Salvages* (1941) the "Perpetual angelus" announcing the Incarnation hovers maternally over the sea of life with its waves of calamity or halcyon calm.

The Incarnation informs and animates the world of *Four Quartets* with its concentric meditations on time. But the way Eliot approaches the mystery is so anchored in the homely, the unheroic responsibilities of human life that the poem conveys a humility befitting the subject. The great meditation on the Word in part V of *The Dry Salvages* is prepared for in the humble, frustrated consideration of the poet's craft in the corresponding movements of *Burnt Norton*, where he finds that "Words strain/crack and sometimes break, under the burden," and in *East Coker* (1940) where he comes to realize that "every attempt/is a wholly new start, and a different kind of failure." In the midst of these unostentatious reflections on the craft of using words breaks the Incarnational moment of *The Dry Salvages*, "the moment in and out of time" where one perceives the ineffable divine visitation as "music heard so deeply/that it is not heard at all, but you are the music/While the music lasts." He understands that a constant state of apprehension of this inbreak of eternity into time is "an occupation for the saint . . . something given and taken in a lifetime's death in love," and this is beyond most of us whose perceptions at best "are only hints and guesses,/Hints followed by guesses." In among these apparitionary intimations breaks the veiled revelation,

> The hint half guessed, the gift half understood,
>   is Incarnation.
> Here the impossible union.
> Of spheres of existence is actual,
> Here the past and future
> Are conquered, and reconciled . . .

sending us back to look for the Incarnation in the shaft of sunlight, the waterfall, the wild thyme under our feet–the places of earth, "Grace dissolved in place." After trying to capture the Incarnational vision in the third quartet, the poet returns in part V of *Little Gidding* (1942) to a calm, humble perception that "every phrase/And sentence that is right" is "where every word is at home,/Taking its place to support the others"– the modest striving for perfection of the life in the life's work.

Four Quartets is a supreme achievement; nevertheless, for all their loftiness, the poems are imbued with a kind of "divine levity" that can make Eliot's lines sparkle. The field mouse that trots across the wainscot in part I of *East Coker* amid the oracular passage on the rise and fall of houses echoing Ecclesiastes, and who gets breathed in as an essential part of a house along with the wall and wainscot in the solemn descanting lyric on the death of the four elements in part II of *Little Gidding* is a whimsical presence. Whimsical too is Eliot's use of the nonce-word "grimpen" in tribute to Sherlock Holmes in the midst of a passage exploring the relation of wisdom and humility in part II of *East Coker*. And what are the "Chairmen of many committees" and "The Directory of Directors" doing in a passage beginning with the impassioned echo of *Samson Agonistes* and ending with an echo of *The Ascent of Mount Carmel*? Many of his most serious passages are interrupted by the voice of Old Possum refusing to take the self seriously while oddly reinforcing the seriousness of the insight struggling to be conveyed. The cosmic lyric of part II of *East Coker* is followed by the comment, "That was a way of putting it–not very satisfactory." And in the third movement in the midst of his elevated paraphrase of St. John of the Cross, and immediately following the lovely inbreak of the timeless moment, he inserts the self-parody, "You say I am repeating/Something I have said before. I shall say it again./Shall I say it again?" These interruptions are temperamentally functional to a poet striving for "the wisdom of humility," whose contentment will be to nourish with his own life "the life of significant soil" (*Dry Salvages*, V). There is moral elevation and spiritual liberation in these poems when we are bid not to "fare well,/But fare forward," and not to think of the fruit of action (*Dry Salvages*, III). It is enormously consoling to be told that "Most of us . . . are only undefeated/Because we have gone on trying" (*Dry Salvages*, V), and that "For us, there is only the trying. The rest is not our business" (*East Coker*, V). In his use of "us" and "most of us," Eliot always identifies the speaker with the ordinary person, not the saint, and yet this ordinary person is given the penetrating spiritual insight to discern the difference between detachment and indifference, wisdom and fear, love and possession.

The themes are crafted as music with continual resolution. The unexplained moments of *Burnt Norton* grow into the "lifetime burning in every moment" of *East Coker*, to the "moment in and out of time" mediated in *The Dry Salvages*, and culminating in the vision of history as "a pattern/Of timeless moments" in *Little Gidding*. The "unprayable/Prayer at the calamitous annunciation" emerges as "the hardly, barely prayable/Prayer of the one Annunciation" (*Dry Salvages*, II). Indeed *Four Quartets* is a celebration of Incarnation, and Eliot deserves praise for being able, like Dante, to "realize the inapprehensible in visual images" ("Dante," *Selected Essays*). Precisely because of this the poems have an appeal for those who do not share his belief. What Eliot says of Herbert's *The Temple* applies as well to *Four Quartets:* "These poems form a record of spiritual struggle which should touch the feeling, and enlarge the understanding of those readers also who hold no religious belief and find themselves unmoved by religious emotion." Eliot notes that the great religious poets of English literature are specialists who can do nothing else. In this respect, Eliot is more in the tradition of his greatest mentor, Dante, who "because he could do everything else, is for that reason the greatest 'religious' poet, though to call him a 'religious' poet would be to abate his universality."

Four Quartets is a stunning coalescence of Eliot's previous poems. The "heart of light" refused in the hyacinth garden of *The Waste Land* is proffered in the rose garden of *Burnt Norton* and confirmed in the resolution of the "crowned knot of fire" in *Little Gidding*. The "multifoliate rose" rejected by "The Hollow Men" blossoms into "the Garden/Where all loves end" in *Ash-Wednesday*

and becomes one with the fire of love in the last quartet. In praising Dante, Eliot says a great poet should be able not only to perceive and distinguish the colors or sounds of ordinary experience but should feel vibrations beyond the range of ordinary people. The poet should be able to make others "see and hear more at each end than they could ever see without his help" (*To Criticize the Critic*). In *Four Quartets* he opens that spectrum for us and marks himself as a great religious poet, "one of those which one can only just hope to grow up to at the end of life" ("Dante," *Selected Essays*).

Eliot, Buddhism, and The Middle Way

Cleo McNelly Kearns
Princeton Theological Seminary

T. S. Eliot maintained a lifelong interest in Indic philosophy and religion, drawing in his poetry both upon the ancient cultural traditions of Hinduism, extending back to the Vedas and the Upanishads, and upon thought and imagery associated with Buddhism. Eliot's curiosity about Indic traditions was first aroused by Edwin Arnold's *The Light of Asia* (1879), a popular poem on the life of Buddha which he discovered in his boyhood and for which he "preserved a warm affection" all his life. In his formal studies at Harvard he encountered sharper, more scholarly distinctions and interpretations, first under Irving Babbitt, and later, as a graduate student in philosophy, with Charles Lanman and James Woods. These men taught Pali, Prakrit, and Sanskrit within a broad philosophical context. Their work was made easier by the respect and attention that had been given Indic philosophy and religion by Harvard's major figures in philosophy, William James, George Santayana, and Josiah Royce, all of whom influenced the development of Eliot's mind and work. Eliot's Indic studies bore fruit in crucial material for *The Waste Land* (1922) and *Four Quartets* (1936-1942), often in images which have parallels within Christian tradition; sometimes the two traditions could be seen as corresponding and easily harmonized, sometimes not.

A major example of Eliot's use of Indic traditions both to enrich and to call into question Western ideas and modes of thought occurs in part

III of *The Waste Land*. Here he draws on the Buddha's Fire Sermon (which, as Eliot notes, "corresponds in importance to the Sermon on the Mount"), both for the title of the section and for one of its primary allusions. The Fire Sermon (found in Henry Clarke Warren's 1896 *Buddhism in Translations*, a collocation of early Buddhist texts from the Pali canon, which Eliot had used in his studies) was reputedly so intense that it prompted sudden enlightenment in its first auditors. It presents, with mounting intensity, the fires in which all humans burn, fires of sense, vanity, lust, hatred, or attraction, even the fire of the workings of the mind itself. This fire generates at once both suffering and liberation. To change in a moment from one to the other it need only be recognized for what it is: the fundamental and inescapable condition of experience in this world. As Eliot put it, in a moment Dantesque as well as Buddhist, "We only live, only suspire/ Consumed by either fire or fire" (*Little Gidding*, IV).

In *The Waste Land* Eliot brings the Buddhist fire into conjunction with St. Augustine's sensual burning in Carthage. The "collocation," to use Eliot's word, of these representatives of Eastern and Western asceticism, the Buddha and St. Augustine, is "not an accident," yet a collocation is not an identity. In so far as this textual conjunction brings into play the Buddhist way, it implies a rejection of what would be seen as rather primitive notions of guilt and expiation, in favor of a far more radical detachment from, even elimination of, all illusory categories of subject and object, self or soul, and other or God. This process of elimination is enacted in the syntax of the poem, from which the grammatical categories of subject and object are gradually deleted to leave behind only the gerund, "burning." In so far as it represents the Christian way, however, even in its most negative form, it implies both the persistence of the (guilty) self and the intrusive, even violent intervention of a savior: "O Lord Thou pluckest me out/O Lord Thou pluckest/burning." Both of these points of view, in part *because* of their very contradiction, contribute to the pain of that fire. The Buddhist dimension helps to generate a view of physical, psychological, and spiritual pain not comprehended if we confine ourselves to the Christian context of the poem.

Eliot's other allusions to Indic texts and traditions provide not only a supplement to Christian insights but a radical and sometimes relativizing second perspective on them, generating by their differences new and more extensive points of view. To take only one example of this effect: Eliot often explores in his poetry the concept of a cycle of lives, each harvesting the fruit of the previous one in a series of returns, punctuated by brief interim periods in which the soul is forced to contemplate its inadequate past and self-ordained future, without, however, the power to alter what it has done. This "in-between state," with its attendant horrors, including the prospect of endless repetition, haunts Eliot's verse, creating numerous Gothic effects. It offers, certainly, very little of the spurious comfort frequently attached to popular notions of reincarnation. It is present in the weary "time for a hundred visions and revisions" contemplated in "The Love Song of J. Alfred Prufrock," in the living death represented by Tiresias in *The Waste Land*, and most markedly in the revelation at the end of *Little Gidding* (1942), where the soul, peregrine in a twilight zone between two worlds, reenacts its failures with hallucinatory and painful vividness. This concept of an in-between or temporary state of recollection after death is reminiscent of course of Christian concepts of purgatory, and gives Eliot's frequent references to Dante's *Purgatorio* a darker twist. It lends special poignancy to Arnaut Daniel's request, alluded to at the end of *The Waste Land*, "bethink you in time of my pain." Here again, however, it is the differences which count and make the two points of view qualify one another. While both Christian and Indic traditions affirm a possible salvation from an endless round of consequences, salvation depends in Christian thought always upon the intervention of the divine. In the most rigorous and learned of Hindu and Buddhist traditions, however, it depends ultimately on the intense, ego-breaking efforts of the self alone. The traditions, logically opposed, are brought together as poetry for the intensity generated by their contradictions. It is as if two poles of a magnet were held by force together.

Eliot's Buddhist readings were primarily in Theravada or early sources and concentrated less on mystical, theological, and philosophical matters than on the human story of a man horrified by the suffering of the world and determined to solve its riddle. The Buddha's enlightenment derives not from superhuman austerities or the intervention of extraterrestrial beings, but from a sudden grasp of the radical insubstantiality of all existence. Because of his eventual rejection of the extreme asceticism of many contemporary Hindu sages, the Buddha's way of approaching ultimate truth came to be called the Middle Way, a phrase Eliot was to employ, not without reference to the Anglican via media, as well as to his own middle age, in *East Coker* (1940).

Irving Babbitt, Eliot's great mentor, stressed the temperance of this Middle Way in his own presentation of Buddhism. His essay "Buddha and the Occident" (most easily found in his posthumously published translation of the *Dhammapada*, 1936) argues, sometimes polemically, the case for early or Theravada over later or Mahayana traditions in Buddhist thought. Babbitt calls the Mahayana schools, with their accretion of multiple divinities, metaphysical debates, esoteric practices, and concatenated mythologies, a form of "extravagant theosophy" and reminds his readers that what he takes to be the earliest Buddhist sources show no traces of this supposed degeneration into mystification. Instead, they teach a liberation from selfishness and from the fear of death through reliance on inner discipline, restraint, and self-control. The Buddha taught his disciples to be "refuges unto themselves," a turning inward which leads to an impersonal strength beyond the need of either ritual or romance. Eliot's famous theory of impersonality, as I have argued in my *T. S. Eliot and Indic Traditions: A Study in Poetry and Belief* (1987), owes much to Babbitt's view of Buddhism, as does his estimation of that quality he called, in a 1921 essay on Andrew Marvell, "wit's internal equilibrium." The point of intersection between Buddhism and Christianity lay for Eliot, as for Babbitt, in the emphasis in both traditions on disciplined meditation.

The same emphasis on peaceful meditation may be found as well in the older Hindu tradition, and the steps toward its attainment are analyzed with clinical precision and practical insight in Patanjali's great treatise, the *Yoga-sutras*, which Eliot studied under Woods at Harvard. The word which best sums up this dynamic peace is the Sanskrit *shantih*, which is at once a technical term in Hindu philosophical tradition for the ultimate realization of the oneness of all things; a mantra, or set of sound-syllables believed upon silent repetition to engender the quality (in this case peace) to which it refers; and the formulaic ending to an Upanishad or sacred discourse. For Eliot, this single word indicates the essence of Indic tradition; of it, the Western "Peace which passeth understanding" is, as Eliot noted, an inadequate translation. When, then, Eliot chooses to conclude *The Waste Land* with the triple repetition

of *shantih*, he is calling into play the ultimate goal of the poem's difficult, disturbed, and distracted meditation, reminding us of the distance, in time, space, language, and frame of reference, between the modern world and that goal, and invoking, with a certain qualified immediacy, its real presence in the poem. He is, moreover, remarkably, redefining his own poem as a kind of Upanishad, a sacred and prophetic utterance in a canon as yet unclosed.

A similar complex and multifaceted use is made in *The Waste Land* of one of the thirteen major Upanishads, the *Brihadaranyaka*, which recounts a parable: three types of creatures—humans, demons, and gods—approach Prajapati, the embodiment of divine wisdom, with ultimate questions about the nature of being. Each group hears in the voice of revelation, the thunder's *Da*, a different answer: *datta*, give; *dayadhyam*, sympathize; and *damyata*, control (yourself). To each interpretation the thunder replies with the great affirmative sound-syllable *Om*, which implies a confirmation of their different, yet true and sufficient insights. Eliot provides within the poem a gloss for each of the three terms, indicating not simply the necessity of, but the dangers associated with, each. Give, he suggests, yes, but giving may be either genuine surrender and sacrifice or mere seduction. Sympathize, yes, but the effort to get inside another's experience, at least through any kind of ratiocinative process, may merely confirm the philosophical solipsism into which our pride and obsession with finding the keys to other minds often leads. Control, yes, but at times we recognize too late that our or another's heart "would have responded" even gaily to "controlling hands" only when the moment to exercise that control has passed.

The *Brihadaranyaka* Upanishad provides a crucial point of recall to essential and universal ethical truths, but the poem must recognize and record as well the modern inability to respond adequately to this challenge. Renouncing as they mostly do any concept of a mediator, this and other Indic traditions alluded to in *The Waste Land* thus present a particularly sharp and disturbing challenge to easy consolations of, or easy interpretations of, Christian mediation. They seem to demand simultaneously the highest level of selfless sacrifice and spiritual transcendence and the most pragmatic charity and common sense and yet offer no set of steps to move from one to another. Their difference, their distance, is marked within the poem by their linguistic strangeness as well as by their thematic content. *The Waste Land* reminds us that many bridges, literal and figurative, are falling down, including some always regarded within Western culture as secure. Hence the poem's deferred *shantih* is dependent, not on the precision of the concept of "peace" to which it refers, nor on any external guarantees of doctrine or identities of meaning, but purely on the depth and intensity of the meditation on very difficult contradictions that precedes it.

His years at Harvard introduced Eliot to a number of crucial concepts and texts besides those of the Fire Sermon, *shantih*, and the *Brihadaranyaka* Upanishad. These included the *Bhagavad-Gita*, Patanjali's *Yoga-sutras*, the Jatakas and Nikayas (birth tales of the Buddha and stories of Buddhist saints), Buddhaghosa's commentary on the *Anguttara-Nikaya* (an important treatise by a major early Buddhist philosopher), and many of the other texts of the Pali canon collected in Warren's *Buddhism in Translations*. Through the lectures of Masaharu Anesaki, a visiting lecturer at Harvard, Eliot also came to know something of the Mahayana or Far Eastern tradition, including the *Saddharma-pundarika* or Lotus Sutra, as well as the thought of Nagarjuna, whose philosophy has remarkable points of contact with that of the Western late idealist philosopher F. H. Bradley, the subject of Eliot's dissertation.

The extent to which Eliot apprehended Hinduism or Buddhism as religions with real and immediate claims on his personal faith and practice is debatable. Of his work at Harvard he wrote in *After Strange Gods* (1934): "Two years spent in the study of Sanskrit under Charles Lanman and a year in the mazes of Patanjali's metaphysics under the guidance of James Woods, left me in a state of enlightened mystification." To have gone further in understanding Indic thought had seemed to require an effort to "erase" from his mind all the categories of Western philosophy, and this, for reasons "practical as well as sentimental," he had been unwilling to do. Moreover, Eliot tended to shy away from religious points of view where he had little feel for the linguistic base and cultural context.

In accordance with these reservations, Eliot, in his preface to Simone Weil's *The Need for Roots* (1952), distanced himself rather firmly from those who could find their way toward religion only through the so-called Mysterious East, remarking on the mistaken universalism of the position that "ultimate and esoteric truth is one," that

all religions "show some traces of it," and that it is "a matter of indifference" to which we adhere. Yet there are indications that in his early years he had traveled some distance toward Buddhism. Stephen Spender recalls him remarking that at the time of writing *The Waste Land* he almost became a Buddhist. Certainly, the depth of a lifelong preoccupation with Indic sources and traditions is well attested in his poetry, plays, and essays. Following his conversion, Christianity was central, yet Eliot's concern with Buddhism and its Hindu foundations never vanished. It appears in the later plays and, for example, in his interest in the work of Hubert Benoit, a psychiatrist and student of Zen, who wrote several provocative works on meditation and Western psychology, and on whom Eliot drew for his 1933 Norton Lectures, published as *The Use of Poetry and the Use of Criticism*. Beyond these unidentifiable reference points lay a widening circle of reading and practice, which led in turn to a deepening appreciation of the relationships among Buddhism, Hinduism, and Christianity as contemplative ways. (Eliot remarked on some aspects of these relationships in a preface to Nagendranath Gangulee's *Thoughts for Meditation*, in 1951.) This conjunction, however, did not imply for Eliot the identity or blurring of different paths, but precisely a middle way between them, able to appreciate each for the difference it could make to another.

The last explicit allusion to Indic traditions in Eliot's poetry is the extended meditation on the *Bhagavad-Gita* in part III of *The Dry Salvages* (1941). Here, with the casual and low-keyed invocation, "I sometimes wonder if that is what Krishna meant," Eliot introduces an extended gloss on the text he called, in his essay on Dante (1929), "the next greatest philosophical poem to the *Divine Comedy* within my experience." In the Gita, Arjuna, the warrior-hero, pauses on the field of battle, struck with fear of acting wrongly, to seek instruction from Krishna, his charioteer and an incarnation of God. Krishna teaches him the yoga or discipline of active passivity or passive action, a practice of detachment and selflessness which enables Arjuna both to fulfill his destiny on earth and to gain his salvation. The teaching culminates in a revelation of Krishna himself as devouring time, bringing all things to their appointed destruction/consummation.

Eliot gives his interpretation of this great text a specifically Buddhist twist in a single couplet with an off-rhyme which has something of the bite of an early Buddhist aphorism. "You can-

Promotional leaflet for the 1988 revival of Eliot's play about the murder of Saint Thomas à Becket

not face it steadily," he says, "but this thing is sure,/ That time is no healer: the patient is no longer here." The sense of the transience of human subjectivity in these and subsequent lines, and the insistence on the constant destruction of all identities we like to take as certain, are fully consonant with Theravada Buddhism. So is Krishna's counsel on how to manage our middle or "between" state, a state which is, we finally begin to grasp, for Eliot the entire and necessary condition of our life on earth: "Here between the hither and the farther shore/While time is withdrawn, consider the future/And the past with an equal mind." That "equal mind" is the Gita's virtue par excellence, and the centered but moving point of Eliot's own middle way.

Deep-running references to Hindu and Buddhist concepts and images qualify and expand many of the most seemingly transparent passages in *Four Quartets*. When the lotus rises "quietly, quietly" from the empty pool in *Burnt Norton* (1936),

and the "surface glittered out of the heart of light," the resulting vision hovers on the border between perception and projection with a destabilizing ambiguity reminiscent of the most profound doctrines of the Middle Way. These lines evoke at once an illusion, a trick of sunlight making the empty pool look full, and a reality, a glitter no less present for the illusion it creates. Nor is it any accident that the pool is empty, a state regarded in Buddhist teaching as the essential precondition for insight. This Indic dimension, however, is not in any way a "key" to the poem, for such a key, to use a phrase Eliot employed in *The Waste Land*, would only "confirm a prison." Rather, it is an intimation, an intimation like those at the end of *Little Gidding*, "heard, half-heard, in the stillness/Between two waves of the sea." Perhaps all the Indic echoes in Eliot's poems are best heard this way, that is, most effectively heard between the lines, qualifying, resonating, extending, and deepening more obvious intentions and points of view.

Eliot's Plays in the English Theater of the 1980s

Katharine J. Worth
University of London

The 1980s were ushered in on a high note for Eliot the playwright by Michael Elliott's resplendent production of *The Family Reunion* (1939) at the end of the previous decade (Vaudeville Theatre, 19 June 1979, previously at the Round House). No play of Eliot's seen in the English theater since then has drawn the same full-throated chorus of praise as that inspired by Elliott's brilliantly inventive interpretation. Even critics such as Francis King (*Sunday Telegraph*, 22 April 1979), who had doubts about the play ("difficult and sometimes even incomprehensible"), nevertheless were persuaded by the production that this was, though "flawed," an "undoubted masterpiece." Readers were urged to hasten to a performance which perfectly reconciled the "warring elements of poetry and naturalism."

Although the play's arrival at the Vaudeville was a special mark of success for a play in verse, its debut at the Round House in April of the same year provided an even more spectacular demonstration of the freeing effect of the directorial approach. I recall the palpable sense of closeness to the ghostly visitants, the Eumenides, when they entered the scene as shapes infiltrated between audience and actors, menacing the audience as much as the characters in the skeletal frame (on the same level as the audience) that represented Wishwood. This single move succeeded at once in involving the spectators in the nightmare in much the way that Harry (played by Edward Fox) is involved. The audience saw what he saw–or something like it–for who knows what contours each individual would supply to the vast tentlike shapes that suddenly loomed over him. It was the kind of terror William Butler Yeats surely had in mind in his poem, "The Apparitions": "Fifteen apparitions have I seen./The worst, a coat upon a coat-hanger." Perhaps there is nothing there but an empty coat–yet for a moment, by a trick of light, an unexpected angle, the dark part of the mind leaps to a more horrific interpretation. So the audience was inside Harry's "neurosis," understood as Mary cannot when he cries in agony on the first manifestation: "Are you so imperceptive, have you such dull senses/That you could not see them?"

The dark, haunted part of the play, then, came over triumphantly. What even admiring critics found harder to take was the move at the end to a state of redemption. Harry setting off in pursuit of the "bright angels" was found less convincing than Harry tormented by guilt: Eliot's own estimation of his character as an "insufferable prig" was quoted with some approval.

What then of the 1980s? There has been only one London production with a director and actors of a caliber comparable to that seen in *The Family Reunion. The Cocktail Party* (1950) of 1986 did not, however, enjoy the same success. Why that should have been so is a question to pursue, but first it might be useful to see if any general pattern emerges over the decade, any indication of preferences and popularity among the plays. From such a viewpoint *Murder in the Cathedral* (1935) holds the field: it remains the play most faithfully and consistently supported. No doubt this is at least partly due to its attractiveness to the religious "faithful," a phenomenon Eliot himself was not too happy about. He was aware that there could be a danger for him as playwright in the predisposition of audiences attending religious festivals and the like to accept plays on the strength of their content, putting up with boredom in the glow of "feeling that they have done something meritorious" simply by attending. But if such attitudes persist, they seem hardly sufficient to account for the regular revivals of the play, especially by young actors. The most recent London production, by the National Youth Theatre, offered a glowing demonstration of the dramatic vitality that can be tapped by players approaching the work in robust spirit.

If *Murder in the Cathedral* has its own place, the later plays sometimes seem to have won theirs on the strength of widespread interest in the playwright's life, stimulated by Peter Ackroyd's 1984 biography of Eliot and Michael Hastings's play *Tom and Viv*. So at least it might appear from reviewers' notices which have increasingly stressed connections between the life and work, as, for instance, when *The Family Reunion* was produced at the Everyman Theatre, Cheltenham, in 1986. The play was given in a "package" with *Tom and Viv*, thus drawing forth many comments on Eliot's source material. Inevitably reviewers were intrigued by the pairing and were inclined to spell out the links. The reviewer for *Plays and Players* (July 1986) suggested that *The Family Reunion* seems to be Eliot's attempt to find "'an objective correlative' for his own suffering and guilt in that tragic relationship." That Eliot's "attempt" resulted in by far the greater play was not always clear from such accounts, though the comparison with *Tom and Viv* did throw up some interesting sidelights. Hastings's play in fact helps to show just how brilliant was Eliot's achievement in realizing through his dramatic persona, Harry, so much not only of his private agonies but also of the imaginative force that drove and possessed him.

The Tom of *Tom and Viv* is not someone easily conceived of as capable of reaching into his own depths to see "eyes" staring at him "from behind the nightingale's thicket" and of finding the words to open up these experiences. Whether Harry in *The Family Reunion* is seen as prig or wounded being, he is always felt to have the antennae of a poet, and a power over words which can capture things in a graphic phrase, as when he bursts out to the assembled aunts and uncles: "how can you say that nothing is changed?/You all look so withered and young." In Hastings's play Viv (Vivienne Haigh-Wood, Eliot's first wife) is by far the more living and interesting character: there can be no complaint about that; indeed, it was what gave the play its special force. But the character of Tom suffered all the more from a context in which he was so much less strongly imagined than the woman he was set against. And this all served as a reminder of how exceptionally difficult it is to find subtle enough dramatic form to make the figure of a poet convincing on stage–how, indeed, it had needed the dramatic (as well as poetic) gift of Eliot himself.

It is always a problem to know how far criticism of a play in performance stems from inadequate performance or directorial concept, and how far from weaknesses in the play itself. Eliot's own severe comments on *The Family Reunion* must seem nowadays, in the light of Michael Elliott's production, to have been due in large part to failures in stage realizations he was able to see. That same production is evidence, if such is needed, against the speculations advanced by some reviewers that the theater might be the wrong medium for metaphysical speculation, the "fragile metaphysical ideas of human experience within and beyond the framework of time," as the reviewer for *Plays and Players* said of the Cheltenham production of *The Family Reunion*. Whether the director, Terry Wale, was able to draw from his actors performances of the requisite delicacy might perhaps have been the more crucial question. James Woolley's Harry, plunging into the part of "a

man demented at full throttle," clearly had much to learn from Edward Fox's "hooded" style (in the 1979 production) with its upper-class reserve, much colored, as reviewers tended to comment, by his celebrated impersonation of Edward VIII on television. Though there were reservations about Fox's tight-lipped rendering, which some found lacking in flexibility, he succeeded well, to my mind, in suggesting the obsessional anxieties and rages lying beneath the repressed exterior: this made the outbursts all the more forceful.

The Cheltenham production demonstrated, however, through some telling scenic effects, the strength of Eliot's underlying theatrical concepts which inspired them. The frozen group of aunts and uncles, held in a long stasis under the house lights as the audience took their seats, was one such moment. It owed its immediate theatrical power to the director and performers but arose very naturally and easily out of Eliot's fundamentally dramatic vision of a frozen Wishwood where nothing changes except to wither. There seems nowadays a growing awareness, among directors at least, that there are powerful theatrical effects to be drawn from Eliot's texts, that they can, despite earlier skepticism on the point, be handled in a modern way as "scenarios" for a total theater approach. Whether audiences, and in particular, reviewers, are equally open-minded is more doubtful. The expectation of the "holy" that made Eliot squirm, has lingered on. In 1979 the *Stage* reviewer was saying of the production of *The Elder Statesman* (1959) at the Malvern Festival: "Inevitably we approach it reverentially, almost as though we were in church." While a reviewer of *The Confidential Clerk* (1954) at Cheltenham in 1978 found it appropriate to comment: "God plays little part in this play by Eliot's standards" (*Financial Times*, 21 September 1978). The 1980s have seen a change in this respect only inasmuch as people have become conversant with and fascinated by the biographical aspects of the plays: psychology then tends to replace theology as a stock approach.

A move to flexibility has been seen in the growth of adaptations and dramatized anthologies of Eliot's work. *Cats* stands on its own here, a runaway popular success that tapped the comicality and rhythmic sprightliness of the "cat" poems to draw out a full-blooded song-and-dance show. *Cats* was a shock to some admirers of Eliot, though perhaps not to those who saw the program presented at the Globe Theatre in 1965 as a memorial tribute to Eliot and enjoyed its piquant mixture of unlike elements; Groucho Marx reading cat poems, John Dankworth supplying the jazz accompaniment for a sparkling version of *Sweeney Agonistes* with Cleo Laine in full throat as Dusty. Programs presenting readings from the oeuvre in quasi-dramatic form, like the Triple Action Theatre's "anthology" *Baptism* (given in Hull in 1974) seem to be gaining hold. The most recent, *Let us go then, you and I*, presented by three distinguished actors, Eileen Atkins, Edward Fox, and Michael Gough, opened at the Lyric, Hammersmith, in 1986 and had success sufficient to take it the following year to the other Lyric in Shaftesbury Avenue, in the heart of the West End. The theatrical force of so much in Eliot's poetry allowed the actors to present characters as well as poems: Edward Fox, for instance, aroused interest in his departure from upper-class norm into cockney voice in *The Waste Land*, and Eileen Atkins was praised for her ability to suggest feeling "below the line." Even those most meditative and inward poems, *Four Quartets*, were drawn into the theatrical ambience by the claim that this was the first ever "staging" of them.

Nineteen eighty-six was a prime year for Eliot the playwright in the West End theater. Hopes ran high for the production of *The Cocktail Party* presented by the New Theatre Company at the Phoenix Theatre, with an esteemed director, John Dexter, and, as reviewers all agreed, a "cracking cast." Alas, the production failed to fulfill the critics' expectations: with one or two exceptions, there was a general view that the play had not worn well (some, of course, thought that it had never been a satisfactory theater piece). Even a discerning critic who was ready to welcome it as manna after "the trivial pursuits of most West End theatres" joined the chorus of doubt. Michael Billington described his experience of watching the play as "like seeing the dust-sheets removed with a great flourish from some heirloom only to discover that it is chipped and mouldy with age" (*Guardian*, 30 July 1986). Others less prepared to take up a sympathetic position talked about "high flown Anglican poppycock" or groaned, "The latest effort to raise the tone of the West End makes you long for something low and musical" (*Financial Times*, 29 July 1986).

From many of these reactions there does emerge, however, the sense of a theatrical experience which somehow touched a live nerve. The play in fact had the power to make people resentful. There was undoubtedly a resistance to the concept of martyrdom as a "higher" way of life than the compromise position of Edward and Lavinia–this despite the fact that John Dexter played down hierarchical moral attitudes as much as he could. In the consulting-room sequence of act 2, for instance, when Reilly is explaining to Celia that he can "reconcile" her to the human condition and she asks if the common routine he describes is a good life, Alec McOwen as Reilly shouted with an emphasis scarcely in Eliot's original, noncommittal line: "It *is* a good life." And he made the most of an egalitarian emphasis Eliot did provide, rolling out with conviction his answer to Celia's later question about the two "ways," "Which way is better?": "Neither way is better./Both ways are necessary."

Yet it is after all no easy matter to persuade the audience that equal value is set on the two ways–whether by Reilly or by Eliot. Lavinia and Edward are so obviously making "the best of a bad job" that their "way" looks rather low in the order of things. Again, the director made strenuous (some thought overemphasized) efforts to bring out the life-affirming qualities in their relationship by showing Lavinia as unmistakably pregnant in the final scene. Perhaps because Celia was also presented as someone full of life, in fact, richly sensuous, even sexy (another of Dexter's unexpected touches), critics were all the more resistant to the idea of her being sent off to martyrdom.

In a way, then, the attractiveness of the production tended to work against the assumptions about sin and salvation embodied in the play. The cocktail-party world was created with great panache: everything promised entertainment; the arresting set, Art Deco with Vorticist touches, the elegant piano accompaniment to the opening chatter, the full-bodied performances of Robert Eddison and Rachel Kempson as spirited eccentrics, running other people's lives for them. Alec McOwen as a dry, Puck-like Reilly contributed mischievously to the comedy, conveying the sense of some great unexplained joke going on in his own mind with his incipient or barely suppressed laughs and gleeful responses. All this made up a world with obvious connections to the theater conventions of the West End in Eliot's day–the smart thriller, the comedy of Noel Coward and his followers–but offering in its pervasive suggestion of parody the prospect of new and strange developments.

For some critics these never came: instead, the play took a nosedive into improbabilities and sermonizing in the austerely skeletal consulting room that replaced the lush decor of the cocktail-party scene. But there were some for whom the frivolities of the first act functioned as Eliot intended, preparing the way for the revelation in the second act of "Eliot's vastly darker and more ambitious design," as Sheridan Morley put it (*Punch*, 6 August 1986). Sheila Gish, as Celia, triumphed, for these critics, in the intensity of her rendering of spiritual need combined with high intelligence. And despite some reservations here and there about a schoolmasterish element in Alec McOwen's interpretation, he too commanded belief as a person to whom such characters as Edward and Lavinia would listen as he confronts them with unpalatable truths about their incapacity for love.

On the psychological level, as distinct from the spiritual (if the distinction can be made), *The Cocktail Party*, like *The Family Reunion*, stirred up thoughts of *Tom and Viv* and the painful life material which lay in the background of the recriminations of Edward and Lavinia. Despite some puzzlement about the casting of a too-youthful Simon Ward as Edward, his scenes with Sheila Allen, an elegant Lavinia, helped to bring home to those who distrusted the religious element the credibility of the "dark chasms in Eliot's comic structure," as one reviewer expressed it (*Financial Times*, 29 July 1986). The fact that Dexter and McOwen had explored in psychiatric territory before, in Peter Schaffer's *Equus*, tended to make those who knew that more ready to accept Reilly in his psychiatrist persona (though as always there was a reverse side, *Equus* not necessarily striking people as an impressive precedent).

From the glossy, starry *Cocktail Party* of 1986 to the presentation of *Murder in the Cathedral* by the National Youth Theatre in 1987 is in some ways a long step. A company of young beginners does not raise the same expectations as a cast of such tried quality as Dexter assembled. The NYT is known for its high standard, however, and for adeptness in choice of play to suit the special needs and talents of its youthful team. *Murder in the Cathedral*, which they gave at Christ Church, Spitalfields, 13 August 1987, proved an excellent choice for them. The production also stimulated questions about the play, in the way that only a lively and well-thought-out production does.

One obvious reason for the choice of this play was the opportunity it gave to a large number of young actors (over twenty in the two choruses of Women of Canterbury and Monks). The complicated setting in Hawksmoor's beautiful church called for a large stage crew, another plus from the company's point of view. Conversely, the play does not demand mature character acting across a range of types, nor, it could be argued, any psychological subtlety in the presentation of character, since the struggle going on in Becket's mind is expressed in the outwardly simple form of the medieval morality play, as argument and debate among symbolic figures.

It was in this way that the play was seen when the company presented it, to many plaudits. The central character was not the Archbishop, announced one reviewer, but "the faltering, doubting, unruly and impassioned Chorus of Women who watch, awestruck and transfixed, as their high priest is butchered before them." The magnificent setting, given theatrical excitement by skillfully deployed scaffolding and lighting, became a rich projection chamber for the women's voices, sounding now here, now there, sometimes, as when Becket is murdered, springing out of the dark in what the *Independent* reviewer heard as "a bizarre polyphony of horror and grief." This was above all a spectacular production, and a musical one, for the choruses had powerful support from the music of Geoffrey Burgon, a composer admired for the remarkable range of his compositions, from requiems and masses to the music for popular television serials such as *Brideshead Revisited*.

The National Youth Theatre scored in its imaginative exploitation of special assets: Hawksmoor church, large numbers for the chorus (something the West End or even the subsidized theater could scarcely afford), artists, such as the composer, with a strong interest in religious themes coupled with theatrical flair and expertise. Eliot's play is among other things a thrillingly imagined ritual, calling for large-scale, flamboyant treatment; its many, unexpected changes of rhythm can gain in force from a "scattering" of voices such as the director, Edward Wilson, orchestrated at Spitalfields. And there are shock effects, like the sudden appearance of the Knights, which can acquire an extra horror when the audience is in the body of the church in which the murder is to occur. So it was, no doubt, at Canterbury when the play was first done, and so it was, with a new charge from youthful vitality, in the NYT production.

But what of Becket himself? The young actor, Jamie Foster, played the part with an impressive dignity and gravity that was appropriate to the extrovert, public style of the production as a whole. He did not attempt to project through style and tone the anguish and terror of the inner struggle that lies behind the symbolism of the Tempters' scene, as Richard Pasco did convincingly in the Royal Shakespeare Company production directed by Terry Hands at the Aldwych Theatre in 1972. It may be that *Murder in the Cathedral* is destined to remain a play performed in churches, though Hands's interpretation–dwelling on the neurotic "escape" element in Thomas's acceptance of martyrdom–suggested that it could have a place in the theater, even the theater of character and psychology. The élan of the NYT production was a promising augury.

It was with this notable amateur production, suitably adapted to a new venue, that Eliot's centenary was celebrated in the live theater in 1988. The National Youth Theatre Company took *Murder in the Cathedral* to the Edinburgh Festival where it was performed in the austere grandeur of St. Giles's Cathedral in August 1988. It was essentially the same production that had been seen in London, with new actors. Becket was played by Conor Grimes, who interestingly brought the vocal sound of Northern Ireland to the part and gave a performance admired for its vigor. The production was counted a highlight of the festival and sold out every night. Thus Eliot the playwright was successfully brought into the midst of one of the most lively, varied, and esteemed international festivals in Europe. From Edinburgh the production went to the Tyne Theatre, Newcastle-upon-Tyne, where it opened on the most auspicious date imaginable–26 September 1988. Its

next destination is Moscow, where it has been invited for April 1989. The National Youth Theatre has indeed done Eliot the playwright proud in a year when the professional theater has been less ready to venture.

Why that should have been so is hard to say, but no doubt a contributing factor was the relatively cool reception afforded to John Dexter's production of *The Cocktail Party* in 1986. Potential producers in 1988 might well have been deterred by the somewhat anticlimactic impact of a production that had seemed destined to succeed more brilliantly. The gap left by the live professional theater was, however, valiantly filled by the BBC, whose Radio 3 program broadcast all the full-length plays, attracting sympathetic critical notice for some strong performances, including Peter Barkworth's Becket. Many people must have heard these accomplished productions who would have been unlikely to see the plays in the theater. So perhaps, after all, Eliot the playwright was well served in the English theater in the year of his centenary.

It is pleasing to be able to leave the 1980s–so far as they have gone–on this note of promise. It has not been a period of great excitement for Eliot's plays in the English theater but the events of the last two years offer encouragement as well as some disappointment. There will surely be an access of interest when the correspondence dealing with the theater years is published. Let us hope that will be soon, and that we may look forward to a more splendid finale to the decade in the performance of Eliot's plays.

Book Reviewing in America: II

George Garrett
University of Virginia
and
David R. Slavitt

"We are not suffering, in the book business, from too much honesty."
–Katherine Dalton, *"Books and Book Reviewing, or Why All Press
Is Good Press,"* Chronicles (*January 1989).*

Agenda

To continue.

We have four general topics in this year's installment of "Book Reviewing in America." Last year we began with a discussion of newspaper reviewing and reviewers, together with some treatment of the kinds of book reviewing to be found in literary magazines and quarterlies. Inevitably this first part elicited some responses and reactions. And, as well, we had to leave some loose ends. So we begin this year's exploration by dealing with some of these responses and tying up some loose ends. Next we take a general view of the year in book reviewing. Then, thirdly, we commence an investigation and evaluation of the place and part of the popular magazines in the book-reviewing scene. Finally, and most important, we continue with the series of interviews, begun last year, with prominent and/or representative figures from the world of book reviewing. The more we examine the subject, the more we are convinced that, with the exception of one or two formidable institutions, such as, say, the *New York Times Book Review* and (maybe) the *New Yorker,* book reviewing in America is more a matter of *people,* good ones and bad ones, than it is a matter of institutions. The power and glory of institutions, or the notable absence thereof, derive mainly from the character, experience, and abilities of the people involved. This year we are able to present what we feel are extremely interesting interviews with two prominent and quite different figures from slightly different aspects of book reviewing. Pulitzer Prize-winning poet Henry Taylor, himself an active and respected reviewer of poetry, gives us an interview with Colin Walters of the *Washington Times,* whose book section we singled out for praise and recognition in last year's essay. And David Slavitt concludes with an interview in depth with longtime book–and cultural–critic John Leonard, whose sometimes controversial views of the literary situation in America have been shaped by years of combat experience in the trench warfare of literary New York. Walters and Leonard are two of the people who, at the very least, influence and help to establish the reputations of new books. Thus, even as we continue to describe and seek to define the forms that book reviewing takes, we must also continue to spotlight the people who, one way and another, run the show.

News from last time

One of the people we heard from following the publication of the 1987 *DLB Yearbook* was Jack Miles, book editor of the *Los Angeles Times* who had been both mentioned and quoted in our piece, but whose *Los Angeles Times Book Review* had not received credit due. One of the pieces we had singled out for special praise, Nikki Finke's "Literary Brat Pack: Young, Brash, Rich," was attributed to the *International Herald Tribune,* where we found it, but was, in fact, reprinted there from the *Los Angeles Times Book Review,* thus proving Miles's point that eastern critics, including ourselves, simply don't pay enough attention to or keep up with the West Coast literary world. Since then, in penance, we have been keeping up with Jack Miles's paper; and it is a pleasure to report that during the past year, the *Los Angeles Times Book Review* has been right on the cutting edge of newspaper book reviewing in America, taking a second place in importance and number of reviews only to the *New York Times Book Review* and, in terms of overall quality of individual reviews, the equal of any. Serious fiction was well represented. Miles's idea of publishing a poem, together with basic biographical and publication information, from new books of poetry has caught on and, it seems, works very well. The quality and range of the reviewers, from staff regulars such as Richard Eder and Georgia Jones-Davis, to occasional reviewers such as Frank Gibney and Michael J. Carroll, are first-rate. Over the year first novels fared well in the *Los Angeles Times*. An excellent example–a serious, full-length review of a fine novel which, for whatever reason, was reviewed late by the *New York Times Book Review* and relegated there to the sad limbo of "In Short"–is Carolyn See's review (28 November) of *Anna L.M.N.O.* (Random House), by Sarah Glasscock. Jack Miles is doing an outstanding job, and the *Los Angeles Times Book Review* has more than earned eastern, as well as local, attention.

Another part of the newspaper reviewing scene which received short shrift from us was the highly individual, hit or miss, and often influential world of the weekly newspapers. One of the best of the reviewers for weekly papers whom we have encountered, and one who has been at it, successfully, over many years, is Eloise Goza Allen. Mrs. Allen writes her column, "Read Any Good (Or Bad) Books Lately?," for the *Madison County Recorder*. There are special problems "in writing a book review column for my little weekly newspaper in this almost-in-Georgia North Florida town." There are also attention-getting tricks of the trade. "I trick my customers by heading the column each week with the name of a local person"; she writes, "where possible I make a connection between our area and the subject book." Offering a single example, she says: "For Peter Taylor's *Summons to Memphis* I snared attention by reminding readers that the King Cotton Hotel in Memphis once had as a manager a favorite local citizen." This is, to be sure, small-scale, grass-roots stuff; but it is also precisely the word of mouth on which the good fortune of serious books in America depends and by which book and author may find new readers. Mrs. Allen ends one typical review, this one of Rosamunde Pilcher's *The Shell Seekers* (St. Martin's Press), with a down-home, personal note: "If I've aroused any interest in the book, then it may be borrowed from me after Hazel McLeod finishes it. I'm asking our director of the Suwannee River system to get a copy for our Pinckney Street library as soon as the books are available here."

Another critic we have been in touch with is Bruce Allen of Kittery, Maine, who must be almost unique in having been since 1969 (and *survived* since then) "self-employed as a freelance writer specializing in book reviews." Allen regularly writes for *USA Today*, *Smithsonian*, several of the quarterlies, and such newspapers as the *Baltimore Sun*, *Providence Journal*, *Chicago Sun-Times*, *Newsday*, *Chicago Tribune*, *Los Angeles Times*, *St. Louis Post-Dispatch*, *Boston Globe*, *Christian Science Monitor*, and, from time to time, the *New York Times Book Review*. He also writes reviews regularly for such magazines as *Library Journal*, *Playboy*, *Nation*, *Saturday Review*, *New Republic*, and *Sports Illustrated*. Allen knows the scene and the subject inside and out; and his observations are worth considering: "In response to 'Book Reviewing in America,' " he writes, "I guess I'd like to offer two observations. One, that it's precisely *because* the chains are overloaded with Garfield and Jane Fonda and Donald Regan et al. that we have a special responsibility to seek out and notice books that don't otherwise get noticed. I do a roundup of 'Neglected Fiction' that appears annually in *USA Today*: it's an opportunity to tell readers about important reprints like the stories of Georgios Vizyenos [*My Mother's Sin*, University of New England Press] or Leonardo Sciascia's almost-forgotten masterpiece *The Council of Egypt* (Carcanet). Also homegrown successes such as Lynda Gray Sexton's *Margaret of the Imperfections* [Persea] or Tom De Haven's *Sunburn Lake* [from a major publisher–Viking–but neglected, nevertheless]. Readers want to know about books like these, and we're their source of information.

"Two, a general principle. I keep hearing that too many reviewers are 'soft' on their subjects; don't apply sufficiently rigorous standards of judgment. I don't buy this. I feel reviewers have to remember we're writing, not for the ages, but for the present. . . . Too many reviewers want to be 'critics,' and I feel many take themselves too seriously."

Allen calls for some kind of record and recognition of the best reviews of a given year: "I'd like to see an annual gathering of the best book reviews–both short pieces (even unto the 150-word briefs that run in *Library Journal* and *Publishers Weekly*) and review essays from the literary quarterlies. The National Book Critics Circle has edged around the idea, in piecemeal fashion, for a few years now, but nothing much has come of it."

News from this year past

In the literary business of America, numbers, often closely guarded and always late in appearance, join with rumor and gossip and simple anecdotal evidence to form present history. *Publishers Weekly* (11 March) offered the first reliable, industry-wide statistics for 1987-1988, indicating that, at present and after considerable previous inflation, the output of "product," that is the number of titles published in a variety of set categories, was roughly the same as the year before. In the category of fiction, including both hardcover and trade paper editions, 5,647 titles were published in 1987 as compared with 5,105 in 1985 and 5,578 in 1986. (Prices crept upward at the same time, averaging, for hardcover books, $15.24 in 1985 and $16.89 in 1987.) A little later in the year (11 June) *Newsweek*, drawing on ongoing research from R. R. Bowker, reported some of the latest publishing statistics–"figures that astound and perplex." During the past year a total of 800,000 books were in print, roughly ten times the number forty years ago. There are 21,000 identified publishers as against 1948's total of 387; though it needs to be pointed out that only fourteen percent of publishers are responsible for ninety percent of the titles. During 1987-1988, some 90,000 *new* titles were listed in *Books in Print*, as compared to 8,000 in 1949-1950. But 50,000 to 60,000 titles fall out of print annually. With numbers such as these to contend with, it is no surprise that the press, in all its forms, can review only a small number of the books published in America. All things considered, the most surprising thing is how, against pure and simple impossibility, critics and reviewers at least try to call attention to serious books, praising and damning as the case may be, discovering and following patterns and trends, giving the latest news of the business and, not least in a society which seems committed to gossip and the publicity of the private and personal, paying close attention to the lives of prominent literary figures.

Not surprisingly, it was a year of biographies in America, and there were a surprising number of literary biographies published and widely reviewed; and not merely major studies of such major historical figures as Chekhov and Tolstoy, Dickens and Zola, Shaw and Rimbaud and O'Casey, but also full-scale biographies of William S. Burroughs, Shirley Jackson, Katherine Mansfield, Anita Loos, Lillian Hellman, Dorothy Parker, Langston Hughes, Richard Wright, Mary McCarthy, Jean Stafford, Truman Capote, John Cheever, Marjorie Kinnan Rawlings, W. H. Auden, Christopher Isherwood, Wallace Stevens, and Ezra Pound, among others. Not to mention such oddities as Ian Hamilton's *In Search of J. D. Salinger* (Random House), which emerged from fires of litigation and publicity as mostly an account of the book Hamilton did not and could not write. *Publishers Weekly* gives its readers a touch of *People* magazine by presenting regular interviews with writers, "PW Interviews." It is not an insignificant gesture that so many of those included in the series are, well- or little-known, serious artists. Among those interviewed in 1988 were Larry Woiwode, Don DeLillo, Elizabeth Spencer, Peter Ackroyd, Clyde Edgerton, Ariel Dorfman, Anne Rice, Jay Cantor, Harry Crews, Madison Smartt Bell, Raymond Carver, Philip Roth, Berry Fleming, J. G. Ballard, Jane Smiley, and Penelope Lively. The "Style" section of the *Washington Post* regularly includes extensive pieces on politicians, movie stars, rock stars, and so on, but not wholly neglected by any means are literary figures such as Anne Rice, Carlos Fuentes, and Louise Erdrich.

Because of the unceasing scrutiny of artists as public figures and private people and with Jay McInerney's latest effort, *Story of My Life* (Atlantic Monthly), on the firing line, one might have expected the young writers of "the Brat Pack" to continue to enjoy the limelight. Which, to an extent, they did, though not in entirely appreciative terms. Perhaps it was the men's magazine *M* which set the year's tone in January with its reference to them in the annual piece "Class: Who Has It Who Doesn't": "The novelist Richard Ford has class. Brat novelists Jay McInerney, Bret Easton Ellis and Tama Janowitz don't, though it looks as though it doesn't matter, since their meteoric careers appear to be in the toilet already." In fairness, McInerney has his admirers, among them Rust Hills of *Esquire*, who featured McInerney in his annual literary issue, "Literary Heat" (July, pp. 51-125), with a lineup also including (among others) Norman Mailer, Don DeLillo, Bruce Jay Friedman, and Joyce Carol Oates. McInerney was allowed to defend himself: "He resents those 'ham-handed' critics with a 'crudity of insight' who herd disparate writers into the Brat Pack corral . . . Norman Mailer's career is a model for McInerney. 'He never rolled over and played dead for them. I admire that.' " Also part of "Literary Heat," and for the first time, under the subtitle "Modern Lit," were six (fairly tame) literary anecdotes—Barry Hannah pulling a gun on his creative-writing class; George Plimpton and Ernest Hemingway thumb-wrestling at the Colony; Mailer and Gore Vidal duking it out (briefly, briefly) at Lally Weymouth's party in 1977; Tama Janowitz's hair catching on fire—*that* kind of thing, not ignoring that wonderful old chestnut, the Ved Mehta/V. S. Naipaul story.

There was no shortage of insult and the ad hominem attacks in 1988. A piece by Joe Queenan (a writer for *Barrons*) for the *American Spectator* (December), "Character Assassins," dealing with the fiction of Ann Beattie, Raymond Carver, Leonard Michaels, Grace Paley, and some others, caught the eyes and attention of journalists and was widely discussed. Nobody escaped his wit and anger. (Of Richard Ford's *Rock Springs* he wrote—"The *Times* calls these stories stunning. Another word might be 'stupid.' ") Queenan concluded strongly: "I hate this stuff. With the exception of Carver, who has a certain morbid charm, I hate this stuff a lot. I hate it because it's boring, condescending, and monotonous, but I hate it even more because it subverts the function of good art: It's a lie."

Not all literary personality pieces, by any means, were negative and critical. Some were sympathetic in the best sense. An outstanding example, linking literary journalism with criticism, was Bruce Weber's "Andre Dubus's Hard-Luck Stories" in the 20 November issue of the *New York Times Magazine*.

Perhaps appropriately, in keeping with a fairly rowdy election year, 1988 saw a good deal of rage manifested by reviewers. Rhoda Koenig's, in *New York*, is more a matter of needling than sharp carving. Here she begins her number on Edna O'Brien's *The High Road* (Farrar, Straus & Giroux): "When it comes to walking the line between sensuality and self-infatuation, Edna O'Brien will never pass a Breathalyzer test. Relentlessly giddy, swarming with hyperbole and pathetic fallacies, her prose has a stranglehold on the ineffable. One seems to read *The High Road* to an accompaniment of sighs—the author's rapturous twitterings and the reader's disbelieving *Oy vays*" (21 November, p. 132). Slick and sassy, *Vanity Fair* is a good place to look for the personal side, if not the "inside," of literary art. The June issue was especially rich, with a large-scale biographical piece on the troubles and triumphs of Jerzy Kosinski, "The Kosinski Conundrum," by Stephen Schiff ("Did the socially ubiquitous Polish-American novelist hire someone to write his

books?"); and with Germaine Greer turned loose ("Women's Glib") to review *The Sisterhood* (Simon and Schuster) by Marcia Cohen, where both the author and some of her subjects got well battered in the clinches. Though Greer had nice things, too, to say about her feminist sisters, Gloria Steinem and Betty Friedan caught a share of zingers. The book's author wasn't lucky either: "The cliché distortion may be unconscious, but Ms. Cohen shows a pretty shrewd understanding of what the average New York *Daily News* reader wants to know about feminists—the size of their breasts, the shape of their ass, their jewelry, their lovers, what they wore to this and that, their strip searches, their mud-wrestling, the whole schmear." In the same issue regular reviewer James Wolcott, in his "Mixed Media" column, takes on the *New York Times* book critics. Of John Gross: "Gross has the soul of an academician, straight from Dullsville. He's the consensus of one"; of Michiko Kakutani: "A graduate of Yale, she's the ultimate A student and all-nighter, an industrious ant who does her homework by the light of the harvest moon. Innocent of idiosyncrasy, she adheres entirely to the standard repertory of the East Coast literary scene, never citing critics out of tenor with the times or the *Times*." And of the distinguished third reviewer on the daily roster of the *Times*, Christopher Lehmann-Haupt: "Years ago he-man street toughs like Jimmy Breslin used to mock Lehmann-Haupt as a sissy who parted his name in the middle."

Spy magazine, though it offers no reviews (directly), is nevertheless a service to the whole literary community with its regular feature "Review of Reviewers." Nothing much is sacred or serious here. James Wolcott is "cowish." Lehmann-Haupt is "lazy." Of writer Ralph Novak of *People* ("the Isaac Asimov of one-paragraph criticism"), *Spy* columnist Ignatz Ratzwikziwzki writes: "Writing, clearly, is not the most time-consuming of Novak's weekly tasks. His mini-essays read like grade-school book reports." Under "Logrolling In Our Time," a regular feature in *Spy*, we are given the words, from blurbs and book reviews, of prominent authors extravagantly praising each other: Anne Tyler on Alice Adams and vice versa; also Margaret Atwood/Marge Piercy, John Irving/Stanley Elkin, Doris Grumbach/Hilma Wolitzer, James Salter/Joy Williams, Robert Coover/T. C. Boyle, and Robert Coover/Angela Carter. The only writer to appear more often than Coover is Paul Theroux, who in 1988 was cited for swapping encomiums with Graham

Greene, Jan Morris, and Anthony Burgess. *Spy* occasionally focuses attention on individual writers and publishers. For example, "So What's Wrong With Being Multi-faceted" (November, p. 56) simply quotes, back-to-back, a series of complete contradictions of fact from interviews with Stephen King. Several literary figures were selected for serious consideration in the *Spy* 1988 Ironman Nightlife Decathalon (under "Party Poop," December), among them Jay McInerney, Harold Brodkey, Gary Fisketjon, and publisher Morgan Entrekin, "still sporting the Farrah Fawcett hairdo that impressed the competition judges last year. . . ." *Spy* also featured Entrekin and McInerney in its "A Cavalcade of Coasters" (June) as "Future Coasters" together with the more solid category of "Literary Coasters," which, among others, listed such luminaries as Ralph Ellison, Allen Ginsberg, Joseph Heller, John Irving, John Knowles, Norman Mailer, Tama Janowitz, Susan Sontag, and Random House's whole line of trade paperbacks–Vintage Contemporaries.

Outside the context of satire and frivolity there were any number of occasions in which the reviewer of a serious book became purely and simply angry. National Public Radio's Alan Cheuse lost his usual soft-voiced cool when on 24 September he reviewed *At Risk* (Putnam's), by Alice Hoffman, for "All Things Considered." Calling the book "emotional pornography, an attempt to titillate the sympathy of mainstream American readers and play on their fears of the awful disease (AIDS) without forcing them to sympathize for an instant with the overwhelming majority of its victims," Cheuse went on to say, " 'At Risk' is not only bad art . . . it's immoral . . . a stupid misstep on the part of a gifted novelist and an insult to its potential readership. A boycott is in order, though I can't throw up a picket line around a book, I can just throw up."

AIDS, of course, was a hotly debated topic during the year. So was the matter of the established literary canon. The subject was treated widely and in depth in many places, perhaps most thoroughly in James Atlas's "The Battle of the Books: Are the Classics Racist and Sexist? Debate Rages Over Which Books Form the Intellectual Heritage of Americans" (*New York Times Magazine*, 5 June, pp. 24-27, 72-73, 75, 85, 94). Not unsympathetic with the notion of revising and reforming the canon to reflect changes in the power structure and the values of ethnicity, Atlas covered both sides of the issue at some of its key academic centers (Duke, Stanford, Princeton, Yale) and, in the best contemporary manner, managed to build his case around the *people* arguing about it, making more public the character and repute of academics such as Frank Lentricchia (Duke), Marjorie Garber (Harvard), Gerald Graff (Northwestern), Margaret Williams Ferguson (Columbia), and especially the inimitable Stanley Fish and his wife, Jane Tompkins, who have, according to Atlas, earned Duke a new nickname–"The Fish Tank."

Whether or not the canon changes on the campuses of America, there was a changing of the guard at the Book-of-the-Month Club which may portend some real changes in the future literary scene, all the more so since, as a matter of course, main and alternate selections of the club are widely reviewed. (Indeed, the reviewing, in a sense, begins *in house; Book of the Month Club News* descriptions of the books, though clearly designed to sell the selections, often partake of many literary qualities of a favorable review and are, for a number of reasons, influential with reviewers, a situation noted in an important article, "The Book-of-the-Month Club and the General Reader: On the Uses of 'Serious' Fiction," by Janice Radway, *Critical Inquiry*, Spring 1988, pp. 516-538.) This detailed study of the system and the cultural role of the club may have had some influence in end-of-the-year changes, which included the resignations of Gloria Norris, Wilfred Sheed, and Mordecai Richler, longtime judges for BOMC with lifetime tenure, and their replacement for at least one year by black novelist Gloria Naylor and nonfiction writer J. Anthony Lukas. The meaning of the changes, above and beyond new brooming, remains to be seen and will surely engage the attention of critics and columnists in 1989.

George Garrett: Reviewing in the Popular Magazines

Keeping up with the overwhelming number and variety of magazines published in America, coming and going swiftly, is an impossible task. And so we are ever more and more dependent upon others, the reviewers of magazines. A case in point is "The Magazine Reader," a regular column by *Washington Post* "Style" section writer Charles Trueheart, who shares his own interests and discoveries. An example of the latter is *The Fessenden Review*, billing itself as "The Noisiest Book Review in the Known World," out of San Diego.

Summarizing its contents, Trueheart concludes: "It has a cranky personality and a bizarre taste in books, but at least it *has* a personality and indulges its taste."

Anyone who spends any time examining the book-reviewing scene in the popular magazines is in for some real surprises. The first major surprise is how much book reviewing actually goes on and how often in unlikely places. That is, many magazines, created for and around certain specific themes or special interests (in its admittedly selective and incomplete listing, "Consumer Publications," *1989 Writers' Market* uses fifty separate categories of magazines and fills up some 590 pages of fairly fine print), while they may not regularly review books, will call attention to books concerning the special topics and interests of the magazine and will also, from time to time, publish reviews of books deemed by the editors to be of probable interest to their readership. Sometimes this can include fiction as well as nonfiction. Thus, occasionally, a magazine such as *Soldier of Fortune: The Journal of Professional Adventurers* will review fiction dealing with combat or the experiences of mercenaries and adventurers. It is not these magazines or their reviews we are dealing with here, but it is necessary to acknowledge their existence and the fact that, outside the more conventional channels of the promotion of commercial publishers, they can sell some books–if those books happen to be in print and available. Quite aside from sales, however, these reviews, early or late, can also result in a growing number of *readers* for a given book or author, a fact sometimes overlooked in examining the sales-oriented publishing seasons. Shelf life in libraries tends to be much longer, and less quantifiable, than shelf life in the bookstores. Thus, in a real sense, notices gained by books in a wide variety of unexpected places may directly influence the literary scene, if not the publishing business.

We are not here examining, either, the special interest and trade magazines specifically concerned with books, publishing, and bookselling. But it needs to be said, at the outset, that both *Kirkus Reports* and the industry's all-around magazine, *Publishers Weekly,* do an extraordinary job (admittedly a losing battle always, but nonetheless amazing) with their advance notices of new and forthcoming books. *Publishers Weekly,* with its "Forecasts" section, is especially fine with its brief, descriptive reviews of fiction which, in spite of overwhelming readership interest in nonfiction, is kept in balance to the distinct advantage of fic-

tion writers and publishers. Nobody does much with poetry anymore; but the commercial publishers can scarcely be faulted when publications ostensibly devoted to the subject do so little themselves. For instance, the *American Poetry Review* seldom, if ever, reviews new poetry, being content, evidently, to serve as a kind of *People* magazine for contemporary verse. At best it is a sort of advertising journal. *American Book Review,* a bimonthly review of books "of literary interest published by the small, large, university, regional, third world, women's and other presses," reviews about as many books of poems and books about poets and poetry as anybody, including *Poetry.* But, as an innocent reader might guess from the statement of purpose quoted above, it is built on a firm political base and bias, both literary and social. Similarly, there are the commercial "book review" magazines (example: the monthly *Book Page,* originating in Nashville, but widely available, and free, at southern bookstores), which have basically descriptive and appreciative notices, more buying guides than book reviews.

We are chiefly concerned here with the more general popular magazines, but there is one thing which all the magazines share, to one degree or another, with each other, regardless of the demographics of real or intended audience. The magazines require a fairly long "lead time" for their materials. This is true even with the newsmagazines such as *Time* and *Newsweek.* Their world and national news is very quickly published, almost as close to events as that of the newspapers. But most of their "back of the book" materials, including books, arts, and cultural affairs reviews, is routinely prepared and scheduled well ahead of time. What this means for the more general magazines is that in order for their book reviews to be published in time to be able to influence the commercial life of the books, the magazine editors and writers have to work from duplications of typescript or from galleys or bound galleys rather than from the finished book. The problem which this presents to the commercial trade publisher is the simple expense of duplicated typescript or galleys. Bound galleys can cost as much as fifty dollars per copy, which is a fair-size little bite out of the promotional budget of many serious books. The choice is whether or not a review in a given magazine can likely result in the sale of five or ten copies of that book. It is no surprise, then, that the basic reviewers' lists for many trade publications do not (automatically) even include a wide range of popular magazines.

Regional and local magazines (the incomplete listing of *1989 Writers' Market* includes 155 entries) vary widely in quality and purpose, and for the purposes of book reviewing they have to depend on the availability of writers who are ready, willing, and able to do some searching and scouting for themselves. For, by and large, these magazines do not regularly appear at all on the basic review lists of commercial publishers, at least for general trade books. Usually, unless the publisher is exceptionally knowledgeable and efficient, editors and/or writers must discover the books of interest on their own and ask for copies for review purposes. Most publishers, though, oddly, not all, are willing to send out review copies on request; but, of course, there is a significant delay in the appearance of the review, a time lag increased by the necessary "lead time" of most of these magazines. Thus, even with the reviews in hand, there can easily be a delay of a month or two before a given review can appear in the magazine. What this means is, first of all, that, like the special interest magazines, local and regional magazines review books too late to have much influence, if any, on the sales of a book scheduled by its publisher to have a shelf life of, ideally, about sixteen weeks. The initial life cycle of a hardcover trade book may very well be over and done with before this particular kind of magazine review appears. In that sense these magazines are not fundamentally different from the literary magazines and quarterlies, themselves "special interest" magazines, except that the audience is potentially wider and more general. On the other hand, regional and local attention can always serve to enhance the reputation of both book and writer, thus influencing the future and, sometimes, the potential of a given book to earn a subsidiary reprinting. Mainly, however, the regional and local magazines operate at a slight distance from the *business* of publishing, even though they may well coordinate their reviews with local and regional bookstores.

Exemplary of the magazines we are discussing are those (with clones all over the nation) such as *Southern Living*, which offers, regularly, brief descriptive reviews of books of regional interest, including some southern fiction. Thus, for example, *Southern Living* of December 1988 (p. 128) offered a brief appreciative review of the first novel, *A Blue Moon in Poorwater* (Ticknor & Fields), by Cathryn Hankla. First novels are hard-

pressed to earn much notice *anywhere*. In this case, subject matter and regional interest and authenticity caught the attention of the editors. *Southern Exposure* is assertively addressed to a more liberal readership and is apt to review books, as well as publishing excerpts from forthcoming fiction, of social and political import. So *Southern Exposure*, in Summer 1988, published "Loyds," an excerpt from a forthcoming novel, "The Big Toe," by Appalachian writer Denise Giardina. (This kind of advance preview of a book to come *could*, in fact, have some influence on sales.)

People often make more difference than policy; or, to put it more accurately, people make the policies. *Southern* magazine, a more hip and energetic competitor for *Southern Living*, coming from Little Rock, Arkansas, has, throughout 1988, had the services of young novelist Madison Smartt Bell, who reviews new books and writes a column–"Southern Lit." During the year, then, *Southern* was at once relevant to and part of the larger literary scene.

Then, among regional and local magazines, there are special cases, not rare enough to be classified as exceptions, but unusual in a combination of location and availability of talent. For instance, *Albemarle*, a slick magazine published six times a year in Charlottesville, Virginia, happens to be located near the University of Virginia and the colony of writers who have come to live in the area. There are usually some local books to notice. Charlottesville is also home for John Howland, Jr., who is, among other things, a regular reviewer for *Newsday* and a member of the National Book Critics Circle. Howland does a column, "Local Readings," for *Albemarle*, usually five pages or more with photographs and sidebars. He tends to build his column around a theme. Typical was his column for April/May 1988, "Books of Exile and Arrival," which treated new books by Isabel Allende (then visiting the university) and local resident Rita Mae Brown. He also considered *Journey of the Wolf*, by English professor Douglas Day, which, he announced, is scheduled for a new 1989 edition.

Since, according to the serious guesstimates of most demographic studies, educated women constitute at least eighty percent of the public for hardcover trade books, many of the general magazines directed primarily at women have some emphasis on books and literature. Sometimes this is strictly limited. For example, *McCall's* lists Helen DelMonte as "Books and Fiction Editor" and does publish both fiction and poetry but does not (certainly not with any regularity) publish book reviews. Somewhat more sophisticated, *Redbook* publishes some moderately adventurous fiction, but no regular book reviews. On the other hand, *Cosmopolitan* (fiction and book editor– Betty Nichols Kelly) makes a good deal out of books, presenting two sections–"Books" and "Fiction and Books"–as regulars among its departments. The "Fiction and Books" section runs excerpts from popular, sometimes mildly serious novels. Their "Books" section for December, by Louise Bernikow, was a survey of picture books on travel, art, cooking, photography, and illustrated biographies of celebrities. The disclaimer introducing a somewhat more serious book is revealing: "For those who prefer thought-provoking tomes in a lighthearted season, consider Joseph Campbell's visually stunning *The Power of Myth*." *Seventeen* has a regular "New Voices" as part of its "In Every Issue" section, which alternates book reviews with book reviews and poetry. And there are short stories, original or excerpts from elsewhere, in each issue. The book reviews are mostly favorable, always brief, and seem aimed at encouraging teenage girls to read. *Vogue* ("Books") and *Harper's Bazaar* ("Book Bazaar") both publish regular book reviews. Neither tends to use space for less than appreciative purposes–praise tends to be lavish; but the reviews, especially in *Vogue*, are intelligent, well researched, factual, and, ironically, are more likely, three out of four times, to be by men than women. Example: December's *Vogue* had book reviews by Peter Buckley, Roy Reed, Herbert Muschamp, and Cathleen Medwick. In a relative sense, *Harper's Bazaar* is, deliberately, a little more lightweight than its competitor. Its comment on books for Christmas says it nicely, with a slight smile: "They look great under the tree, around the hearth–and even better on the shelf." *Lear*, the new magazine begun by Frances Lear "for the woman who wasn't born yesterday," has as yet no book editor and no book reviews. They use the talents of serious writers. Kurt Vonnegut, Jr., and Timothy Foote contributed pieces to the December issue, and authors sometimes enter the scene as celebrities. Perhaps that is a function of editor Lear's television background.

Similar magazines, though aimed at a slightly younger consumer, *Glamour, Mademoiselle, Taxi,* and *Elle*, regularly have book reviews and deal with literature and the literary situation. *Glamour* ("Books, Trends") is the lightest of the four, offering sound byte-size reviews by editors Laura

Mathews and Janet Rosen. (Exemplary critical reaction: Laura Mathews on *The Phantom of the Opera Pop-Up Book*–"Who needs Broadway, when you can get a book that performs?") *Mademoiselle* has a "Books" section, edited by fiction and book editor Eileen Schnurr, which is not intended for real or potential intellectuals, but is at once entertaining and earnest. The December column was not without bravado and style, presenting "Hip lit: The New Journals," by Joyce Maynard, a brisk and breezy introduction to such trendy, heavyweight literary magazines as the *Paris Review, Granta, Grand Street,* and the *Quarterly* (pp. 92, 94). Of her experience reading through issues of the *Paris Review,* Maynard writes: "What does emerge, overall, is that there is a world of people out there who enjoy spending the odd hour reading the letters of Gertrude Stein or an essay on the life and work of a little-known Russian poet. And though I may not be one of those people myself, I'm glad they exist." *Taxi* ("Fashion, Trends & Leisure Living") is new and slick and, judging by its advertisements and photo features, aggressively, if very expressively, campy and "off-the-wall." "Books" is a regular part of the "On Duty" department, and serious books are considered with individual full-page reviews. For example, the October 1988 issue reviewed, in sequence, two books about the crisis and tragedy in South Africa–David Turnley's photographic volume, *Why Are They Weeping?* (Stewart, Tabori & Chang), and William Finnegan's *Dateline Soweto* (Harper & Row). The point of view, though in context clearly exemplary of what Tom Wolfe dubbed "radical chic," is honest and serious. The issue on the newsstands at year's end, the February 1989 issue (*Taxi* seems to be on an eccentric time scheme), continues the sociopolitical pitch with reviews of *Imelda: Steel Butterfly of the Philippines* (McGraw-Hill) and treats two forthcoming novels, Salman Rushdie's *The Satanic Verses* (Viking) and Brad Leithauser's *Hence* (Knopf), stories without a lot in common except a left-wing political stance (passionate on Rushdie's part), a distrust of both technology and the masses, and, as reviewer Wendy Smith puts it, they are "equally obsessed with the big question: the future of the human race." Despite all the trendy pretensions and all the evidence of the conventional, if complex, hypocrisy of the comfortable who would like a more caring and compassionate world, *Taxi* has some real potential in book reviewing. From the point of view of book reviews the most interesting and successful of these slick-papered, fancy magazines for certain kinds of women is *Elle*. Issues regularly have current, if brief, book reviews under "Faces/Books"; as, for example, in the October issue there were short reviews of William Shawcross's *The Shah's Last Ride* (Simon and Schuster) and Kristin McCloy's first novel, *Velocity* (Random House). Somewhat more space was devoted to another first novel, Margaret Diehl's *Men* (Soho Press). The December issue was impressive, with seven strong reviews and articles on books and writers, among them reviews of new work by Don DeLillo, Edward Hoagland, Ultra Violet, Alex Shoumatoff, Nadine Gordimer, and Jonathan Spence. David Rieff's review of Don DeLillo's *Libra* (Viking) is broad and inclusive, even containing a brief survey of American paranoia–"a fundamental trope in American art and American life." Feminist critic, editor, and story-writer Christina Baker characterizes the reviews in *Elle* as "By far the most interesting, intelligent and thorough treatment of books of any women's magazine."

Perhaps this is the best place to mention the slick, coated-paper male (or unisex) equivalents to the women's magazines. *Esquire* is, of them all, perhaps, the best known and still among the most influential magazines in the literary world, though lately it is hard to see exactly why. Guided, in a *literary* sense at least, by editors Rust Hills and Will Blythe, the magazine publishes a modest amount of good fiction from a small stable of writers; and, of course, there is the annual literary issue, published sometime in the summer. This special issue has calmed down a bit since the old days, a fact noticed, with nostalgia, by Hills in the August 1987 ("The Big Guns of August") issue. "Twenty-four years ago," he wrote, "the pages of this and other magazines bristled with the self-righteous indignation of postwar rebels. Norman Mailer used this very forum to attack his friends and colleagues, and people invited the man to their homes only if they were willing to invest in an umbrella policy." But Hills, not without a certain creaky sadness, was still willing to draw up an only half-facetious map of the brightest stars in the literary cosmos ("a cosmic mess but cosmic nevertheless"). By July 1988 ("Literary Heat") Hills had reduced himself to half a page to talk about the old days and, as well, "our own glorious Manifest Destiny. . . ." *Esquire* used to review books. Now they publish fiction and literary anecdotes and seem to be running on fumes. *GQ* (*Gentleman's Quarterly*) has the services of Tom Jenks, a former assistant to Hills,

and he publishes good fiction, mostly fishing the same small pool as his old boss. There is also a "Books" section, one which does not (yet) transcend the stated general purpose of the magazine, namely "emphasizing fashion, general interest and service features for men ages 25-45 with a large discretionary income." *M–The Civilized Male*, though almost passionately chic and upscale, doesn't do a whole lot with books or things literary. It might (does) point out that George Plimpton, Gore Vidal, and John Irving attended Exeter while Louis Auchincloss is a graduate of Groton. Books sometimes pop up for instant notice in the regular "What's Hot Now" section. Here, for example, is the complete treatment (minus a color reproduction of the jacket) of Anne Tyler's *Breathing Lessons* (Knopf): "With the movie of her last book already filming, Anne Tyler's new book for Knopf is the hot read this fall. 'Breathing Lessons' is the story of a 28-year-old marriage in which the more things change the more they remain the same." *Fame*, whose premier issue appeared in November, is "gender free," edited by Gael Love and featuring Clint Eastwood and Marlon Brando as cover portraits for its crucial first couple of issues. *Fame* has a regular "Books" column (so far) as a part of its regular "Fame says it all about" section, which includes, as well, columns on "Business," "Art," "Theater," "Film," "Music," "Media," and a contribution by "Critic at large" Carlin Romano, who happens also to be a book critic for the *Philadelphia Inquirer*. "Books," however, is by David Streitfeld. The first issue offered mainly an article based on interviews (with William Styron, John Sayles, Tillie Olsen, Leonard Gardner, Robert Pirsig, William Gass, and Richard Price) entitled "Writers in Limbo: William Styron, John Sayles, and others answer the burning question: 'Where's the book?' " In the second issue of *Fame* Streitfeld produced three full pages ("Prophet of Doom") on J. G. Ballard and four more pages ("Booked for the Holidays") of his choices of "the best picture books of the season." *Fame* has some possibilities.

More plain than their fancy brothers and sisters are *Ms.* and *Mother Jones*. *Ms.* has a "Books" section for every issue. The reviews tend to be thoughtful and intelligent, are generally favorable, and always have a distinctly feminist slant. Thus a review of Arianna-Stassinopoulos Huffington's controversial biography *Picasso: Creator and Destroyer* (Simon and Schuster), while lamenting the unsophisticated and unscholarly approach, nevertheless praises the book's exposure of the darker, misogynistic side of Picasso's genius. *Mother Jones* has few frills or flounces and is calmly revolutionary. There is a regular "Books in Brief " feature, and there are full-scale feature articles on major, and especially Latin American, writers–Carlos Fuentes (November), Isabel Allende (December), and Mario Vargas Llosa (January 1989). The tendency is to review political and historical books or fiction with a socio-political framework; though sometimes a novel is examined for the instruction it may provide. For example, in May, regular reviewer Adam Hochschild linked John Updike's *S.* (Knopf) with Bharati Mukherjee's *The Middleman and Other Stories* (Grove), a juxtaposition which allowed him to comment on Mukherjee's characters in contrast to Updike's: "With one eye out for the INS agents, these are the people who cook the meals and clean the houses and clerk in the malls of Updike Country." In December a review by Georgia Brown ("Look at Me! The Writer as Flasher," pp. 46, 47) of Ellen Gilchrist's *The Anna Papers* (Little, Brown) allowed the reviewer to reiterate the Old Left's caution against too much loose-limbed individualism: "Anna the writer kills herself to avoid pain–and I take this as Gilchrist's avoidance too, a romantic, easy way out, as well as a grandstand play." Whatever else, *Mother Jones* doesn't surround its texts with advertisements for luxury goods. Typically the advertisement section, "Ways & Means," mostly classifieds, begins with the same ad–"Sexual Aids/How to order them without embarrassment/How to use them without disappointment"–and includes other ads for things such as "Buddhist Meditation Supplies."

The degree of the politicization of American magazines is somewhat surprising and has a definite effect on book reviewing. The element of surprise derives from the absence of any serious debate or even argument *within* the magazines themselves. The magazines certainly speak to and of each other, but behind the front lines most assumptions go strictly unquestioned. Hence a given magazine is seldom persuasive to others, either antagonists or the uninitiated, and probably not intended to be. Most often, the magazine is a kind of cheering section (with the editors as cheerleaders) for whatever it is the magazine believes in. Books seldom escape the resulting strictures and inhibitions; but, paradoxically, books are important weapons and so, though often distorted beyond original purposes, are seldom ignored.

Victor Navasky's *Nation* remains relentlessly topical and political, but publishes a good deal of material about books and the arts. Poet Thomas Disch is a regular on theater, opera, and general culture. John Leonard is responsible for dealing with fiction. Novels are not a large part of the magazine's bill of fare, but Brina Caplan reviewed Allison Lurie's *The Truth About Lorin Jones* (Little, Brown), Robert McPhillips dealt with Anne Tyler's *Breathing Lessons,* and Eric Bentley explicated Tomas Eloy Martinez's *The Peron Novel* (Pantheon). Leonard was responsible for a couple of outstanding reviews: one of DeLillo's *Libra,* in "Scripts, Plots and Codes," 19 September, pp. 205-208; and his thorough critique of Milorad Pavic's *Dictionary of the Khazars* (Knopf), 5 December, pp. 610-613. "Think of *Dictionary*," he argued, "as a counteranthropology at least as interesting as any Levi-Strauss field trip to Bororo or Nambikwara." The *New Republic* has only a few reviews per issue and nonfiction predominates, but the reviews are relatively lengthy, two or three thousand words. And there is some excellent literary reviewing, first-rate pieces such as David Denby's "The Gripes of Roth" (review of Philip Roth's *The Facts,* Farrar, Straus & Giroux), 21 November, pp. 37-40. The 19 December issue featured a review, by Israeli writer Hillel Halkin, of Pavic's novel which, by form if nothing else, rivals Leonard's *Nation* review. Halkin did his review in imitative dictionary form, beginning with "Borges, Jorge Luis (1899-1986)" and ending with "Publishing" ("A branch of manufacture concerned with the production and sale of books").

Commonweal brings a Catholic perspective to books, including a good deal of fiction. Among the novels reviewed were Thomas Flanagan's *The Tenants of Time* (Dutton), William Kennedy's *Quinn's Book* (Viking), Gabriel García Márquez's *Love in the Time of Cholera* (Knopf), Chinua Achebe's *Anthills of the Savannah* (Doubleday), and J. F. Powers's *Wheat That Springeth Green* (Knopf). Genuinely outstanding reviews of the year, anywhere, would have to include Barbara A. Bannon's review of *The Truth About Lorin Jones* (16 December, pp. 690-691) and Peter LaSalle's critical look at *Libra* (4 November, pp. 598-599). LaSalle noted "some real problems," including the book's "sheer pretension," its many "leaden one liners," and a plethora of "tough guy spy dialogue that would embarrass even Frederick Forsyth on a bad day." *Commentary,* Jewish and neoconservative, has lengthy notices in its "Books in Review" section, though next to no fiction except in articles. There *are* solidly literary articles, such as Joseph Epstein's "Who Killed Poetry?" (August) and Carol Iannone's "Adultery, from Hawthorne to Updike" (October). The *New Criterion* is a monthly that looks and acts like a quarterly. Reviews are relatively long and thorough essay reviews. Among the best in 1988 were regular Bruce Bawer's "Jean Stafford's Triumph," a review of David Roberts's *Jean Stafford* (November, pp. 61-72), and David Gurewich's "Glasnost, Ho!," a review of *Children of the Arbat* (Little, Brown) by Anatoli Rybakov (September, pp. 77-81).

Once upon a time, not so long ago, both the *Atlantic* and *Harper's* exercised a real literary influence, in part on account of their book reviewing. Book reviews have almost vanished in the new format of *Harper's*.The *Atlantic* published important "literary" short stories as well as serious nonfiction articles and essays. But the "Books" section these days is limited to a couple of essay reviews, and the familiar "Brief Reviews" section treats maybe ten to a dozen (at most) titles in reviews ranging from one hundred to two hundred words. The choices for this section inevitably seem whimsical, but that very quality can result in oddly interesting moments. *Item.* The December *Atlantic* devoted most space (roughly three hundred words) in "Brief Reviews" to a not-much-noticed novel, Nicholson Baker's *The Mezzanine* (Weidenfeld & Nicolson), "an odd, clever novel" of thirty seconds spent on an ascending escalator. Only the simple fact that, in this context, anything will do as well as any other, allows for this kind of adventure in reviewing. The main point is, however, that over a year these once influential magazines review fewer titles, and not much more promptly, than the literary quarterlies. Determinedly conservative, the *National Review* makes more of books than the *Atlantic* and yet less than one might have expected. It is a scattershot method. There is the first-rate, intelligent column, "The Right Books," by senior editor Chilton Williamson, Jr., built upon a topic and a new book touching on it. There are "Random Notes," very brief notices of books which, often and elsewhere, might receive no attention at all; and, also, previews of books coming out in the month or so ahead. The regular reviews, found in "Books Arts & Manners," are various, favor nonfiction heavily, and run roughly twelve hundred to fifteen hundred words (about one-half of the length of the competitive *New Republic*). Good people regularly write for this section, peo-

ple such as D. Keith Mano, M. D. Aeschilman, staff members such as John Simon and Richard John Neuhaus. Finally, there are, from time to time, general articles with a literary base. The December issue sets up a debate, an "exchange" between Roger Scruton and Arianna-Stassinopoulos Huffington about her Picasso biography and its implications. Scruton's reaction is mixed, if strong, and concerns itself with larger problems of biography as manifested in this book; "Serious biography is therefore suspicious of facts, and at war with scholarship. If Picasso emerges from Mrs. Huffington's chatter as demeaned and diminished, this is not because she emphasizes the demeaning side (though she certainly does), but because she does so unremittingly, and at enormous length, until Picasso is entirely buried beneath the case against him." The author's reply is largely ad hominem, though she makes some valid, if debatable points about the relationship of art and morality. The significant and surprising thing is that the *National Review* opened its pages to a serious debate, one based on the power of a book. Perhaps it should not surprise, since William F. Buckley, Jr., a public figure who loves public debate, is editor in chief. But the balance and fairness of it goes against the grain of the usual assumptions concerning the rigidity of conservative publications.

Which leads to another modest discovery. Some of the most emphatically conservative publications in this country, editorially hard-knuckled and hard-nosed, are among the most enlightened and interesting of book reviewers. The *American Spectator* made something of a splash with the Joe Queenan article on contemporary short story writers, "Character Assassins" (December, pp. 14-16), but the regular "Book Reviews" section was composed of seven essay reviews; and the special section, "Books for Christmas," recommended a wildly disparate library of things old and new, including novels such as Dominick Dunne's *People Like Us* (Crown), David Markson's *Wittgenstein's Mistress* (Dalkey Archive), Tom Wolfe's *The Bonfire of the Vanities* (Farrar, Straus & Giroux), and Laura Ingalls Wilder's *The 'Little House' Boxed Set* (Harper & Row). *Chronicles: A Magazine of American Culture*, edited by classicist Thomas Fleming, is published by the Rockford Institute. The quiet admonition at the bottom of the copyright page— "The views expressed in *Chronicles* are the authors' alone and do not necessarily reflect the views of the Rockford Institute or of its directors"— seems to be a simple statement of fact. The reviews and reviewers of any given issue (in this case January 1989) are various. David Slavitt writes roughly twenty-five hundred words in review of Richard Eberhart's *Collected Poems 1930-1986* (Oxford University Press) and *New and Collected Poems* (Harcourt Brace Jovanovich) by Richard Wilbur. With one major exception (see below) nobody in the commercial magazine world paid any printed attention to either of these books. Paul T. Hornak reviews *Collected Letters of John Randolph of Roanoke to Dr. John Brockenbrough 1812-1833* (Transaction); Gregory J. Sullivan finds provocative and intelligent things to say about the life and career of Lionel Trilling, starting from the Twayne series' *Lionel Trilling*, by Stephen Tanner. An earlier issue (June 1988) presents two extensive, somewhat contradictory reviews of Tom Wolfe's *The Bonfire of the Vanities*, an essay review of *Trump: The Art of the Deal* (Random House), another essay review of *Uncivil Religion–Interreligious Hostility in America* (Crossroad), and a brief notice of Times Books' *Buying Into America,* by Martin and Susan Tolchin.

Any doubt that serious conservatives tend to take books and literature seriously, and more as points of departure than (as in the case of the *Nation* and the *New Republic*) as metaphorical Molotov cocktails to be hurled at the opposition or (coming from the other side) expeditiously extinguished, vanished in consideration of one of the most extraordinary magazines in America–*The World & I,* a monthly published by the Washington Times Corporation. This magazine, awash with color photographs and reproductions, averages about seven hundred pages per issue, of which roughly one hundred pages are devoted to "Book World," exclusively given over to in-depth reviews (averaging about three thousand words) of a variety of books. Books are also regularly reviewed as a part of other topical sections, such as "The Arts" and "Currents in Modern Thought." Usually ten to twelve books are reviewed, one or more of these being a "featured book," which allows for an excerpt from the book and more than one response to it. The June issue, which had more reviews of novels than usual, featured Márquez's *Love in the Time of Cholera,* together with an excerpt and four essay responses. Nine other books were reviewed in "Book World," among them Thomas Flanagan's *The Tenants of Time,* Herbert Gold's *California Dreaming* (Fine), and Faith Sullivan's *The Cape Ann* (Crown). For the last two these reviews are surely the most thor-

ough they will receive. Flanagan may earn as much or more space and attention in a literary magazine. In the "Currents in Modern Thought" section, seventy-five pages were given to the topic "Literary Modernism: From Hardy to Pound," with essays by Denis Donoghue, Hugh Kenner, Eugene Goodheart, Jeffrey Meyers, and others. Although new work is paramount in "Book World," there are exceptions. The April issue reserved something close to seventy-five pages for "Remembering James Baldwin." Only the *New York Review of Books* matches *The World & I* for in-depth book reviewing, and the reviews in *The World & I* seem much more various in subject and far less dominated by any consensual ideology. *The World & I* book editors, Lynn Criner and Doug Burton, are doing a commendable job, performing a major service in the contemporary literary scene.

In publishing, however, all roads do, finally, lead to and from New York City. And it is there that the greatest impact and influence of book reviews takes place. It is said, with authority, that the intellectual influence of the *New York Review of Books* remains strong, despite the clubby (or, anyway, cliquish) character of its regular writers, despite their age and cranky predictability. They have the services of some excellent writers, acknowledged experts; and these writers are given space enough to go beyond the usual limits and thus to develop larger themes and to establish critical relationships. In general, however, fiction receives casual, almost perfunctory attention these days (one of the few habits the editors share with that imaginary and critical mass–middle America). A clear exception to the rule is the critical work of Robert Towers, whose review of Louise Erdrich's *Tracks* (Holt) and *Breathing Lessons* by Anne Tyler (10 November, pp. 40-41) is typically excellent, at once appreciative and critical, not ignoring problems, but responsive to the most subtle currents of feeling, the most delicate gestures of art. A kind of lower Manhattan answer to the *New York Review of Books* is the *Village Voice Literary Supplement,* consisting of forty pages in large, tabloid format. It has its own best-seller list ("Our Kind of Best-Sellers") garnered from independent bookstores only. There is a lot of advertising, chiefly for commercial trade paperbacks and books from university and small presses. A typical issue has eight to ten short reviews, "Brief Encounters," and ten or more essay reviews, with also a short story or two. Nonfiction, perhaps because it offers more elbow room for ideological star turns, gets much more attention than fiction. The writing is uneven, but seldom less than lively. The advertising probably has more influence.

Of special interest in the context of New York are those ostensibly locally oriented magazines which are, in fact, national in scope, depending upon the apparently unshakable conviction of Americans coast to coast that somehow New York City is *their* city too, a sort of national theme park which it is their bound duty, as much as their privilege, to honor and maintain by tourism and taxes. These magazines–*New York, Vanity Fair*, and preeminently the *New Yorker*, subscribed to and available on newsstands everywhere–are, each with slight differences, possessed of a wonderfully ambiguous stance. On the one hand, they must have a national audience to earn the advertising profits by which they rise or fall. (The *New Yorker*, in its new regime, has taken to national advertising of itself–on television!) But part of their national appeal is the sense of being "in," of being all that we locals and yokels imagine. Similarly, within the precincts of their own region, these magazines must be authentically local and authoritative. What is required is an elegant double standard, a sort of self-reflexive sophistication, poised on the razor's edge of being an inherent contradiction–for how can *true* sophistication be self-aware without being also self-conscious? Leaving them (and their readers) with the pains and pleasures of this delicate problem, we need only to remark that since the American publishing industry, at least in a primary editorial and a secondary service sense, is still chiefly centered in New York, book reviewing which originates there has a local as well as a national influence. In a chummy, close-knit if competitive business like publishing, where the principals see each other face to face with some regularity, local reputation weighs heavily. And national success and repute without a corresponding sense of local honor (if only for the clever capacity of being able to manipulate the responses of country bumpkins–the mainstream of middle America) is empty, ashes on the tongue. At the absolute minimum, then, the book reviews in these local/national magazines have the power to create conversation in the trade, "in house" as it were.

All of which is to say that these particular magazines have a good deal of power in the book world, more than they may be aware of, indeed more than they may wish for. *New York* is, of the three, more regionally oriented; for in

large part it is an ongoing listing of places, events, and activities in the city. But the book reviews are a regular section, under "Arts," chiefly featuring the work of contributing editor Rhoda Koenig and a few others. Serious fiction earns a surprisingly high percentage of the reviews, one or two per issue. In general the reviews, roughly 500-750 words, are efficient and amusing, requiring, by intent, an awareness of the reviewer in action as an object of attention as much as the given book. At once exemplary and representative is Koenig's review of John Updike's *S.* which, in fact, made some bright and quick observations, points often missed by other, more plodding reviewers. But, at the same time, Koenig, not atypically, had to establish her own (and the reader's) sense of timely, "with it" sophistication at the slight expense of Updike and his book. "The subject of *S.* is, obviously, pretty stale (doesn't 'nude encounter group' now sound as remote as 'stereopticon'?) but Updike's magic fingers massage a lot of life into this journey down the well-worn path to enlightenment." Good for a shared grin or a giggle, if not a full belly laugh. And the review's conclusion is a little trope more inclined to cuteness than criticism. "*S.* is full of sass and spirit, a springy book to curl up with while we wait for the first crocus and this year's cuckoo." True to form, or anyway to the cockamamy spirit of our times, *New York* made its grandest literary gesture of the year with a cover story, "The Genius: Harold Brodkey And His Great (Unpublished) Novel," by Dinita Smith (19 September, pp. 54-62, 64-66), an essay on the signs and wonders of a novel which is not only unfinished and unpublished, but may not actually exist. The title of this possible masterpiece is "Party of Animals." The monthly *Vanity Fair* is more aggressively literary. The basic book column is James Wolcott's "Mixed Media," which, as titled, may or may not be about books or strictly literary. During 1988, for example, he wrote columns on such subjects as Burt Reynolds, "spooky Phil Spector," "Oprah, Phil, and the talk show confessionals," the critics of the *New York Times*, and Robert Altman's *Tanner '88*, and, most relevantly to this piece, "Partisans Reviewed: Left, right, and center, the party lines of commentary magazines" (November, pp. 28, 32, 36-37). (His conclusion? that the *New Republic* is "the most entertaining and intellectually agile magazine in the country.") But Wolcott also reviews new books. The occasion for the Phil Spector piece (January 1989) was Mark Ribowsky's *He's a Rebel* (Dutton).

Other reviews are constructed on themes. In "The Laugh Pack" he reviewed a group of writers earlier described by *Newsweek* as the "new breed of literate humorists": Roy Blount, Jr., Ian Frazier, Frank Gannon, George W. S. Trow, Veronica Geng, and some others. "The Good-Bad Girls" (December) reviewed short-story writer Mary Gaitskill and first novelists Margaret Diehl and Kristin McCloy. As in the case of Rhoda Koenig, the reviewer-as-actor is a required role: "Now don't get me wrong. I'm a guy. I've been around. I peeked under the tent when the circus came to town and saw the bearded lady in her bath. . . ." *Vanity Fair* also uses critic James Atlas, from time to time, to write literary articles–"The Survivor's Suicide," concerning the late Primo Levi (January 1988)–and reviews of books, for example, "The Abbess of Oxford" (March), a full-scale essay review and interview with Iris Murdoch, whose new book was *The Book and the Brotherhood* (Viking). And there are regular profiles of various literary figures. For variety it would be hard to beat that same March issue, which featured "Queens of the Road" by Dominick Dunne, celebrating Joan and Jackie Collins; and Pete Hamill's "Love and Solitude," a lengthy interview with Gabriel García Márquez.

After all is said and done, however, like it or not, neither *Vanity Fair* nor *New York* nor, indeed, any other similar magazine, can touch the *New Yorker*. Even under new, and not necessarily improved, management and editorship, the quality of writing and thinking in the *New Yorker*, especially in their book reviews, is uniformly high. Somewhat less obvious is the fact that in a steady and cumulative (if not always timely) fashion, they do manage over the course of a year to take notice of a surprising number of good books; and of this surprisingly thorough coverage, since the "Briefly Noted" section is usually divided into three parts–"Fiction," "General," "Mystery and Crime"–fiction is given considerably more coverage than in most other popular magazines. Those books which earn a full-scale essay review are seriously benefited. With Terrence Rafferty (see the 1987 *DLB Yearbook*) writing regularly, spelled by John Updike, Clive James, Lis Harris, David Thomson, Brad Leithauser, and others, including poetry critics Helen Vendler and Edward Hirsch, there were many important reviews in the *New Yorker* during the year. Rafferty was at his best in essay reviews on Carlos Fuentes's *Myself With Others* (Farrar, Straus & Giroux) and *The Art of the Novel* (Grove) by Milan Kundera (16

May); pop novels *The Icarus Agenda* (Random House) by Robert Ludlum and *Rock Star* (Simon and Schuster) by Jackie Collins (20 June); *The Hearts and Lives of Men* (Viking) by Faye Weldon (1 August); *Libra* by Don DeLillo (26 September); and in the 19 December issue he produced an excellent (and very rare) examination of several first novels: Jonathan Franzen's *The Twenty-Seventh City* (Farrar, Straus & Giroux), Michael Tolkin's *The Player* (Atlantic Monthly Press), and ("the most adventurous and original American first novel of recent months") Ellen Akins's *Home Movie* (Simon and Schuster). Among John Updike's best efforts were his review of *Curfew* (Weidenfeld & Nicolson) by José Donoso and *Anthills of the Savannah* by Chinua Achebe (13 June); and, in the 4 July issue, a review ("Small Packages," pp. 81-84) of several short novels from Europe: Raymond Queneau's *Pierrot Mon Ami* (Dalkey Archive), Patrick Suskind's *The Pigeon* (Knopf), and Emmanuel Carrere's *The Mustache* (Scribners). Clive James's moving and unsentimental essay, "Last Will and Testament" (23 May, pp. 86-92), on Primo Levi's *The Drowned and the Saved* (Summit), becomes a meditation on the meaning and implications of the Holocaust: "Our only legitimate consolation is that, although they [catastrophes like the Holocaust] loom large in the long perspectives of history, history would have no long perspectives if human beings were not, in the aggregate, more creative than destructive. But the mass slaughter of the innocent is not a civics lesson. It involves us all, except that some of us were lucky enough not to be there. The best reason for trying to lead a decent life is that we are living on borrowed time, and the best reason to admire Primo Levi's magnificent last book is that he makes this so clear." A minor catastrophe at the *New Yorker* concerned a long "Critic at Large" essay (18 July, pp. 72-82) on the life and works of James Agee, written by the distinguished and venerable John Hersey. After its appearance there was a little firestorm of publicity indicating that parts of the essay were, perhaps inadvertently, plagiarized.

The two principal weekly newsmagazines, *Newsweek* and *Time*, have long been powerfully influential in many aspects of contemporary culture, including literature; and although they have both cut back on the space allotted for book reviews and, thus, on the number of books reviewed in a year, both have outstanding critics on their editorial staff and, on the whole, do a better job of covering the literary scene and its events than might be expected, especially in spotlighting the major new works of serious fiction. At *Time* senior writers Paul Gray and R. Z. Sheppard and contributors such as Stefan Kanfer produce a lively book section. But *Time* does other things as well. Given a page to write about the literary excitement of Hispanic culture in the special issue on that subject (11 July), Paul Gray adroitly focused on the prominent translator Gregory Rabassa, who has translated the work of many of the chief writers of Latin America. On the other hand, *Time* missed the opportunity to discuss the work of many of the Hispanic-American writers whose work is, indeed, breaking out of the barrio, albeit by means of the university and small presses. *Time* also produces literary features from time to time. Witness Richard Lacayo's "Profile: Stand Aside Sisyphus/Make Way for Susan Sontag" (24 October, pp. 86-88). In a purely relative sense *Time* had some moments of high literary adventure. Nobody, least of all these newsmagazines, spends time or space on the beleaguered art of contemporary poetry. But Paul Gray managed an intelligently executed piece ("A Testament to Civility," 9 May, pp. 84-85) on Richard Wilbur and his *New and Collected Poems* (Harcourt Brace Jovanovich).

Newsweek (senior writers Walter Clemmons and Peter S. Prescott, general editor Laura Shapiro, and others) awards a little less space to its "Books" section, but was often somewhat more adventurous overall. *Newsweek* produced a literary cover and story–"Tom Clancy, Best Seller"–for its 8 August issue, with an extensive piece by Evan Thomas on "The Art of the Techno-Thriller" (pp. 60-65). Most surprising was an article by Walter Clemmons, "The Joyously Versatile Thomas Disch" (11 July, pp. 66-67), which, using the occasion of the publication of a children's book, *The Brave Little Toaster Goes to Mars* (Doubleday), publicly "discovered" and praised this little-known poet, novelist, and man of letters. The very existence of this piece, especially in a newsmagazine, but, in plain fact, anywhere in the world of the popular magazines, is simply astonishing. Paradoxically it leads directly to an awareness of the greatest limitation of all the popular magazines, that, all things considered, these magazines are not and cannot be instruments of discovery. With the notable exception of a radically critical magazine like *The World & I*, they have to make a virtue of the necessity of dealing with easily recognizable, if not only well-known, books and authors. Thus the magazines become, far

more than the nation's newspapers, a front line for the defense of the literary establishment. And they have a deep interest, more essential than vested, in the preservation of the status quo. The most that they seem to be able to do–though, judging by this past year, they do this rather well–is, despite the constant critical mass of the purely commercial, to call attention to and to celebrate some worthy and serious literary art and artists.

Henry Taylor–An Interview with Colin Walters

The *Washington Times* began publication in the late spring of 1982, under controversial circumstances: the capital behind it was furnished by members of the Reverend Sun Myung Moon's Unification Church, and there were a couple of years during which many people had a hard time taking the paper seriously–a fact of life to which the paper responded with a brief advertising campaign featuring people reading the paper with bags over their heads. Now, though its slant is conservative, it has established its editorial independence from its ownership. Its book section has grown from a page and a half in a magazine section to a healthy proportion of the Monday "Life!" section; one or two additional reviews run on Tuesdays and Thursdays on the op-ed page. The section has gained increasingly a reputation for seriousness and literary quality.

Though I have been reviewing poetry for the *Washington Times* since early in 1983, when the paper was less than a year old, I have never sat down for an extended conversation with Colin Walters, who has been editing the book review pages for all but the first five weeks of the paper's existence. Most of the books in his office are arranged on shelves, though there are a few stacks of larger things–coffee-table books–on the floor at the base of the shelves. These, it turns out, make good steps, which Mr. Walters uses often to reach the top shelf. There is not the faintest suggestion of inundation or disorder.

Walters is a medium-sized man in his early fifties; his increasingly Americanized British accent, his well-trimmed, curly hair, and his reading glasses all give a somewhat professorial impression which is strengthened by the range and energy of his regular column, "On Books"; but his association with academe has been usually–even refreshingly–limited.

"I was born in Weston-super-Mare, in Somerset; the only person currently of note to have been born there was John Cleese. It was in Somer-

Colin Walters (photograph by Ross Franklin/
The Washington Times)

set; it's now in a new county area called Avon. A few years ago there was a fit of redistricting, which altered historical associations; you wouldn't like it if you knew all about it.

"I went to elementary school there, passed the standard eleven-plus and went to the grammar school, which I left at sixteen. I did not subsequently have the advantage of a university education. I passed six O-levels, as they were called, but by the time I was seventeen I was in the army. When I was eighteen years old, I was a sergeant, on a boat departing for Suez in 1956; we never got there, of course; we were ordered back. I stayed in the army for nine years. In the course of that time I did do some A-Level studies in literature and ancient history, through Wolsey Hall, Oxford, which is not part of the University, but it's a very respectable institution, and made these correspondence courses available. I never took any exams, because by the time I might have I was too busy settling in here, trying to become an American."

His first stint in the United States was at the British Embassy, as an army payroll supervisor holding the rank of sergeant; he returned to England for a year when he left the army and was back in the United States late in 1964, looking for a job, which he found in the poverty program.

"I quickly found that I was among people some of whom were willing to let me do quite a lot of work; a year later I was running the budget office, and a year after that I was special assistant to the executive director, and that set me up as a 'professional' in the United States sense. I went from job to job doing budget work, and quietly on the side got in some writing. For eight years I was associated with the Washington Center for Metropolitan Studies, Atlee Shidler's organization; it's now called the Greater Washington Research Center. I wrote the occasional monograph on things like subway costs.

"Meanwhile I'd been harboring this desire to be a writer—all my life, in fact. When I left school at sixteen, I was doing well; I was always near the top of my class, and it was a bit of a shock to discover that I wasn't going to go to Oxford or Cambridge after all. But of course it was a different world then—a very different world. My family had neither the means nor the expectations to indulge much of that kind of thinking. I did have this sense of a door slamming on me; so I was sort of tinkering about.

"In 1961 I had some poems published by a kind of cooperative—a guy in Dulwich village had this press, and I got these poems—juvenilia, really, I was still a child—printed up in a handsome little edition." He rummages behind his desk and hands me a copy of *Songs To Myself* (Outposts Publications), which is better than he makes it sound.

"When I was over here, still in the army, I wrote a letter to Robert Evett, who was then the literary editor of the *New Republic*. He befriended and encouraged me, and I kept scribbling away; he commissioned a review from me, of a book by Benjamin DeMott, and then never ran it; it obviously wasn't good enough. He didn't ask me for another book review for about eleven years. He had by then been to the *Atlantic*, and had returned to the *Washington Star*, for whom I ended up doing a review just about every weekend for a year or two. I rather learned the basics of the trade there. I was still free-lancing—a Sunday reviewer, if you will, since this was still in the think-tank part of my life.

"But Bob died and the *Star* began its eclipse; remember when Joe Albritton bought it and put everybody on a four-day week and fired all the stringers? Then, I didn't get to write another book review for another seven years. But the *Washington Times* came along, and Anne Crutcher–she had been Bob's boss at the *Star*, part of that large *Star* contingent that came over here–asked me how I'd like to come be the book review editor, and I jumped at it. I had left the institute, Atlee Shidler's think tank, in 1979, and was for a short time one of [Washington, D.C.] Mayor Marion Barry's top aides, assistant city administrator for financial management; I was technically and politically out of my depth. I left there for the University of the District of Columbia, in the last days of Lisle Carter's administration, and started a small institute for district affairs; that lasted from 1980 to 1982, and that's what I left to come here.

"I got here in June of 1982, five weeks into the paper's publishing life. After the army, it's the longest job I've had. What you might reasonably call a third career.

"I edit the book pages and write a weekly column. I also do a radio book review for a small syndicate, Radio America." He rummages again, in a box full of cassettes. "Here's one from July 25th–I have boxes and boxes of these things, and I have no idea what I shall ever do with them. But let's see–the tape contains the whole program, and there's this little three-minute segment of mine–yes. Jean-Paul Sartre's *Mallarmé: Poet of Nothingness*. They let me do pretty much what I like, you see.

"Each week, now, we run eight or nine reviews on Monday, and one each on Tuesday and Thursday, in the commentary pages; that's a solid ten a week, or 520 a year. The briefs, the shorter notices, amount to our noticing another 350 books. But it hasn't always been this way; we have now about two and a half times as much space for books as we had at the beginning.

"At first, you never saw us on the cover of the magazine section, and then in 1985 we began to get covers, and began to be proud of the magazine. We were ambivalent about the switch to the broadsheet, the regular section, which came along with some other format changes in 1987–purely mechanical considerations, having to do with the specs of the presses and what they can and can't crank out.

"But there is one advantage to the broadsheet format. It gives me a little more time, because the pages don't have to be set up as far in advance of publication. And that's very important to me, because I'm trying to compete with the *Washington Post* and the *New York Times* with respect to timing, and they tend to get the books more quickly than I do. That's less true than it was five years ago, but there are still some publishers from whom it is not easy to get review copies early. So the shorter lead time makes me competitive. On the whole, we do pretty well, when you balance out the things we still have to do that they have already done, and the things we do two or three weeks ahead of them.

"Any book editor has to bear in mind, though, not only the extent to which he can compete nationally, but what the competing local claims are on the space. We have the so-called 'Washington book,' which comes in various shapes and sizes, and we have to see what we make of them: Neil Sheehan's Vietnam book is obviously not to be ignored; and sometimes, neither is a novel by a congressman's wife. Then, there's an overlapping circle, a set of books on American politics–not Washington stuff explicitly, but Washington's business. Or by Gorbachev, who has just cranked out another screed. Then local ones in the truly local sense–area writers ought to be noticed in their own home town, if possible. So location does tilt things somewhat; but allowing for all that, I try to color in with as broad a spectrum as I can, and I like to cover intellectuals' books and university presses as well as I can, and we do a fair amount of poetry.

"I like to find things of unusual quality that are likely to be overlooked elsewhere; maybe I'm proudest lately of having found David Markson's novel *Wittgenstein's Mistress*, which went unnoticed for weeks after my review; but then the *New York Times* picked it up, and others, and now maybe it will be published in England by Jonathan Cape; so that's been pleasant. Now that the review section is about as big as it can be, it's great to have this 'On Books' column, because in there I can be as eccentric as I like. Nobody else seems to want to write about Mallarmé, as I do once in a while.

"I try to be daring, in the books we choose and the people we choose to have a go at them; I want an interesting juxtaposition of book and reviewer, much more than I want a particular point of view; I have my range of comfort, of course, which is fairly broad and centrist, but I'm much more concerned that a review be interesting than that it take a particular tack.

"I'm not trying to be bold enough to make a constant stream of enemies; if I weren't here, I couldn't do any of it, so I won't go out weekly looking for the reviewer who is likely to make an author want to shoot me.

"But I always am trying for interesting matchups between writer and reviewer, and I encourage reviewers to be critical, really to be critics, which is one of the biggest problems with having writers review other writers. Quite aside from whatever personal feelings there may or may not be, the writer has a sensitivity to the difficulties, or a sympathy with them, that gets into the review and discourages criticism. I think reviewers ought to be smart, clever, and feisty, and they shouldn't have to conceal their cleverness from the reader.

"I have the luxury of being able to think this way, because I have enormous freedom, and the support of my supervisors. This situation, I think, tends to obtain more often in youthful institutions. I do not have a battle with anyone here, trying to establish that books can be newsworthy. I don't have anyone telling me that this or that book must be reviewed, though I feel sure that I could jeopardize my position with constant foolishness; but that's not the same as a need to play it safe. I don't have to do that, maybe because this paper is still young. If you're worried about not doing something wrong, you find it harder to do things right.

"Another thing I'm glad to have established here is a books committee, several staff people, who have been involved with the book section–a group that can meet and talk a little about the books that come in here, since no book editor can pretend to be expert in everything that's worth talking about. How good are you, for example, on theologians? Exactly.

"And, not really paradoxically at all, this distributed responsibility makes it easier for me to indulge my interest occasionally in the eccentric item. Recently there was a reprint of a 1905 book by a man named E. P. Evans, a history of *The Criminal Prosecution and Capital Punishment of Animals*. This was a big thing in the medieval period; it was a matter of exorcism, and things had to be done right. If the pig must be hung wearing human clothes, then the point is that leaving the pig undressed will not get the devil out of him. Anyway, I reviewed this reprint, and then *Insight*, the newsweekly that's published by this company, picked it up, and then I began getting calls from librarians, asking me what I meant by get-

ting the public excited about books they didn't have. Most popular review I did all year long.

"What's the point of reviewing books? Is it to give judicious advice about whether to buy a book or not? Or is it to give people something edifying to think about for a few minutes? Clearly, both. Ask yourself how many people get their general liberal arts education out of book reviews, and never go near even a secondary text. Newspaper generalist reviewers are pretty well down the intellectual ladder, perhaps, but one of their functions is to use a book as an occasion to make clearer to the public some topic, idea, recent episode, or whatever–for the benefit of those who will not go near the book. I don't mean that reviewers should write about something other than the book, only that readers can learn much by reading the book page, even if they don't read the books. And, if what we tell them is all they'll ever hear, we should watch what we say, shouldn't we?

"The conventional wisdom is that only the *New York Times* can run reviews that will affect sales, unless you're reviewing local presses where dozens of copies constitute a significant number. In the case of poetry, that can matter, can't it?

"One of the things I have to demonstrate in my annual budget hearing is something called proof of presence–evidence that people know and care that we're here. And one of the things I do in support of that is to collect blurbs that quote us–in catalogs, paperback reprints, and so on." He shows me a photocopy of an ad which quotes his paper. "This is just a thriller here, you see, but that's commercial evidence, though sufficiently indirect to be hard to pin down. Clearly the publishers care, and maybe that's because they think they should."

Proof of presence! It occurs to me that the phrase applies to a sort of Holy Grail, indefinable and desirable, which writers themselves are seeking whenever they scan the pages of a book section. When I started out reviewing poetry for the *Washington Times*, I did so on the condition that I should never feel edited politically; I haven't been. A few friends of mine told me I was doing the wrong thing, even that the association would ruin me; but no poet has ever scolded me for praising a book in these pages, or even for finding it wanting. There is a feeling of independence about reviewing for Colin Walters, and the exhilaration of knowing he will do his best not to print a boring review.

David Slavitt–An Interview with John Leonard

To say that John Leonard has been all around the block is hardly to suggest the range of experiences he's enjoyed or, on occasion, suffered. He was, from 1971 to 1975, editor in chief of the *New York Times Book Review*, which made him, automatically, the most powerful person in the book reviewing game in America–or for that matter, figuring in the size and affluence of the American marketplace, in the world. He had been, before that, a member of the editorial staff of the *New York Times Book Review* (1967-1969), and a daily book critic (1969-1970). And when he stepped down from the editor in chief's chair, it was to be the chief cultural correspondent (1976-1982), which included the writing of some of those daily book reviews as well as his "Private Lives" column and his "Critic's Notebook" work.

But then the axe fell. Or more particularly, John Leonard reviewed, unfavorably, a book that had been dedicated to Abe Rosenthal, who was at the time the executive editor of the *Times*–the dedication didn't appear in the bound galleys Leonard had been sent, but that didn't let him off the hook. It was unforgivable that he'd been unkind to Betty Friedan and to her book *The Second Stage*, and Mr. Rosenthal was displeased. Leonard was relieved of all his duties, not fired but, even worse, forced to come in every day and sit there, watching the hands drag slowly around the dials of the wall clocks. There were men in the basement, typesetters, members of the printers' union, who were doing similar kinds of Sisyphean chores as a result of some labor contract's job security provision. The *Times* had gone over to computerized typesetting of the stock tables, but the printers came in every day from somewhere in outer Queens, sat at old Linotype machines, set the tables, and then, at the end of their shift, smashed the type, or threw it back in the vats that hold the molten lead.

At least they had something to do, a way of filling up the hours they had to put in. Leonard was just sitting there, watching the clock, feeling absurd, and also feeling angry because he knew that nothing he wrote was going to get into the paper. And worst of all, it wasn't his fault. In any fair and reasonable universe, this kind of interference from upstairs isn't supposed to happen–especially not at the *Times*. This isn't because that paper is owned and run by finer human beings than other newspapers, but only because they are

John Leonard (photograph by Sam Falk / The New York Times)

so much more pretentious and self-righteous. But one can't always rely on other people's vices.

At that particular moment, the revived *Vanity Fair* was organizing itself, a Newhouse undertaking that was going to be competition for the *New Yorker*. And they offered him a job in which he could do actual writing that might even appear in print in the pages of the publication. One doesn't usually leave the *Times* and its security and prestige, but Leonard didn't think he had much choice. He cleaned out his desk and made the move.

And it was a disaster. The Newhouse people were less patient than they had led the editor, Richard Locke, to expect. He was fired and a new one came in, with new ideas or at least a set of new names and faces that could create an illusion of change. Leonard was out in the cold.

He has managed to recoup and, indeed, is now riding high, operating as a television critic for *New York* magazine, reviewing books for *Newsday*, the Long Island newspaper that is making its foray into the New York market. Leonard also does book reviews for "Fresh Air" on National Public Radio, is the Media columnist for *Ms.* magazine, and reviews fiction for the *Nation*. And he has been appearing now on CBS-TV's "Sunday Morning" where he can talk about pretty much anything he wants to, books or anything else that has happened to catch his attention.

A diminutive, bespectacled, bewhiskered John Leonard–he looks a bit like a leprechaun–opened the door of his townhouse in the east Seventies, an impressive building although somewhat in need of maintenance, and ushered me past his workroom and up to the homey front parlor on the second floor. When we had seated ourselves, I asked him about his new constellation of jobs. The *Nation*, for instance, seemed an interesting place to begin, because its book reviewing had struck me as somewhat tendentious, rather too engagé and insufficiently belle-lettrist. How had he managed to make them understand that they needed him?

"Well, it's just funny," Leonard said, allowing himself a small and wry smile. "Elizabeth Pochoda [literary editor of the *Nation*] is an old friend of mine. I do a weekly book review for National Public Radio for "Fresh Air" which comes out of Philadelphia, and that's the way I've basically been keeping my hand in, plus reviewing for *Newsday*, which is frustrating because it's always their idea. The relationship was never such–and I can see why book editors suspect this–that if I wanted to review something, I could call somebody up and get the book. They have a regular rotation of daily reviewers, and for the Sunday section, Nina King was the editor and she's now gone to the *Washington Post*, and Jack Schwartz, who left the culture desk of the *Times*, is the book editor at *Newsday*. And they have a Sunday section which is six pages, seven pages, something like that. And it's pretty good. And that's what I was reviewing for. And it was fun.

"I mean, I'd decided that I needed to get back into reviewing books. I didn't for a long time–I had a long problem with alcohol. I'm now dry for two and a half years, but I felt that I could review anything else but I would not review books, because every book I read I was reading myself into instead of paying attention to what the author was all about. I took everything personally and my reactions were all skewed...."

"Is that wrong?" I asked. "Are we not supposed to do that?"

"Well, but we have to be conscious of our skewing," he answered, holding his palms up as if to show that he was concealing nothing. "Obviously, I read through left-wing eyes; I read with a Freudian gleam. But I'm conscious of it and try to correct for it. But I was reading books out of a personal need and not out of disinterestedness,

and that bothered me. It doesn't bother me, writing about television or anything else, but it bothered me about books. But I got that taken care of. I got that cleared up."

I told him I liked that distinction. "To bring any sort of intelligence at all to television is more than they deserve, and to hell with them?"

"You're also writing out of a kind of swound anyway," he said. "It's one big circus. It was a stream of consciousness reviewing a stream of consciousness, and it didn't seem to matter a lot. It matters a great deal with books. So I said to *Newsday*–because I'd been doing a weekly column for them–that I wanted to do some books, and they had some odd choices for me. The first thing I did for them was the two biographies of Sartre, which took me forever. And then they sent me Lech Walesa's autobiography . . . things like that. It was a lot of fun but it was always a surprise, and I had the feeling that I wasn't sinking my teeth into things that mattered most to me. I was giving them very short reviews. And an NPR review is a page and a half, double spaced. So I went to Betsy [Pochoda] and I told her that, financially, I was now in a position to be able to afford to write for the *Nation*–they pay in the high two figures. And she gave me Tom Wolfe's book [*The Bonfire of the Vanities*] and the special issue of *Dissent*. And I did that and they were very pleased. And I did I. F. Stone. And then Victor [Navasky, the editor] and Betsy came and said, 'Look, if you really want to do this, we would like to have you in on a regular basis, but of course we can't afford to pay competitively. But what we can do is that we can say, you can review the fiction of your choice at whatever length you want, as often as you want–we'd like it at least once a month. And for anything you want to do, our pages will be open for you.' And that was wonderful. As it turned out . . . I did the DeLillo [*Libra*] and then, I didn't find anything. I was reviewing fiction regularly for National Public Radio, and I read the Heller novel [*Picture This*] and I said, 'Do I want to write at length about how bad this is?' No, that's not where my energies should be put. A lot of books came along that were interesting, but nothing that I wanted to spend 2,000 words thinking about. But now there'll probably be a whole bunch of them. The Salman Rushdie, which looks wonderful, and the Doctorow's coming out. And a Margaret Atwood, which may or may not be good. It depends. She's up and down."

During the years when Leonard was not reviewing books, and even now that he's taken it up again, some publishers were less openhanded than others with review copies, he recalled rather amusedly. "On the other hand, I've been very bad about sending back catalogues. Some people always sent me books, even after I left the *Times*. Simon and Schuster and Knopf have always sent me books. Some people pay no attention to you when you review for radio. It doesn't count to them. I've got two hundred stations, but you can't see it and so it doesn't count. The minute the announcement appeared in the *Nation*–which has a circulation of 80,000!–then they started sending books."

I suggested that he could send the publishers copies of what he'd said on the radio, so that there would be a physical object, a piece of paper to put into those scrapbooks that publicists keep. Leonard agreed that that might work, but he shook his head at its impossibility. "You see, what I do for a living is the *New York Magazine* piece every week on television, and I do the *Newsday* column on whatever I feel like–politics, family living, or whatever. And I do these book reviews. And I do a monthly column for *Ms.* And now I'm on CBS "Sunday Morning" with Kuralt, which turns out to be a lot of fun, an enormous amount of fun. And it pays funny money–the opposite side of National Public Radio or the *Nation*. They pay way too much for not very much work. Of course, I've seen everything on television for *New York Magazine* and I don't have to work very hard. That [*New York Magazine* media column] has been my principal source of income for the last five or six years, and those other things I just sort of added on. And along comes CBS–and you're just struck again by the way rewards are distributed in this society. It is ridiculous!"

I asked Leonard to expand a little on that "along comes CBS," and tell me what actually happened. It was, he said, "odd. When they started 'Sunday Morning,' ten years ago, they called me and asked whether I'd be interested in doing something like that. I was working for the *Times* and I knew there was no way the *Times* would permit me to do the two things. And there was no way I was going to leave the *Times* to go into television. It didn't interest me much and also I had quite reasonable doubts about whether I'd be any good at it. And I suggested Jeff Greenfield, because I knew him to be the kind of person who can speak instantaneously in sentences and is funny and who knows a lot about television. And he was a wow. It was a great mistake for CBS to let

him go, but he wanted to do more and more politics, so they lost him to ABC. It was just ridiculous! And then they got Ron Powers, who had been the TV critic for one of the Chicago papers, to do nothing but television–which he did until last spring. And then he had some book projects and a fancy teaching post. And that's when they called me.

"But I'd left the *Times* after sixteen years, and the one thing that I'd promised myself was that I'd never again be owned by an institution. Never again! I'm entirely free-lance! And CBS wanted to own me–we started talking last March–and I would have to ask permission of them. I mean, they would pay an enormous amount of money, but I would have to ask permission of them to do anything else. I'd have had to give up *New York Magazine* and give up *Newsday*–that's ridiculous! I'm a writer; I'm not a media personality. It didn't make any sense, and I said so. I said that the only way I could possibly do it was as a free-lance. And what's more, I didn't think it could be sustained being only about television. It would have to be about movies or occasionally a book, or theater when it had a national pertinence. And that was the last I heard about it, for a long time. But then, about two months ago, they called and said, 'We'll do it your way, if you're still willing to do it.' And I thought, why not? What I didn't know, or had no way of knowing . . . I assumed I'd be walking into a pill-popping, paranoid, hectic place, every image one has of television. But 'Sunday Morning' was not like that. 'Sunday Morning' is presided over by the Buddha-like Charles Kuralt, and it has its own serenity and it goes for an hour and a half and ends with its nature essay and babbling water. And they have been warm, and it's been fun, and I have fucked up and they have covered for me."

Even on his terms, the arrangement with CBS is apparently openhanded. "I just reviewed [Milorad Pavic's] *The Dictionary of the Khazars* for the *Nation*," he said. "I loved it, but it was a lot of work, and I turned in a long review and . . . you get paid a hundred and fifty or two hundred dollars, and then you spend four minutes on CBS and get paid fifteen hundred to two thousand dollars, and you say, 'What . . . what is this?' I've got a year's contract, and it's fine. The money will go for . . . we need a new kitchen and we need a new front door, and if anything happens after that, all right. But my kids are out of college and this house has been paid for so that I no longer have to work for money, which is why, when the *Nation* came by, I agreed to do this. The only thing I really wanted now was space, so that I could wander, I could compare, I could quote, and I wouldn't have a hassle with the editors. I'm a prima donna with my copy, often not to my benefit. But until I work with an editor who can spell, I don't trust them with anything else. I need someone who can identify an unattributed reference to Shakespeare or John Donne that we take for granted because we were educated in the fifties rather than the seventies [Leonard went to Harvard and to Berkeley]. . . . So I don't let them fiddle with my copy unless I'm convinced that their culture is thick enough for them to have the right to judge. So it's fun, and I'm still doing the NPR because there are a lot of books, and there are a lot of nonfiction books, and I read five or six books a week, and every couple of weeks I decide on a couple to review—and I have carte blanche to do whatever I want. And that keeps me roughly current. I do one a week for NPR and one a month for the *Nation*. If it's an ambitious piece, one a month is all I can do right now. I've got my own novel to finish—I'm writing a series of mysteries. I've got contracts for three of them and outlines for seven, all with the same character. I'm writing them for fun; this is not art. I didn't want to try to write a great novel. One, I probably can't, but, two, I didn't want to put the pressure on myself, now that I'm two-and-a-half years sober. I go to A.A. and all that. But I don't want to have to write a perfect book. But I do want to write some fiction, because I enjoy making this stuff up, so I entered into this contract. One a year is due. Every time I have a chance, I work at it, and pages roll out, and there are jokes, and I'm having a good time.

"What it has meant with the *Nation* is that I now won't do free-lance book reviews. I would do a review here or there, for the L.A. *Times* or wherever. And that's not necessary anymore. That's not even desirable, because nobody can be as comfortable as I am with this little magazine."

I told him that it seemed to be an ideal arrangement, doing his trawling for NPR and finding one book a month to write on at greater length for the *Nation*. Leonard nodded and said, "And everybody understands, too. I mean, that was up front. Betsy knew what I was doing, and I said to National Public Radio, 'Look, every once in a while, you're going to see little bits and pieces of something I did for you in the middle

of this whale of a review—and I don't want you to get upset that this is what I'm doing.' "

His review, then, of DeLillo's *Libra* in the 19 September *Nation* was preceded by a shorter discussion of that book on NPR's "Fresh Air," but even that fairly long review in the magazine had been cut down, Leonard remembers. "You remember, there's that section, that one long paragraph in which I sum up his entire career. But each of those sentences had been at least one long paragraph—and I thought, nobody really needs this. You never can do everything. You shouldn't put everything in!"

When I congratulated him at having contrived so flexible and elegant an arrangement, he acknowledged that things had worked out well indeed. "If I have an opinion and I can't fit it in one place, I can find another place for it," he said, chuckling.

It was, I suggested, a kind of ideal outcome, a situation even better than anything he could have imagined back in what must have been his darkest days—when the *Vanity Fair* job evaporated. "I've got no gripes," he said. "I like what I'm doing and I've got time to do it, so there's a sense of rhythm and reward."

But because I had alluded to it, he took up the subject and said, "The *Vanity Fair* thing was, for so many of us, a disaster that it is a cause for endless autopsies among a small group of people. The fact of the matter was that for people like Walter Clemmons and me and Elizabeth Pochoda and Steve Rubin and a lot of other people, whatever job we had, we wanted out. And when *Vanity Fair* came along, what it seemed to promise was not only *out* but the opportunity of being on the ground floor of creating a really good magazine out of our brains. If we had had any opportunity to see beyond that opportunity to get out and just step back and ask, 'What is a Newhouse magazine? What is likely to happen to this magazine? Where is the real authority in this magazine? Do we have any reason, looking at all the other magazines they publish, to think that what we want is what they want? Are the two in even remote approximation?' we wouldn't have done it. But we did it, all of us. Renata Adler was there, and Pat Towers. People left the *Boston Phoenix*. But three months into it, they fired the editor—we didn't know that Richard [Locke] hadn't been exactly straight with us. We didn't know that he was running scared with people like Alex Lieberman looking over his shoulder. Locke was the editor of the magazine and had been my assistant editor at the book review. And he'd been under enormous pressure, which he didn't let us know. He tried to carry the whole thing alone, and then, suddenly, he was out and there was Leo Lehrman–I'd known Leo for years–and he was clearly an interim editor. He wanted *Vogue*. I was in Israel, writing about the Peace Now movement, and that's not what he wanted."

" 'Peace Now' is not so bad," I suggested, "but if you could have changed that first word to 'Your Hair,' he might have gone for it."

Leonard laughed, but there was nothing funny about the story, to which he returned. "So, you know, I lasted six months. Walter lasted eight months. Betsy lasted nine months. Betsy went back to the *Nation*, and Walter went back to *Newsweek*. I certainly couldn't go back to the *Times*. So I went to *New York Magazine*, but . . . shellshocked. It was not a good period. And I look at the magazine now, every once in a while, and I say, 'Yeah, that's what they wanted.' "

When I asked him about the Newhouse takeover of the *New Yorker* and how that fit into his scheme of things, he thought a moment, called the appointment of Robert Gottlieb "inspired," approved enthusiastically of Sonny Mehta's appointment to Gottlieb's old job running Knopf, and pointed admiringly at Andre Shiffrin's curious ability somehow to make money with "the goddamndest list" at Pantheon. "And as long as he continues to make money, they'll probably let him alone. And if Random House wants to compete with Simon and Schuster, they get Joni Evans, who publishes big, huge schlock, commercial books at the same time as she publishes very good and very serious literary books. She knows how to publish. We all worry about the *New Yorker*, but there again, it seems to me that, if the *New Yorker* can manage to sustain itself, they might not fiddle with it. It was, after all, a going concern. And if the *New Yorker* had called me and Walter Clemmons and Betsy Pochoda and asked how we'd like to come to work for them, it probably would have been a more successful experiment in career change. A shrewder move!"

I asked him for his view about Peter Prescott's impression that the trouble with book reviewing was that no editors really cared about it, that it wasn't an enterprise taken seriously by the very people who are commissioning the reviews, and that the state of affairs now is perceptibly worse than that which obtained a generation ago, when his father, Orville Prescott, was one of the daily reviewers for the *New York Times*. Leonard's

first reaction was not surprising, considering we had been discussing the bumpiness of his career's road. "It varies so widely," he said. "I think a hell of a lot depends on who the boss is."

A playful black cat named Papaya came wandering through the living room as Leonard toyed a little with the question. "There are always two people who know whether you've done it well or not. You're one, and the author is the other. There is no question that most newspapers and magazines that I know of aren't hiring people and paying them to review books as a responsible or even sometimes profound piece of literary work; they're paying for the entertainment value of the writer's style. On the other hand, I could tell the difference even at the *Times*, and it's an annoying difference. . . . When Dan Schwartz was the Sunday editor, he didn't care what was in the *Book Review* because he didn't read the books. And the publisher didn't care. The publisher would show up once a year and ask me for books– and he was quite specific about it–that he could take on his annual boat trip and, when he was finished with them, throw over the side. And I once complained to a friend and said how lovely it would be if the publisher of the *New York Times* asked for a copy of a book that we'd put on the front page of the *Times Book Review*, and he looked at me and said, 'You don't want that! If he starts reading the books you put on the front page, you'll have to put something else on the front page.' And maybe he was right. Dan Schwartz let me do whatever I wanted. And then Max Frankel came in as Sunday editor, and Max is very interested in books, and he's a man of considerable culture with strong opinions and very strong interests. And what we published was of considerable concern to him. And it made it more difficult. It made it a little more challenging, because I wasn't dealing with somebody who was a lightweight, but he cared deeply about what was published and how we selected our reviewers, and whether the treatment was fair. He had passions, deep passions."

I asked whether my impression was correct about how the front page of the *Times Book Review* had changed since Leonard's time. My recollection was that there hadn't been all those essays, literary, nonliterary, or even antiliterary (about writer's block or overrated classics), taking up space that might better be devoted to book reviewing.

"We would run an essay on the front page," he said, "if there wasn't a book that we felt that week deserved a front-page review. I was opposed to a split front page. Now you have two books on the front page, plus the essay–generally speaking. I believed, rightly or wrongly, that that was our column-six headline, our declaration that this is of most importance in the literary culture this week. You can be uncomfortable. You may not be happy. Half the time people weren't saying what I thought they should be saying about the books they were reviewing. But I had my say, I'd had my shot. I mean, I'd sent them the book. So, they disagreed with me. That's as far as you carry it. Nevertheless, you found something that had a feel of *This is the book!* and that, for better or worse, people were going to want to pay attention to on a certain serious level. I mean, you don't automatically put a best-seller there. Well, Max was much more involved in that process, much more interested in even how we played the first six pages. That was interesting, tension-causing but interesting.

"When I was a daily book reviewer, it all depended on who my editor was, whether anybody paid attention to what books we were covering and what books we weren't, or what we said about them. A guy like Sy Peck was very serious, and there'd be give and take. 'Why are you reviewing another one of these? Why is [Christopher] Lehmann-Haupt reviewing yet another book on Wall Street? Why are you reviewing yet another book on Nixon? Isn't there something else?' That's fine! That's an engagement. Whether it was ever different? I can remember when Peter's father and Charles Poore were the book reviewers. Were they taken more seriously? Not by anybody I knew. Were they taken more seriously by the paper? Nobody ever cared at all! Nobody ever bothered them. They reviewed books on their publication dates. That's how they divided them up! They didn't even discuss it, themselves. They took publication dates so seriously–alone, in the western world, so far as I can tell–that if a book was published on Tuesday, it would be reviewed by Prescott, and if it was published on Wednesday, it would be reviewed by Poore. And people would publish books, picking the day to get the reviewer they preferred. To a degree, I found Prescott one of the most reliable book reviewers in the country, even though I almost never agreed with him, because I knew exactly where he stood. I knew it was time to read Philip Roth when he attacked him. There was something to bounce off of. And for a regular critic, that's terribly important."

That made sense to me, and I referred to Dr. Johnson, who was almost always wrong but was nonetheless a splendid critic.

Thinking about what splendid criticism was and is, or ought to be, Leonard suggested some of what he looks for. "You've got to quote. You've got to synopsize. If you care passionately, you've got to write a short story, because you've got to re-create in the mind of your reader exactly those subjective feelings that you had on reading this book. You restructure. You seduce them! The kids I used to teach [in the Columbia College of General Studies] who had come over from the School of Journalism used to drive me batty. They wanted a formula. I said, 'There isn't any formula. It's much more like a short story. You can begin in the middle. Your job is seduction. You want to lead the reader in and make the reader experience what you experienced. And then you clinch that argument. You have to know when to stop. Each time, it's an act of language that collaborates with the act of language that is the book in front of you.'

"This is book reviewing. You're never going to get more than a thousand words to make your point. And you've always got to quote. It always used to make me furious that Anatole Broyard would be very clever, if he hated a book, in not quoting at all, if it was well written. That's what he did to Renata Adler's novel, *Speedboat*. Because if he'd quoted even a sentence or two, there would have been readers who could have said, 'That has a tone, that has a rhythm, that's interesting.' And you could respond that way. But he closed that book out.

"But it seems to me that the best critics have always to some degree inhabited the skin of the writers they were writing about, so that, if anything, you would hope, especially if you're admiring, that some of the writer's rhythms are going to enter into and inform the way you've created your response. Look at the way Edmund Wilson, at his best, was in and out of the books, in and out, and it all seemed seamless. Now that's in celebration. It's mostly in demonstrating an affinity. If you're angry, then your prose works against it, and should–if you feel that something is sloppy and sentimental, or over-wrought, then you're going to cut it short. Saul Bellow was writing about some black writer and he quoted a very long passage that was pretty bad, and at the end of this long passage, he had a one sentence paragraph of his own, and he said, 'One of the nice things about *Hamlet* is that Polonius gets stabbed.' Vicious! Terminal! Wham!

I think what the reviewer owes the reader is essentially what the reviewer owes the editor, in the sense of a consumer-guide synopsis and a literate, apprehensible presentation of the materials. But then there is the larger obligation that if you really want people to want this book, you work harder in the review to perform this seduction. And then–and I'm not sure whether this is a good thing or a bad thing–there is writing for the writer of the book. You realize the writer has taken certain chances. You want to prove that you've read this book. You don't have the space, but you've got a joke that would take too long to explain to the average reader. That can be exhibitionistic or parochial, but on the other hand, that can be kind of fun, to say to the writer, 'Look, I really am paying attention.' "

I confessed I didn't see anything so wrong with that. After all, if one is seducing, one is also seduced and has to signal that in some way. That seemed to me in no way dishonorable.

"It's not dishonorable. It depends on how much you're doing it on the reader's time. All kinds of things bother me if I sit back and put on a professional hat and ask how ought this to be done. I find this . . . I won't say I'm flabbergasted, but I'm very surprised when a book like *Khazars* is reviewed by a heavyweight like Robert Coover in the Sunday *Times* and then several days later in the daily *Times*, and both these people begin with the presumption that this guy [Pavic] made all this up, that the Khazars are a mythical middle European tribe that disappeared in the tenth century. And that means that neither of these reviewers, who were paid to do this, even bothered to consult the Encyclopaedia Britannica. It doesn't matter that Toynbee has written about the Khazars. It doesn't matter that Arthur Koestler has written a whole book, a wrong-headed and weird book, *The Thirteenth Tribe*, that was only published ten or twelve years ago, about the Khazars, and that they did convert to Judaism in the eighth century, and nobody knows why. Nor does anybody know why they disappeared two centuries later. Koestler's thesis is that they disappeared into the Ukraine and Poland and places like that, and that, in fact, most of the European Jews who were destroyed in the Holocaust were really originally Khazars. So much for the Chosen People! So much for a genetic definition of Judaism! A controversial thesis– but it's all been written about and discussed. It ex-

ists in intellectual discourse. And this guy takes off from that and proposes in one third of the book that they converted to Judaism, and in another third that they converted to Islam, and in the other third that they converted to Christianity. And what he's playing with is the different consequences. It's a novel, it's entertaining. . . . But nobody's done any homework! It's the kind of thing maybe that nobody's going to notice, but maybe you and the author. But if you don't do it, then you damn well ought to be very embarrassed when you pick up me in the *Nation* or Paul Gray in *Time*, who at least says they were real people. And you ought to be embarrassed because what else are you paid to do? Especially, if you're Michiko [Kakutani]! That's what you're paid for. You have no other demands on your time.

"No book comes to us innocent of history or social context or historical placement. What Michiko does–she does her homework. She's a graduate student, essentially, and so when she gets a book, she can be relied on–and that's often very useful–to read everything that she can possibly find about the author, so she'll have every other critical review. But this guy's never published a book here before. So maybe all she had to go on was Coover. . . ."

Perhaps cued by his reference to graduate students, I asked Leonard if he was still teaching. "I liked teaching," he said, "but I simply ran out of time. I was requiring a paper a week. And I always had a maximum of fifteen students. And I was very careful, responding at length to each paper, and when it got to the point where it was eating up two days a week, I couldn't afford it. And I had one last semester where the students were all so wonderful that I thought, 'Let's go out on this.' "

I asked Leonard whether he had any regrets or dissatisfactions, and he said he was to some degree troubled by the possibility that there were worthy books he might be missing. "I'm an eclectic reader, and I look at everything that comes into the house, but that doesn't mean I'm getting everything I should get. I should be working harder at that. But I don't want to go back to having lunch every day with publicity people who are poring over catalogues." He used to get a lot of help from publicists, he cheerfully admits. "Those people weren't stupid. And their help was valuable to me. They were in this business because they cared about books, and they had their own discoveries. And you knew who you could trust and who you couldn't, so that you weren't entirely wasting your time if you took their advice. I was steered correctly by lots of people I came to respect and trust. But I can't do that now. I don't have the time or the patience, and I don't have the physical stamina . . . I can't go to those parties. I cannot drink. I simply cannot use my time that way. So it's much more hit or miss. On the other hand, what I'm doing now is much less important to the whole book community. And I'll have to live with that. I don't know that anyone can explain how the concatenation of reviews and subject can suddenly produce respectable sales, but I do think that, insofar as the insular publishing community perceives what is important for their own identity, that *Times* review is preeminent. The remarkable thing about the *Times* is that it is the newspaper that people in this part of the country who are serious about keeping up with the world will read, whether they like it or not. And therefore, a *Times* review of a book will be for a whole lot of people, their only connection with that book. And that's sad, when you know how haphazard the process is. It is inhibiting, as a responsibility, when you're in the middle of that process. But on the other hand, I've felt some frustration."

He spoke of a long, complicated first novel about Wittgenstein, Bruce Duffy's *The World as I Found It*, that he'd liked and had reviewed for *Newsday* and NPR. Richard Eder then reviewed it for the L.A. *Times* and the publisher kept plugging away at it. Finally, the *New York Review of Books* got around to taking notice of it. And its author got some recognition and a grant from somewhere. It was, all things considered, a kind of success story. "But the frustration was that I knew perfectly well that if I had reviewed that book in the daily *Times*, it would have been a very different story. It would have been on the agenda. People might not have gone out and bought it, but they damned well would have known that it existed. There would have been some recognition, when somebody else talked about it, so that the third time someone mentioned it, then you'd be inclined to go and take a look. It's like the front page of the *Times*, and if a story is there, somebody in the president's cabinet has to pay attention to it. It's that kind of agenda setting function that nobody else seems to have the power to command."

Raymond Chandler Centenary

Margaret Slythe
Dulwich College

Any centenary provides an opportunity for significant reassessment. This focus, bestowed upon Raymond Chandler in 1988, attracted the attention of many who perceived the need to reevaluate the man and the writer.

Chandler was born in Chicago on 23 July 1888. His parents met after his mother, Florence Dart Thornton, had emigrated from Ireland to Nebraska where she had relatives. His father, Maurice Benjamin Chandler, worked as a railway engineer. After Raymond's birth he and his mother lived with relatives or in hotels when, in order to see Maurice, they moved from place to place, wherever his work took him. Maurice, who was from Pennsylvania, had one Irish parent, so Raymond Chandler was three-quarters Irish (and wholly Quaker). When he was seven years old, his parents separated and later divorced. With his mother he went to Upper Norwood, in South London, England, and soon after to 77 Alleyn Park Road, within sight of the impressive buildings of Dulwich College, designed by Charles Barry, the younger. Dulwich had been founded in 1619 by the actor-manager, Edward Alleyn. The Barry buildings had been completed in the 1870s to accommodate the Victorian expansion in education.

In September 1900, at age twelve, Chandler entered Dulwich College. By midsummer 1901, in the Upper II, he won his first prize, the first of many in Maths, Classics, and Modern Languages. The master of the college was Arthur Gilkes, a published author with high moral and critical standards. Chandler remembered Gilkes's ideals all his life and claimed that the strength of morality and fair-mindedness of his detective hero, Philip Marlowe, was based upon the teaching of Gilkes. Many years after leaving Dulwich, Chandler described his legacy from the college as "literacy and intellect." His classical education, he claimed, had saved him from being fooled by literary pretentiousness.

After leaving Dulwich, Chandler spent a year in France and Germany to enhance his chances in the examination for the civil service, a

Raymond Chandler at Dulwich College, circa 1903 (courtesy of the Wodehouse Library, Dulwich College)

career which his lawyer uncle felt would provide security. He won a job in the Admiralty, but due to loneliness and frustration he quit after six months. Chandler longed to return to the United States, but because of his devotion to his mother he resisted this impulse until low earnings from his magazine writing convinced him that America was where he should be. He served in the Gordon Highlanders in World War I, preferring a Canadian uniform to an American one in part because his mother, a British citizen, would be eligible for a pension in the event that he were killed. After the war he went into the oil business, eventually becoming a high-salaried executive. In 1924 he married Pearl Eugenie Hurlburt Pascal ("Cissy"), nearly eighteen years his senior, and remained with her until her death in 1954.

His first novel, *The Big Sleep*, was immediately recognized as a refinement of the American hard-boiled detective novel, invented by Dashiell Hammett. It appeared in 1939, when Chandler was fifty-one years old. The later books, especially *Farewell, My Lovely* (1940) and *The Lady in the Lake* (1943), and the often indifferent films made from his stories confirmed his reputation.

Chandler's July birthday, beyond the school year at Dulwich, provided a perfect opportunity to celebrate the whole year as the centenary. Alan Road's parody, "Dames, Dudes, and Dulwich" (*Observer*, 12 October 1987), set the tone for what was to follow. In late February 1988 Dulwich College presented *Down These Mean Streets*, a theatrical production based on the author's life and work written by Bill Morrison, and an exhibition of books, manuscripts, photographs, and other memorabilia was opened by Chandler's literary executor, Graham Carleton Greene. In March, *Bay City Blues*, an adaptation of *The Little Sister* (1949) by Bill Morrison, was performed in the college theater and later toured Canada and the United States. Media coverage was intense, involving journalists and television crews from many parts of the world. The relationship between Chandler's education and the creation of his fiction was a central focus of the centenary celebration and allowed for a new awareness of the source of Chandler's and therefore Marlowe's personal code of behavior. The values of the Christian gentleman, exemplified by Gilkes and learned from the study of classical literature at Dulwich, reveal the true roots of Marlowe.

The British Broadcasting Corporation's World Service has featured Chandler on several occasions during the year, especially in their "Meridian" program, and the BBC celebrated the centenary throughout the week of 23 July; a high point was the broadcasting of the only known recording of Chandler's voice, which survives in an interview with Ian Fleming, creator of James Bond. It was originally broadcast in 1959, the last year of Chandler's life. All the ingredients of this complex man were present: the humor, the quality of friendship and confidences bestowed upon him, the confusion between Chandler himself and Marlowe. On the centenary itself the main BBC drama production of the week was Bill Morrison's radio adaptation of *Farewell, My Lovely* with Ed Bishop as Marlowe. The National Film Theatre showed his films; Hamish Hamilton published new hardback editions of his six novels and two collections of short stories; Penguin Books produced a new paperback edition of his work as a boxed set. In the fall London Week-End TV presented a major assessment of Chandler's life and work in their prestigious "South Bank Show." The director, David Thomas, a Dulwich graduate himself, spent several weeks in Los Angeles with a crew filming the city which Chandler seemed so much to make his own. Dutch, German, Swedish, and Japanese TV crews have visited Dulwich College as part of their own centenary acknowledgment. In addition, radio arts programs from several countries, including Australia and India, sent recording journalists. In La Jolla, California, where Chandler lived, the local public library displayed his work. The *San Diego Tribune* presented its readers with articles in its "Scene" supplement, with contributions by *Tribune* editor Neil Morgan, who knew Chandler for many years, and staff writers Gregory Nelson Johnson and Arthur Salm. The annual Anthony Boucher Memorial Mystery convention paid tribute to Chandler during October. The Chandler Archive at UCLA, which was set up with the author's assistance, and which provided much material for the Dulwich exhibition, displayed original and manuscript material in its library during late September. In a major new documentary series the KCET-TV station in Los Angeles featured Chandler and his work as a historical aspect of Los Angeles.

In the mid twentieth century the detective writer in America was "below the salt," declared Chandler. No one has done more to change that than Chandler himself, and thirty years later he would be delighted that his technical skills and stylistic originality are appreciated by scholars and read in many languages.

Dulwich College has established a permanent memorial to Raymond Chandler, and the Chandler estate plans to have a gathering of all those who have affectionate connection with him. In addition, the Fulbright Commission has established the Raymond Chandler Arts Fellowship Award in Detective and Spy Fiction, which will enable a British Citizen interested in writing crime fiction to study in the United States. Details may be obtained from Sarah Newhouse, Programme Development Administration, Fulbright Commis-

Dulwich College in 1903 (courtesy of the Wodehouse Library, Dulwich College)

sion, 6 Porter Street, London W1M 2HR. May the language and brilliance of Raymond Chandler move gracefully into its second century.

A TRIBUTE

from MICHAEL AVALLONE

He was sixty and I was thirty when I closed in on him at the New York Headquarters of Mystery Writers of America in the summer of 1955. A cocktail party in his honor, deservedly so. All I could say to him, first crack off the bat, was: *"I envy you your talent."* His comeback was *"I envy you your youth."* His handshake was pure Marlowe. Nothing half-hearted or insincere. He autographed my copy of *The Long Good-bye,* and I gave him my signed *The Tall Dolores.* Raymond Chandler also granted me the right to use the last portion of his timeless essay on mystery writing, "The Simple Art of Murder," that section which so stirringly delineates what a private detective hero in fiction *ought to be.* I wanted it for a future Ed Noon novel, as a tribute to the Master of the Form. To me, those words are the Star-Spangled Banner, Custer's Regimental, and the Twenty-Third Psalm of Private Eye Sacred Writings. *". . . the detective in this kind of story must be such a man. He is the hero, he is everything. . . ."* And a glorious and so on.

Not even Spade's valedictory in *The Maltese Falcon*—*". . .when a man's partner dies he has to do something about it. . . ."*— tops this. Sam was talking about his *business;* he was not a white knight at all. Philip Marlowe was and is, a million mean streets later still, no matter how many of today's players pretend he isn't and yet imitate him ad nauseum. And imitate him they still do; I can name you at least ten pretenders to the throne. No one can imitate Sam Spade. Which is probably the biggest reason Hammett never put him in another novel. The Falcon caper is pure art, as far as I am concerned. Nobody did it better. Or ever will. *De profundis,* 1988.

But the other one and only is Chandler.

My recorded thumbnailer on *Farewell, My Lovely,* my favorite Marlowe, goes like this: "King of the First-Person Narrators. Writing style, liveliness and *panache* with *brio,* remarkable to this day. The literal blueprint for the *genre. . . ."* No, no contradiction there. Listen. *First Person,* voice over, the hero as narrator, in book form and on film, the *noir,* baby, of all *cineastes* everywhere. Me included. Sam Spade is third person all the way down the line. So call for Philip Marlowe when you need that kind of shamus heart to help you out of your particular darkness. Not only a brain but a *soul.* Moose Malloy knew and so did Miss Fromsett, and Terry Lennox and General Sternwood and the little sister from Manhattan, Kansas. I am continually amazed at the paucity of literary experts and mandarins who can make this distinction between Hammett and Chandler and fail to do so. Apart from working the same side of the street, both writers are as unalike as diamonds and rhinestones; and the Barbaras, Stanwyck and Streisand. Consider:

Chandler was funny. Hammett was not. Make them laugh? Not Sam Spade!

Hammett was genuinely hard-boiled. Chandler was not. Philip Marlowe rarely carried a gun.

Chandler could toss off an explosively apt simile or a wondrously vivid metaphor with a tongue-in-cheek toughness that was more style than reality, whereas Hammett played it uncompromisingly straight, no tricks or games, with rock-hard *substance,* using all the street-smart conviction at his command, which was considerable.

I shared a couple of letters with Chandler when he was in La Garda in the south of Italy before that historic Mystery Writers of America cocktail party. Later, when his beloved wife Pearl died and he attempted a miserable suicide, he tried to sue me for using the piece he had so willingly given permission to use. Dorothy Gardiner, the late but great executive secretary of MWA, made the peace between us. Not much later, he was dead. I still have the *Times* obituary I cut out of the paper on a sad day in March of 1959—a write-up that gave him the top cards so clearly merited.

Only last spring, I wrote the following fade-out to an article I was doing on the art of writing mystery fiction in the hard-boiled school. The guy who wrote *"She smelt the way the Taj Mahal looks by moonlight"* and *"she had the sort of figure that could make a priest kick a hole through a stained-glass window"* was also capable of this: The closing lines of *Farewell, My Lovely,* Class of 1940. Read and learn, eclectics and copycats out there:

I rode down to the street floor and went out on the steps of City Hall. It was a cool day and very clear.

You could see a long way—but not as far as Velma had gone.

They still haven't topped that—or even matched it.

A TRIBUTE
from JAMES ELROY

Raymond Chandler was to me primarily a stylist—the writer who illuminated the Los Angeles that lived immediately before my birth. He made me want to go back and revel in it, love it, *know it.* Of the "BIG 3" detective writers (Hammett, Chandler, Ross McDonald) he is the one who thrilled me most with pure hard language, who *taught me* the language of dangerous romance.

A TRIBUTE
from JOE GORES

The three American novelists alive during my youth whom I will always regret not seeking out are Hemingway, Hammett, and Chandler. Hemingway was my first writing inspiration; I followed Hammett into the detective trade; and I emulated Raymond Chandler as a writer until I found a style of my own.

Hammett turned the pulp-born private-eye tale into literature by writing with a spare, savage realism; a reader could strike matches against his prose, break bones against his protagonists. They were hard, unsentimental men whose sole dedication was to The Job. They read no books, they sired no children, they loved no women—or did so only fleetingly.

With Philip Marlowe, Chandler made the detective novel fun. His first-person tales brought poetry and grace—and a great deal of conscious humor—to the genre. Marlowe was as hard, as lonely as Spade or the Op; but he was aware of his aloneness. When he says goodbye to a dead friend in *The Long Good-Bye,* he does it in a peculiarly hard-boiled way, with a mixture of hard-nosed toughness and blatant sentimentality.

Chandler also made Marlowe's Los Angeles as vivid as Holmes's London. He showed us the City of Angels, once a tough, beautiful, lonely town on the edge of the Pacific, becoming a gridlocked megalopolis full of smog and angry people.

He came late to his craft, in his fifty-first year when *The Big Sleep* appeared; but his man

> **5724. CHANDLER, Raymond Thornton,**
> *b.* 23 Aug. 1888, *s.* of –, Mrs., "Whitefield
> Lodge," 77 Alleyn Park, W. Dulwich ; L. Apr.
> 1905 ; R. Great War, L/Corpl. Gordon
> Highrs., Canadian Infy.

Chandler listing in The Dulwich College Register, 1619
to 1926

Marlowe immediately stepped out of the shadow of Hammett's Sam Spade and Continental Op forever. For the next twenty years Philip Marlowe was the standard against which all other hard-boiled heroes had to be judged.

I quit detecting after twelve years, not because I had become disillusioned at the gap between the reality of detection and its fictional portrayal, but because I had become impatient to write my own stories full-time. Besides, for me Chandler forever bridged the gap–and explained it–in "The Simple Art of Murder." He made us see that his fictional detective *couldn't* be real, because he was the guy real detectives wished they could be: the archetypical American Hero. Those of us writing in the hard-boiled tradition continue, like Chandler, to try and portray this hero in our novels.

Come to think of it, Chandler's own words in the essay are not a bad epitaph for the man himself:

> Down these mean streets a man must go who is not himself mean, who is neither tarnished nor afraid. . . . He must be a complete man and a common man and yet an unusual man. He must be, to use a rather weathered phrase, a man of honor. . . .
>
> The story is this man's adventure in search of a hidden truth, and it would be no adventure if it did not happen to a man fit for adventure.

A TRIBUTE

from WILLIAM F. NOLAN

Imagine him: Chandler at 100. A fierce, bitter-tongued old man in a seamed, time-bent body. Skin like weathered hickory. A blowing fire of white hair. Hands like the claws of a bird. Glittery eyes, deep-sunk in the ridged skull. But he was gone at 70, three full decades short of his 100th birthday. Writers wither and die–but their creations live on. If the writer is any good, that is. And he was better than good; he was a master. So Marlowe is still very much with us.

Marlowe. Still young or youngish, still walking those mean streets, still hard-muscled and hard-minded–the tough, tarnished knight within a splendidly drawn portrait of Los Angeles in the Thirties and Forties. Still as quick as ever with his wisecrack wit.

He's in the pantheon, thanks to Chandler. He'll never age and die, any more than Holmes will, or Sam Spade, or the gods of Olympus. The passing decades can't put a glove on him. Open any page of a Chandler novel and he's there, vitally, kinetically alive in Chandler's rhythmed prose, a confirmed cynic-romantic, a lonely, embattled warrior in a corrupt environment, forever tilting at the windmills of society.

Chandler imitators have produced a thousand pseudo-Marlowes since *The Big Sleep*, but they are lost in his shadow. Marlowe remains unique. He stands alone as the personalized, individualistic product of a very special mind–the mind of Raymond Thornton Chandler. Time has not dimmed the force and freshness of Chandler's creation, nor the power of his singing prose. We *believe* in Marlowe's Los Angeles because Chandler made it real for us, just as we believe in the chess-playing, pipe-smoking detective who can't be bluffed or bought off, whose unbending moralistic code may not be in fashion in the 1980s (it never really was!) but whose dedication and integrity never waver.

We celebrate the creator and we continue to mourn his loss in the closing years of this century– but Philip Marlowe doesn't give a damn about some dead guy named Chandler. He's got things to prove, places to go, a case to solve. *The Big Sleep . . . Farewell, My Lovely . . . The High Window . . . The Lady in the Lake . . . The Little Sister . . . The Long Goodbye . . . Playback . . .* Just open any page and you'll see what I mean.

New Literary Periodicals:
A Report for 1988

Richard R. Centing
Ohio State University

The following report on new literary periodicals, the second in a series of annual surveys scheduled to appear in the *Dictionary of Literary Biography Yearbook,* documents scholarly journals, annuals, newsletters, reviews, and indexes launched in 1988, along with some 1987 titles that had not come to our attention by press time last year. Any 1988 titles that we missed will be covered in the 1989 *Yearbook.*

These descriptions are not meant to be evaluative. By highlighting outstanding facets of each serial, we intend to bring them to the attention of librarians and scholars for purposes of collection development and scholarly submissions. Following the first discussion of a new title the publisher's address is provided in parentheses after the title.

The year 1988 was one of retrenchment and reallocation in American libraries. According to the Association for Research Libraries, periodicals are now consuming sixty percent or more of library acquisition budgets. Methods for serial cancellation projects are promoted while ideas for new subscription funds are not forthcoming. That is the bad news. The good news for literary scholars is the unstoppable growth of new literary periodicals, providing networks of communication and outlets for new critical approaches. It is the hope of this report to keep the scholarly community regularly informed about the burgeoning growth of serial publications, and to alert indexing services of the need for the inclusion of new titles in their core lists. Please contact the author with any comments on the report for 1988 or suggestions for inclusion in the 1989 report.

The *Yearbook of Langland Studies* (Colleagues Press, Inc., P.O. Box 4007, East Lansing, MI 48826) is published annually. Volume 1 (1987) is a handsomely produced 197-page hardbound. Devoted to William Langland (circa 1330-1386), author of *Piers Plowman,* the journal also welcomes articles and notes that deal with related poems in the tradition of didactic alliterative verse. The in-

Volume 1 Number 1
Autumn 1988

Cover for the journal devoted to the author of
Pilgrim's Progress

augural issue consists of eight essays, including "Langland's and Chaucer's Prologues" by Helen Cooper (Oxford). Besides publishing original scholarship, the *Yearbook* includes a fully annotated, annual bibliography of secondary articles and books in the field of Langland studies. The "Reviews" section has eight long, signed reviews of scholarly monographs published from 1985 to 1987. Each annual also has shorter notes and concludes with a detailed index.

Envoi: A Review Journal of Medieval Literature (AMS Press, Inc., 56 East 13th Street, New York, NY 10003) appears twice a year and is produced in association with the Department of English and Comparative Literature at Columbia University. The first issue arrived late in 1988. The editor, Paul Spillenger, announces his manifesto for *Envoi* in his preface, stating his goals of reviewing books on medieval literature within a year of publication and providing a forum for "open discussion" of the field, bringing it "more fully into the realm of modern literary discourse." The early book reviews are playing catch-up, covering 1986 and 1987 titles; later issues hope to achieve currency. Around fifty book reviews and notices form the bulk of the first 266-page issue, although substantial essays are also included, most notably two bibliographic essays on recent scholarship on medieval drama and Dante studies and "Medieval Readers and Ancient Texts: The Inference of the Past" by Christopher C. Baswell (Barnard College). Concluding with a long "Books Received" column, *Envoi* appears to be a major resource tool for scholars and librarians concerned with collection development.

The Shakespeare industry has generated numerous journals devoted to scholarship on the world's best-known poet/playwright. The *Spear-Shaker Review* (P.O. Box 913, RR 1, Napanoch, NY 12458) is a quarterly devoted to the belief that the true author of the Shakespeare plays is Edward de Vere, seventeenth earl of Oxford (1550-1604). The editor/publisher, Stephanie Caruana, a former real-estate broker and writer from Brooklyn, believes the historical evidence supports her view. The first issue of the review (Fall 1987) contains essays reviewing the case against Shakespeare, notices of new books, excerpts from previous writers on the controversy, and news of the Shakespeare Oxford Society (P.O. Box 147, Clarksville, MD 21029) and the De Vere Society (Hertford College, Oxford, England OX1 3BW). "The truth will out" proclaims their masthead, and "Shake-speare" will be unseated by the *Spear-Shaker Review.*

Bunyan Studies: John Bunyan and his Times (Counter Productions, P.O. Box 556, London SE5 ORL, England) is an author-specific scholarly semiannual devoted to John Bunyan (1628-1688). The advertisement for the journal claims that his "*Pilgrim's Progress* has been more widely read than any other work in English except the Bible." *Bunyan Studies,* founded in the tercentenary year of the poet's death, will focus primarily on Bunyan but will include relevant articles on his contemporaries. The journal includes scholarly reflections on the critical response to Bunyan's works, descriptions of important Bunyan archives, book reviews, and a section called "News and Reports" that includes everything from conference summaries to notes on fugitive documents. The illustrated journal is edited by W. R. Owens (The Open University, London). Researchers will be pleased by the annotated bibliography, "Recent Articles on Bunyan."

Renaissance Studies (Oxford University Press, Walton Street, Oxford, England OX2 6DP), a multidisciplinary semiannual founded in March 1987, is a publication of the Society for Renaissance Studies. The society, founded in 1967, welcomes contributions for the journal on history, art, architecture, religion, literature, and language of any European country or any country influenced by Europe during the period of the Renaissance. The articles, which exhibit a strong historical bias, have ranged from a study of the posthumous reputation of Henry VII to a paper on John Milton as a translator of poetry. The "Reviews of Books" section typically includes about a dozen long, signed book reviews, covering subjects such as the plague in fifteenth-century Florence, Elizabethan music, and French emblem literature. Each illustrated issue concludes with a "Reviews of Exhibitions" section, documenting major exhibitions such as the 1986 show in Florence mounted to celebrate the six-hundredth anniversary of the birth of Donatello, and a review of an exhibition in the Netherlands on Sir Philip Sidney that contains useful notes on new books on Sidney published in Holland. The editor, Gordon Campbell (University of Leicester Department of English), is a Milton scholar.

An interesting story in the *New York Times* (8 October 1988), "In Glasnost, Echoes of the 18th Century," documents the worldwide study of the Enlightenment, citing developments in China, Russia, and Eastern Europe. International scholars of this field will welcome the following journal. Century-and-genre specific, *Eighteenth-Century Fiction* (University of Toronto Press, Journals Department, 5201 Dufferin Street, Downsview, Ontario M3H 5T8) is devoted to the historical and critical analysis of imaginative prose of the eighteenth century, broadly defined as 1660-1832. Published by the University of Toronto Press for McMaster University, the premier issue of this quarterly (October 1988) packages four essays and seven lengthy reviews in eighty-two pages. Patricia Meyer Spacks (Yale University) offers "Energies of Mind: Plot's Possibilities in the 1790s," and Donald Greene (University of Southern California) has the lead essay, "The Original of Pemberley," concerning place names in Jane Austen's *Pride and Prejudice*. The Austen piece is illustrated with detailed maps and a superior color reproduction of an eighteenth-century painting. Alistair M. Duckworth (University of Florida) surveys recent studies of the period in a bibliographical essay that should be invaluable to beginning graduate students. Open to both French and English contributors, one essay in the first issue is in French: "De Prévost à Sade" by Jean Sgard (Université des Languer et Lettres de Grenoble). The editor is David Blewett (McMaster University).

Another manifestation of eighteenth century scholarship is *The Age of Johnson: A Scholarly Annual* (AMS Press, Inc., 56 East 13th Street, New York, NY 10003), featuring essays and reviews on all aspects of the world of Samuel Johnson (1709-1784). The focus is from about 1735 (the beginning of Dr. Johnson's literary career) to about 1800 (when most members of his circle ceased to be active). The first volume, which is copyrighted 1987, was released on 10 March 1988. At 482 pages, the hardbound journal corrals a wide mixture of expert research covering numerous particulars about Johnson as well as authoritative investigations of William Cowper, Edward Gibbon, Charlotte Smith, George III, and Laurence Sterne. Included is Margaret Anne Doody's "The Law, The Page, and The Body of Woman: Murder and Murderesses in the Age of Johnson," a beautifully crafted exploration of the literature of crime. The editor, Paul J. Korshin (University of Pennsylvania), welcomes longer essays that exceed average journal length yet are too short for publication in book form. One essay runs forty-six pages. Throughout, the annual is studded with pertinent tables and illustrations, and each essay finishes with extensive footnotes. The book reviews are mini-essays, scrupulous in their digesting of research preceding the book under review. One fifteen-page review is an exacting analysis of booksellers' and exhibit catalogs issued during Johnson's bicentenary, with commentary on the importance of various Johnson collections in England and America. Overall, *The Age of Johnson* must be acknowledged as one of the best of the new literary annuals.

The *Mark Twain Circular* (The Citadel, Charleston, SC 29409) is a monthly newsletter

Cover for the interdisciplinary quarterly edited by Peter Stitt

sent at no charge to subscribers to the *Mark Twain Journal*. Individual subscriptions to the circular are also available via a five-dollar membership in the Mark Twain Circle of America, an organization founded at MLA in December 1986. The first six-page issue is dated January 1987. It is intended as a timely supplement to the semiannual *Mark Twain Journal* which was founded in 1953 as a successor to the *Mark Twain Quarterly* (1936-1953). While the journal publishes scholarly articles, the primary focus of the new circular is on short notes and queries, letters, conference information, calls for papers, and announcements of new books. The circular has already deviated from this policy by publishing a paper in the December 1987 issue by the late John Tuckey delivered at an MLA meeting in December 1979 on the theme of "Mark Twain's Last Years." A valuable feature of the *Mark Twain Circular* is the ongoing secondary bibliography of articles about Twain in scholarly journals and popular magazines; these are fully annotated. The editor, James S. Leonard, is an assistant professor of English at the Citadel and the joint author (with C. E. Wharton) of *The Fluent Mundo: Wallace Stevens and the Structure of Reality* (University of Georgia Press, 1988).

A single-author newsletter has been created concerning the life and career of Malcolm Cowley (1898-　), the American poet, critic, editor, and literary historian whose *Portable Faulkner* (1946) lifted Faulkner out of critical obscurity. Taking its title from a line in a Cowley poem, "Farmhouses curl like horns of plenty," *Horns of Plenty: Malcolm Cowley and his Generation* (2041 West Farragut Avenue, Chicago, IL 60625) is a quarterly edited by Bill Butts. Cowley's generation is defined as those writers born between 1891 and 1905. The Spring 1988 initial number offers an introduction to Cowley's work in thirty-two pages, featuring modestly sized articles on narrow topics, along with book reviews and queries for information.

Harold Pinter (1930-　) is recognized as one of the most important dramatists of this century and as Britain's most significant living playwright. The *Pinter Review* (University of Tampa, Box 11F, Tampa, FL 33606) is an annual dedicated to research on this English dramatist and screenwriter who has also published essays and poetry. Members of the Harold Pinter Society, an organization founded at the December 1986 MLA, receive a subscription with their membership. The first annual for 1987 was issued in 1988. Its eighty-six pages contain a history of the Pinter Society, an "Editor's Column" that outlines the future goals of the journal, several essays on Pinter's work, and an introduction to Pinter's unpublished novel "The Dwarfs" (along with a first printing of a selection from the manuscript). The contributors are noted Pinter scholars, such as Katherine H. Burkman (Ohio State University), who has published two books on Pinter. The review concludes with a comprehensive Pinter bibliography covering 1986 and 1987, citing translations, productions, films, reviews, and scholarly books and articles. The editors are Francis Gillen (University of Tampa) and Steven H. Gale (Missouri Southern State College).

Talisman (P.O. Box 1117, Hoboken, NJ 07030) is an independent, semiannual little magazine specializing in contemporary poetry. It takes its title from a literary annual edited by William Cullen Bryant, Robert Sands, and Gulian Verplanck between 1827 and 1830. The original *Talisman* was one of the first magazines established primarily to publish new work by American writers. The new *Talisman* continues this tradition, focusing on a major modern poet in each issue along with a sampling of other active poets. Alice Notley (1945-　) is the featured poet in the inaugural number (Fall 1988). Of particular note is the inclusion of a twenty-two-page interview with Notley and the first publication of a work in progress. The editor is Edward Foster.

Another little magazine of exceptional merit is *Turnstile* (Turnstile Press, 175 Fifth Avenue, Suite 2348, New York, NY 10010), edited by Amit Shah, a native of Calcutta, India. This semiannual of poetry, fiction, and graphics publishes a roster of unknowns alongside underground leaders such as Arthur Winfield Knight. A number of Manhattan-based publishing professionals are involved, so *Turnstile* may tap some excellent new writing. A welcome touch of satire infuses some pieces, such as Robert Meldrum's "Cowboy Poetry." Meldrum is cited in the notes on contributors as the "Geraldo Rivera of literary criticism." The first issue was dated Winter 1988.

Founded in Spring 1987, the *Northern Review* (Academic Achievement Center, Room 018 Learning Resources Center, University of Wisconsin-Stevens Point, WI 54481) is a multipurpose, semiannual journal featuring essays, fiction, poetry, and photographs "all focused on the diversity as well as the connections within this broad area we call the North." Included are a short story from the promising new writer Bret Lott and, advancing the northern theme, Wendy Larsen's poem "Night Sounds in Alaska," which speaks of salmon, seals, and Gambier Bay. The noncreative inclusions are diverse, ranging from an interview with the CEO of a paper products company to the first publication of a pioneer diary. The editorial advisory panel includes distinguished authors such as Donald Hall and X.J. Kennedy. Richard Behm is the managing editor.

A more ambitious interdisciplinary review is the *Gettysburg Review* (Gettysburg College, Gettysburg, PA 17325), a quarterly mixing literary analysis, graphics, and cultural critiques with original poetry and fiction. Around two hundred pages an issue, with an impressive editorial board of luminaries, including Robert Penn Warren and Donald Barthelme, the review is attractively produced and exactingly edited by Peter Stitt, an English professor at Gettysburg College who specializes in American poetry. The contents range from a survey of recent Hemingway biographies to poetry by Rita Dove (winner of the Pulitzer

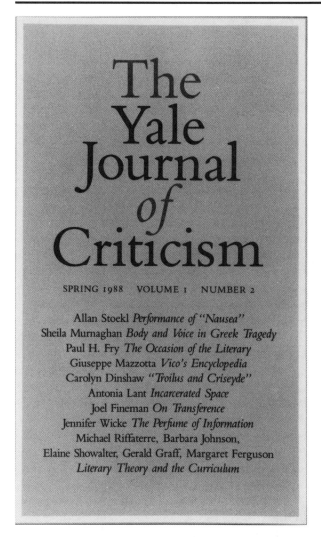

The Yale
Journal
of
Criticism

SPRING 1988   VOLUME 1   NUMBER 2

Allan Stoekl *Performance of "Nausea"*
Sheila Murnaghan *Body and Voice in Greek Tragedy*
Paul H. Fry *The Occasion of the Literary*
Giuseppe Mazzotta *Vico's Encyclopedia*
Carolyn Dinshaw *"Troilus and Criseyde"*
Antonia Lant *Incarcerated Space*
Joel Fineman *On Transference*
Jennifer Wicke *The Perfume of Information*
Michael Riffaterre, Barbara Johnson,
Elaine Showalter, Gerald Graff, Margaret Ferguson
Literary Theory and the Curriculum

Cover for the semiannual journal that seeks to broaden the base of literary criticism to include aspects of sociology, legal discourse, philosophy, and other humanistic disciplines

Prize for Poetry, 1987). Dan Pope's "The Post-Minimalist American Story, or What Comes After Carver" is a timely discussion of the short-story scene. Writings by David Ignatow, Frederich Busch, and Linda Pastan can also be encountered in the *Gettysburg Review*, already a competitor to the long-established quarterly reviews.

Launched in May 1987, the *South African Theatre Journal* (P.O. Box 27927, Sunnyside, 0132, South Africa) is published in May and September each year. Created as a forum for the academic discussion of performance studies and the performing arts, especially in southern Africa, the subjects have ranged from production history to the methodology of theater research. Kelwyn Sole's "Identities and Priorities in Recent Black Literature and Performance: A Preliminary Investigation" is a seventy-page treatment of the phenome-

non of black literature and performance in South Africa. This major essay relates theater to the growth of black trade unions, the rise of black-consciousness organizations, and the "resurgence of organizations of a non-racial, progressive orientation." A number of other articles also confront the dominant ideology of the nation but in a non-polemical tone. Many articles advocate a deeper awareness of the need for theater research in higher education, rather than just preparing students for the professional theater. A study of colonial and postcolonial influences on Nigerian drama in English also touches on the problem of presenting African drama abroad. The September 1987 issue concludes with a select bibliography of journal articles on South African theater, mostly from South African journals, followed by a listing of theses and dissertations on theater from South African universities. Each issue reviews new books from abroad as well as from local publishers.

The *Australian & New Zealand Theatre Record* (Australian & New Zealand Theatre Studies Center, The University of New South Wales, P.O. Box 1, Kensington NSW, 2033 Australia) is a monthly which began publication in January 1987. Modeled after the *London Theatre Record* (1981), it reproduces published reviews of professional theater productions. While eighty Australian playwrights are covered in the 1987 issues (according to *Index 1987*, its annual cumulative index), you can also locate the full text of reviews of Alan Ayckbourn, Ben Jonson, Neil Simon, and William Shakespeare. There is even a review (reprinted from the *Financial Review*) of an adaptation of *Four Little Girls*, a play by Pablo Picasso about his children. The coverage of New Zealand began in April 1988. The editor, Jeremy Robin Eccles, was born in England but has become a noted critic in Australia. He wrote the report "Theatre Criticism in Australia," which is published as an appendix in *Index 1987*. The *Australian & New Zealand Theatre Record* is illustrated with production photographs.

Edited by a group of younger members of the Yale faculty, the *Yale Journal of Criticism* (Yale University Press, 92A Yale Station, New Haven, CT 06520) is a major addition to the new, interdisciplinary journals of critical theory that are attempting to broaden the base of literary criticism to include insights from sociology, legal discourse, philosophy, and other humanistic disciplines. Issued twice a year, the combined semiannual issues exceed four hundred dense pages.

Christopher Norris gave extended treatment to the *Yale Journal of Criticism* in the *Times Literary Supplement* (10-16 June 1988). His favorable review focuses on the first number (Fall 1987) and concludes that it embraces "a wide range of interests while not falling into catch-all eclecticism." The most recent number (Fall 1988), however, does verge on the eclectic, encompassing studies of the influence of obstetrics on Mary Shelley's *Frankenstein*, camp definitions of culture, the iconography of China's Great Wall, and an in-depth probing of V. S. Naipaul's *The Enigma of Arrival*. An article from Spring 1988 by Antonia Lant, a teacher of cinema studies at New York University, examines Margarethe von Trotta's film *Rosa Luxemburg*, claiming that this "revolutionary woman [Luxemburg] is transformed into an unnecessarily mythic and nostalgic character," and relates this film to the problem of understanding postwar German culture. The journal has also published a number of vital articles that contribute to the debate on curriculum and canon formation.

The quarterly *Journal of Poetry Therapy* (Human Sciences Press, Inc., 72 Fifth Avenue, New York, NY 10011) is an "interdisciplinary journal of practice, theory, research and education" concerning the use of poetics as a psychotherapeutic agent in clinical settings. The editor, Nicholas Mazza (Florida State University), is from the field of social work. The editorial board includes poets, teachers of library science, English professors, and hospital workers. The first sixty-four-page issue (Fall 1987) includes a variety of articles on the art of haiku, the psychiatric treatment of a schizophrenic male suffering from delusions that he was Darth Vader (from the Star Wars movies), the process of writing poems, and the therapeutic benefits of poetry to help resolve grief. A section called "Journal File" provides abstracts for articles from other journals that would be of use to poetry therapists. Some original poetry concludes the journal, which is sponsored by the National Association for Poetry Therapy.

Sponsored by the International Association for the Fantastic in the Arts, the *Journal of the Fantastic in the Arts* (M. E. Sharpe, Inc., 80 Business Park Drive, Armonk, NY 10504) defines the "fantastic" in its broadest sense as "that which is not real." While covering traditional science fiction, the journal also wants to cover the omnibus subject as it is reflected in all the arts, such as film, painting, and dance. The first six essays range in coverage from an examination of postmodernism

and the fantastic to an exegesis of C. S. Lewis's *The Magician's Nephew* (1955). Critic and author Brian Aldiss gives some insider opinions on the role of the fantasy writer. The editor is Carl B. Yoke (Kent State University). The book-review editor is listed as Robert A. Collins (Florida Atlantic University) although no book reviews appear in the first number. The interdisciplinary journal, which exhibits exceptional printing standards, is projected as a quarterly.

Its title clearly defines the *International Journal of Lexicography* (Oxford University Press, Walton Street, Oxford OX2 6DP England). Concerned with both theoretical and practical aspects of lexicography, this quarterly, edited by Robert Ilson (University College London), is interested in lexicographic projects, dictionary publishing, and lexicography as a profession. The first issue (Spring 1988) features such articles as "British and American Grammatical Differences," "Contrastive Analysis of Terminological Systems and Bilingual Technical Dictionaries," "The Lexical Entry of Biblical Hebrew *Hu* in Monolingual Dictionaries," and "Lexicography in Simple Language." The concluding book reviews are of new dictionaries, including foreign language dictionaries. Organizations associated with the journal are the European Association for Lexicography and the Dictionary Society of North America.

Advocates of women's concerns will be the primary users of *Feminisms* (Ohio State University, Center for Women's Studies, 207 Dulles Hall, 230 W. 17th Avenue, Columbus, OH 43210), the newest version of the quarterly that replaces *Women Studies Review* (1979-1987) and *Women Are Human* (1972-1979). Launched with the Winter 1988 issue, *Feminisms* is primarily a reviewing service, with noted scholars reviewing new books by and about women. It is edited by a changing cadre at the center, whose director is Susan Hartmann. Books of the social sciences predominate, although literary topics are included, such as a review of a new edition of Lorraine Hansberry's plays and of paperback reprints of novels by women. Less visible, although a continuing feature of the journal, is the publication of new short stories and poetry by women, giving *Feminisms* the role of a literary review. There are also interviews with faculty of the center, some of whom have joint appointments in Women's Studies and the Department of English, bringing news of academic developments that should be of interest to all scholars.

Focusing on sexuality and gender in art, literature, film, and history, *Genders* (University of Texas Press, Journals Department, Box 7819, Austin, TX 78713) is an advanced theoretical triannual "developing the range of possibilities offered in discourse analysis, historical interpretation, literary and art criticism, semiotics, and psychoanalytic theory." The first 134-page issue (Spring 1988) contains seven long essays. Subjects covered include a study of anal imagery in the paintings of Jasper Johns, the application of the Prostestant discourse on circumcision to George Eliot's *Daniel Deronda*, and the subtleties of desire between men as expressed in Tennyson's *In Memoriam*. Libraries that have a call for journals of theory such as *New Literary History* will be the primary market for *Genders*, whose complex texts assume a working knowledge of thinkers from Plato to Lacan. The editor is Ann Kibbey, Department of English, University of Colorado at Boulder.

On Learning To Write

Gerald Petievich

The first mystery-writing class I attended was at an unaccredited institution in Paris also offering night classes in weaving, pottery, and modern dance. As a U.S. Secret Service Agent assigned to a liaison job at the American Embassy, I didn't really fit in.

The classroom was on the third floor of a musty, dilapidated building on the Left Bank. I was the only male in a small class comprised mainly of embassy wives and American women whose husbands were business executives working in France.

The instructor was a kind, sixtyish American expatriate who said she'd once worked for a correspondence school of creative writing.

The format of instruction was one to which I would become accustomed. After the teacher would lecture for a few minutes on some topic of interest to mystery writers, the students would, one by one, read aloud from their work. I found this to be a torturous experience then just as I would now, having authored six novels.

One student in the class, an embassy secretary, was writing a mystery involving characters stranded at a ski lodge in Switzerland. In a typical chapter someone would be found dead near the fireplace in the chalet, then the characters would go outside and find another body in the snow. As they were examining the body, one of the group would drop dead. The group would hurry back inside and someone would drink poison. These events would be sandwiched between long stretches of meaningless flashbacks and musings.

Another student, a husky embassy wife, proudly read aloud each week from a meandering tale in which the detective, a handsome, affable man named Zack, incessantly cleaned his pipe and solved his cases by discussing clues with his slender wife, whom he loved more than any man has ever loved any woman. The student's husband, an aloof, intolerant dunce who smoked cigars, frequently accompanied her to class.

A good portion of class time was taken up with student explanations of their work. After a student would read aloud, the instructor would make some comment about how the writing could be improved. Then the student would go through a defensive song and dance about how the work would be more understandable if it was taken in context. For instance, the writer of the ski lodge mystery explained that the reason there were so many murders was that she didn't want to write a mystery like all the others. She was, as she called it, "breaking ground."

The goal of breaking literary ground is shared by many novice writers. I think this is because writing fiction is so difficult. When toiling at the keys it is easier to believe one is conquering Mt. Everest rather than believing that everything has already been written.

Gerald Petievich (photograph by Lyn Smith)

One woman consistently refused to read out loud and preferred instead to hand out photocopies of the latest neatly typed chapter of her novel, a locked-room mystery told from the point of view of a cat named Prunella.

I broke out in a cold sweat when it came my turn to read aloud from the police-procedural novel I was working on. There I was, a G-man sitting in a room reading beginner's hard-boiled prose to a group of bored women. My first writing, as I recall, was a lot like the investigative reports I had been trained to write in the Secret Service: just the facts in chronological order.

But no one ever criticized me for that. They just listened, or feigned listening, and when prodded by the instructor, said something noncommittal like "Gee, it's not the kind of thing I read, but I like it."

After a couple of class meetings I came to ascertain why the instructor treated all the students

with great deference and her criticism of student work was never stronger than a few pointers on grammar and punctuation. It was because she had no advice to offer. The whole process of writing fiction was as much a mystery to her as it was to me and the others. The highlight of the course was a classroom lecture on "getting published" given by a guest speaker, a hippie who had once sold an article to *Penthouse* magazine.

Shortly after the term ended, my Secret Service tour of duty in Paris came to a close, and I was transferred back to the United States. I immediately signed up for a university seminar in mystery writing.

In this class several students were obeying the maxim *one must write about what one knows* quite literally. For example, a diminutive, balding architect was writing about an architect-detective who solved his cases by wandering through skyscrapers he'd designed and finding clues in blueprints.

A civilian police radio dispatcher in the group was finishing work on a mystery written entirely in police radio-call dialogue.

An elderly female student who always brought her Siamese cat to class was struggling with an Oedipal mystery set completely within the confines of the secondhand shop where she was employed.

The most prolific writer in the group was a middle-aged woman churning out stacks of pages about candle-carrying Druids wandering about at night at Stonehenge. They did little else than carry candles because she said she didn't want to write a lot of action and then have to discard it later when she changed the plot.

In this class superstition about publishers was widespread. Like the ancient high-school rumor about the woman who had bees living in her beehive hairdo, everyone believed in some story or other about a writer who had chanced into getting published. The longest discussions were held not on how to improve the quality of one's writing in order to get published but on discovering the magic formula that will induce a publisher to buy one's mystery novel. Some of the stories circulating in the class were as follows:

1. The writer traveling by air who happens to sit next to a well-known New York mystery editor. The editor reads a few pages of the writer's manuscript and makes an offer on the spot.

2. The writer who got published by submitting her manuscript under a pen name and tricked the publisher into thinking she was the

wife of a famous author whom the publishing house was dying to publish.

3. The writer who submitted his manuscript to forty publishers simultaneously, created his own bidding war, and sold his manuscript for millions.

In all of the above rumors no one was able to remember the name of the actual writer or book.

A number of students had acted on these and other myths. For example, the architect was typing his novel in italics because he thought by making it distinctive he would have a better chance of a publisher choosing it from a stack of unsolicited manuscripts.

The secondhand shop lady, convinced that the manuscript itself had little to do with getting published, submitted her work to potential publishers with a detailed plot outline, a lengthy letter of introduction, and a photograph of herself sitting on the beach with her portable typewriter–and her cat.

There was interminable chatter about how to find a literary agent. It was believed that they hid from writers and never accepted new clients. Some thought it was impossible to get published without one. Others had already submitted their work to several literary agents and been rebuffed. The Druid lady had bragged that she had retained the services of a literary agent: a man in Arkansas to whom she had mailed a fee of four hundred dollars. The police dispatcher was more than happy to share a three-word missive sent to him, along with his returned manuscript, by a well-known New York literary agent. It read: "This is trash."

The class instructor, who said she had once worked for a publisher, gave the same advice week after week: *Keep on writing*–an instruction which I realize now is about as valuable as the Music Man's exhortation to *Think music*.

Though I gained nothing during the class, a fellow student helped me a great deal. One night after class she told me she thought my problem was that my book had no plot. I thought about it and realized she was right.

Over the next few months, after outlining entire crime novels scene by scene to see how other writers did it, I finally worked my story into an outline. This seemed to help a lot. By this time I was getting up at four A.M. each day in order to put out a page or so before I went to work at the Secret Service office, and I was spending all my weekends and vacations writing.

Using my outline, I forged ahead with the first draft of what would eventually be my first novel. As I plugged away at the typewriter every day I continued to take writing classes.

I spent one memorable semester studying in a class run by the group method. The students were encouraged to criticize each other's work. It was very homey. Everyone was careful not to hurt one another's feelings and to encourage each other *to keep on writing*.

The fear of plagiarism was rampant in the class. Everyone had heard of a writer somewhere whose book had been stolen by an unscrupulous publisher and printed under another title. Some students were experts on the ins and outs of getting copyright protection. One, a reclusive man working diligently on a western novel in which all the cowboys were homosexuals, was so fearful of plagiarists that he had retained a literary lawyer.

For some reason, it seemed those most fearful of being ripped off were the ones with the least chance of being published.

Finally, I came to a point in my writing where I was making the same mistakes over and over again. I *kept on writing* but it just wasn't getting any better. As the draft of my novel grew, the obstacles–point of view, handling time, developing character (the toughest of problems writers face)–grew bigger. I attended writers' seminars and picked up a few pointers here and there, but found that, just like the faculty of the creative writing classes I'd attended, the instructors knew very little about writing. Eventually I met that fate often visited upon many a struggling writer. I had written myself into a corner.

The last class I took was taught by an authentic published mystery writer, Joseph Hansen. The makeup of the group was similar to the others I had joined: more lonely women writing Zack stories; a barber who introduced himself to the class as a police officer and maintained the guise throughout the semester; a lady who based her mystery characters on the actors whom she wanted to play their parts in the movie to be derived from her yet-to-be-completed book; an obnoxious lawyer who proudly informed everyone that, rather than using a typewriter or word processor, he was dictating his mystery novel at the rate of forty pages a day.

The difference was that the instructor, because he was a published novelist, actually knew what he was talking about. During the first few sessions he answered the questions I had wrestled with for years. Thirteen months later, with Hansen's editing and advice along the way, my novel *Money Men* was scheduled for publication by Harcourt Brace Jovanovich.

Looking back on this strange education, I'd guess that few, if any, of the students I came in contact with during these classes ever saw their novels published. I don't know whether this is because they weren't as obsessed with the goal of writing as much as they needed to be, whether they just didn't have the requisite ability with words required to reach the goal, or whether most of them were just a little crazy and were using writing as an outlet, a substitute perhaps for catatonia or television addiction. Maybe it was all the fault of the respective educational institutions for not hiring instructors who knew enough to teach the subject.

I've also wondered if there is some secret combination of personality factors, as well as technique, needed to make the grade as a novelist; an artistic drive, a requisite obsession, a mental aberration perhaps.

Nevertheless, I have always admired the writers I met in these classes. After all, while everyone thinks they can write, they actually mustered the courage to come to a classroom, read aloud, and bare themselves. Wherever they are now, I wish them well.

The Royal Shakespeare Company at the Swan

George L. Geckle
University of South Carolina

Although theatergoers regularly have opportunities to see performances of Shakespeare, they seldom get to see the works of his contemporaries. Two of these, for example Christopher Marlowe (1564-1593) and Ben Jonson (1572-1637), were enormously popular in their own time (indeed, at times exceeded Shakespeare's popularity) and wrote plays that seem today to be sometimes more modern and relevant than Shakespeare's. Within this context, the Royal Shakespeare Company's 1987-1988 season in Stratford-upon-Avon was of great interest. The main house, the Royal Shakespeare Theatre, included a standard selection of Shakespeare's plays: *The Taming of the Shrew, The Merchant of Venice, Julius Caesar, Twelfth Night*, and *Measure for Measure*. For many theatergoers and reviewers, however, the real excitement was the repertoire at the Swan Theatre, which opened in April 1986 and is dedicated to plays from the period 1570-1750: rarely performed plays by Shakespeare, his contemporaries, and playwrights influenced by him.

The Swan, an intimate theater with a seating capacity of 460, has been built within the shell of the old Shakespeare Memorial Theatre, erected in 1879 and destroyed by fire in 1926. The promontory stage, about twenty feet wide, thirty-five feet deep, and three feet high, thrusts out into the audience seated in the front row and provides these patrons and the majority of those spectators seated in the surrounding three galleries a sense of real intimacy with the actors. The houselights are never fully extinguished, so both the actors onstage and the audience are always visible to each other, thus enforcing the sense of intimacy and even interaction. It is a stage obviously influenced by what is known about Elizabethan stages, for instance the Arend van Buchell drawing of the 1596 Johannes de Witt description of the original Swan Theatre.

The opening season at the new Swan, 1986-1987, included *The Two Noble Kinsmen* (first produced circa 1613) by Shakespeare and John Fletcher; *Every Man in His Humour* (1598) by Ben Jonson; *The Fair Maid of the West* (part 1 circa 1597-1610, part 2 circa 1630-1631) by Thomas Heywood; and *The Rover* (two parts, 1677-1681) by Aphra Behn. The second season included *Titus Andronicus* (1594) by Shakespeare, *The Jew of Malta* (circa 1590) by Marlowe, *The Revenger's Tragedy* (circa 1606) by Cyril Tourneur (or Thomas Middleton, as some scholars argue), *The New Inn* (1629) by Jonson, and *Hyde Park* (1632) by James Shirley. It is the last four plays, very rarely performed, that were of particular interest.

*Interior of the new Swan Theatre (*Hyde Park by James Shirley: A Programme/Text with Commentary by Simon Trussler, *1987)*

The RSC opened its 1987-1988 season at the Swan on 7 April with *Hyde Park*, a Caroline play. The Caroline period of English drama was ushered in when Charles I became king in 1625, which is the same year James Shirley wrote his first play. Shirley (1596-1666) became the leading playwright for the King's Men in 1640, following the death of Philip Massinger, who had himself succeeded John Fletcher, who had succeeded Shakespeare. He was a prolific writer best known today for his comedy *The Lady of Pleasure* (1635) and his tragedy *The Cardinal* (1641), two frequently anthologized plays. Previous to his connection with Shakespeare's old company, Shirley was writing for Charles I's wife's company, Queen Henrietta's Men, and it was during this period that he wrote *Hyde Park*, performed by the Queen's Men in 1632 at the Phoenix Theatre in Drury Lane. The play was probably popular in the 1630s, and it was later mentioned by Samuel Pepys, who saw it at the Theatre Royal in Drury Lane in 1668. Other than that, there seems to be no stage history until the revival at the Swan Theatre.

Hyde Park is a play structured around the courtship of three women: the seemingly man-hating Mistress Carol, ancestor of Shakespeare's Beatrice (*Much Ado About Nothing*) and predecessor of Congreve's Millamant (*The Way of the World*), wooed by Rider, Venture, and Fairfield (and won by the last); Fairfield's sister Julietta, wooed by Trier, who truly tries her fidelity by setting the lecherous Lord Bonvile upon her; and Mistress Bonavent, who is courted by Trier's friend Lacy. The comedy, which a dedicatory epistle says "was presented . . . upon first opening of the Park" and which has some scenes set in Hyde Park, contains such serious topical issues as class conflict and the romantic versus commercial aspects of courtship and marriage. Director Barry Kyle, however, set the play in 1920s Bloomsbury and the players in Edwardian dress. Some reviewers seemed to accept this, for example Michael Billington in the *Guardian* (17 April 1987): "I found no problem in seeing the play bifocally both as a Caroline comedy and as a comment on Bloomsbury on a bender. Mr. Kyle's treatment also throws into sharp focus the central relationship between Fiona Shaw's Mistress Carol, an amorous sheep in Virginia Woolf's clothing, and Alex Jennings's prim suitor [Fairfield], who, with his greatcoat and loosely-knotted scarf, has the faintly fogeyish look of the young men who do architectural films on Saturday Review." Other reviewers found the setting confusing. Paul Taylor notes in the *Independent* (17 April 1987), the scene "in which the lecherous nobleman Bonvile [played by John Carlisle] tries to seduce and rape the virtuous Julietta [Felicity Dean]; but is at the last moment converted to goodness by her impassioned, eloquent reminders of the moral obligation entailed by his high rank." If this scene is to be understood as a political allegory, a "benign and unbloody dress rehearsal of the Civil War, with Julietta (who represents town-integrity) teaching a stern and much-needed lesson on personal responsibility to the selfish, wayward court," Taylor wonders, then why have Bonvile "turn a portrait of Charles I on horseback face to the wall, as though averting the gaze of a political pin-up . . . from something shameful. . . . Why, in an essentially Bloomsbury ambience, is there all this fuss about Charles I?" Further, as Taylor concluded: "although Pippa Guard (Mistress Bonavent) chokes back most movingly her disappointment at having to give up Lacy [Richard McCabe] for her returned husband [Paul Webster], we feel that, in this Bloomsbury atmosphere of insipient liberation, she would have found some other less meekly submissive solution."

Criticism of the Bloomsbury setting was also voiced by such major reviewers as J. C. Trewin in the *Birmingham Post* (16 April 1987)–"Surely we should get a better idea of what James Shirley was like if we could see his play in its proper period"–and by John Peter in the *Sunday Times* (19 April 1987)– "if you want to introduce an unknown classic, you must respect its idiom. . . . Shirley, for example, had things to say about contemporary life, about the morals of court and town, but no one would suspect it who hasn't read the play." Peter concluded by pointing out that the Swan Theatre program "contains eight pages of excellent commentary [by Simon Trussler], and a full text of the play," both of which no doubt provided (ironically) the incentive for Peter's and Taylor's adverse remarks.

A better Caroline play in all respects, and certainly in terms of its production by the Royal Shakespeare Company, was *The New Inn* by Ben Jonson. Written in the early years of the reign of Charles I but in the latter years of Jonson's career as an author, *The New Inn* was initially performed by the King's Men at their indoor theatre, the Blackfriars, in January 1629. Unfor-

tunately for Jonson, "sick and sad," as he says in the epilogue, the play was a complete failure because of poor acting and had only that one performance, its only professional production until John Caird's RSC revival opened at the Swan Theatre on 4 November 1987.

Like *Hyde Park*, Jonson's comedy reflects serious topical themes dealing with sexual, social, and economic issues, the most notable being its concern with Neoplatonism, the subject of a fashionable coterie headed by Queen Henrietta Maria. Neoplatonic concepts, ultimately derived from Plato's *Symposium* and such Renaissance sources as Baldassare Castiglione's *The Book of the Courtier* or Edmund Spenser's *Four Hymns*, are evident in Jonson's play, not only in the themes but also in the structuring of the various love affairs, from one of the highest level, that of Lovel and Lady Frampul, through those of such intermediates as Lord Latimer and Prudence (Lady Frampul's chambermaid), Lord Beaufort and Laetitia (Lady Frampul's long-lost sister, disguised as Frank, the host Goodstock's son), and Nick Stuff (tailor) and his wife, Pinnacia, who dresses in her betters' gowns for vicarious (and kinky) sexual adventures. It is a play replete with echoes of Shakespearean comedic situations and plot devices (long-lost relatives, disguises, mistaken identity, fortuitous and happy discoveries), as well as typically Jonsonian low-life characters (Jordan, Bat Burst, Hodge Huffle, and others) and frauds (Sir Glorious Tipto and the Stuffs) for which the author of *The Alchemist* and *Bartholomew Fair* was and is famous.

Set in the Light Heart Inn at Barnet (on the Great North Road), the action takes place in one day in this microcosm of English life and reflects Jonson's preoccupations with the unities of time, place, and action as the events focus on a Court of Love presided over by Prudence (played by Deborah Findlay). Although the long discourses on love and valor by the melancholic Lovel (played by John Carlisle) are rather tedious on the printed page, many of the reviewers agreed with J. C. Trewin's opinion (in the *Birmingham Post*, 11 November 1987) that the play's "best theatrical speeches are two fullscale dissertations, . . . which John Carlisle . . . expresses splendidly." The speeches also achieve results, for as Michael Coveney (in the *Financial Times*, 12 November 1987) described it: "The virginal Lady Frampul (Fiona Shaw) is quite undone and melts. Miss Shaw, a temperamentally non-submissive actress, registers the onset of passion with a wild-eyed panicky confusion." Coveney, who found the play "a real surprise, and a real treat," made another shrewd observation: "Dressing up leads to character revelation. The host [played by Joseph O'Conor] is no more what he seems [he turns out to be Lord Frampul] than is the old Irish beggar woman [played by Darlene Johnson, who turns out to be Lord Frampul's wife] who nurses his supposed son [Frank, played by Sonia Ritter, who turns out to be Laetitia]. A family is reunited, marriages proposed. The ephemeral chill felt by Lovel at the end of his ordeal, as of 'a court removing or an ended play,' is a prelude to the promise of happiness he has earned. . . . The company inhabits the play and the theatre (the two coalesce) with an irresistible relish, much aided by Sue Blane's glorious Caroline costumes."

As Caird, who had directed a highly successful production of Jonson's *Every Man in His Humour* at the Swan for the RSC's 1986-1987 season, said in an article in *Plays and Players* magazine (November 1987): "You can empty a main house with a Jonson play–even a known one. The space has to be right. When the Swan was built, the right of Ben Jonson's plays to be performed there was ungainsayable. And one of the main reasons that this particular play has not been performed is that, like a lot of Jonson's work, it's very difficult to read. But as soon as you start to rehearse it, it springs into brilliant, violent technicolor."

Whereas *The New Inn* reads badly and yet plays well, *The Revenger's Tragedy* (printed 1607) reads well and yet plays problematically. Perhaps this state of affairs is appropriate for a play of uncertain authorship (current scholarship attributes it to either Cyril Tourneur or Thomas Middleton) and a nonexistent stage history between its first performances by the King's Men in the early years of James I's reign and several productions in the twentieth century. Beginning in the 1950s *The Revenger's Tragedy* has had both amateur and professional productions, the most famous being Trevor Nunn's 1965-1966 RSC production starring Ian Richardson in the title role as Vindice. The 1987-1988 RSC version, which opened at the Swan Theatre on 2 September 1987, was directed by Di Trevis and starred Antony Sher as Vindice.

This Jacobean play, as its title indicates, is one of a subgenre of English Renaissance tragedy sometimes called by modern scholars "revenge tragedy" or "Italianate tragedy of intrigue." More famous non-Shakespearean plays

Arend van Buchell's drawing of the original Swan Theatre, based on Johannes de Witt's 1596 description (Bibliotheek der Rijkuniversiteit, Utrecht)

within this category include Thomas Kyd's *The Spanish Tragedy* (circa 1585-1590), Marlowe's *The Jew of Malta*, and John Webster's *The White Devil* (1612) and *The Duchess of Malfi* (1614). As with most of the plays in the tradition, *The Revenger's Tragedy* is set in Italy (notorious at the time for revenge, Machiavellianism, and general decadence) in a corrupt court presided over by a murderous, lecherous Duke and his ambitious, adulterous Duchess. Most of the other characters have symbolic Italianate names, such as the Duke's sons Lussurioso (lecherous) and Spurio (bastard); the Duchess's sons Ambitioso (ambitious) and Supervacuo (superfluous); the main character, Vindice (a revenger of wrongs); Vindice's sister Castiza (chastity); and their mother, Gratiana (grace). The plot, which is as sordid as the characters' names imply (in fact, one of Lussurioso's followers is named Sordido), includes murder, rape, adultery, and the attempted seduction of Castiza. The action is punctuated by several sardonic tirades by the malcontent Vindice, a character who comes right out of a tradition of satire exemplified in such contemporary Jacobean plays as John Marston's tragicomedy *The Malcontent* (1604) and Ben Jonson's dark comedy *Volpone* (1606), both of which also have Italianate settings. Vindice, in disguise as Piato, leads the attempt on his sister in a much grimmer version of the Julietta/Trier/Bonvile incident in *Hyde Park*.

It is a splendidly grotesque world that is created in *The Revenger's Tragedy*, a play so macabre that T. S. Eliot in a 1930 essay on Tourneur declared that "its motive is truly the death motive, for it is the loathing and horror of life itself." It is not a play to everyone's taste, as Irving Wardle in the *Times* (12 September 1987) illustrated when he asserted: "It is a highly effective guignol narrative snapping up every pretext for macabre gags. But, outside the closed world of plot, there is no examination of what forces produce a malcontent nor of what is being satirized, apart from the absurdity of plays like *The Revenger's Tragedy*." Perhaps for the nonspecialist theatergoer Wardle makes a valid point. Nonetheless, as J. C. Trewin said in the *Birmingham Post* (14 September 1987) about this period piece: "The affair must certainly have been something for the Jacobean connoisseur who did not mind such names as Lussurioso, Ambitioso, and Supervacuo, or such an agreeable piece of quiet chat as 'Talk to me, my lord, of sepulchres and mighty emperor's bones.'" These lines were delivered by Lussurioso, played "magnificently" by Nicholas Farrell, said Andrew Rissik in the *Independent* (12 September 1987), "as an ice-cold hypocritical gangster, the Michael Corleone of this depraved court."

Vindice, who appears in the opening scene at court—where everyone looked overpainted and overdressed and somewhat like rotting mannequins—with the skull of his fiancée, Gloriana (a name long associated with Queen Elizabeth, who had died in 1603), poisoned nine years before by the Duke for rejecting "his palsy-lust," was played compellingly by Antony Sher, who, as Rissik rightly said, "acts him the only way you can act this character: with all the stops out, as a psychopath pursuing an obsession. He is driven by ferocious analytical logic, and his ultimate goal is not revenge but moral justice." It is this sense of "moral justice" outraged in a world peopled by such as Lussurioso and Spurio (wonderfully performed by Phil Daniels, "mocking the rhetoric of his betters, picking each word off

like a scab," quipped Michael Ratcliffe in the 20 September 1987 *Observer*) that leads Vindice into his own psychological nightmare as he panders for Lussurioso, tests the virtue of his mother (played by Linda Spurrier) and sister (played by Stella Gonet), and finally succumbs, after avenging himself on the Duke and Lussurioso, to hubris by revealing his cleverness to the new ruler, who promptly sends Vindice and his assistant revenger-brother off to execution, the final grim joke in this peculiar Jacobean revenge tragedy.

Whereas the RSC's production of *The Revenger's Tragedy* left one with a slight sense of moral ambiguity and emotional unease, *The Jew of Malta*, the most exciting and interesting Swan Theatre production, was even more unsettling. Although the dating and early stage history are rather uncertain, it was probably written after the two parts of *Tamburlaine* (circa 1587-1588), because the prologue spoken by Machevil refers to the death of the Duke of Guise, who was assassinated on 23 December 1588. In his diary Philip Henslowe recorded thirty-six performances between 26 February 1592 and 21 June 1596 (mainly at his Rose Theatre by Lord Strange's Men, the Admiral's Men, and others). In an inventory of properties for the Admiral's Men taken on 10 March 1598, Henslowe recorded "*Item*, j cauderm [that is, 1 cauldron] for the Jewe," no doubt a reference to the cauldron into which Barabas falls at the end of the play. Another relevant contemporary allusion is found in Robert Greene's *A Groatsworth of Wit bought with a Million of Repentance* (1592), a deathbed pamphlet in which Marlowe is accused of atheism and is asked: "Is it pestilent Machivilian pollicy that thou hast studied?"

According to a dedicatory page in the first printed edition (1633), titled *The Famous Tragedy of the Rich Jew of Malta*, Edward Alleyn, who had previously starred as Tamburlaine, played the title role. In the nineteenth century Edmund Kean starred in an adaptation of the play, but it has rarely been performed in the twentieth century. The last major productions were given by the RSC in 1964 (Clive Revill as Barabas, Ian Richardson as Ithamore, and Glenda Jackson as Bellamira) and again in a revival in 1965 (Eric Porter as Barabas, Peter McEnery as Ithamore, and Patsy Byrne as Bellamira). The 1965 production was done in conjunction with *The Merchant of Venice*, as was the 1987-1988 production at the Swan, which opened on 7 July 1987.

The Swan is a theater perfectly suited for a play such as *The Jew of Malta*, in which the main

Phil Daniels as Spurio and Julie Legrand as the Duchess in the 1987 Swan Theatre production of The Revenger's Tragedy
(The New Inn by Ben Jonson: A Programme/Text with Commentary by Simon Trussler*)*

character speaks forty-nine percent of the lines and which is absolutely brimful of soliloquies and asides. When John Carlisle as the ghost of Machevil appeared (in a long black shroud that looked like a funnel of smoke) out of a trapdoor symbolizing hell's mouth and, swinging above the stage, opened the play with an expository soliloquy–"to present the tragedy of a Jew,/Who smiles to see how full his bags are crammed,/ Which money was not got without my means"– the cynical tone of the production was established. It was immediately reinforced as Barabas in an opening soliloquy of forty-seven lines was shown counting his wealth in a roomful of packing cases–"Infinite riches in a little room." Utilizing a clever concept, the set designer, Bob Crowley, used a tower of crates to form a central column that served as a backdrop for Barabas's house, castle walls, nun's convent, Bellamira's bordello, and a drawbridge from which Barabas descended in the last scene (while grasping a rope) into the same pit from which Machevil had appeared to open the play. After Barabas's demise, a statue of a nun descended from the flies to the strains of religious music as Ferneze, the Christian Governor of Malta, dressed in a white gown,

intoned the final lines of the play–"So, march away, and let due praise be given/Neither to fate nor fortune, but to heaven"–and then removed his wig and revealed himself to be (as everyone who had carefully watched the prologue already knew) Machevil.

While Robert Hewison in the *Sunday Times* (19 July 1987) quipped that the play "is a sort of revenger's comedy" and then groused about the production and argued that "there is no point in asking an audience to watch a play that you can only make work by sending it up," Sean French in the *Observer* (19 July 1987) asserted that "the play is profoundly and irredeemably anti-semitic" and that it provided "an evening that disturbs in the wrong way." Reflecting a more appreciative reaction to the production were comments by Andrew Rissik in the *Independent* (16 July 1987) and David Nathan in the *Jewish Chronicle* (24 July 1987). Rissik saw "a violently funny, beautifully dovetailed and unpompous piece of theatre, which suggests–as Eliot once did–that Marlowe's gift to the English stage was his appetite for a dreadful and desperate farce." Nathan found "a savage laughter in the play that derides Jew, Christian and Turk alike, the exuberance of the Jew's villainy contrasting warmly with the icy, patronizing and even more treacherous Christians." Nathan, who later reviewed the production for *Plays and Players* (September 1987), was particularly impressed with Carlisle's "commandingly satanic Machevil" and "haughty Ferneze," Janet Amsbury's "fetching, white-socked Abigail," Phil Daniels's "slithery Ithamore [who] looks as if he was born to die in a dark alley," and, most important, Alun Armstrong's Barabas, "superbly transforming the energy of the text into a physical reality that makes this purveyor of wholesale death the most vibrant life on view."

Armstrong's Barabas was a brilliant portrayal. From the opening scene in his counting-house, wearing a black homburg and flinging "paltry silverlings" aside while gloating over his gold coins, to his exaggerated (and fake) weeping when Ferneze and the other Knights of Malta seize his goods to pay tribute money to the Turks, to his immediate turn to villainous behavior after being stripped of his wealth, to his disguise as a French musician in a straw hat with a ukulele, Armstrong exhibited tremendous vitality and relish for his role. At the Swan, which encourages such possibilities because of the closeness of the front rows to the stage, Armstrong played outrageously and effectively to the audience with the use of the play's many asides (Barabas has forty-eight), as well as ad-libs and a few raised eyebrows. His exchange with Phil Daniels as Ithamore in which each tried to outdo the other in relating past villainous deeds was a comic masterpiece. Even the poisoning of the nuns and the tricking of the friars was played for and elicited laughs from the audience.

But *The Jew of Malta* is also a play in which not only are Jews fleeced by Christians but also one in which slaves are sold and bought and in which people are murdered. These facts of the plot are what led Michael Billington in the *Guardian* (16 July 1987) to declare that "while Mr. [Barry] Kyle's new production is full of vivacious villainy, it lacks underlying seriousness." On the other hand, Irving Wardle in the *Times* (16 July 1987) saw topical seriousness in the "modern-dress production [which] swarms with Marlovian equivalents of Shiite militiamen, Maronite Christians and Hassidic zealots. The analogy cannot be pushed to the point of jihad, as Marlowe was writing under religious censorship. But that, indeed, is what lends the piece its greatest impact. Under cover of displaying a gross and palpable Jewish vil-

lain, Marlowe succeeds in exposing his nominally virtuous Christian adversaries as the real enemy."

Wardle's point is a good one, especially if one happened to see *The Merchant of Venice* in the main theater during the same season. As Wardle noted: "In Shakespeare you see ordinary sympathetic people turning like a pack of wolves against an outsider. In Marlowe you see them from the outsider's viewpoint, as stone-faced pharisaical hypocrites, preaching Barabas out of his possessions and finally dumping him into the furnace he had prepared for their enemies (while also availing themselves of the other side of his plot, and leaving the Turkish army to fry to death, as planned)." Nonetheless, as Billington made clear in his *Guardian* review, the overall effect of the two plays was clear-cut: "[director] Bill Alexander treats Shakespeare's comedy as a racist tragedy, while Barry Kyle directs Marlowe's tragedy as a brutal farce."

Whereas Shylock, played by Antony Sher in a brilliant performance, was as single-minded as Shakespeare's text indicates, he had more than ample reason to want to exact his "pound of flesh" from Antonio, who, played by John Carlisle as a melancholy homosexual with an unrequited longing for Bassanio (played by Nicholas Farrell), was an incredibly cold and vicious anti-Semite who spat upon Shylock at every opportunity and even showed overt distaste for the convertite Jessica in the concluding scene. Bassanio, who used his friendship (love that dared not speak its name?) to get the money he needed to pursue the quest of Portia, was more passionate than Antonio but just as vicious, as were the rest of the Christian males, toward Shylock. Phil Daniels as Launcelot Gobbo provided some moments of respite from the somber tone of this production, and Portia (Deborah Findlay) and Nerissa (Pippa Guard) were more sympathetic than some reviewers indicated (the audience delighting in their put-downs of the nasty fiancés who had given their engagement rings away), but overall the production, set in seventeenth-century Venice and highlighted by a graffito Star of David and an altarpiece of Madonna and child on the backdrop at the rear of the stage, was a disturbing one.

The question, as with *The Jew of Malta*, is: did the RSC's *Merchant of Venice* disturb in the right way? Shakespearean purists could be outraged at the idea of turning a comedy into a tragedy, thereby losing almost all of the romance in the play and making the last act not the closure of the love relationships but a final comment on how racist attitudes can permeate all societal and personal relationships. Although there is frequent criticism of the RSC's interpretation of classical drama in order to make relevant social and political points for modern audiences, one must consider such attempts in terms of success or failure. The productions of *The Jew of Malta* and *The Merchant of Venice* worked in Stratford and were again successful when they were transferred to the RSC's main theater in London, the Barbican Theatre, in the spring of 1988.

Whereas the reviewers who saw the production of Shakespeare's play at Stratford had rather mixed reactions to it and especially to Antony Sher's Shylock, all of them took it as a serious play dealing with serious issues. By the time it got to London it had been made tighter and better. As J. C. Trewin said in the *Birmingham Post* (28 April 1988): "As I remember it, much in this production has matured considerably since the opening of Stratford. At this time it is almost a routine response to under-value *The Merchant*, but at The Barbican the players keep its tension even when one knows every move on the board." Perhaps one example will suffice to corroborate Trewin's point. It is the final moment in the final scene. In the Stratford version Nerissa dropped her newly acquired crucifix and walked off the stage. Antonio picked it up, looked at her departing back, and appeared to be about to call her, but then changed his mind and kept the crucifix. In the London version she dropped it, saw him pick it up, and waited for him to hand it to her, but instead he taunted her with it. As Jeremy Kingston in the *Times* (27 April 1988) said of this final tableau: "images like this take hold of your mind."

What took hold in *The Jew of Malta* was somewhat the same, that is to say, the Christians were once again more immoral than Barabas, or the Turks, for that matter. But whereas *The Merchant of Venice* production left one feeling depressed about the negative aspects of the human race, the final emotional moment in *The Jew of Malta* production was, if anything, a feeling of neutrality. Perhaps, as Victoria Radin said in a *New Statesman* review (1 April 1988): "Cheeky and swift and cunning and, as the programme note suggests, Ortonesque–Kyle's staging is expert in assessing the cool temper of our times." Or, perhaps, to place the production in a less morally neutral context, the following comment by Charles Spencer in the *Daily Telegraph* (25 March 1988) is more apropos: "With its casual acts of violence and concentration on material values, 'The Jew of Malta' is the Marlowe play which has most in common with the spirit of the latter half of the 20th century."

Perhaps, finally, it is a sad commentary on our times if the last two reviewers quoted above are correct, but if plays centuries old can be produced in ways that excite and provoke modern audiences both emotionally and intellectually, they are still vital and relevant. The RSC showed in its productions of *The Jew of Malta*, *The Revenger's Tragedy*, and *The New Inn*, certainly, that the past can still speak to the present.

The author thanks the staff of the Shakespeare Centre, Stratford-upon-Avon, for providing reviews and helpful assistance. This work was supported by a grant from the University of South Carolina Research and Productive Scholarship Fund, and the author thanks the Research and Productive Scholarship Committee for the award.

The Nobel Prize and Literary Politics

Jeffrey Meyers

University of Colorado at Boulder

In 1925, just before Wyndham Lewis unleashed his six major works of the late 1920s, he jokingly asked Ezra Pound, who had forsaken France for Mussolini and the crackpot economic theories of Major Douglas: "Could you get me the Nobel Prize next year? or do you want it for yourself?" Both inveterate outsiders were destined to remain virtually excluded from public recognition and honors, while their close friend Tom Eliot received the Order of Merit and the Nobel Prize in 1948. When Lewis heard of Eliot's award, he commented on the irony of their lives and told Pound, who had been charged with treason, declared insane, and confined to St. Elizabeths hospital in Washington: "You might almost have contrived this climax to your respective careers: yours so Villonesque and Eliot's super-Tennyson."

The strange careers of Pound and Lewis illuminate the central paradox of the Nobel Prize. The literary award that includes a dignified royal ceremony (on 10 December, the anniversary of Nobel's death), grants the largest amount of money ($390,000 this year), engenders the most publicity, and carries the greatest prestige, has frequently been awarded to mediocrities. Most of the greatest writers of the twentieth century have not won the prize. An understanding of who makes the decisions and who has won the prize helps to explain why the losers are often more impressive than the winners.

Joseph Brodsky, though an unusual choice for last year's prize, tends to confirm this negative trend. The forty-seven-year-old Russian-Jewish poet is young, was arrested in 1964, was exiled from the Soviet Union in 1972, was sponsored by W. H. Auden and Robert Lowell when he arrived in the West, and now lives in New York. He is not as well-known as his compatriots and rivals, Andrei Voznesensky and Yevgeny Yevtushenko; and he has not equaled the achievement of last year's finalists, V. S. Naipaul and Octavio Paz. He does not have a major reputation and is not widely read. A comparison of Brodsky to the four previous Russian winners

shows that he is an exile like Ivan Alexejevich Bunin, a complete antithesis to the official propagandist Mikhail Sholokhov, a critic of the regime like Boris Pasternak, and (for eighteen months) a political prisoner like Aleksandr Solzhenitsyn. Like several other winners during the last decade—Vicente Aleixandre, Odysseus Elýtis, Jaroslav Seifert, Claude Simon, and Wole Soyinka—he is earnest but obscure. In political terms, the award is a criticism of Russia, an honor for America, and a recognition of all writers in exile. But, as I shall argue, Brodsky is not at all equal to the strongest candidates for the prize.

The money for the prize was donated by Alfred Nobel, the inventor of dynamite, whose testament decreed that it should be given to the author who has produced "the most outstanding work of an idealistic tendency." Nobel's equation of idealism and literary merit has bedeviled the choices from the start and frequently led to the selection of the monumental as well as the banal. The winners are chosen each fall by the eighteen members of the Swedish Academy, and about thirty candidates are seriously considered. Members of the Swedish, French, and Spanish Academies; fellows of other humanistic institutions and societies; and "teachers of aesthetics, literature and history at university colleges" may nominate candidates, but few American professors exercise this right.

Nobel wanted to give the winners complete financial independence so that they could devote themselves entirely to their work, but almost all the writers were well-off by the time they won the award. Only eight previous authors—Rudyard Kipling, Maurice Maeterlinck, Romain Rolland, Sigrid Undset, Sinclair Lewis, Eugene O'Neill, Pearl S. Buck, and Albert Camus—won the prize when they were still in their forties and relatively young. The academy, which has become increasingly conservative about age, prefers to give the award to moribund writers such as Eric Axel Karlfeldt, John Galsworthy, Aleixandre, and Seifert.

The Nobel Prize was first awarded in 1901. The subsequent eighty-five winners (there were four double prizes and seven war years without an award) from twenty-nine countries can be somewhat subjectively divided into five general categories: I (A & B). great international reputations; II. serious and important; III. third-rank and often middle-brow; IV. obscure, unreadable, and forgotten; V. the Scandinavian contingent. (See table.) This division reveals that only sixteen of the eighty-five winners (less than one-fifth) are now recognized as great authors while forty-one are no longer read. The most unfortunate choices were the low-brow Pearl Buck (Hemingway, in China, spoke of "the bad earth"), Sholokhov, who was accused of plagiarism, and Knut Hamsun, who became a Nazi collaborator in World War II.

When the Nobel Prize was first awarded, many of the greatest writers of the nineteenth century were still alive. Instead of choosing Tolstoy or Chekhov, Meredith or Swinburne, Hardy or Zola, Twain or James, or even the local favorites, Ibsen or Strindberg (none of whom ever won the prize), the Swedish Academy immediately revealed its limitations by a controversial award to Sully Prudhomme. World opinion protested against the neglect of Tolstoy, and forty-two Swedish authors signed a tribute to his genius. The despotic disposition of Carl Wirsén, the first permanent secretary (chairman) of the Swedish Academy, who died in 1912, was largely responsible for the inexpiable sins of omission during the early years. He accused Tolstoy of "narrow-minded hostility to all forms of civilization," declared that "Hardy's deep pessimism and inexorable fatalism were not to be reconciled with the spirit of the Nobel Prize," was violently opposed to Ibsen, and hated Strindberg, who had satirized him in *The New Kingdom* (1882).

During the next six years the prize (including a double award in 1904) went to Theodor Mommsen, Björnstjerne Björnson, Frédéric Mistral, José Echegaray, Henryk Sienkiewicz, and Giosuè Carducci. The early winners were all establishment figures. Sully Prudhomme, Anatole France, Henri Louis Bergson, Echegaray, Verner von Heidenstam, and Karlfeldt were members of the French, Spanish, and Swedish Academies (the Swedes have been exceptionally generous to their own countrymen); Mommsen, Carducci, and Rudolf Eucken held university chairs at Berlin, Bologna, and Jena. Kipling, in 1907, was the first distinguished writer—and the youngest ever—to win the prize.

The national distribution is also strangely unbalanced. France and the United States lead with twelve and nine awards, followed by Germany with seven; Sweden with six; Italy and England with five; Spain and the Soviet Union with four; Norway, Denmark, Poland, and Ireland with three; Chile, Greece, and Israel with two. It is clear that British authors have been seriously neglected, and Scandinavians and Poles inflated. Austria (including Czech-born, German-language writers of the Austro-Hungarian Empire) has the greatest grievance, for none of its major writers—Rainer Maria Rilke, Robert Musil, Franz Kafka, and Hermann Broch, as well as Ludwig Wittgenstein, Hugo von Hofmannsthal, Karl Kraus, Stefan Zweig, and Georg Trakl—has ever won the award.

In addition to the ten nineteenth-century masters and the four best Austrian writers, there are forty other immensely distinguished authors who did not win the prize. Fourteen authors (Joseph Conrad, Ford Madox Ford, E. M. Forster, James Joyce, Wyndham Lewis, Virginia Woolf, D. H. Lawrence, Auden, Robert Frost, Wallace Stevens, Pound, Marcel Proust, Paul Valéry, and André Malraux) are as good as the winners with the most secure reputations (group IA), and twenty-six (H. G. Wells, Aldous Huxley, Robert Graves, George Orwell, Evelyn Waugh, Arthur Koestler, F. Scott Fitzgerald, Robert Lowell, Giovanni Verga, Italo Svevo, Gabriele D'Annunzio, Benedetto Croce, Giuseppe Ungaretti, Giuseppe di Lampedusa, Primo Levi, Anna Akhmatova, Isaak Babel, Vladimir Nabokov, Bertolt Brecht, Paul Celan, Antonio Machado, Federico García Lorca, Constantine P. Cavafy, Nikos Kazantzakis, Mohammed Iqbal, and Yukio Mishima) are as good as the winners in group IB or II. Minor masters like Katherine Mansfield, Jorge Luis Borges, Elizabeth Bishop, Sir John Betjeman, and Philip Larkin have never been seriously considered.

Though voting records are not kept and the choices of the Swedish Academy are as secret as those of the Vatican (one waits with equal eagerness for the puff of smoke from the log-burning Jotul stove), it is possible to give a partial explanation of the selection process. Unlike the more objective awards in science, the Nobel Prize for Literature is based on subjective judgments. Like any academy composed of elderly, stuffy, and conservative members, the Swedes tend to choose old, safe, well-established, and even popular writers. Like most literary prizes, the Nobel most frequently goes to the consensus candidate–a blackball immediately eliminates a controversial contender and a double prize indicates a compromise–or to the choice of the most adamant judge. Swedish translators are often persuasive lobbyists for their own authors. Previous winners have also been instrumental in obtaining the prize for their friends. Thomas Mann helped Hermann Hesse, Martin du Gard helped André Gide, and Solzhenitsyn–who has great moral as well as literary authority–most likely helped Heinrich Böll get the prize, two years after he himself had won it.

Writers in uncommon languages may enhance their reputations and become candidates for the prize if they are sponsored by famous writers in major languages. Authors who write in or have been translated into English–today's universal language–have the best chance. The most original and idiosyncratic writers lose most in translation, and for this reason there have been more winners in prose than in poetry. Though some authors wrote in several genres and some categories overlap, the eighty-five winners can be generically divided into forty-nine novelists, twenty-three poets, eight playwrights, three philosophers (Eucken, Bergson, and Bertrand Russell), and two historians (Mommsen and Sir Winston Churchill).

The criminals and crazies, the rebels and extremists in ideas and behavior (Pound, Henry Miller, Louis-Ferdinand Céline, Brecht, Jean Genet, Dylan Thomas, and John Berryman)–authors whose presence might have disrupted the solemn proceedings–had absolutely no hope of winning. The academy safely but unwisely chose Jacinto Benavente but not Lorca, Seferis not Cavafy, Yasunari Kawabata not Mishima, Böll not Günter Grass, Seifert not Milan Kundera.

But there have been a few extraordinary choices. Gide, whose defense of homosexuality in *Corydon* (1911) had kept him out of the French Academy, won in 1947. Samuel Beckett's dark and disturbing vision, far more pessimistic and fatalistic than Hardy's, was ignored in the citation of 1969, which claimed that in his works "the destitution of modern man acquires its elevation." And the Swedes aroused the wrath of their powerful neighbor by giving the prize to Pasternak and Solzhenitsyn, who had criticized and defied the Soviet Union.

Like college admission boards, the academy is influenced by regional distribution and likes to spread the wealth among the smaller countries. A mediocre writer from a remote region, like a bright student from North Dakota, is more likely to be chosen. For this reason, competition among English-language writers is much fiercer. Ten of the sixteen best winners and eleven of the fourteen best losers wrote in English.

Politics also influence the choices, and it is no accident that Saint-John Perse, Seferis, and Pablo Neruda were diplomats. William Butler Yeats won the award two years after Ireland became independent. The first Finn, Frans Eemil Sillanpää, won in 1939, the year his country was invaded by Russia. Sweden–which remained neutral during the war, sold iron ore to Germany and allowed armed Nazi troops to pass through their country while invading Finland in 1941–worked off some of its guilt by giving the 1944 prize to the Dane, Johannes Jensen, who could not go to Stockholm because his country was occupied by the Germans. Hesse, a German author whose dubious moral position was analogous to Sweden's, won the first postwar prize despite his compromise with the Nazi regime.

Graham Greene was considered too friendly with left-wing dictators such as Fidel Castro and Omar Torrijos. Malraux (whom Camus felt should have won the prize in 1957) was considered too right-wing, and his biographer, Jean Lacouture, explains that "the Nobel Prize for Literature was withheld from him because he was for so long a minister in a [Gaullist] government regarded as semi-fascist by a few puritan professors of the Stockholm jury." Auden said time would pardon Kipling and Claudel, pardon them for writing well, but Auden himself was not pardoned. In 1964 he was Dag Hammarskjöld's candidate and had an excellent chance to win. But the Swedes disliked his introduction to Hammarskjöld's *Markings* (1964), which referred to the author's "exceptionally aggressive super-ego," and Auden was told he would have to change this if he wished to remain in favor. But, according to his biographer, Humphrey Carpenter, Auden "was adamant. He printed the introduction without changing anything, remarking philosophically and without bitterness: 'Well, there goes the Nobel Prize.'" When an African was due for the award, tribal politics influenced the decision. It was given to Soyinka, from the dominant Yoruba tribe of Nigeria (like Solzhenitsyn, he had been imprisoned for political reasons), instead of to the better writer, Chinua Achebe, a minority Ibo who had supported the independence of Biafra during the civil war.

The academy, naturally cautious about making premature judgments, often gives the award to a writer several decades after his best work has been done. (Kipling, Yeats, Bernard Shaw, Mann, O'Neill, Solzhenitsyn, and Saul Bellow were among the very few winners who continued to produce impressive new works.) They presented it to William Faulkner and to Ernest Hemingway, who had done their finest writing in the 1920s and 1930s, as they were composing or soon after they had completed their most bogus and bathetic books: *A Fable* (1954) and *The Old Man and the Sea* (1952). Hemingway, superstitious about "the Swedish thing," felt it frequently put an end to a writer's career. Eliot believed it was more an epitaph than an honor: "The Nobel is a ticket to one's funeral. No one has ever done anything after he got it." Camus, and many other writers, felt guilty about receiving the award during a period of sterility, and unworthy when subjected to the overwhelming publicity and flattery.

The academy's insistence on "idealism" has sometimes led it to select writers such as William Golding (a contentious choice), who strain for profundity and moral uplift. Faulkner also succumbed to this temptation in his embarrassingly pompous acceptance speech: "when the last dingdong of doom has clanged and faded from the last worthless rock hanging tideless in the last red and dying evening, even then there will still be one more sound: that of [man's] puny inexhaustible voice, still talking." By contrast, Hemingway's speech, which diagnosed the dangers of literary life even as he reaped its rewards, was a sad acknowledgment of solitude, uncertainty, and personal failure: "Writing, at its best, is a lonely life. Organizations for writers palliate the writer's loneliness but I doubt if they improve his writing. He grows in public stature as he sheds his loneliness and often his work deteriorates. For he does his work alone and if he is a good enough writer he must face eternity, or the lack of it, each day."

A knowledge of the selection process makes it possible to predict which writers might win the prize in the next decade. Countries which have never been given the prize–including Austria, the Netherlands, Portugal, Romania, Hungary, South Africa, Canada, Mexico, Argentina, Brazil, Turkey, Indonesia, and China–have a good chance of winning with a halfway decent candi-

date. From the geographical point of view, Eugène Ionesco (who writes in French) of Romania, Paz and Carlos Fuentes of Mexico, Jorge Amado of Brazil (a much better writer than Mario Vargas Llosa), and Yasher Kemal of Turkey have an outside chance. Though Naipaul–a superb writer and prickly personality–is more pessimistic than idealistic (but not more negative than Beckett), three extraliterary considerations make him a very strong candidate. He is Indian (which would please the Asians), he was born in Trinidad (which would satisfy Caribbean and Central American interests), and he lives in England.

Grass (Germany), Kundera (a Czech living in Paris), Voznesensky (Russia), Alberto Moravia and Leonardo Sciascia (both Italy) are serious contenders. But the leading candidates, American and English, are better writers than the most recent winners from their countries: Isaac Bashevis Singer (1978) and William Golding (1983). The most distinguished Americans are Arthur Miller (whose plays are constantly produced all over the world and whose recent autobiography, *Timebends*, is a major work), the prodigiously talented Norman Mailer, and the intelligent and accomplished William Styron. The most impressive British authors are Graham Greene (probably hors de combat), Angus Wilson, Anthony Burgess, and Harold Pinter, and the two finest poets in the English language, Geoffrey Hill and Seamus Heaney. (Ted Hughes did his best work long ago, and Doris Lessing ruined her chances by lapsing into science fiction.)

Only two homosexuals, two Asians, five Jews, and six women (the last, in 1966, was Nelly Sachs, a naturalized Swedish citizen) have won the prize, and a woman might soon get it. Now that a Nigerian has won the award, the prize could go to a white South African writer. Nadine Gordimer, like Kundera, a worthy opponent of an unpopular regime, is earnest, serious, respected–and rather dull. But Iris Murdoch's keen intelligence, high seriousness, philosophical ideas, richness of imagination, technical skill, monumental achievement, and moral vision, as well as her gender, make her the most worthy and promising candidate for the Nobel Prize.

Table

IA. Yeats, Mann, Gide, Eliot, Faulkner, Hemingway, Camus, Solzhenitsyn.

IB. Kipling, Shaw, O'Neill, Russell, Sartre, Beckett, Montale, Bellow.

II. Mommsen, F. Mistral, Carducci, Maeterlinck, Hauptmann, Hamsun, Bergson, Bunin, Pirandello, Hesse, Lagerkvist, Mauriac, Churchill, Pasternak, Quasimodo, Saint-John Perse, Andrić, Seferis, Agnon, Sachs, Kawabata, Neruda, Böll, White, Singer, Elýtis, Márquez, Simon.

III. Prudhomme, Sienkiewicz, Lagerlöf, Tagore, Rolland, A. France, Benavente, Deledda, Undset, S. Lewis, Galsworthy, Martin du Gard, Buck, G. Mistral, Laxness, Jiménez, Steinbeck, Sholokhov, Asturias, Aleixandre, Milosz, Canetti, Golding, Seifert, Soyinka, Brodsky, Mahfūz.

IV. Echegaray, Eucken, Heyse, Spitteler, Reymont.

V. Björnson, Heidenstam, Gjellerup, Pontoppidan, Karlfeldt, Sillanpää, Jensen, Johnson, Martinson.

John O'Hara's Pottsville Journalism

Apprenticeships are always instructive to students of literature. John O'Hara's first writing job was on the *Pottsville Journal* from summer 1924 to late 1926. Since Pottsville became the fictional Gibbsville, O'Hara's early journalism has potential biographical and critical value. It is therefore regrettable that there is no located run of the *Pottsville Journal* for this period–although the other years of the paper survive in bound volumes. Until recently only one of O'Hara's *Journal* articles ("A Cub Tells his Story," 2 May 1925) had been found. Now five by-lined O'Hara sports pieces in the *Journal* have been acquired by Charles Mann, Curator of Special Collections at the Pennsylvania State University Library.

The most interesting of these new pieces are O'Hara's defense of Red Grange's decision to turn pro and O'Hara's report on the exhibition game between the Pottsville Maroons professional football team and the former Notre Dame team. Grange's choice of foregoing his senior year at the University of Illinois to play for the Chicago Bears was a matter of national debate during an era of athletic innocence when college stars were expected to play for the joy of the game.

O'Hara's pregame color story on the Maroons-Notre Dame game documents the events surrounding the 1925 National Football League championship. After the Maroons won the championship by beating the Chicago Cardinals, the Pottsville team played a postseason exhibition game against the barnstorming Notre Dame All-Stars (former Notre Dame players including the Four Horsemen), which the Maroons won 9-7. Since the exhibition game was played in Shibe Park, Philadelphia, the local Frankford Yellowjackets claimed an invasion of their territorial rights. The Cardinals were then permitted an extra game against a weak team and were awarded the championship–a matter that still generates wrath in the Anthracite Region. The 1925 Maroons included extraordinary players: Charlie Berry (who also played for the Philadelphia Athletics), Russ and Herb Stein (the first brothers to be selected as All-Americans), Walter French, Jack Ernst, and Tony Latone (O'Hara's selection as the best ball-carrier he ever saw).*

M.J.B.

* Information about the Maroons has been drawn from Doug Costello's 1985-1986 articles in the *Pottsville Republican.*

HOW THE CUP LOOKED TO ONE WHO HAD NOT SEEN IT PREVIOUSLY

Thought It Was All Bull Until
He Saw Wonderful
Trophy

COSTLIER THAN DAVIS CUP

(By John O'Hara)

Why so much publicity should be attached to the mere presentation of a loving cup, even though it did represent the winning of the Anthracite football championship, was more than we could understand. We could readily see how important it was to gather about the famed festive board to bid a final good-bye and wish a final good luck to the Maroons, but all this talk about the cup, the cup, the cup, seemed to us inordinately out of proportion. BUT, we had not seen the cup.

About the only thing we have seen (pictures of) that can compare with the immense Mug that was presented last night to the Champions of the Anthracite Region is the Longwood Bowl, maybe the Davis Cup, but they are of international fame. Englishmen in flannels practice all year in South Africa for the chance to compete for the honor of holding for a year (only for a year, unless they win it again) the cup which is emblematic of the world's championship in tennis. The same Davis Cup has been contested for since Pete Henry's mother first firbade him to kick a football in the house. And that is the only cup to which the Curran and Meade trophy can, to our mind, be compared. It's bigger than the international polo championship cup and if Dr. Striegel ever turns to polo he'll have a cup big enough for a pony to drink from.

The cup, to our unpracticed eye, looked to be about, well, very near a yard from top to bottom. It is about a foot in diameter at the mouth and weighs, without the wooden pedestal, about fifteen pounds. Our guess is that it would bring at least a thousand dollars from the most conservative pawn-broker. (That is for its intrinsic value; pawn-brokers, as we remember, refuse to consider the sentimental value of watches, banjos, and Championship cups.) The sentimental value of this cup may be found by adding the horse-power of the heart-beats that went into the winning of it; the untiring energy that was expended by Dr. Striegel and his associates in bringing together and holding together the champion Maroons; the sincere support of the fans, and the individual efforts of the players themselves. The Curran and Meade trophy is worthy of possession by such a team: such a team is worthy of the possession of such a cup.

Ray Curran, again you proved that you do not do things by halves.

19 December 1924

O'HARA'S OPINIONS OF TWO BIG GAMES

As one who had never before seen the renowned New York Celtics display their wares, we were naturally a good deal more than casually interested in last night's game.

Coming for the P. H. S. Summit Hill tilt we were a little afraid after having seen the very exciting scholastic game that the Big Five affair would come as a sort of anticlimax. Not so. The "big" game only made it sustained suspense. We'll bet that there wasn't a more thrilling high school game anywhere in the country last night, and the Celtics affair was certainly the most thrilling professional game we have ever seen.

The poise acquired in hundreds of games—when each victory for the opposing team meant added prestige, while to the Celtics it meant only another to their long string of wins—that poise was the first thing we noticed when the Celtics stepped nonchalantly on the floor and just as nonchalantly tested the backboard. We passed the time before "Gick" Tracey called the game by learning which was Holman, and which was Lopchick, and who was this man and who was the man who looked like Blue Bonner.

The game itself is history, but we have seldom known forty-five longer seconds than when Pottsville led and when every move was watched by the stands as though each rooter were in the arena, waiting for the thumbs-up or down signal from the haughty Roman emperor.

It was without a doubt the fastest and hardest-played, the most thrilling and most exciting professional game we have ever seen. And the best feature was that we won.

19 February 1925

PUNTS & PASSES

Joe Spagna, a former Frankford Yellowjacket, has been recalled from Florida to help out for the Pottsville game. He probably will play right guard, Seidelson to be shifted to left end, if Chamberlain is unable to play. There are rumors of other Frankford additions.

—

Larry Conover was severely injured in the Cleveland-Chicago Bears game of a few weeks ago. That is why he was out of the lineup for the last two games.

It is hoped he will be in shape by the time Cleveland comes here.

—

Pottsville would benefit by scheduling a game at New York. The Maroons' standing warrants it, but it looks as if the famous Giants are not ready to meet Pottsville until they feel certain of victory.

—

The Anthracite region calls Pottsville cheap, because conditions preclude a baseball team, but when we step out with one of the greatest football teams in America they say we are going over our heads. Charming inconsistency.

We'll keep the football, as long as we can.

—

Irvin Heintz, a former Pottsvillian now of Stamford, Connecticut, will attend Saturday's game at Philadelphia. He says he will contribute to the Maroon's volume of cheering.

Mr. Heinz never misses a chance to see the great club representing his old home town. He was one of the promoters of Pottsville's 1922 team.

—

Fans again have been discussing the relative merits of professional and collegiate football teams and the possibility of a Maroon victory in an imaginary game between Red Grange and Pottsville.

The discussion can amount only to that, despite rumors that a leading professional team and a leading college team would be a great attraction at the Sesqui-Centennial in Philadelphia next year.

But there are some angles of a pro-college game which are worthy of consideration. The pro player would not be tricked through ignorance of the rules or by an ancient fluke play. Last week in the Yale-Maryland game Captain Johnny Joss, of Yale, drew a heavy penalty on his team by talking to his quarterback immediately upon entering the game as a substitute. We have not seen a high school team so far forget the rules as to incur that penalty this year. Yale also was fooled on an onside kick. The talking-to-quarterback penalty cost Yale an early-in-the-game lead–always a handicap.

Another thing, not a single shoestring has been pulled against the Maroons during the present season. Akron was set for one several times, but Hoot Flanagan or Barney Wentz was on the alert each time.

Rudimentary football can be taught to seniors who have been on the football squad for four years but very seldom are teams as good as the Maroons in need of coaching in the elementary phase.

But then, you might say, there are mighty few teams in this vale of tears which are as good as the Maroons. Right!

(John O'Hara)
13 November 1925

WHY SHOULDN'T RED MAKE A FORTUNE?

If His Reputation is Worth a Million He Has Right to Capitolize It

---

WEALTHY SHOULDN'T KICK

(By John O'Hara)

If I were Red Grange and I could make a million dollars on my reputation, I'd make that mil-

Staff of the Journal, *1925. O'Hara is between the two girls at left (courtesy of the Historical Society of Schuylkill County).*

lion and consider that I have mighty good reasons for capitalizing on my fame.

In the first place, he owes it to his father. According to the story of his life, it was rather a tough struggle for the father to pay Red's way through the University of Illinois. Now that Grange has the chance, he ought to pay back that money–with interest. At the very least it cost his father $6,000 to send Grange through the university.

Why shouldn't Red capitalize on his name? If he were known only as Harold Grange, student of the University of Illinois, whose sonnets have been stirring the literary world, rather than Grange, the Touchdown Maker, whose athletic prowess has stirred even those who know little of football, no one would object to his profiting by

what he has learned at the university. If he were an engineer, or a lawyer, the same would hold. True, he is not supposed to go to college to play football but he learned more about football and how to play it well than many law students learn about law and how to practice it. Why, then shouldn't Red establish a fortune when he can?

It is all very well for Louis Stoddard to be sickened by the tales of fat offers made to Grange but Mr. Stoddard, unless I am mistaken, has enough money to play polo and a polo pony is worth almost as much as a ton of coal, (in strike times.) An illustrious name is an illustrious name, but $25,000, as John D. Rockefeller would say, is $25,000.

20 November 1925

MAROONS GETS WARM RECEPTION AT SHIBE PARK; FRENCH PLAYS

Hundreds Of Fans Pay Tribute To Pottsville Team As Players Reach Field Early

BOX OFFICE IS CROWDED

Hoot Flanagan, In Uniform Has "Chipped" Shoulder Bone Instead Of A Fracture

By JOHN O'HARA

(Pottsville Journal Staff Reporter)

Shibe Park, Philadelphia, Dec. 11 (Special Wire to Journal)–The Maroons arrived here at one o'clock to dress for their game with the Four Horsemen.

Walter French met the team at the park and is in shape to play. Hoot Flanagan, who was thought to have suffered a broken shoulder at Chicago, will be in uniform as further examination showed the shoulder bone was slightly chipped instead of fractured.

Clarence Beck was at the Reading Terminal when the team arrived. Dick Stahlman accompanied the Maroons. It is not known whether he will play. The players entered the press gate and hundreds paid homage to the Pottsville eleven.

The crowd at the box office bore a stronger resemblance to a collegiate crowd than any professional game seen this year by the writer. Despite the October weather, fur coats were in the audience.

The press box is sure to be the hottest place in Philadelphia in summer and the coldest in winter. Upon arriving at Philadelphia this morning the team taxied to the new Elks' Home where they lunched and rested until twelve-thirty. They changed clothes at Shibe Park. The entire team inspected the field before dressing.

Movie Camera Man on Scene

The ground is springy but dry. A movie camera man is on the scene. WIP is broadcasting the game. Reminiscent of the crowd on the bank of the creek at Minersville is a cluster of fans on housetops past right field. The game was started at two o'clock.

Jack Bergen, millionaire automobile man, of Newark, called to congratulate the Pottsville team.

The Providence game is apparently off, because the Steamrollers would not pay the guarantee agreed to, insisting on the new arrangement which was unsatisfactory to Pottsville. This was done as late as 7:30 o'clock this morning. There still is a chance that Providence will wire accepting Pottsville's proposition but Dr. Striegel thinks not.

The Maroons are scheduled to play at Atlantic City December 20th, but some of the regulars may play their last game for Pottsville today. Berry, Osborne, French and Ernst are due to report to Callahan's team in Florida early next week.

St. Francis Xavier's Band, which visited Pottsville for the Frankford game, is on the field.

12 December 1925

OBITUARIES

Raymond Carver

(25 May 1938-2 August 1988)

William L. Stull
University of Hartford

See also the Carver entry in *DLB Yearbook: 1984.*

In life, art, and even death, Raymond Carver's double, mentor, and companion soul was Anton Chekhov. Like Chekhov (1860-1904), whose grandfather bought himself out of serfdom and whose father's grocery shop went broke, Carver was a child of the working poor. His father, Clevie Raymond Carver ("C. R."), rode the rails from Arkansas to Washington state during the dust-bowl days of the 1930s. C. R. became a saw filer in the lumber mills–and an alcoholic who was dead at fifty-three. His wife, Ella Casey Carver, was no stranger to domestic violence, and she supplemented the family income by working as a waitress and retail clerk. Raymond Clevie Carver, nicknamed Junior, Frog, and Doc, was born on 25 May 1938 in Clatskanie, Oregon, a logging town of seven hundred on the Columbia river. The family returned to Washington in 1941, and Carver grew up in Yakima, a hub town of twenty thousand in "The Nation's Fruit Bowl," the fertile valley east of the Cascades.

Carver was a belated child of the Great Depression, and well into times of postwar prosperity his house lacked an indoor toilet. His poem "Shiftless" (1986) lays out the economics of his childhood: "The people who were better off than us were *comfortable*. . . . / The ones worse off were *sorry* and didn't work." Like Chekhov, Carver knew intimately the marginal lives of hardship and squalor from which he crafted luminous stories of empathy, endangerment, and hard-won affirmation. "They're my people," he said years later of the inarticulate laborers and service workers who form his submerged population. "I could never write down to them."

Before Chekhov, there were fables, tales, and sketches. But there were no short stories, no "plotless" evocations of human subjectivity on the threshold of perception. Chekhov created the modern story in the 1880s, partly out of journalistic necessity, by fusing realistic detail and roman-

Raymond Carver (photo by Marion Ettlinger)

tic lyricism. The result was a lambent mode of fabulation that teases out the mysteries of "normal" life. In stories such as "Misery" (1886), "Anyuta" (1886), and "The Kiss" (1887), the Chekhovian moment, albeit half-grasped and fleeting, encapsulates a soul. Chekhov's restrained yet resonant manner became standard practice for twentieth-century storytellers, including Carver's American mentors Sherwood Anderson, Ernest Hemingway, and John Cheever. By the late 1960s, however, nonmimetic, formally experimental "superfiction" had become the favored mode of the literary avant-garde. Realistic stories, like the "totalizing" novel, had been declared outmoded, if not obsolete.

During these same years, in the backwaters of Washington and Northern California, Raymond Carver had married at nineteen and fathered two children by the time he was twenty. Juggling "crap jobs," fatherhood, and eventually "full-time drinking as a serious pursuit," he eked out time to write. "Get in, get out. Don't linger. Go on," were the bywords of his life. Of necessity, they shaped his art. "I needed to write something I could get some kind of payoff from immediately," he later said. "Hence, poems and stories."

Chekhov would have understood. At nineteen he had moved from provincial Taganrog to Moscow and taken charge of his impecunious family. Although a full-time medical student, "Papa Antosha" earned much-needed cash by writing dry-humored sketches for mass-market weeklies. In a letter of 10 May 1886 he ticked off guidelines for what small-minded critics a century later would call "minimal" fiction: "(1) no politico-economico-social verbal effusions; (2) objectivity throughout; (3) truth in the description of characters and things; (4) extreme brevity; (5) audacity and originality—eschew clichés; (6) warmheartedness." Working under similar conditions of "unrelieved responsibility and permanent distraction," Carver found Chekhov's precepts congenial, and during the 1960s and 1970s he reinvented short fiction along Chekhovian lines. In the process he laid the groundwork for a realist revival in the 1980s. "In a literary sense," novelist Douglas Unger said shortly after Carver's death, "his story exists as a kind of model of the resurrection of the short story."

Few would dispute Carver's claim that Chekhov was "the greatest short-story writer who ever lived." Nor would many question Charles May's judgment, voiced in *A Chekhov Companion* (1985), that the most Chekhovian of contemporary writers was Raymond Carver. As artists and as men, the two led parallel lives. Tragically, the parallels converged during 1988, as Carver followed Chekhov in succumbing, far too early, to an illness emblematic of his age. In Chekhov's case the malady was tuberculosis, which claimed his life at forty-four. In Carver's instance it was lung cancer. The writer who once described himself as "a cigarette with a body attached to it" died on 2 August, two months past his fiftieth

birthday. Two years earlier novelist Robert Stone had called Carver "the best American short-story writer since Hemingway." Speaking at Carver's memorial service in New York City on 22 September, he offered a higher compliment. Borrowing a line from his own essay on Chekhov, Stone termed Carver "a hero of perception."

Throughout his writing life, first in poems, later in essays, and always in his fiction, Carver kept in contact with his Russian mentor. In the title poem of his second book, *Winter Insomnia* (1970), for example, he called on Chekhov to prescribe him "three drops of valerian, a glass/Of rose water—anything," to calm his frazzled nerves. In an essay, "On Writing," collected in *Fires* (1983), he praised the "simple clarity" of Chekhov's moral awakenings: abrupt, often negative epiphanies signaled by phrases such as "and suddenly everything became clear to him." The same phrase appears, all but verbatim, in Carver's story "The Pheasant," collected in the same book.

Surely Carver's boldest tribute to Chekhov came in "Errand," a prize-winning story that also proved to be his last work of fiction. "Errand" begins in biography, with an artfully telescoped account of Chekhov's final months, culminating in his drinking a glass of champagne minutes before dying in Badenweiler, a spa in the Black Forest. The hard facts told, the story continues as Chekhovian fiction. With mounting lyricism Carver recounts the "human business" attendant upon Chekhov's death. After a night-long vigil Chekhov's widow instructs a young bellman to locate a proper mortician. Respectful if half-comprehending, he listens as she outlines his errand. Before leaving, however, the young man bends, discreetly, to retrieve the champagne bottle's fallen cork. This gesture, at once honorable and unremarked, brings the story to a faultless Chekhovian close.

"Errand" appeared in the 1 June 1987 *New Yorker*. The following spring it won the O. Henry Award and appeared in *Prize Stories 1988*. During the same period, however, Carver's life imitated his art—with fatal consequences. In September he found himself spitting blood. In October two-thirds of his left lung was removed. Over the next nine months, as Carver waged a brave but losing battle against cancer, Chekhov became his ghostly double. "When hope is gone," he wrote in his journal, "the ultimate sanity is to grasp at straws." Chekhov too had grasped at straws, boasting less than a month before his death that he was "beginning to grow stout." By March 1988 the cancer had spread to Carver's brain. Before beginning radiation therapy, he wrote a meditation on Chekhov's "Ward No. 6" (1892). Explicating a patch of dialogue between the disaffected doctor, Andrey Yefimitich, and the imperious postmaster, Mihail Averyanitch, he noted how even in Chekhov's godforsaken madhouse "a little voice in the soul" arises, urging "belief of an admittedly fragile but insistent nature."

Carver's fiftieth birthday was fast approaching, and in May he received a host of accolades. These included a Brandeis University creative arts citation, an honorary doctor of letters degree from the University of Hartford, and induction into the American Academy and Institute of Arts and Letters. It was also in May that *Where I'm Calling From*, a collection of his new and selected stories, was published by Atlantic Monthly Press. (*Elephant*, containing his seven latest fictions, followed in England on 4 July.) *Where I'm Calling From* received glowing notices from coast to coast, including front-page coverage in the *New York Times Book Review*. More important, the retrospective occasion prompted critics to reassess Carver's career and reputation. Although widely acknowledged as "one of the great short-story writers of our time," he had been tagged a "minimalist," a dismissive label untrue to the spirit of his work. Packed with thirty-seven stories written over twenty-five years, *Where I'm Calling From* gave Carver's so-called minimalism the lie. "Carver has not been a minimalist but a precisionist," David Lipsky wrote in the *National Review* (5 August 1988). Reviewers for the *Washington Post*, the *San Francisco Chronicle*, and the *Times Literary Supplement* concurred. "It goes without saying that Carver is a master," Roger K. Anderson observed in the 19 June 1988 *Houston Chronicle*. "But now a new generosity of spirit is unmistakable. Achieving this may be the keystone of his career–a new level of tranquility."

In June the cancer reappeared in Carver's lungs. As he acknowledged in a poem entitled "What the Doctor Said," the diagnosis was a death sentence. Given a similar verdict, three years before his death Chekhov had responded by marrying the actress Olga Knipper. (The wedding date, duly noted in "Errand," was 25 May, Carver's birthday.) Outdoing his mentor in audacity, on 17 June Carver married his companion and collaborator of the past ten years, the writer Tess Gallagher. The wedding took place in Nevada, in the Heart of Reno Chapel, and Carver de-

scribed it with gusto as a "high tacky affair." True to the tragicomic occasion, Gallagher went on to a three-day winning streak at roulette.

Returning to Port Angeles, Washington, their home of the past five years, Carver and Gallagher hurried to assemble his last book of poetry, *A New Path to the Waterfall* (1989). In this unusual collection, Carver's verses speak in dialogue with work by other poets–and with prose poems gleaned from Chekhov's fiction. Together, the two "companion souls" make a "last, most astounding trip" that recapitulates a life lived prodigally but well. Reprinting a number of his early poems, Carver recalls the heady but numbered days of his youthful marriage. He revisits his parents' kitchen, catching a glimpse of his father in an adulterous embrace. Invoking Czeslaw Milosz's "Return to Kraków in 1880," he questions the value of his work: "To win? To lose?/ What for, if the world will forget us anyway." In poems of searing candor, he struggles to say "what really happened" to his loved ones and to him. Finally, in the closing pages, he confronts the "stupendous grief " of his impending death. The life journey ends in the Chekhovian twilight of "Afterglow," a portrait of the artist mugging for the camera, his cigarette at a "jaunty slant." The book's coda, "Late Fragment," voices Carver's hard-won self-acceptance:

> And did you get what
> you wanted from this life, even so?
> I did.
> And what did you want?
> To call myself beloved, to feel myself
> beloved on the earth.

The manuscript completed, Carver and Gallagher made a fishing trip to Alaska and planned a "dream visit" to Moscow. "I'll get there before you," he joked while in the hospital. "I'm traveling faster." Released into his wife's care, Carver spent the last afternoon of his life on the porch of his newly built house, overlooking his roses. That evening he and Gallagher watched the movie *Dark Eyes* (1987), Nikita Mikhalkov's Chekhovian pastiche. At 6:20 the next morning Carver died in his sleep.

Without revealing the urgency of his condition, during the last months of his life Carver told interviewers what he hoped might be his epitaph. "I can't think of anything else I'd rather be called than a writer," he said, "unless it's a poet. Short-story writer, poet, occasional essayist." After family services on 4 August he was buried

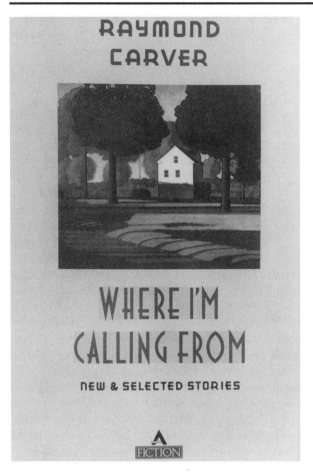

Dust jacket for the 1988 collection of short stories that prompted David Lipsky to write in the National Review, *"Carver has not been a minimalist but a precisionist." Other critics joined him in this reassessment.*

in the Ocean View Cemetery in Port Angeles. The grave overlooks the Strait of Juan de Fuca, the deep blue channel that Carver had plied in his boat and celebrated in three books of poetry, *Where Water Comes Together with Other Water* (1985), *Ultramarine* (1986), and *In a Marine Light* (1987). On Sunday, 7 August, the London *Times* combined a front-page review of *Elephant* with a hastily drafted obituary. Raymond Carver had revealed "the strangeness concealed behind the banal," affirmed "the individuality that survives mass-produced goods and look-alike lifestyles," and extracted "a poetry out of the prosaic," wrote Peter Kemp. The title of his article was "The American Chekhov."

As his uncanny kinship with Chekhov suggests, there was about Raymond Carver an abiding doubleness. "I really do feel I've had two different lives," he told the *Paris Review* in 1983. The "line of demarcation" was 2 June 1977, the day that after ten years of progressive alcoholism

Carver had stopped drinking. The changeover was, in his view, nothing short of miraculous. "Toward the end of my drinking career I was completely out of control and in a very grave place," he recalled. By his thirty-ninth year alcohol had shattered his health, his work, and his family. (He and his first wife, the former Maryann Burk, separated in the summer of 1978 and were divorced in October 1982.) What followed over the next ten years was, in the words of a poem that appeared in the *New Yorker* a few weeks after Carver's death, "Pure gravy."

At a writers conference in Dallas in November 1977, Carver, still new to sobriety, had met Tess Gallagher, a poet who like himself was a native of the Pacific Northwest, the child of an alcoholic father, and a survivor of a broken marriage. Nine months later the two met again in El Paso, where Carver was a visiting distinguished writer at the University of Texas. After a Chekhovian courtship, including a date during which Gallagher nervously tore an earring through her lobe, the two became housemates. First in El Paso and Tucson; then in Syracuse, New York (where both taught at Syracuse University); and finally in Gallagher's hometown of Port Angeles, Carver and Gallagher lived and worked together. The two writers became each other's first readers. When their books appeared–some twenty-five between them over the next ten years–they became each other's dedicatees. Eventually, they became coauthors, sharing credit for *Dostoevsky: A Screenplay* (1985). As mutual influences, each pointed the other in new directions. Established as a poet, Gallagher produced a collection of stories, *The Lover of Horses* (1986). Carver, who had made his mark in prose, brought out book after book of verse and received *Poetry* magazine's Levinson Prize in 1985. "This second life has been very full, very rewarding," he told an interviewer in 1986, "and for that I'll be eternally grateful."

Carver's gratitude spilled over from his life into his work, not only in poems such as "For Tess" (1985) and "The Gift" (1986) but also in stories such as "Cathedral" (1981), "If It Please You" (1981), and "A Small, Good Thing" (1982). During the 1980s his once spare, skeptical fiction became increasingly expansive and affirmative–in Mona Simpson's phrase, "more generous." In *Fires* he restored to original length several of the stories he had shortened for his so-called "minimalist" masterpiece, *What We Talk About When We Talk About Love* (1981). True to its title, *Cathedral*

(1983) explored the transcendental dimensions of everyday experience, much in the manner of Chekhov's quietly religious stories "Easter Eve" (1886) and "The Student" (1894). Last came the new work in *Where I'm Calling From*: seven stories written during the final years of Carver's life. Once again his work was changing. Stylistically, his fiction was growing longer and looser, novelistic in the manner of Chekhov's late works "The Lady with the Dog" (1899) and "In The Ravine" (1900). The subject matter of his stories was changing, too. "Now they deal not just with husband and wife domestic relationships," he told Paris-based *Frank* in 1987, "but with family relationships: son and mother, or father and children." Moreover, as Carver noted in a posthumously published introduction to *American Fiction 88*, he had grown less interested in conclusiveness than in "the tapestry of relationship and event."

Through it all a certain doubleness persisted. "In this second life, this post-drinking life, I still retain a certain sense of pessimism," Carver said, echoing the speaker of his story "Intimacy" (1986), who likewise holds to "the dark view of things." From 1984 to 1988 he and Gallagher both lived in Port Angeles, but they shuttled between two houses, his in a blue-collar neighborhood, hers in an upscale development. The doubleness appeared as well in the faces Carver showed the world. In the jacket photo on *Ultramarine*, he sports a shiny suit and looks every inch the famous author. On *Where I'm Calling From*, he hunches in a well-worn leather jacket, his only ornament a black onyx ring. "There was always the inside and/the outside," run the opening lines of a poem in his first book, *Near Klamath* (1968). "Part of me wanted help," says one of his characters two decades later. "But there was another part." From such persistent self-divisions, Carver wrought an art of haunting ambiguity.

During what he later called his "bad Raymond days," Carver twice went bankrupt. But he was efficient even in his prodigality. He packed two lives into the space of less than one, insisting up to beyond his dying day that he was twice-born and happy. "Don't weep for me," the speaker of "Gravy" tells his friends, "I'm a lucky man." Born into unpromising circumstances, Carver made virtue of necessity by following a pragmatic aesthetic set forth in his poem "Sunday Night." (First published in 1967, it is included in *A New Path to the Waterfall*.) "Make use of the things around you," the poet tells himself, noting the rain outside his window, the cigarette be-

tween his fingers, and the sounds of a drunken woman stumbling in the kitchen. "Put it all in,/ Make use." Early on, Carver crossed the "tell-it-as-you-see-it" poetics of William Carlos Williams with the unblushing candor of Charles Bukowski. "You are not your characters," he told an interviewer in 1978, "but your characters are you." In later years he repeated Rainer Maria Rilke's dictum, "Poetry is experience." Without symbolic fanfare or confessional hysteria, he invested personal experience with mythic resonance. "If this sounds/like the story of a life," he says in one of his poems, "okay."

Carver was the son of a craftsman, and his writerly development followed the stages of a craftsman's training. After moving his family from Yakima to Paradise, California, in 1958, he enrolled at Chico State College. There, he began an apprenticeship under the soon-to-be-famous John Gardner, the first "real writer" he had ever met. "He offered me the key to his office," Carver recalled in his preface to Gardner's *On Becoming a Novelist* (1983). "I see that gift now as a turning point." In addition, Gardner gave his student "close, line-by-line criticism" and taught him a set of values that was "not negotiable." Among these values were convictions that Carver held until his death. Like Gardner, whose *On Moral Fiction* (1978) decried the "nihilism" of postmodern formalism, Carver maintained that great literature is life-connected, life-affirming, and life-changing. "In the best fiction," he wrote "the central character, the hero or heroine, is also the 'moved' character, the one to whom something happens in the story that *makes a difference*. Something happens that changes the way that character looks at himself and hence the world." Through the 1960s and 1970s he steered wide of the metafictional "funhouse" erected by Barth, Barthelme and Company, concentrating instead on what he called "those basics of old-fashioned storytelling: plot, character, and action." Like Gardner and Chekhov, Carver declared himself a humanist. "Art is *not* self-expression," he insisted, "it's communication."

First under Gardner, then under the mentorship of Professor Richard C. Day of Humboldt State College, Carver began writing stories. The earliest of them, revised and collected in *Will You Please Be Quiet, Please?* (1976) and *Furious Seasons and Other Stories* (1977), show him testing his voice among the echoes of his predecessors. His first published story, "The Furious Seasons" (*Selection*, Winter 1960-1961), is a long-

Early drafts of Carver's O. Henry Prize-winning story "Errand," first published in the 1 June 1987 New Yorker *(courtesy of Tess Gallagher)*

Room Service   *or "Champagne"*

Anton Chekov's sister, Maria, born in 1863, three years younger than the writer, visited him in a Moscow clinic during the last days of March 1897. The hospitalization — it was the first such treatment for the tuberculosis that would kill him in 1904, at the age of 44 — followed a ~~hemorrage~~ *hemorrhage* that occured the evening of March ~~21st~~ *21* in the dining room of the Hermitage, Moscow's most fashionable restaurant. (Chekov, who was not wealthy by any reckoning, and never ostentatious, nevertheless owned two houses by this time and was building a third at Yalta.) He had gone to dinner at the invitation of his friend and confidant, Alexei Suvorin, an immensely rich newspaper and magasine publisher, a reactionary, a self-made man whose father had fought at Borodino as a private and who, like Chekov, was the grandson of a serf. *(Chekov was)*

Chekov, *as always,* meticulously dressed ~~as usual~~ *in a dark suit and waistcoat* his ~~usual~~ pince-nez in evidence, had just been seated at the table and was doing something with his napkin when blood began gushing out of his mouth. Suvorin and two waiters helped him to the gentlemens' room and tried, unsuccessfully, to stanch the flow of blood with ice packs. Chekov was agonizingly embarrassed about what had happened. Later, back at his hotel, ~~he~~ *he referred to the "scandal" at the restaurant but* persisted in denying the gravity of the situation. "He laughed and jested as usual," drawn experiment in Faulknerian polyphony. His next, "The Father" (*Toyon*, Spring 1961), offers a tight-lipped Kafkian fable of fewer than five hundred words. Like nearly every writer of his generation, Carver was pulled into Hemingway's orbit. In 1963, the year of his graduation from Humboldt State, he vascillated between reverence and rebellion, publishing both a workmanlike Hemingway imitation, "Pastoral" (*Western Humanities Review*, Winter 1963), and a deconstructive parody, "The Aficionados" (*Toyon*, Spring 1963).

For Professor Day, the story that "marked" Carver as a writer was "The Hair." (First published in the Spring 1963 *Toyon*, it is reprinted in *Those Days* [1987] a small-press book of Carver's early writings.) Here as in "The Father," Carver's topic is a young man's identity undone by a seemingly harmless irritant. Over the course of an outwardly normal workday, the hair caught between Dave's teeth erodes his composure, rendering him feverish by nightfall and leaving his wife nonplussed. But whereas "The Father" is brisk and impersonal, given almost wholly in dialogue, "The Hair" is leisurely and lyrical. Although Kafkaesque in its theme, stylistically the story calls to mind Chekhov's early accounts of normality disrupted: "An Upheaval," for example, or "Panic Fears" (both 1886). Further experiments in the Chekhovian lyrical/objective manner followed. A pair of stories, "The Ducks" (first published as "The Night the Mill Boss Died," *Carolina Quarterly*, Winter 1963) and "The Student's Wife" (*Carolina Quarterly*, Fall 1964), trace the nightmarish "awakenings" of, respectively, a stolid working man and a sensitive young woman, each of whom sees feelingly the awful emptiness of routinized existence.

Carver had found his register. As Michael Koepf wrote in 1981, "There's a Chekhovian clarity to Ray Carver's stories but a Kafkaesque sense that something is terribly wrong behind the scenes." Nonetheless, throughout the 1960s Carver practiced other modes and styles. He spent the academic year 1963-1964 at the Iowa Writers Workshop. (Lack of funds prevented him from staying a second year to complete his M.F.A. degree.) In 1966 he published in the *December* magazine a long, Jamesian story, "Will You Please Be Quiet, Please?" that Martha Foley included in *The Best American Short Stories 1967*. He flirted with classicism ("Poseidon and Company," *Toyon*, Spring 1963) and with fantasy ("Bright Red Apples," *Gato Magazine*, Summer 1967). He experimented with unreliable narrators, first-person retrospec-

tion in the manner of Sherwood Anderson, and Hemingwayesque regionalism.

"It was important for me to be a writer from the West," Carver recalled of the period that led up to the publication of his first book of poems, *Near Klamath*, by the English Club of Sacramento State College in 1968. During the middle 1960s he worked as a night custodian at Mercy Hospital and sat in on classes at Sacramento State with a third mentor, the poet Dennis Schmitz. What with his appearance in the respected "Foley collection," the impending publication of his first book, and the death of his father, 1967 was a landmark year. Moreover, in the summer of 1967 Carver accepted his first white-collar job. Moving his family from the California midlands to the San Francisco suburbs, he became a textbook editor at Science Research Associates (SRA) in Palo Alto. Over the next several years, Carver's writing took on the coloration of his new milieu, becoming dryer and more sophisticated. The change can be seen in "A Night Out" (*December*, 1970; retitled "Signals" in *Will You Please Be Quiet, Please?*), a black-humored account of a feuding couple's dinner at a glitzy restaurant. Fittingly, the final story of Carver's apprenticeship looks both backward and ahead. Published in the Autumn 1970 issue of *Western Humanities Review* as "Cartwheels," it chronicles a city-dweller's abortive return to the hinterland of her youth. Retitled "How About This?" in the obsessively interrogative *Will You Please Be Quiet, Please?* (1976), it can also be counted the first work of his journeyman period.

By 1970 Carver had gained control of his medium and defined his "obsessions" (he disliked the word *theme*). Following the example of Tolstoy's *The Death of Ivan Ilyich* (1886), he had taken for his province unheroic lives, "most simple and most ordinary and therefore most terrible." Drawing on Chekhov and Kafka, he had focused on hypnagogic moments during which socially constituted identity totters. His Jamesian donnée was marriage, in particular "a certain terrible kind of domesticity" that he termed "dis-ease." Perhaps most important, in both poetry and fiction he had tapped a vein of "menace." As Marc Chénetier notes, this "motherlode of threat" runs beneath the polished surface of Carver's middle work like a seismic fault.

Carver's apprenticeship ended abruptly in September 1970, when his job at SRA was terminated. The upheaval proved to be fortunate. Thanks to severance pay, unemployment benefits, and an NEA Discovery Award, for the first time in his life he could write full-time. Over the next nine months, he produced more than half the stories that went into *Will You Please Be Quiet, Please?* In the process, he began to see himself as a writer. "I discovered that if I went to my desk every day and applied myself I could seriously and steadily write stories," he later said. Moreover, his fiction underwent a sea change. "Something happened during that time in the writing, *to* the writing. It went underground and then it came up again, and it was bathed in a new light for me. I was starting to chip away, down to the image, then the figure itself."

It was also during this period that Carver became associated with the mentor of his journeyman decade, Gordon Lish. Through the 1960s Carver had followed John Gardner's advice and published solely in "little" magazines: respected quarterlies like *December* that paid in copies rather than cash. Lish, formerly Carver's Palo Alto neighbor, had in 1969 become fiction editor of *Esquire*, perhaps the "slickest" of the large-circulation magazines that paid real money. Breaking with precedent, Carver sent one of his new stories, "The Neighbors," to *Esquire*. Lish accepted it, cut the title by a word and published "Neighbors" in June 1971. It was a turning point.

"Neighbors" tells the tale of an outwardly average couple, Bill and Arlene Miller, who gradually turn the apartment of their out-of-town neighbors, the Stones, into a psychosexual rumpus room. Furtively at first, then with abandon, the caretakers invade the Stones' privacy: nipping from their liquor cabinet, cross-dressing in their clothes, and unearthing snapshots that promise voyeuristic thrills. Flushed and lusty, the Millers make what promises to be a climactic visit to the Stones' apartment—only to find that Arlene has locked the key inside. Abruptly barred from their fallen paradise, husband and wife huddle outside the door, feeling an ill wind.

Without being altogether different from Carver's earlier fiction, "Neighbors" exhibits a surer control of structure, style, and audience. Carver himself allowed that it had "captured an essential sense of mystery or strangeness," which he attributed to the story's polished style. "For it is a highly 'stylized' story if it is anything," he noted, "and it is this that helps give it its value." Textual revisions in *Will You Please Be Quiet, Please?* indicate that Carver developed this style under Lish's influence. "He had a wonderful eye, an eye as

good as John Gardner's," Carver later said. But whereas Gardner had advised Carver to use fifteen words instead of twenty-five, Lish advocated a more radical aesthetic: the "minimalist" conviction that less is more. "Gordon believed that if you could say it in five words instead of fifteen, use five words." Under Lish's mentorship, Carver's fiction grew leaner and more laconic, iceberg-like in its hidden depths. His subject matter changed as well. Editor Lish's interests were "paralysis, death, family, home, the things people live with, the violence that is in us," as well as "flight" from all of the above. These concerns became the obsessions of Carver's journeyman stories, which appeared not only in the glossy pages of *Esquire* and *Harper's Bazaar* but also in a host of respected quarterlies and annuals. Indeed, the titles of Lish's *Esquire* anthologies, *The Secret Life of Our Times* (1973) and *All Our Secrets Are the Same* (1976), suggest a leitmotif of Carver's middle work. "You're told time and again when you're young to write about what you know," Carver later said, "and what do you know better than your own secrets?" With rare exceptions, his stories of this period end in devastating moments of exposure. "Are you there, Arnold?" asks the wife of a character who has tangled his identity in a web of his own making. "You don't sound like yourself."

Surely the high point of Carver's journeyman years should have been the appearance of *Will You Please Be Quiet, Please?* Published in March 1976 by McGraw-Hill under its new Gordon Lish imprint, this collection of twenty-two stories was targeted to introduce an "increasingly influential" writer to a wider public. It succeeded admirably, bringing Carver a National Book Award nomination in 1977, the same year that a second collection of his stories, *Furious Seasons*, appeared from Capra Press. But the truth was that the author's own secret life had brought his career to a standstill. Estranged from his wife and children, Carver was four times hospitalized for alcoholism during 1976-1977. "I was dying from it, plain and simple," he later said, "and I'm not exaggerating."

Miraculously, on 2 June 1977 the drinking stopped. Carver acknowledged the help of Alcoholics Anonymous, but he never found an explanation equal to the fact. "I guess I just wanted to live," he later said. Having come so close to death, he counted his first life over. What at the time he called "The Other Life"–"The one without mistakes"–had yet to begin. But as he noted in "Rogue River Jet-Boat Trip," a poem dated Independence Day 1977, his trip "upriver" had commenced.

As ever, Carver's writing followed the curve of his experience. He had passed through a personal inferno, and his works from this period–poems with titles such as "Distress Sale," "Alcohol," and "Marriage," collected in a book called *Fires*–have about them a purgatorial intensity. Even after he celebrated his fortieth birthday and began his "second life" with Gallagher, Carver was unsure what remained to him. "At the time I felt it was okay, it really was, if I never wrote again," he later said. "But Tess was writing, and that was a good example for me."

Over the next five years Carver undertook a wholesale reassessment of his fiction. What emerges as a dialectic of expansion, contraction, and restoration extends over five interlocking books: *Furious Seasons* (1977), *What We Talk About When We Talk About Love* (1981), *Fires* and *Cathedral* (both 1983), and *If It Please You* (1984). Between 1978 and 1981 Carver wrote and published in magazines nearly a dozen new stories dealing with the wrenching vicissitudes of alcoholism and the long-drawn dissolution of a marriage. In the first of these, "Why Don't You Dance?" (*Quarterly West*, Autumn 1978), a "desperate" man, presumably abandoned by his wife, conducts a yard sale in his driveway. Drunk to the point of anesthesia, he sells a young couple his marriage bed–and tacitly bequeaths them the hopes of his youth.

These new stories and several earlier ones, including five from *Furious Seasons*, Carver next cut "to the marrow, not just to the bone" to create *What We Talk About When We Talk About Love*. Donald Newlove's capsule review in the April 1981 *Saturday Review* suggests the arresting unity of voice and vision in that slender book: "Seventeen tales of Hopelessville, its marriages and alcoholic wreckage, told in a prose as sparingly clear as a fifth of iced Smirnoff." The stories in *What We Talk About When We Talk About Love* won Carver fame as "a full-grown master," a "minimalist," and a capital-letter Influence on a new generation of writers coming of age in the 1980s. Indeed, one younger writer, Jayne Anne Phillips, termed them "fables for the decade" in the 20 April 1981 issue of *New York*.

In retrospect, however, Carver's best-known collection emerges as his least representative book. For him, the bare-boned "minimalism" of *What We Talk About When We Talk About Love*

marked not a destination but a turning point. "Any farther in that direction and I'd be at a dead end," he later said. What followed over the next two years was an artistic turnabout, "an opening up" during which he restored and expanded the work he had pared down under the influence of editor Lish, Hemingway's "theory of omission," and his own purgative impulses. Two small-press books, *Fires* and *If It Please You*, display the outcome of this process. In addition, Carver wrote a dozen new stories in a higher, more hopeful key. The first of them, "Cathedral" (*Atlantic Monthly*, September 1981), he termed "totally different in conception and execution" from his previous work. In this quietly redemptive story, a blind, not wholly welcome houseguest helps his host see life anew. Guest editor John Gardner included "Cathedral" in *The Best American Short Stories 1982*, and in September 1983 it became the title story of Carver's third major-press book. Reviewing *Cathedral* on the front page of the *New York Times Book Review* (11 September 1983), Irving Howe observed that several of Carver's stories could already be numbered among the classics of American short fiction. What struck him in the new book, however, was the author's growth. "*Cathedral* shows a gifted writer struggling toward a larger scope of reference, a finer touch of nuance."

Cathedral brought Carver nominations for the Pulitzer Prize and National Book Critics Circle Award. More important, it marked his graduation from the school of Gordon Lish. As Jonathan Yardley wrote in the *Washington Post* (4 September 1983), "The stories in *Cathedral* leave no doubt that [Carver] has moved away from the 'minimalist' style into one that is more expansive, inclusive, and generous." Although it took less percipient reviewers several more years to recognize the fact, Carver's journeyman days were over, as was his long revisionary interlude. With *Cathedral*, he declared his independence as a master. In the five years that remained to him, the only "outside" influences on his work were Gallagher and Chekhov.

Carver's independence gained financial support in May 1983 when the American Academy and Institute of Arts and Letters granted him one of its first Mildred and Harold Strauss "Livings" awards. A side effect of the award, which brought him five years of tax-free income, was celebrity status. Carver was profiled in the *New York Times Magazine, Vanity Fair*, even *People*. Feeling besieged by the East Coast "hubbub," he fled west in January 1984. Carver moved into Gallagher's newly built "sky house," then standing empty in Port Angeles. Once again, his life and work were changing. Intending to write fiction, he found himself drafting poems. "No one could have been more surprised than I was," he later said, "because I hadn't written any poetry in over two years. I would write myself out every day, then at night there was nothing left. The bowl was empty. I went to bed at night not knowing if there would be anything there the next morning, but there always was."

The result was *Where Water Comes Together With Other Water*, followed in short order by *Ultramarine* and, finally, *A New Path to the Waterfall*. (*In a Marine Light*, a conflation of the first two books, appeared in England in 1987.) In Carver's early poetry, collected in *Near Klamath, Winter Insomnia*, and *At Night the Salmon Move* (1976), his element had been the earth—the fields and forests of central Washington, the region's down-to-earth inhabitants. The poems in *Fires*, written during his turbulent middle years, had been alternately hell-bent and penitential, the record of a phoenix-like rebirth. ("Friends, I thought this/ was living," he testifies in "Luck.") Now, working in Gallagher's glass-walled study above the strait, Carver took for his element the water. His new poetry celebrated the riparian landscape of the Olympic Peninsula. At the same time it charted the riverine currents, eddies, and whirlpools of his own two lives. Despite undeniable losses and a pressing sense of mortality, Carver felt himself renewed by the healing waters. "I felt that way—increased, spiritually increased—for being out here alone and being quiet."

The new poems were "a great gift." Written unhurriedly, day by day, they were quieter than Carver's earlier poetry. They were also less polished and more intimate. ("It's the tenderness I care about," he says in "The Gift.") Indeed, the aesthetic distance between experience and expression appeared so slight in them that some readers questioned whether they were poems at all ("journal entries with a ragged right edge," grumbled Jonathan Dee in the 25 June 1985 *Village Voice*). Others, however, heard uncommon resonance in Carver's common language. "Mr. Carver is heir to the most appealing American poetic voice, the lyricism of Theodore Roethke and James Wright," wrote Patricia Hampl. For Greg Kuzma, the heart-stopping power of *Ultramarine* lay in its unquestionable authenticity: "experience delivered smoldering like newborn calves."

Photograph of Carver that appeared on the dust jacket of Ultramarine, *his 1986 volume of poetry (© Jerry Bauer)*

During these years that now must be counted his last, Carver also worked as a critic and anthologist. He edited *The Best American Short Stories 1986* and judged the stories in *American Fiction 88*. With Tom Jenks he compiled *American Short Story Masterpieces* (1987), a sequel to Robert Penn Warren and Albert Erskine's *Short Story Masterpieces* of 1954. In essays, interviews, and introductions, Carver encouraged two developments that he had largely set in motion: the short-story renaissance of the 1980s ("the most eventful literary phenomenon of our time") and the concurrent "resurgence, not to say new dominance, of realistic fiction." In the wake of postmodern formalism, he articulated a set of values that harkened back not only to Gardner's moral fiction, but to Tolstoy's "sincerity" and Roman *gravitas*. Carver called for "fiction of *occurrence* and *consequence*" and praised "an honest story, well told." The test of his principles was always his practice, the stories that set and changed the standards of his time. Indeed, as Marilynne Robinson observed of *Where I'm Calling From*,

"The process of Mr. Carver's fiction is to transform our perception."

When John Gardner died at forty-nine in a 1982 motorcycle accident, Carver termed the loss to literature "beyond figuring." Surely the same can be said of Raymond Carver's too-early death. With good reason Carver felt confident that *Where I'm Calling From* had secured his place among the American short-story masters. ("We're out there in history now, babe," he said to Gallagher.) To the end, however, he insisted that his best work lay ahead. "I've got fish to catch and stories and poems to write," he told the *New York Times* two months before his death. Even the masterful stories of his last years–"Boxes," "Elephant," and "Errand" among them–Carver judged transitional. "In truth I feel like all the stories I've written in the past six or eight months were not really, in some strange way, the stories I intended to write," he said in 1986. "The other stories, the ones I will write, are the harder stories."

Sadly, the hardest story proved not to be fiction. "Ray did grieve to be leaving his life so early," Tess Gallagher told some two hundred friends and admirers gathered at Carver's memorial service in New York City. "If will alone could have prevailed, he'd be alive today and with us." But if Carver's death cuts his story short, there is about his life, his lives, a sense of consummation. "Ray was a man who believed in the inviolability of great literature," recalled his friend and fellow writer Richard Ford. Speaking on National Public Radio shortly after Carver's death, Ford told how in the halcyon spring of 1987, after the publication of "Errand," but before the discovery of Carver's cancer, he and Carver had visited V. S. Pritchett in London. Born in 1900, the distinguished man of letters was still writing, at the time completing *Chekhov: A Spirit Set Free* (1988). Alive since Chekhov's day, Pritchett had lived to read Carver's work. Ford recalled that Carver left the meeting "electrified," feeling himself part of a great tradition.

Raymond Carver proved that literature has room for second acts, and in his second life, the life of "pure gravy," he came full circle. He returned to the Pacific Northwest, to poetry, and to Chekhov. He moved beyond Hopelessville toward a small, good thing that he knew to be lasting. "I'm just bearing witness to something I know something about," he said. "In a way, I've come back to testify." In his last months, Carver spoke of "blessing," "grace," and "mystery." But asked whether he was a religious man, he answered with inborn equivocation. "No," he said, "but I have to believe in miracles and the possibility of resurrection."

New Books:

The Stories of Raymond Carver (London: Picador, 1985);

Dostoevsky: A Screenplay, with Tess Gallagher (Santa Barbara: Capra, 1985);

Early for the Dance (Concord, N.H.: Ewert, 1986);

My Father's Life (Derry, N.H.: Babcock & Koontz, 1986);

Ultramarine (New York: Random House, 1986);

Those Days: Early Writings, edited by William L. Stull (Elmwood, Conn.: Raven Editions, 1987);

In a Marine Light (London: Collins Harvill, 1987);

Intimacy (Concord, N.H.: Ewert, 1987);

Where I'm Calling From (New York: Atlantic Monthly Press, 1988);

Elephant (Fairfax, Cal.: Jungle Garden, 1988);

Elephant and Other Stories (London: Collins Harvill, 1988);

A New Path to the Waterfall (New York: Atlantic Monthly Press, 1989).

Other:

The Best American Short Stories 1986, edited by Carver with Shannon Ravenel (Boston: Houghton Mifflin, 1986);

Joel Gardner, *Batavia*, contains an untitled essay by Carver (Burlington, Vt.: Shadows Editions, 1986);

American Short Story Masterpieces, edited by Carver and Tom Jenks (New York: Delacorte, 1987);

American Fiction 88, introduction by Carver (Farmington, Conn.: Wesley Press, 1988).

Periodical Publications:

"Coming of Age, Going to Pieces," *New York Times Book Review*, 17 November 1985, pp. 3, 51-52;

Contribution to "A Symposium on Contemporary American Fiction," *Michigan Quarterly Review*, 26 (Fall 1987): 710-711;

Untitled essay, *Poetry*, 151 (October-November 1987): 204-207.

Interviews:

"David Sexton Talks to Raymond Carver," *Literary Review* [London], 85 (July 1985): 36-40;

Larry McCaffery and Sinda Gregory, *Alive and Writing* (Urbana: University of Illinois Press, 1987), pp. 66-82;

Nicholas O'Connell, *At the Field's End* (Seattle, Wash.: Madrona, 1987), pp. 76-94;

David Applefield, "Fiction & America," *Frank* [Paris] 8/9 (Winter 1987-1988): 6-15;

Stewart Kellerman, "Grace Has Come into My Life," *New York Times Book Review*, 15 May 1988, p. 40;

Penelope Moffet, "Raymond Carver," *Publishers Weekly* (27 May 1988): 42, 44;

Kellerman, "For Raymond Carver, a Lifetime of Storytelling," *New York Times*, 31 May 1988, p. C17;

William L. Stull, "Matters of Life and Death," in *Living in Words*, edited by Gregory McNamee (Portland, Oreg.: Breitenbush, 1988), pp. 143-156;

Michael Schumacher, *Reasons to Believe* (New York: St. Martin's, 1988), pp. 1-27.

Bibliography:

William L. Stull, "Raymond Carver: A Bibliographical Checklist," *American Book Collector*, 8 (January 1987): 17-30.

References:

John Biguenet, "Notes of a Disaffected Reader: The Origins of Minimalism," *Mississippi Review*, 40/41 (Winter 1985): 40-45;

Michael J. Bugeja, "Tarnish and Silver: An Analysis of Carver's *Cathedral*," *South Dakota Review*, 24 (Autumn 1986): 73-87;

Gordon Burn, "Poetry, Poverty, and Realism Down in Carver Country," *Sunday Times* [London] (17 April 1985): 12;

David Carpenter, "What We Talk About When We Talk About Carver," *Descant*, 56/57 (Spring-Summer 1987): 20-43;

Andrea Chambers, "Love, Literature, and Solitude Link Mutually Admiring Authors," *People*, 28 (23 November 1987): 81-82, 84;

Marc Chénetier, "Living On/Off the 'Reserve': Performance, Interrogation, and Negativity in the Works of Raymond Carver," in *Critical Angles* (Carbondale: Southern Illinois University Press, 1986), pp. 164-190;

Jürgen Donnerstag, "Amerikanische Alltagsmileus und ihre Sprache in Zeitgenössichen Short Stories," *Anglistic & Englischunterricht*, 31 (1987): 67-76;

Erich Eichman, "Will Raymond Carver Please Be Quiet, Please?," *New Criterion*, 2 (November 1983): 86-89;

Mark A. R. Facknitz, " 'The Calm,' 'A Small, Good Thing,' and 'Cathedral': Raymond Carver and the Rediscovery of Human Worth," *Studies in Short Fiction*, 23 (Summer 1986): 287-296;

Facknitz, "Missing the Train: Raymond Carver's Sequel to John Cheever's 'The Five-Forty-Eight,' " *Studies in Short Fiction*, 22 (Summer 1985): 345-347;

Norman German and Jack Bedell, "Physical and Social Laws in Ray Carver's 'Popular Mechanics,' " *Critique*, 29 (Summer 1988): 257-260;

Patricia Hampl, "Surviving a Life in the Present," *New York Times Book Review*, 7 June 1987, p. 15;

Kim A. Herzinger, "Introduction: On the New Fiction," *Mississippi Review*, 40/41 (Winter 1985): 7-22;

Tom Jenks, "Together in Carver Country," *Vanity Fair*, 49 (October 1986): 114-117, 139, 141;

Peter Kemp, "The American Chekhov," *Sunday Times* [London] (7 August 1988): G1-2;

Michael Koepf, "The Collapse of Love," *San Francisco Review of Books*, 6 (May-June 1981): 16;

Greg Kuzma, "*Ultramarine*: Poems That Almost Stop the Heart," *Michigan Quarterly Review*, 27 (Spring 1988): 355-363;

David Lipsky, "News from an Unremarked World," *National Review*, 40 (5 August 1988): 50-52;

Marilynne Robinson, "Marriage and Other Astonishing Bonds," *New York Times Book Review*, 15 May 1988, pp. 1, 35, 40-41;

Kathleen Westfall Shute, "Finding the Words: The Struggle for Salvation in the Fiction of Raymond Carver," *Hollins Critic*, 24 (December 1987): 1-9;

Allan Lloyd Smith, "Brain Damage: The Word and the World in Postmodernist Fiction," in *Contemporary American Fiction*, edited by Malcolm Bradbury and Sigmund Ro (London: Arnold, 1987), pp. 38-50;

Michael Vander Weele, "Raymond Carver and the Language of Desire," *Denver Quarterly*, 22 (Summer 1987): 108-122;

Alan Wilde, *Middle Grounds: Studies in Contemporary American Fiction* (Philadelphia: University of Pennsylvania Press, 1987), pp. 111-112, 117-120.

Papers:

Carver's manuscripts and letters from the years 1978 to 1984 are housed in the Charvat Collection at Ohio State University. Except for scattered materials in private hands, all earlier papers have been lost or destroyed. Papers from more recent years are currently in the possession of Tess Gallagher.

A TRIBUTE

from FREDERICK BUSCH

Ray Carver was a generous and unassuming man, more eager to recognize than to be recognized, and dedicated to what counts most: love and work. He was a fine student and an influential teacher–is any writer more emulated, these days, than he?–and he brought the art of Ernest Hemingway into real touch again with contemporary readers and writers. There are two ways of working with the surfaces of life in fiction: the easy superficial (see what is called by literary journalists "postmodern" or "minimalist" fiction), or metaphor. Ray Carver used action and speech as metaphors for the seething actual interior. The tension between what his narrative persona knows and can tell–one almost sees the twitching jaw, the glow of the sucked cigarette, the standing veins of the forehead and neck–makes for an acute sense of danger, need, often courage, even heroism, that charges Carver's work. Although he latterly wrote and spoke about Chekhov, sending a hundred students and teachers back to *him*, he was Ernest Hemingway's student and his own achievement, a creator of strong implications, a voice and not a gesture. Raymond Carver was a passionate lover of the passionate, his fiction a living rebuke to the pretentious, gelid work errantly connected with the solid, true fiction of this good writer who was such a good man.

A TRIBUTE

from HAYDEN CARRUTH

In spite of the popularity of his work–or possibly because of it–Raymond Carver's writing had not at the time of his death received any worthwhile critical attention, as far as I know. A great deal has been said about his "minimalism," his "naturalism," etc. This is nonsense. His selected stories, *Where I'm Calling From*, contains all his fiction that he wished to preserve; it is, in effect, his collected fiction, though it contains only thirty-seven stories. But what a copious work it is! Car-

ver's range of mood, topic, theme, his whole imaginative scope, is far broader than most people recognize, and far deeper too. Like his master, Anton Chekhov, to whom he paid homage in his final story, "Errand," Carver uses apparently simple means to achieve complex ends. It would be impossible to epitomize the fundamental values and emotions embodied in even the most obvious of his stories without injustice. One always hesitates to speak for futurity, but to my mind *Where I'm Calling From* is the only certifiable masterpiece produced in the United States during the past quarter-century, and will be acknowledged as such for as long as anyone is interested in American literature.

So his death at an early age is an inestimable loss, and all the more to those of us who were his personal friends, for he was nearly as good a storyteller in speech as he was in writing. Every conversation with him was memorable: spirited, funny, full of human understanding, and often touched by pathos. As his stories show over and over, his ear for the idioms and rhythms of speech was acute, and he had an abiding interest in language as such, an interest always evident in his pungent and witty speech. I have never known anyone like him, and I don't expect I ever will.

A TRIBUTE

from GARY FISKETJON

"Beats all I saw or heard of this life," Ray said to me in the early eighties after things were going his way and specifically after a rainy, seemingly cabless Manhattan evening when we'd hailed and were taken up in a semidecrepit limousine. The driver's irrepressible nature and simple kindnesses made us feel that *anything* was possible, and that the two of us were as far from Oregon, where we both came from, as Dorothy ever was from Kansas.

Throughout Ray's first forty years there were many black days, when the temptation to give in to despair must have been overwhelming. His father before him, toward the end of *his* life, broke down utterly, reduced to mute silence and an empty room. Having stepped into such a place, one can never leave it entirely behind. This is the room where many of Ray's characters find themselves, and doubtless where he imagined finding himself too many times to even think about. When told that Richard Brautigan was said to have shot himself, Ray wrote me that

"Even if he did it, it was the booze thing, sure. I entertained that same way out myself on many occasions, back in those dark days."

But he saved himself, never forgetting what it is like to have no prospects whatever. "Working, praise be," was a refrain in his letters. "At my station." He suffered no illusions about his calling–"Nobody ever asked me to be a writer," he said–and took more pride in his work than in how it was received. He also filled a room with a spirit to match his considerable size. Giving someone a leg up or a kind word, congratulations or consolation, loyalty and kindredness ... these acts and qualities *were* Ray, and he showed them countless times–in a letter, a phone call, a packet of smoked salmon sent through the mail. His life was something of a miracle, and none of us is willing to admit that it has ended.

A TRIBUTE

from TOBIAS WOLFF

I can't do justice to my friend Raymond Carver by pulling a long face and speaking in pained, lugubrious tones. It doesn't work. Ray can't be remembered that way. What happens instead, whenever I start to talk about Ray with another of his friends, is that after a few moments of ritual gravity we begin to remember him as he was, smart and funny and kind, boyish, loyal, tough, peasant-shrewd, fragile. We can't talk about Ray without telling stories, recalling things he said and did, not a few of them in the realm of outlawry, and then almost in spite of ourselves a strange joy, even hilarity, comes over us. And that is as it should be, because Ray made us feel this joy when he was alive and we most truly remember him when we let his memory bring it back to us.

Ray was the happiest man I ever knew. He was happy as we can only be happy when we have been brought to the brink of death and then spared for a while. He used to love telling the story about Dostoyevski's last-minute reprieve, and I always had the sense he was talking about himself too. He took nothing for granted. Every new day, every moment with his friends, every new story and poem was an astonishment to him. The good and loving life he shared with Tess Gallagher, the extraordinary respect his work inspired in all kinds of people–to Ray, these were miracles. At moments of particular happiness he would look around with pure wonder. "Things could be worse," he'd say.

He was entirely without pretense. Jim Heynen once told Ray a story about something strange that had happened to him. As Jim was coming out of a bank a bald eagle dropped a salmon bang on the hood of his car, which salmon Jim took home and ate. Not long after Jim told Ray this story he read a poem of Ray's in which an eagle drops a salmon at the poet's feet while he's out taking a walk. Later Jim asked Ray about it, asked if by chance Ray had made use of his story. "Well, Jim," he said, "I guess I must have, because I don't take walks."

Ray had this bedrock honesty about himself, and the effect was that you could be equally honest without fear of being judged. He took you as you were, with as little sanctity or heroism as you owned, so long as you did not pretend to more than you owned. There was absolute freedom in his company. One could, and did, reveal anything–Ray had an insatiable, uproarious appetite for stories on the human scale, stories about the endless losing war our good intentions wage against our circumstances and our nature. He was so greedy for these stories that one day I found myself confessing to something I hadn't done, just for the pleasure of seeing him shake his head and say, "It's a jungle out there, Toby, it's a jungle out there."

Chekhov wrote of his character Vassilyev that "he had a talent for humanity." Ray had that talent. Whatever was human interested him, most of all our struggle to survive without becoming less than human. This struggle shaped his life. His understanding of it, compassionate and profound, made him the great writer that he was, and the great friend.

Charles E. Feinberg
(27 September 1899-1 March 1988)

Gay Wilson Allen

Charles E. Feinberg, one of the world's leading book and art collectors, died on 1 March 1988 at his winter home near Miami, Florida. Though best known for his Walt Whitman collection, he also assembled many Jewish religious objects, as well as books and manuscripts of several other major twentieth-century authors, including Robert Frost, T. S. Eliot, James Joyce, and Dylan Thomas.

Feinberg, who was born in London, England, in 1899, immigrated to Canada with his father while still a child. After attending elementary schools in Ontario, he moved to Detroit in 1923. There he was manager of the Regal Shoe Company from 1923 to 1925; manager of the Silent Automatic Corporation from 1925 to 1928; vice-president of Argo Oil from 1928 to 1951; and vice-president and president of Speedway Petroleum from 1951 to 1962. He prospered in these enterprises, enabling him to buy the rare books and manuscripts that form an important part of his enduring legacy.

He was also active in a number of civic and philanthropic organizations, including B'nai B'rith, American Friends of Hebrew University, the National Commission on Jewish Americans, the Jewish Historical Society, the Bibliographical Society of America, the Michigan Historical Commission, the Detroit Historical Society, and the Boy Scouts of America. In addition, he was a "friend" of libraries at Princeton, Columbia, and Syracuse universities, the Detroit Public Library, the Free Library of Philadelphia, and the Hebrew University Library in Jerusalem. In 1958 he founded the Lubavitch Foundation of Michigan, which was later incorporated into the international Lubavitch Foundation. He made donations to various U.S.I.A. libraries and exhibited books and gave lectures at branches in London, Paris, and elsewhere.

Feinberg's note in *An Exhibition of the Works of Walt Whitman* (Detroit Public Library, 1955) explains how he became interested in Whitman as a

Charles E. Feinberg in the library of his Detroit home

boy in London: "It began with a book. An old bookdealer who took an interest in what a boy was reading, one day said to him, 'Here, boy, buy this book and see if you like it—bring it back if you don't.' The book was called *American Poems* and contained a selection of poems by Whitman. I was the boy. It's hard to remember why you are stopped by a word or a line or a page—but that was the beginning of my interest in Walt Whitman."

During 1955, the centennial of the first edition of *Leaves of Grass*, Feinberg repeatedly demonstrated that he had not only become one of the leading Whitman collectors but also one of the most knowledgeable scholars of Whitman's works. He had read every book and manuscript

214

he had bought and also studied and investigated its background. Though Feinberg never published a complete bibliography of his holdings, no one knew Whitman bibliography better than he did. He began his collection in 1918, and over the next seven decades he bought practically every letter and manuscript, even postcards, that came on the market, either through his agent David Kirschenbaum or by personal bids at auctions.

The use he could make of his collection of Whitman holographs was demonstrated in a remarkably valuable article, "A Whitman Collector Destroys a Whitman Myth," first read at a meeting of the Bibliographical Society in New York in January 1958 and published later that year in *The Papers of the Bibliographical Society of America*. The myth he destroyed was that the poet had worked as a carpenter, like Jesus of Nazareth, while writing the poems of his first edition. Several early biographers of Whitman exploited this myth, and most readers of Whitman had accepted it as true, believing that he had learned the trade from his carpenter father. Among Feinberg's purchases was a large batch of financial records, including bills, receipts, account books, promissory notes, correspondence regarding interest due or paid, and other monetary matters. These prove conclusively that Whitman himself did not work as a carpenter but was an employer of carpenters, a contractor, and a speculator in real estate.

Though there has never been a more enthusiastic admirer of Whitman than Charles Feinberg, what he admired was the poet of worldwide influence in both art and culture. As a true scholar, though this was a title he did not claim and in fact spurned, he wanted to separate truth from myth and have Whitman known for what he actually was. This principle also guided him in searching out and assembling these records of Whitman's actual life.

Whitman himself, Feinberg points out, was responsible for much of the mystery and misunderstanding of these years; he mislead his first biographer, John Burroughs, and later Dr. Richard Maurice Bucke about the length of time he spent in St. Louis in 1848 and the extent of his "western" travels. Whitman not only supplied information to these two biographers but he read and revised their manuscripts. Some of this exaggeration I noted in my biography of Whitman, *The Solitary Singer* (1955), but Feinberg's article is the most definitive treatment ever published on these years.

The earliest receipt in Feinberg's collection, for purchase of a lot on Prince Street in Brooklyn from Austin Reeves, is dated 20 November 1844. Other receipts show that he bought and paid for other property. Some of the bills and receipts also clearly indicate that he was the main supporter of the family, for which he bought clothing and other essentials, as well as some "frills," such as daguerreotypes and a piano for his brother Jeff. Most of the bills and receipts, however, were for building materials and carpentry labor. During these formative years Whitman was also engaged in journalism, both as correspondent and editor, and he operated a book and stationery store as well as a printing shop, but he was always busy buying and selling, making deals, and doing his best to keep up with his debts, both for himself and his family.

Feinberg concludes his article: "Some biographers have treated Whitman as a careless idler, a drifter, a loafing dreamer, who never took his meals on time and worked only when he felt like it. What I have tried to say is that Whitman was a very practical young man, devoted to his family, making money to support them and being modestly successful in business matters. By 1855, he felt that he was ready to publish his *Leaves of Grass* and deliberately turned his back on all his money making ventures, to do what he felt he was born to do, to be a writer, the poet and singer of America's songs, the architect of the American Dream."

I have dwelt on this one article because it reveals clearly Feinberg's purposes for collecting Whitman and the uses he made of his collection. He was also generous with all Whitman scholars. Everyone who has written seriously about Whitman since the 1950s consulted him and made use of his material.

When the late Sculley Bradley and I began the edition of *The Collected Writings of Walt Whitman* for New York University Press, Feinberg immediately offered us (as well as the editors of individual volumes) unrestricted use of all his manuscripts, even though dealers believe, probably with reason, that printing a manuscript diminishes its commercial value. In addition, he furnished frontispiece photographs for each of the volumes (he had also assembled the finest collection of photographs of the much-photographed poet). Modern Whitman scholars owe a greater debt to Charles Feinberg than to any other man,

Feinberg and Robert Frost

and anyone interested in studying or writing about Whitman will miss this generous collector. Fortunately, he had turned over most of his collection to the Library of Congress before his death, with the exception of a few items which are contracted to be delivered later. This collection is the grand monument to the memory of Charles E. Feinberg.

A TRIBUTE

from JOHN C. BRODERICK

Charles Feinberg's love affair with the Library of Congress began in the 1950s. As in most love affairs of long duration, there were some spats and disagreements. The library did not always do what Charlie thought it should, and he did not always do what the library thought he should. But there was a bond between the man and the institution, strengthened on his side by his awareness that both Thomas Harned and Horace Traubel wanted the greatest Whitman collection to reside in the national library. With Charlie's cooperation, eventually it did.

Charlie opened the library's 1955 exhibit with a talk on Whitman collections and collectors, printed as the introduction to the library's 1955 Whitman catalog. Shortly thereafter, discussions

began on the terms by which the Feinberg Whitman Collection could be made part of the national collections. Eventually, it seemed possible to accomplish, and a ten-year purchase agreement was executed, which was fulfilled 1969-1979. The opening of the Whitman sesquicentennial exhibit in 1969 was undoubtedly the highest moment of all, when a substantial number of the Feinberg Whitman treasures went on display in the library's magnificent Great Hall. The collecting did not stop in 1969 or in 1979 but continued almost to the day he died. And there were important gifts to the library, over and above the arrangement leading to the acquisition of the Whitman Collection: Karl Shapiro and John Ciardi manuscripts, a fund to purchase new Whitman material, and, above all, the papers of Horace Traubel, the indispensable adjunct to study the good gray poet.

Many individuals and institutions can rightly claim Charles Feinberg as one of their own, but none more than the Library of Congress. As honorary consultant in Walt Whitman Studies 1972-1981 and as unofficial adviser to the library for nearly forty years, he numbered a succession of library officials among his circle of intimates. Generous and irrepressible, Charles Feinberg was enthusiastic and intellectually active to the end. A friend of all libraries, he will be missed most at the national library, which he loved enough to try to improve–and frequently did.

A TRIBUTE

from MATTHEW J. BRUCCOLI

I met Charles Feinberg in the late 1950s when I was a graduate student and he lectured on Walt Whitman for the Bibliographical Society of the University of Virginia. He was the first prominent book collector who encouraged me. The others advised me that I wasn't rich enough to become a serious collector. Mr. Feinberg told me that he started buying books with money earned by shining shoes. Over the years we became friends; the longer I knew Charlie, the more I cherished him. He was the most generous collector I have known. His books and manuscripts were available to scholars who needed to use them. The peak of his generosity was the donation of the greatest Whitman collection in the world to the Library of Congress because he was grateful to America for making it possible for a poor, uneducated immigrant to succeed. He supported the growth of his Whitman collection after it went to the Library of Congress, and he made money available for future acquisitions.

The last time I spoke with him was when he called me to discuss a cataloging problem at the library. Although Whitman was closest to his heart, Charlie's library ranged over American literature and was strong in poetry. His Robert Frost collection–which he presented to Hebrew University–was superb.

The recipients of his benefactions included many libraries in America and abroad as well as charitable organizations. Charlie quietly financed many Whitman research projects. He was a founder of the American Friends of Hebrew University and the founder of the Lubavitch Foundation of Michigan, and he was active in the National Jewish Committee, the Boy Scouts of America, the Friends of the University of Detroit Library, the Michigan Historical Commission, and the Detroit Historical Society.

Charles Feinberg was patriotic, charitable, scholarly, and devout. The Charlie I knew best was the bibliophile, and I learned some of the best lessons in bookmanship from him: "You regret only the books you don't buy." And, "If you don't buy it now, you may never get another chance." And, "It costs more today than it did yesterday, but tomorrow it will cost even more."

Charles Feinberg once said, "My life would have been a desert without books." Charlie abhorred spiritual deserts.

Nancy Hale

(6 May 1908-24 September 1988)

Anne Hobson Freeman
University of Virginia

See also the Hale entry in *DLB Yearbook: 1980*.

In the late 1970s Nancy Hale used to come to my writing class once every semester. She would sweep regally into the classroom–back ramrod straight under a smartly cut suit, angel hair billowing above her finely chiseled face. The students would be speechless with surprise, and Nancy with shyness, as I struggled lamely to introduce her.

Silence would then fall upon the room. Nancy, sitting next to me at the end of the long seminar table, would unfold her tortoise-shell half-glasses and set them just below the rise of that magnificent nose. Peering down its slope, she would then begin to read something she had written.

Her well-chosen words–so pure, precise, and yet endlessly surprising–intoned by that inimitable voice, with its hollow echoes and occasional broad *a*'s, would carry us back to the Boston of her childhood. And *up*, too, toward a standard of expression that every writer in that room longed, someday, to achieve. The standard was, quite simply, perfection.

By that time she had published eighteen books and scores of short stories, primarily in the *New Yorker* magazine. And she was now hard at work on a historical novel based on the life and letters of her great-uncle Charles Hale. The chasm of achievement that separated her from us seemed unbridgeable, until her words began to work their magic.

By the time she took those reading glasses off and folded them back into their case, the students knew and loved, and now, inexplicably, felt obliged to protect the vulnerable soul that had been so starkly revealed.

In the aftermath of revelation, Nancy was surprisingly relaxed. As she responded to questions on her favorite subject–the mystery of writing–her spontaneity, frankness, and total engagement suggested that she saw herself as just another writer talking to her equals.

Nancy Hale (University of Virginia, Department of Graphics, Photo 5256)

The students loved her for it. They would go home and write into their journals words like "gutsy," "queenly," "dangerously honest," or "as beautiful inside, as she is on the outside." One, who later became a fiction editor at *Mademoiselle*, wrote, "I wish that Nancy Hale was my grandmother. Then I could talk to her like that anytime I wanted to."

A fact that always surfaced in those classroom discussions was that the fiction writer must be brave enough to probe for the very personal discovery, the inner secret that turns out to be the main reason the fiction writer writes and the fiction reader reads.

218

Nancy Hale made this observation more formally in *The Realities of Fiction* (1962) when she said: "Stories of mine that have made readers say, 'Why! That's just the way it is with me!' seem, to my surprise, to be about what I should have thought most private, most personal to myself. Just so I seem to do better by the world when I am acting for what is most inwardly myself."

That statement might be used now as a touchstone to determine which among the hundred short stories, forty-odd memoirs, and seven novels Nancy Hale published over half a century will be lasting contributions to the world of letters.

As long as she remained in contact with the well of feeling, deep below the surface, and let that feeling generate the form of her writing, she produced wonderful short stories, and memoirs that broke new ground for the prose elegy. But when she came at writing from the opposite direction, from the head and not the heart, she was much less successful. The intellectual constructs she felt obliged to impose on her novels and many of her stories–theses based on rigid and reductive assumptions about the northerner's versus the southerner's response, or the academic's versus the artist's–diminished the power of her talent.

Admittedly these contrasts fueled some brilliant satire. One of the funniest scenes in modern literature is the literary cocktail party in New York attended by the author from Virginia in *Dear Beast* (1959). Small wonder William Faulkner went out of his way to compliment "Miss Nancy" on that particular performance. Yet even here, in her satire, the touchstone can be applied to distinguish the shallow kind that masked her anger and antagonism from the all-embracing kind that sprang from pure delight in human foibles. Her most daring experiment in satire, *Heaven and Hardpan Farm* (1957), is set in a mental institution. Yet it works, because her portraits of the patients and their Jungian doctor are bathed in that redemptive delight.

In reality as well as fiction, Nancy Hale indulged in at least two kinds of laughter–a tinny social laugh which signaled lack of ease and a deep and lovely rumble that bubbled from her soul. When all is said and done, though, it was not in satire but in celebration that her talent found its fullest expression.

The books I find myself going back to reread now are the quiet and deliciously sensuous stories in *The Earliest Dreams* (1936), *Between the*

Nancy Hale, 1929

Dark and the Daylight (1943), *The Empress's Ring* (1955), and *The Pattern of Perfection* (1960), the odes to childhood in *A New England Girlhood* (1958) and *Secrets* (1971), and the elegies to her parents and her aunt in *The Life in the Studio* (1969).

The writer of a tribute in the London *Times* the week after her death concluded that "Nancy Hale was a miniaturist whose imagination was at its best when playing on everyday problems and minor tragedies. . . . On the whole Miss Hale was not as successful on the larger canvas of the novel as she was in the short stories. The carefully polished prose, so effective at setting scenes . . . tended to drown in over luxuriance when asked to explore powerful conflicts and deep emotions."

Her best-known novel, *The Prodigal Women* (1942), is, however, a notable exception. Though the writing of that book consumed five years of her life and wrecked her health, it was a critical success as well as a best-seller. And it proved that her talent could be stretched to the wide canvas.

As André Maurois pointed out in his preface to the French translation of the novel, like Tolstoy, she knew "how to develop a company of numerous destinies and to move them in an authentic social setting."

Mary Lee Settle, in her introduction to the New American Library edition of *The Prodigal Women* (published in the fall of 1988), commented on the author's "gift of making places resonate behind her characters and become a part of them" and said of the portrait that she presents of the years between 1922 and 1940:

> It is a view that can be found nowhere outside of good fiction, neither in the certainties of history nor in the lesser novels by contemporary writers who did not use their senses to record their surroundings. . . .
>
> Her recognition of the power of simple objects can release a magic memory when *The Prodigal Women* is read today. Details glisten with recognition, and for those of us who have any memories of the time, they evoke a piercing recall. A woman spits into a mascara box to dampen the little brush that came with it, and a whole world flashes into a new reality: the mixture of coal smoke and clean linen which was the smell of a thirties train, the scent of *Evening in Paris,* the feel of silk stockings, the swish of a short beaded skirt that those grand and gallant girls of the twenties slipped into . . . while we peek at them dressing and the talcum powder flies. . . .
>
> All of these images are enhanced by her acute visual sense. Nancy Hale was trained first as a painter and it shows in every scene she writes.

The author herself was slightly apprehensive about the reissue of *The Prodigal Women.* She had come a long way spiritually, as well as technically, from the thirty-five-year-old sophisticate who had wrestled with that rich, unwieldy book. In her maturity, she learned to use her gift—for bringing scenes and characters abundantly to life through color, shape, texture, smell, and sound—with greater discipline.

In *The Life in the Studio*, perhaps her finest work, there is a remarkable passage in which Nancy Hale approximates in writing the technique that her mother, Lilian Westcott Hale, the artist, had developed for defining snow in her charcoal drawings—negatively—by bold strokes of black to indicate the trees and buildings behind the snow. Here the artist's daughter uses strokes of sound to define the silence that has descended

Charcoal sketch of Hale drawn in 1946 by her mother, Lilian Westcott Hale

on the house where she, a child, is lying sick in bed while her mother is working by a window in the hall, trying to catch the image of the snow falling outside with sharp strokes of her charcoal pencil:

> Then, gradually and by imperceptible degrees, consciousness would descend upon me—or perhaps it was that I would begin to support the consciousness—of silence. My book slipped back among the litter of other books upon the counterpane, and I would lie there and listen to the stillness and to those tiny sounds that accented the stillness. The house itself made minute, mysterious sounds—the drop of the merest splinter upon the attic floor overhead; a sigh in the walls where some old joist had further settled; the little, complaining creaks a flight of stairs makes, as though recovering from being climbed up. . . .
>
> In the long hour of stillness I could hear the sound even the smallest leaf made as it skittered, scratching, across the crust of snow.
>
> From far away in the back of the house came faint domestic sounds—the coal range being shaken down, the black iron door to the oven opened and shut. . . .

And from closer, in the hall,

IX 4 Lida

X 4 Lida — up to marriage & left.

XI Betsy — in Boston — Ogden affair — rep. — Henry Kunz — to N.Y.

XII Betsy in N.Y. affairs — marries Wolcott — watched he — disintegration separation but no divorce

XIII Maizie up to breakdown & Va. — Dr. G. & Mrs J in Boston —

II

XIV Betsy in N.Y. — work & affairs — speakeasy-lift girl — lots of detail — manly girl — petrified

XV Betsy & O'H — newspaper man — lovely in love summer — dying — admission — Lafayette — hell — to Reno.
O'H mountain

XVI Lida on train to Reno — Betsy in Reno evolved & saintly — Lida at Riverside & he her obj. as trying all new things — she very important now — she is starting some new career — 6 weeks —

XVII Betsy back to O'H — Hell again — to Folly Cove — hell — 1st child — then he marries her — Her growing strength — 2nd child begins — life in F. C. hard V. Dimitrios & rage

XVIII Lida with Lambert in Va — They are going to try sketch —
Shock works — Maizie jires about Lida — Lambert
mountain gives up Lida for Maizie — but she divorces him & Lida is through too — he is ruined —

XIX Maizie's careful life — Oscar justiation permanently — Betsy's
V' hard strong triumphant life contrasted

XX Last chap — Lida — Going into politics — live in others — But Gordon still doesn't like her — Mr. Jekyll — See Mrs. Jekyll — came to close Hampton horse-poetry

Page from Hale's notes for The Prodigal Women *(Nancy Hale Papers, Special Collections Department, Manuscripts Division, University of Virginia Library)*

the sharp, steady sawing of charcoal (sharpened to a needle point with a razor blade) up and down against the sheet of Strathmore board on my mother's easel as she worked on a snow scene from the windows of the front hall.... There would come a pause in the sawing, and a faint rattle, while she rummaged around in the blue-edge box that French charcoal came in. A clack—she had dropped something on the floor. If it was charcoal, it fell with a small explosion. Then a scratchy, rubbing sound, which was the careful filing of the sides of her stick of charcoal against the board covered with fine sandpaper.... A pause. Then would recommence the sawing of the point drawn rhythmically up and down. I would go back to Miss Brontë, or make a stab at arithmetic, but every now and then I would give myself over again to rest in the long morning's silence.

Later she describes another long silence:

when tiny sounds become brilliantly distinct—the occasional *clunk* of the electric clock on the wall of the kitchenette in that small, peaceful apartment; the creak, as my great-grandfather's sea chest in the parlor settled a bit; the sound of a chunk of wet snow as it slid off the roof onto more wet snow; the sound of a car passing outside, coming to us muffled, as though from far away.

I have felt a sense of silence like that one in one other place—in a big church to which I did not even belong. It was during Communion, and there was a hush that was merely accentuated by the sound of the priest's voice murmuring over and over, "The Blood of our Lord Jesus Christ, which was shed for thee...." The Communicants filed up in silence; those who had returned knelt silent in their pews. The vast structure was as still as death; even when the Gloria was sung it came only as the quietest awakening "Lamb of God ... that takest away the sins of the world...."

Since in the church I was surrounded by hundreds of people, I must suppose that the similarity of those silences has more to do with me than with my mother, for her reactions to going to church were anything but restful....

It dawns on me that the silences I knew with my mother came to me not from being alone at all but from being close to her. They may have emanated out of her solitude, but for her being alone did not mean silence. She was listening, calmly rapt, to that humming dynamo, her secret source.

By the juxtaposition of those two silences, rather than by overt statement, which she es-

chewed in her best writing, Nancy Hale suggests that the artist's task is not wholly unrelated to the celebrant's.

In 1980 a stroke changed Nancy's life dramatically. For fifty years writing had been her raison d'être. Now it was relegated to secondary status as she struggled to regain the use of the left side of her body.

For the first time in her life, she developed a passionate interest in athletics. Physical therapy came first now, before even her writing, every morning. By the end of a year, she had managed to regain eighty-five percent of her physical powers, but she would walk with a slight limp and a cane for the rest of her life.

There were falls and other setbacks still to come. And breakthroughs, too. As she explained in an unpublished essay on her illness, "You don't speak of a stroke as anything you have totally conquered. It is work in progress."

Through the fall and winter of 1980-1981, despite the rigors of her physical therapy program, she doggedly pushed through to completion the second draft of "Charlieshope." "A novel-in-history" is the term she coined for this ambitious work. It was a blending of the letters of her uncle Charles Hale, former editor of the *Boston Daily Advertiser* and U.S. consul general to Egypt, with her own memories of the tales her father used to tell her about the slightly Bohemian household he and his brothers and sisters—known in Boston as "the Dirty Delightfuls"—had grown up in.

The book gave her a chance to celebrate the childhood of her father, the painter Philip Hale, and to portray her grandfather, the leonine and beloved Unitarian minister who wrote *The Man without a Country* (1863). But it also sapped her energy at a critical point in her recovery and depressed her spirit as she relived (through the writing of the last few chapters) her great-uncle's final debilitating illness. She began to believe that his illness might have been a punishment for sins earlier in his life.

The oppressive morality of the Victorians, Nancy Hale would be the first to admit, has no place in modern fiction. Yet she identified, too closely probably, with the characters she wrote about, and at that point in her own life she lacked the energy to resist the negative pull of that particular book. In the throes of those last chapters, she began to question the value of writing as a way of life and to wonder if it might not be "a sinful occupation."

Nancy Hale and Fredson Bowers (photo by Jim Carpenter for the Daily Progress, *Charlottesville, Virginia)*

In May 1981 her editor sent back the second draft of "Charlieshope" with suggestions for a final editing, and Nancy decided that she did not have the strength, physically or psychologically, to run the manuscript through her typewriter again. She returned the advance and thereby bought her freedom from the book and ultimately from the despair that was associated with it.

Her decision was a wise one, for within a month she was hospitalized again with an aftermath of the stroke, an illness whose acronym was SIEADH and whose symptoms brought her to the brink of death. Every modicum of energy she still retained, she needed to pull herself back from that, the severest of her setbacks.

Yet she had meant what she said in a newspaper interview: "I'd rather choke, than stop writing." For her, writing was as essential as breath-ing; it was the means by which she had learned to cope with the harshest realities of life. As she wrote once in her notebook: "Creative writing is for me the sublimation of the unendurable." And so, despite the stroke and SIEADH, through the 1980s she continued to produce short stories and memoirs in a thin but steady stream.

In "Tastes," which appeared in the Autumn 1982 *Virginia Quarterly Review,* she explored the positive reaction to debilitating illness which her widowed Aunt Nancy exemplified. The memoir opens with the statement: "Increasingly–perhaps because there are so few of her sort around any more–I think of my Aunt Nancy. My first, strong picture of her is before she was married: golden, curly hair ablaze, singing in her high and happy voice, 'Yip I Yaddy I Yoodly Yay.' It was about 1913; I would have been five."

It closes with a visit to the "infinitely cheer-less" nursing home where her aunt lay confined to her bed with osteoporosis, looking over old family photographs and postcards.

> To her apparently they were perennially fresh and interesting.... After we had spoken about how we missed my mother, we turned to other memories and laughed a lot. At one point, suddenly, incredibly, Aunt Nancy exclaimed, "When I first wake up in the morning I'm so happy I could *squeal*."
>
> Yip I Yaddy I Yoodly Yay.

Coming when it did, right after her own illnesses, the piece represented a spiritual breakthrough for its author. She had managed to reverse the negative direction of her thoughts about old age and illness and writing as a way of life. And she did it by connecting, once again, with her secret source.

Afterwards, when she recalled her despair after the writing of "Charlieshope," she said, "When I'm writing well, I don't feel sinful. I feel *blessed*."

By 1984 she had found out that her grandsons were dyslexic and was trying to find out how she could help them—and children like them—learn to love reading the way she always had. In the process, she discovered that there is a dearth of emotionally satisfying stories with the short sentences and strong narrative thread such children need to get them started. And so she set about to write some for them.

After studying the material the Center for Dyslexia in Charlottesville sent to her, she wrote to one of their tutors, Sheelah Scott: "The description of unhappy, *losing* children in the teaching book touched me deeply. There is something about a child who feels he is failing which is absolutely unbearable. I'm so glad you can help them and hope I can too."

In the end she produced eighteen children's stories, drawing details from her own childhood and that of her children and her grandchildren. Frequently she used the old stone house and studio, Howlets (her summer home in Folly Cove, Massachusetts), as the setting. Her aim was always to encourage the child who was having difficulty adjusting, but also to make the story attractive. As she saw it, "the trouble for many of these children [was] that reading just hasn't been made seductive to them.... Children want to fly in fancy. Over the most trivial matters."

"Birds in the House" was the first of the three booklets published in Charlottesville by the Learning Center in 1985. In it a ten-year-old girl identifies with two birds that are temporarily trapped in her house. Eventually she finds relief from her own disappointment by climbing to her favorite place in an apple tree and writing in her journal. The story ends triumphantly with the girl's discovery that no matter what happened to her "she could always do that–look at the things around her and write them down."

In the second story, "Wags," written for an even younger reader, a cocker spaniel very narrowly escapes drowning at Folly Cove. The author, trying to confine herself to one-syllable words, said that she experienced a thrill of victory when she thought of describing the glacial boulders in the cove as "Ice Age rocks."

Nancy Hale's last published work was "Miss Dugan," an homage to her high-school English teacher, in the anthology *An Apple for My Teacher* (1987, Algonquin Books). She claimed that Miss Dugan had "saved her life" her first year at the Winsor School in Boston by taking an interest in her poetry when she was "drowning in seas of inferiority, shyness (that unfortunately did not look like shyness but rather antagonism), and despair."

At the end, the author reciprocates many years later, when the two of them are swimming in a stone quarry up the road from Folly Cove. To Nancy Hale the image of water–whether it was in the sea, a quarry, or even a swimming pool–represented the unconscious, the chaos that threatens all of us, but particularly artists who have to plunge into it every day to do their work. In her notebook she had written: "There isn't any question (in my feeling) but that the world is more attractive than to create, i.e. I'd rather live than write. But without creation one would get lost in the unconscious–the sea."

Neither Nancy nor Miss Dugan was a very confident swimmer. On this occasion they had strayed perilously close to the deepest water, where the shelf of granite, almost six feet underneath them, was abruptly sheered. Miss Dugan had been happily floating on her back when:

> Suddenly I observed something queer. Miss Dugan was making so little effort to swim that she was, actually, sinking. Her legs were drifting downwards so that they were almost vertical. Her head, tipped back, was beginning to sink. Her chin was under water.
>
> I realized abruptly that unless I did something, quick, Miss Dugan was going to drown .... I've got to save her, I thought. By letting my feet down I found I could just touch bot-

tom on tiptoe. Reaching out, I took hold of Miss Dugan's inertly drifting hand. "Hold on to me" I commanded her. I was not sure she could hear. "Just don't grab me! If you hold my hand I can pull you in."

Miss Dugan held on. For a moment it seemed infinitely perilous–I was so near the brink of the really deep water, where I would not be able to help her. Then I found surer footing, and began pulling Miss Dugan, whose body moved lightly in the water, on to the shore. She told me afterward she had only been repeating Blake.

The method Nancy Hale used to rescue her old teacher was a very light one, all that she could manage, imperiled as she was by her own lack of strength in the deep water. It resembles very closely the method that she used in her best writing and attempted to describe when an English bibliographer asked her for a comment on her work: "I am averse to making statements on my work," she wrote, "because I have found by experience that fiction is so protean that today's aim can be tomorrow's anathema. But I may make the comment that in general I have striven to conceal the purpose underlying my work with 'the light touch' since nothing seems to me so self-defeating as overt earnestness. Yet I can assure readers of my work that its purpose is earnest, indeed painful."

In April 1988 she suffered a second, minor stroke and spent most of her last summer at Folly Cove overcoming the indignities of it. She had virtually won that battle, too, by the time she and her husband, Fredson Bowers, returned to Charlottesville at the end of August.

As I sat beside her on the airplane coming home–while her husband drove the car, packed to the roof with their belongings and their works-in-progress–I suddenly turned to her and said, "You really are a good sport, Nancy."

"I have no alternative," she said quietly.

The week before she died, she urged her physical therapist to give her harder exercises, started on a series of Italian lessons, and dictated the first draft of a story. She was fully alive and fighting back the only way Nancy Hale knew how to fight, which was with all her might, when the final stroke carried her away on the twenty-fourth of September 1988.

As I was leafing through an old *Who's Who* the next morning for biographical facts to include in the obituary notice, I came upon a statement which Nancy, herself, had appended to her entry: "After a long and reflective life, my impression is that the life itself is seeking a goal & whether in art or in reality, the sign of creation having been present . . . is a sensation of pure joy."

Those last two words, "pure joy," cut right to the core, as Nancy's words could do, beyond the sense of loss and grief, to suggest the final response of her friends and many of her readers to her presence on this earth for eighty years.

A TRIBUTE
from JOHN C. COLEMAN

Almost immediately after coming to Charlottesville to teach undergraduates at The University of Virginia, now nearly forty years ago, I met Nancy Hale. We rapidly became good friends.

After teaching required basic English courses for my first few years at the University I was given a course for undergraduates listed in the catalogue as ADVANCED COMPOSITION, ENGLISH 21-22. During the first semester my students wrote expository themes, during the second semester narrative. I soon found that in the latter semester reading and discussing with students short-short stories, those under three thousand words, from the *New Yorker* and other magazines, was helpful. Two stories which I used repeatedly to spark their imaginations were Nancy Hale's "Entrance into Life" and Richard Wilbur's "Game of Catch." When I spent part of one afternoon with Nancy and another with Wilbur telling them what I thought their stories were really about, stating theme, discussing dénouement, and so forth, each burst out laughing, insisting that for them the stories were simply accounts of what they saw: in Nancy's "Entrance into Life," a group of seniors at The University of Virginia marching down the Lawn to receive their diplomas; in Wilbur's "Game of Catch," some kids throwing a ball back and forth in a vacant lot. At any rate, that was their report– but I didn't believe a word of it.

Although I admired Nancy's novels, I preferred her short stories, a form of narrative in which I felt she was especially successful. I was particularly interested in those stories which ultimately appeared in two collections: *The Empress's Ring* and *The Pattern of Perfection.* But to me Nancy's most original, impressive, and challenging work is *The Realities of Fiction,* in which she explains the role of the imagination in the creative process and discusses the work of writers ranging from Tolstoy and Dickens to Hemingway and Faulkner, from Jane Austen to Katherine Mansfield and Virginia Woolf. However, it is her autobiographical and biographical *The Life in the Studio* for which I feel the greatest affection. It is not only a touching memorial to her distinguished parents, Philip and Lilian Westcott Hale, but also a moving account of the author developing a new perspective, a new understanding about herself and others which many of the characters in her fiction try to achieve but often fail to do so.

I saw Nancy and her husband, Fredson Bowers, several times in London and once or twice at Oxford. I remember vividly going to the Courtauld Gallery in Woburn Square with her to view that superb collection of French paintings and listening intently to the comments of the daughter of parents who had dedicated their lives to that form of art. Later when Nancy and I spent a day together at Oxford I was much impressed by her stating that she enjoyed riding about Oxfordshire in the local buses, not so much to see the villages and countryside but to look at the people on the bus and to hear their voices. I was reminded of her comment when I read recently that Edgar Dégas had told a young friend who was trying to summon a hansom cab to take them to a restaurant, "I don't like cabs. You don't see anyone. That is why I love to ride in an omnibus. We were created to look at one another, weren't we?" To that statement I am sure Nancy Hale would have agreed.

A TRIBUTE

from PHILIP HAMBURGER

When one loves the work of a writer, as I love the writings of Nancy Hale, certain passages remain foremost in the memory. For example, in what is perhaps my favorite of all her books, *The Life in the Studio,* I can never forget: "What I am trying is to clue the reader in on the game any number can play, of looking into a mirror that reflects looking into a mirror that reflects. Down at the far end I hope what will be seen is not death at all, but the life in the studio." And there is her memory of memory: "My pieces, although their background is the scenery and characters that bounded my childhood, are intended less about the real and ascertainable past than about the memory of it; and memory as a mode of thinking tends to burst spontaneously into fantasy at every turn." Nor can one forget those five-pound stone jars of strawberry jam from S. S. Pierce, or

how (as she relates) she would startle a dull dinner party by casually remarking of her father, Philip Hale, "My father used to spend the summers at Giverny, where he knew Monet." If Nancy Hale was lucid, beautiful, understanding, and deeply human in her writing, she was even more so as a friend. Her friendship—always supportive, always generously given—would enter one's life at needed moments with the bright tonic quality of the purest mountain air.

A TRIBUTE

from MARY GRAY HUGHES

When I met Nancy Hale, an elegant sixty-four, in England in 1972, I was struck by her charm, the freshness of her excitement about writing, and her marvelous legs. There was always something extra about her. A sense of risk along with the beautiful manners, of staring unabashed at life whatever was included. It is accepted and standard to describe Nancy Hale as a talented and prolific writer. She published stories extensively in the *New Yorker* and ranged in her work from polished and seemingly effortless fiction to a scholarly biography of Mary Cassatt and affectionate, informative memoirs of her artist parents.

But the magnetizing pull was that extra quality of something unexpectedly deeper, of being rooted in life with all its complexity. Nothing in her writing shows this more clearly than her classic short story "A Full Life." As simple and profound as a work by Chekhov.

She was passionate about art and life and a firm believer that an artist must first be a good person and lead a full life. She relished hers.

I saw her last, so it turned out, in May 1988 in her home in Virginia. She was irresistibly gracious although not strong. She wanted to talk about writing and plans of writing. She was acute and interested and eager for whatever was ahead. And had marvelous legs.

A TRIBUTE

from WILLIAM MAXWELL

The child of painters, Nancy Hale was brought up in a world where it was inconceivable that beauty of one kind or another would not be an essential part of art. Her writing reflects this assumption. Her descriptive powers are remarkable but seldom used in the service of the merely visual. For example: "The sound of the horses' feet was like a confused heartbeat on the swampy ground. They both felt it. They used to get off their horses, without having said a word, and helplessly submerge themselves in each other's arms, while the sweat ran down their backs under their shirts." Writing like that doesn't age. Though she had much of the personality of a poet, her style remains firmly anchored in prose–lucid, unobtrusive, well-shaped, and with an implied voice. Only when the reader detaches himself from the emotional hold that the story has on him is he likely to become aware of how flawless the writing is. Her subject matter is the bedrock of human experience. A senile old woman crying out endlessly to her sister, dead for fifty years. A pair of lovers locked in what was once a radiant marriage but is now destroyed by illness. A little boy driven by the ostracism and cruelty of his schoolmates to put a noose around his neck. Part of the richness of her fiction comes from her social knowledge–from the fact that she is at home in, though not actually committed to, the world of good manners. Gone now, of course, and therefore all the more fascinating to read about. What linens, what flowers, what kind of silver were considered necessary to a proper establishment. Her two best stories, surely, are "Midsummer," which is about an adolescent girl in a delirium of love for an Irish groom in a riding stable, and "The Bubble," which is about a young woman's absorption in her first child. Both stories break your heart. And were meant to. Her best book is, I think, *The Life in the Studio*–the studio in question being her parents'. In it one finds an understanding painfully arrived at and a sad wisdom. What she really cared about, as a writer, was feeling. In a period where the intellectual content of fiction has been more valued than the emotional, it must have seemed to her that her work, in later years, had gone largely unappreciated. At the moment Willa Cather isn't read as much as she once was. One can depend on time to correct myopia of this kind.

A TRIBUTE

from JOHN FREDERICK NIMS

In the early '60's, soon after the death of her mother, Nancy Hale wrote me about her feelings at the time: "Isn't it extraordinary how easy it is to not remember the past but just plain be *in* the past, for an hour or a half an hour? I mean it's all in the mind, but so is now; and one can move just as easily [there as here]. . . ." When I

think now of her own vivid presence I feel I am in that past in which I knew her: the summers at Bread Loaf, the visits to Woodburn, the handsome house that she and her husband Fredson Bowers built near Charlottesville, its wide windows panoramic on the Blue Ridge Mountains to the west, or the other visits to their summer home on the steeply wooded hillside at Folly Cove on Cape Ann, its comfortably sprawling two-storied studio still a repository for the easels and oil paintings of her celebrated mother.

"Vivid" is probably the word that comes first to mind when I think of Nancy, the vividness not only of her distinguished beauty, but of her spirit, her wit, her play of phrase. On first meeting her, one might have a sense of aristocratic reserve, but one soon felt the warmth and empathy beneath it, and, as one got to know her, the mischievous drollery and love of mirth that showed itself in her spontaneous earthy laughter. Both qualities, the frivolous and the grave, come through in a letter she wrote me not long after the one I have quoted above. The letter itself is now in the Lilly Library at Indiana University, together with the other letters and cards I received from her, but, as I remember, it was written on the blank spaces of a gaudy advertising insert she had found in one of the glossy magazines. After a madcap opening, it winds up with a serious and sensitive account of a visit to San Juan with her husband.

The Cathedral in San Juan was kind of touching. I mean it was such a lousy little colonial cathedral, acting so big in the façade and nothing behind it; beside, a minor dead saint under a glass bell, sent on (rather patronizingly, one felt) from Rome a couple of hundred years ago.

San Juan gave me the slight creeps, although I had a good time there (a better time than poor Fred, who got exhausted lecturing on the Bard to blank Latin-American faces; I sat behind one student at a lecture of his and copied down what she had written in her notebook. It was all she *had* written. The title of his lecture was "Death in Victory: Shakespeare's Tragic Reconciliations." All she had written down was "Trasic Recomciliation. . . ."

The reason it gave *me* the creeps was the tropic lassitude, which was faintly alarming, but more just what-the-hellish. The night Fred was in Mayagüez lecturing and I stayed in S.J., I sat out in front of the hotel in a lovely little park, on a bench under a vast live oak. The little trade wind that blows *all the time* was blowing, and it seemed almost vocal, it spoke so definitely of the trivial; of what does it matter; it was just the most inconsequential wind I ever heard. At that point the cop on the beat came and sat down on the bench and tried to pick me up, so I retreated into the hotel. Which was a beautiful place made out of an old convent by a rich Woolworth (redundant) with a patio made from the old cloister, and rooms opening off the galleries with, on the outside, balconies looking over, in my case, a back street that was steps. The first morning I was there I looked out of my window and there was an old man sitting on one of the steps among the passers-by, shaving himself. Another man, younger, was holding a pocket mirror for him. . . ."

Nancy Hale's evening talks to the writers at Bread Loaf were composed and delivered with more style than the rest of us had at our command. She was one of those who believe, with Michelangelo, that trifles make perfection—and that perfection is no trifle. If, in this reminiscence, I have availed myself of her own words more than of my own, it is because I felt they bring her in focus more vividly than I could do. She did all such things better than most of us.

Marguerite Yourcenar

(8 June 1903-17 December 1987)

Steven Serafin
Hunter College of the City University of New York

See also the Yourcenar entry in *DLB 72: French Novelists, 1930-1960*.

"It's just a little book," said Marguerite Yourcenar, referring to the publication of her first novel. "You never know what will happen, but still, now I'm a writer, I have my place alongside everyone else who has ever written in French." At the time she was twenty-six and living in Paris. Published in 1929, the novel, *Alexis; ou, Le Traité du vain combat* (revised edition, 1965; translated as *Alexis*, 1984), earned for her critical as well as popular attention. More important, it marked the beginning of an unprecedented literary career which spanned over half a century. Assessed by Mavis Gallant, her œuvre stands "as testimony to the substance and clarity of the French language and the purpose and meaning of a writer's life." At the age of seventy-six Yourcenar was given the distinction of being elected to the Académie Française, the first woman in the 346-year history of the institution to be so honored. When she died on 17 December 1987, Roger W. Straus, the president and chief executive officer of her American publisher, Farrar, Straus and Giroux, gave full measure to the place in literature to which she had aspired and

now rightfully belonged: "Marguerite Yourcenar was without question or doubt one of the great writers of the 20th century. She is a great loss to the literary community, but her words will be read and remembered forever."

Known primarily in the United States as the author of the acclaimed novel *Mémoires d'Hadrien* (1951; translated as *Memoirs of Hadrian,* 1954), Yourcenar was accomplished as a poet, short-story writer, dramatist, and essayist as well. In addition, she was well respected as both a translator and a classicist. Within the framework of modern fiction she possessed an uncommon if not solitary artistic voice. Her language has been accurately depicted by Gallant as "carved, etched, chiseled, engraved: simply, a plain and elegant style, the reflection of a strong and original literary intellect" (*New York Review*, 5 December 1985). A naturalized American citizen since 1947, she remained a productive writer throughout her life, while actively maintaining her interest as an environmentalist.

Yourcenar was born Marguerite de Crayencour in Brussels of a Belgian mother, the former Fernande de Cartier de Marchienne, and a French father, Michael de Crayencour. She never knew her mother, who died shortly after child-

Marguerite Yourcenar

birth. Inheriting the French citizenship of her father, who assumed responsibility for her upbringing, she enjoyed a unique childhood governed by a curious mixture of privilege and eccentricity. She was raised at Mont Noir, the family home near Lille, and traveled extensively between Paris and the south of France. Immersed in a classical education supervised at home by her father, she read aloud with him first in French and later in Latin, Greek, and English. Her father began as her mentor and became by her own estimation her intellectual companion. "He lived for the caprice of the moment," she once said of him. "He was an extraordinarily free man, perhaps the freest man I have ever known."

Encouraged by her father, she began to write verse at fourteen years of age. In 1921 he arranged for the private publication of her first book, *Le Jardin des chimères*, a dramatic adaptation of the Icarus legend, which she later dismissed as having "the virtue of childish simplicity." This was followed the next year by a collection of poems, *Les Dieux ne sont pas morts*. It was during this time that her father assisted in the invention

of her anagrammatical pseudonym, which in 1947 she adopted as her legal name.

Yourcenar was twenty-four when her father died. Conditioned by her own sense of independence as well as financial security, she decided soon after his death to devote herself exclusively to travel, study, and literature. Determined to establish herself as a writer, she began to contribute poetry and critical essays to a variety of literary periodicals prior to the publication of *Alexis; ou, Le Traité du vain combat*.

Her second novel, *La Nouvelle Eurydice* (1931), was less well received than her first. Autobiographical in part, it was conceived by the author in reaction to the "usual novels of love, ambition, or vanity." Generating interest as well as praise from what Yourcenar has referred to as her "loyal admirers," it failed to attract a larger audience to her work and was generally considered misguided and amateurish. She herself was displeased with the work and later admitted to misgivings concerning the publication. "It was as if a painter with some talent, who had already done some fairly good work, set out to learn technique in the studio, started painting according to the rules, and wound up producing work of the most tedious academic sort."

In contrast, the publication of *Denier du rêve* reinforced her emerging literary reputation and clearly accentuated her inherent inventiveness as an author. First published in 1934, the novel was revised and expanded in 1959 and was translated into English in 1982 as *A Coin in Nine Hands*. Political in design, the novel is atypical of Yourcenar in her utilization of a contemporary setting as well as an ensemble cast rather than a single, dominating protagonist. Witness to the social and political turmoil consuming prewar Italy, she attempted in the novel "to confront the hollow reality behind the bloated facade of Fascism" while simultaneously probing the mystery of perception and the permeance of evil within the infrastructure of modern society. Representing "the symbol of contact between human beings each lost in his own passions and in his intrinsic solitude," the coin of the title symbolically passes from one person to another tangentially connecting their lives in a cycle of unspoken retribution. Acknowledged as a substantial departure in relation to her body of work, the novel nonetheless is characteristic of thematic concerns which unify and distinguish her artistic vision, the exploration of self, the mastery of deception, and the delicate fusion of dream and reality.

The favorable reception given to *Denier du rêve* led to the publication of *Feux* (1936; revised edition, 1974; translated as *Fires,* 1981), which Yourcenar later described as "a sequence of lyrical prose pieces connected by the notion of love." Further demonstrating her assertiveness as well as her versatility as a writer, this was followed by the publication of *Nouvelles orientales* (1938; revised edition, 1975; translated as *Oriental Tales,* 1985), a collection of highly original and interrelated short stories. Then returning her attention to the novel, she produced what is generally considered a major work within her body of literature, *Le Coup de grâce* (1939; translated as *Coup de Grâce,* 1957). Set amid the Baltic civil strife which erupted in the wake of the Russian Revolution, the novel presents a vivid depiction of the brutal and often incomprehensible consequences of political confrontation. Similar in context to her later historical fiction, the novel is regularly cited as a precursor to the more accessible *Mémoires d'Hadrien* and similarly hailed with justification as a masterwork of short fiction.

Yourcenar as a young woman

Published shortly before the outbreak of World War II, *Le Coup de grâce* essentially marked the end of a distinct and highly significant period in Yourcenar's literary career. Having completed the novel while living in Italy, she returned to Paris in August 1939 and was there when war was officially declared. Disheartened by the imminent invasion of France, she left Europe for the United States at the invitation of her American friend Grace Frick. Although conceived as a temporary measure, her displacement quietly surrendered to permanence "largely owing to the force of events." Accepting her situation as a new beginning in her life, she nevertheless found herself at a point of personal as well as literary transformation.

In comparison to the previous decade, the years from 1939 to 1948, which she later described as an "interval of retirement," were relatively unproductive and of questionable merit in advancing her career. With her family inheritance depleted, she turned to more practical if less gratifying means to earn her livelihood. She translated into French works by Virginia Woolf and Henry James as well as a collection of Negro spirituals which had earlier attracted her artistic sensibility. In addition, she began teaching in 1942 at Sarah Lawrence College in Bronxville, New York, to which she commuted from her home in Hartford, Connecticut, an experience which she later admitted left her emotionally and intellectually unsatisfied. That same year, however, she and Frick began to summer in Maine, where in 1950 they purchased what became their permanent residence in Northeast Harbor, on Mount Desert Island.

What essentially constituted the turning point in her career occurred in 1948 when Yourcenar resumed work on a character study of the Roman Emperor Hadrian, a creative inspiration which evolved into the novel designated by critical consensus her most significant achievement. Drawn to Hadrian as the embodiment of what Flaubert had prescribed "a unique moment in history," she sought to capture the essence of a man "existing alone and yet closely bound with all being." Written in the form of a letter to his adopted grandson and future heir, Marcus Aurelius, *Mémoires d'Hadrien* is at once a rumination on the protagonist's life as well as a symbolic confrontation with the finality of death. Mirrored in antiquity, Hadrian is by circumstance and design a singular entity whose presence transcends into the modern world with vibrancy and precision. He speaks with a voice that "seems, authentically, overheard" (*Saturday Review*, 12 June 1976), offering in apologia the fruit of wisdom as well as folly. Within the intimacy of the novel Hadrian is allowed to address the consequence of his own mortality and simultaneously to explore the emotional depth of the human experience.

Described by the author as "a psychological novel and meditation on history," *Mémoires d'Hadrien,* when first published in France, received critical acclaim as a work of major literary importance. Translated into English by Frick in collaboration with the author, the novel was the first of Yourcenar's works to be published in the United States and is noteworthy for introducing her to an American audience as well as initiating her long-standing association with Farrar, Straus and Giroux. The greatest achievement of the novel, as noted by Louis Auchincloss, "lies in the sense conveyed of the essential loneliness of the man who has gained the supreme power and learned to use it humanely."

The publication of *L'Œuvre au noir* (1968; translated as *The Abyss*, 1976), a novel similar in

context and methodology to *Mémoires d'Hadrien,* further enhanced Yourcenar's stature. Set in northern Europe in the mid sixteenth century, it is designed as a vehicle for introspection. The protagonist of the novel is the fictitious Zeno, "an intellectual on the edge of modernity" and in perpetual search of enlightenment, at once elusive and forbidden by decree of the Inquisition. In an age gone mad with zealotry and fear, Zeno emerges as "a priest of the life of reason." Inviting comparison to Hadrian, Zeno was aptly described by Frank Kermode (*New York Review of Books*, 14 October 1976) as "the second deity in this author's cult of the full man, endlessly inquiring, ever skeptical, considerate of the body as of the spirit, of the future as well as the present." Following the physician-alchemist-philosopher "from his illegitimate birth in Bruges to his death in a jail of that same city," the novel essentially diffuses the concept of intellectual and spiritual freedom within a bleak landscape of repression. Without question, the novel is a work of major proportion which serves to demonstrate the full scope of an author at the height of her creative powers. As stated by Stephen Koch, "Marguerite Yourcenar writes squarely in defense of the very highest standards and traditions of that enlightened humanism which Hadrian promulgated for an empire and to the agonized rebirth of which her Zeno dies a martyr."

It was at this point in her life, with her literary reputation firmly established, that Yourcenar was to experience the tremendous personal loss of Grace Frick, who after years of illness died in 1979 of cancer. A remarkable woman in her own right, Frick will undoubtedly be remembered for translating into English Yourcenar's major works, *Mémoires d'Hadrien, Le Coup de grâce,* and *L'Œuvre au noir.* Of equal importance, however, she remained throughout their relationship a source of inspiration and encouragement in a unique collaboration of mind and spirit.

Shortly after Frick's death Yourcenar was unexpectedly cast in the unfamiliar role of literary celebrity. Her nomination for membership to the Académie Française, proposed by the novelist and former editor of *Le Figaro,* Jean d'Ormesson, generated heated debate from those wishing to deny admission to a woman as well as frivolous controversy concerning her ceremonial attire. Despite fervent opposition, she was elected on 6 March 1980 and formally inducted on 22 January 1981. At her reception she eulogized, as tradition ordered, the author Roger Callois, whose

Yourcenar at work

death created the vacancy which she filled within the forty-member body; more important, she paid tribute to the influence of women throughout the history of French letters, citing from among them the contributions of Mme de Staël, George Sand, and Colette. "This uncertain, floating me, whose existence I myself dispute," she said, "here it is, surrounded, accompanied by an invisible troupe of women who perhaps should have received this honor long before, so that I am tempted to stand aside to let their shadows pass."

Largely the result of becoming France's first *académicienne,* the demand for her work in the United States prompted publication of her earlier fiction, including *Feux, Denier du rêve, Alexis, Nouvelles orientales,* and *Comme l'eau qui coule* (1982; translated as *Two Lives and a Dream,* 1987), as well as *Sous bénéfice d'inventaire* (1962; trans-

lated as *The Dark Brain of Piranesi and Other Essays,* 1984) and *Mishima, ou la vision du vide* (1980; translated as *Mishima: A Vision of the Void,* 1986), a study of the Japanese writer Yukio Mishima. Scheduled for publication is an American edition of a second collection of essays and literary criticism, *Le Temps, ce grand sculpteur* (1983; published in Great Britain as *That Mighty Sculptor, Time,* 1987) and three volumes of her autobiography.

Marguerite Yourcenar holds a unique position within contemporary literature. By definition she is generally acknowledged as a writer of historical fiction. Her work, however, virtually defies classification. "I've always waited until what I was writing was sufficiently a part of myself," she said, "so as to blend in with my own memories." Merging the past with the present, her fiction evokes a quality of agelessness as well as timely significance. "She seems to have come straight out of the seventeenth century," stated Mavis Gallant. "Her mind, her manner, the quirks and prejudices that enliven her conclusive opinions, the sense of caste that lends her fiction its stern framework, her respect for usages and precedents, belong to a vanished France." Jean d'Ormesson, however, characterized her as "one of the few writers of the 20th century who do not consider happiness the ultimate goal of life. The most striking aspect of her work is her use of specific historical situations to express the universal condition of man."

Yourcenar received numerous honors throughout her career. In addition to membership in the Académie Française, she was elected to the Academy of the French Language and Literature of Belgium and the American Academy and Institute of Arts and Letters. In France she was awarded the Prix Femina-Vacaresco for *Mémoires d'Hadrien*, the Prix Combat, the Prix Femina for *L'Œuvre au noir*, the Grand Prix National des Lettres from the French Ministry of Culture, and the Grand Prix de l'Académie Française. She won the prestigious Erasmus Award in 1983 and three years later both the National Arts Club's Medal of Honor for Literature and the Medal of the Commander of the French Legion of Honor. Yourcenar received honorary degrees from Smith, Bowdoin, and Colby colleges and from Harvard University. In addition, she was frequently mentioned as a possible candidate for the Nobel Prize in Literature.

At eighty-four Yourcenar was still writing. "Age means nothing," she once said. "If anything I feel that I'm still a child: eternity and childhood are my ages." She lived her life in much the same way as she accepted the inevitability of her death. She preferred, like Hadrian, "to enter into death with open eyes" and, like Zeno, to experience death as a final act of passage. "One must toil and struggle to the bitter end," said Yourcenar; "one must swim in the river that both lifts us up and carries us away, knowing in advance that the only way out is to drown in the vastness of the sea." This was her legacy, in her life and in her literature.

Literary Awards and Honors Announced in 1988

ACADEMY OF AMERICAN POETS AWARDS

LAMONT SELECTION
Mary Jo Salter, "Unfinished Painting" (forthcoming 1989, Knopf).

LANDON TRANSLATION AWARD
Peter Hargita, *Perched From Nothing's Branch: The Selected Poetry of Attila József* (Apalachee, 1987).

LAVAN YOUNGER POET AWARDS
Marie Howe, Naomi Shihab Nye, John Yau.

WHITMAN AWARD
April Bernard, *Blackbird Bye Bye* (Random House).

NELSON ALGREN AWARD FOR SHORT FICTION

Steven Schwartz, "Madagascar."

AMERICAN ACADEMY AND INSTITUTE OF ARTS AND LETTERS AWARDS

WITTER BYNNER PRIZE FOR POETRY
Andrew Hudgins.

E. M. FORSTER AWARD
Blake Morrison.

GOLD MEDAL FOR BIOGRAPHY
James Thomas Flexner.

SUE KAUFMAN PRIZE FOR FIRST EDITION
Kaye Gibbons.

ROME FELLOWSHIP IN LITERATURE
Edward Hirsch.

RICHARD AND HINDA ROSENTHAL FOUNDATION AWARD
Thomas McMahon.

JEAN STEIN AWARD
Andre Dubus.

MILDRED AND HAROLD STRAUSS LIVINGS AWARDS
Diane Johnson, Robert Stone.

BANCROFT PRIZES

Peter Kolchin, *Unfree Labor: American Slavery and Russian Serfdom* (Harvard University Press).

Michael S. Sherry, *The Rise of American Air Power: The Creation of Armageddon* (Yale University Press).

BAY AREA BOOK REVIEWERS ASSOCIATION AWARDS

CHILDREN'S LITERATURE
Marilyn Sachs, *Fran Ellen's House* (Dutton).

FRED CODY MEMORIAL AWARD FOR LIFETIME ACHIEVEMENT
Jessica Mitford.

COMMUNITY SERVICE
Institute for Food and Development Policy, *Don't Be Afraid, Gringo: A Honduran Woman Speaks from the Heart,* by Elvia Alvarado, translated and edited by Medea Benjamin.

FICTION
Herbert Wilner, *The Quarterback Speaks to His God* (Cayuse Press).

NONFICTION
Randy Shilts, *And the Band Played On* (St. Martin's Press).

POETRY
Edward Kleinschmidt, *Magnetism* (Heyeck Press).

CAREY-THOMAS PUBLISHING AWARD

New American Fiction Series (Sun & Moon Press).

HONORS CITATION
Algonquin Books.

SPECIAL CITATIONS
Oxford University Press & Pocket Books.

CURTIS G. BENJAMIN AWARD

Nat Wartels.

BENNETT AWARD

Yves Bonnefoy.

IRMA SIMONTON BLACK AWARD

Audrey Wood, *Heckedy Peg*, illustrated by Don Wood (Harcourt Brace Jovanovich).

ELMER HOLMES BOBST AWARDS

FICTION
Toni Morrison, Reynolds Price.

DRAMA
Edward Albee.

PUBLISHING
Robert Giroux.

BOOKER PRIZE

Peter Carey, *Oscar and Lucinda* (Faber).

BOSTON GLOBE-HORN BOOK AWARDS

FICTION
Mildred Taylor, *The Friendship*, illustrated by Max Ginsburg (Dial).

NONFICTION
Virginia Hamilton, *Anthony Burns: The Defeat and Triumph of a Fugitive Slave* (Knopf).

PICTURE BOOK
Dianne Snyder, *The Boy of the Three-Year Nap*, illustrated by Allen Say (Houghton Mifflin).

CALDECOTT MEDAL

John Schoenherr, illustrator of *Owl Moon*, by Jane Yolen (Philomel).

CALDECOTT HONOR BOOK
John Steptoe, *Mufaro's Beautiful Daughters* (Lothrop, Lee & Shepard).

JOHN DOS PASSOS PRIZE FOR LITERATURE

Lee Smith.

1987 GOLDEN KITE AWARDS

FICTION
Lois Lowry, *Rabble Starkey* (Houghton Mifflin).

ILLUSTRATION
Arnold Lobel, *The Devil and Mother Crump*, by Valerie Scho Carey (Harper).

NONFICTION
Rhoda Blumberg, *The Incredible Journey of Lewis and Clark* (Lothrop, Lee & Shepard).

THE GOVERNOR GENERAL'S LITERARY AWARDS

CHILDREN'S LITERATURE
(ILLUSTRATION)
Marie-Louise Gay, *Rainy Day Magic* (Stoddart).

CHILDREN'S LITERATURE (TEXT)
Morgan Nyberg, *Galahad Schwartz and the Cockroach Army* (Douglas & McIntyre).

DRAMA
John Krizanc, *Prague* (Playwrights Canada).

FICTION
  M. T. Kelly, *A Dream Like Mine* (Stoddart).

NONFICTION
  Michael Ignatieff, *The Russian Album* (Viking).

POETRY
  Gwendolyn MacEwan, *Afterworlds* (McClelland & Stewart).

TRANSLATION
  Patricia Claxton, *Enchantment and Sorrow: The Autobiography of Gabrielle Roy* (Lester & Orpen Dennys).

DRUE HEINZ LITERATURE PRIZE

Reginald McKnight, *Moustapha's Eclipse* (University of Pittsburgh Press).

O. HENRY AWARD

Raymond Carver, "Errand" (*New Yorker*, 1 June 1987).

HUGO AWARDS

JOHN W. CAMPBELL AWARD FOR BEST NEW WRITER
  Judith Moffett.

NOVEL
  David Brin, *The Uplift War* (Phantasia).

NOVELLA
  Orson Scott Card, "Eye for Eye" (*Isaac Asimov's Science Fiction Magazine*, March 1987).

NOVELETTE
  Ursula K. LeGuin, "Buffalo Gals Won't You Come Out Tonight" (*Magazine of Fantasy and Science Fiction*, November 1987).

SHORT STORY
  Lawrence Watt-Evans, "Why I Left Harry's All Night Hamburgers" (*Isaac Asimov's Science Fiction Magazine*, July 1987).

INGERSOLL PRIZES

T. S. ELIOT AWARD FOR CREATIVE WRITING
  Walker Percy.

RICHARD M. WEAVER AWARD FOR SCHOLARLY LETTERS
  Edward Shils.

IOWA SHORT FICTION AWARD

Sharon Dilworth, *The Long White* (University of Iowa Press).

JANET HEIDINGER KAFKA PRIZE FOR FICTION

Gail Godwin, *A Southern Family* (Morrow).

ROBERT F. KENNEDY MEMORIAL BOOK AWARDS

Toni Morrison, *Beloved* (Knopf).

Pauli Murray, *Song in a Weary Throat* (Harper & Row).

RUTH LILLY POETRY PRIZE

Anthony Hecht.

LOS ANGELES TIMES BOOK PRIZES

Eric Foner, *Reconstruction: America's Unfinished Revolution, 1863-1877* (Harper & Row).

William Greider, *Secrets of the Temple: How the Federal Reserve Runs the Country* (Simon & Schuster).

Brenda Maddox, *Nora: The Real Life of Molly Bloom* (Houghton Mifflin).

Gabriel García Márquez, *Love in the Time of Cholera* (Knopf).

Richard Wilbur, *New and Collected Poems* (Harcourt Brace Jovanovich).

ROBERT KIRSCH AWARD
Thom Gunn.

JOHN D. & CATHERINE T. MACARTHUR FOUNDATION AWARDS

Andre Dubus, Thomas Pynchon.

EDWARD MACDOWELL MEDAL

William Styron.

NATIONAL BOOK AWARDS

FICTION
Pete Dexter, *Paris Trout* (Random House).

NONFICTION
Neil Sheehan, *A Bright Shining Lie: John Paul Vann and America in Vietnam* (Random House).

NATIONAL BOOK CRITICS CIRCLE AWARDS

BIOGRAPHY/AUTOBIOGRAPHY
Donald R. Howard, *Chaucer: His Life, His Works, His World* (Dutton/William Abrahams).

CITATION FOR EXCELLENCE IN REVIEWING
Josh Rubins, *New York Review of Books, Nation, New York Times Book Review, Times Literary Supplement.*

CRITICISM
Edward Denbly, *Dance Writings* (Knopf).

FICTION
Philip Roth, *The Counterlife* (Farrar, Straus & Giroux).

GENERAL NONFICTION
Richard Rhodes, *The Making of the Atomic Bomb* (Simon & Schuster).

POETRY
C. K. Williams, *Flesh and Blood* (Farrar, Straus & Giroux).

NATIONAL JEWISH BOOK AWARDS

CHILDREN'S LITERATURE
Sonia Levitin, *The Return* (Atheneum).

CONTEMPORARY JEWISH LIFE
Paul Cowan, with Rachel Cowan, *Mixed Blessings: Marriage between Jews and Christians* (Doubleday).

FICTION
Philip Roth, *The Counterlife* (Farrar, Straus & Giroux).

HOLOCAUST
Susan Zucotti, *The Italians and the Holocaust: Persecution, Rescue, Survival* (Basic Books).

ILLUSTRATED CHILDREN'S BOOKS
Miriam Chaikin, author, and Charles Mikolaycak, illustrator, *Exodus, Adapted from the Bible* (Holiday House).

ISRAEL
Shabtai Teveth, *Ben-Gurion: The Burning Ground 1886-1948* (Houghton Mifflin).

JEWISH HISTORY
Robert Chazan, *European Jewry and the First Crusade* (University of California Press).

JEWISH THOUGHT
Rabbi Marc D. Angel, Ph.D., *The Orphaned Adult: Confronting the Death of a Parent* (Insight Books/Human Sciences Press).

SCHOLARSHIP
Daniel M. Friedenberg, *Medieval Jewish Seals from Europe* (Wayne State University Press).

VISUAL ARTS
Lester D. Friedman, *The Jewish Image in American Film* (Citadel Press/Lyle Stuart).

NATIONAL MEDAL FOR LITERATURE

Carlos Fuentes.

NEBULA AWARDS

GRAND MASTER AWARD
Alfred Bester.

NOVEL
Pat Murphy, *The Falling Woman* (TOR).

NOVELLA
Kim Stanley Robinson, *Blind Geometer* (Cheap Street).

NOVELETTE
Pat Murphy, "Rachel in Love" (*Isaac Asimov's Science Fiction Magazine*, April 1987).

SHORT STORY
Kate Wilhelm, "Forever Yours, Anna" (*Omni*, July 1987).

NEUSTADT INTERNATIONAL PRIZE FOR LITERATURE
Raja Rao.

NEWBERRY MEDAL

Russell Freedman, *Lincoln: A Photobiography* (Clarion).

HONOR CITATIONS
Norma Fox Mazer, *After the Rain* (Morrow).

Gary Paulsen, *Hatchet* (Bradbury).

NOBEL PRIZE IN LITERATURE

Najīb Mahfūz.

SCOTT O'DELL AWARD FOR HISTORICAL FICTION

Lyll Becerra de Jenkins, *The Honorable Prison* (Dutton/Lodestar).

PEN-NEW ENGLAND

PEN/SCHAEFFER EATON AWARD
Allen Grossman.

PEN AWARDS

PEN/BOOK-OF-THE-MONTH CLUB TRANSLATION PRIZE
Madeline Levine and Francine Pross, *A Scrap of Time*, by Ida Fink (Pantheon).

FAULKNER AWARD FOR FICTION
T. Coraghessan Boyle, *World's End* (Viking).

ERNEST HEMINGWAY FOUNDATION AWARD
Lawrence Thornton, *Imagining Argentina* (Doubleday).

RENATO POGGIOLI TRANSLATION AWARD FOR A WORK IN PROGRESS
James Morris, *The Empty Valice*, by Sergio Ferrero.

NELSON ALGREN FICTION AWARD FOR A WORK IN PROGRESS
Jack Driscoll, "The Hermit Journals."

PEN MEDAL FOR TRANSLATION
Ralph Mannheim.

ØBK'S CHRISTIAN GAUSS AWARD

Leonard Barkan, *The Gods Made Flesh: Metamorphosis and the Pursuit of Paganism* (Yale University Press).

EDGAR ALLAN POE AWARDS

BIOGRAPHICAL/CRITICAL STUDY
Leroy Lad Panek, *Introduction to the Detective Story* (Popular Press, Bowling Green State University).

FACT CRIME
Richard Hammer, *CBS Murders* (Morrow).

FIRST NOVEL
Deidre S. Laiken, *Death Among Strangers* (Macmillan).

GRAND MASTER AWARD
Phyllis A. Whitney.

JUVENILE NOVEL
Susan Shreve, *Lucy Forever and Miss Rosetree, Shrinks* (Holt).

NOVEL
Aaron Elkins, *Old Bones* (Mysterious Press).

ORIGINAL SOFTCOVER NOVEL
Sharyn McCrumb, *Bimbos of the Death Sun* (TSR).

ELLERY QUEEN
Ruth Cavin.

PRESENT TENSE/JOEL H. CAVIOR LITERARY AWARDS

BIOGRAPHY/AUTOBIOGRAPHY
Dan Vittorio Segre, *Memoirs of a Fortunate Jew* (Adler & Adler).

FICTION
Philip Roth, *The Counterlife* (Farrar, Straus & Giroux).

HISTORY
David Sorkin, *The Transformation of German Jewry, 1740-1840* (Oxford University Press).

RELIGIOUS THOUGHT
Nehema Aschkenasy, *Eve's Journey: Feminine Images in Hebraic Literary Thought* (University of Pennsylvania Press).

SPECIAL CITATION FOR LIFETIME ACHIEVEMENT
Cynthia Ozick.

PULITZER PRIZES

BIOGRAPHY
David Herbert Donald, *Look Homeward: A Life of Thomas Wolfe* (Little, Brown).

EDITORIAL CARTOONS
Doug Marlette, *Atlanta Constitution* and *Charlotte Observer*.

FICTION
Toni Morrison, *Beloved* (Knopf).

GENERAL NONFICTION
Richard Rhodes, *The Making of the Atomic Bomb* (Simon & Schuster).

HISTORY
Robert V. Bruce, *The Launching of Modern American Science 1846-1876* (Knopf).

POETRY
William Meredith, *Partial Accounts: New & Selected Poems* (Knopf).

REA AWARD FOR THE SHORT STORY

Donald Barthelme.

REGINA MEDAL

Katherine Patterson.

DELMORE SCHWARTZ MEMORIAL POETRY AWARD

Deborah Digges.

JOHN SIMMONS SHORT FICTION AWARD

Michael Pritchett, *The Venus Tree* (University of Iowa Press).

WHITBREAD BOOK OF THE YEAR AWARD

Christopher Nolan, *Under the Eye of the Clock* (Weidenfeld & Nicolson).

WHITING AWARDS

Michael Burkard, Lydia Davis, Bruce Duffy, Gerald Early, Jonathan Franzen, Mary La Chapelle, Li-Young Lee, Sylvia Moss, Geoffrey O'Brien, William T. Vollman.

LAURA INGALLS WILDER AWARD

Elizabeth George Speare.

Checklist: Contributions to Literary History and Biography, 1988

This checklist is a selection of new books on various aspects and periods of literary and cultural history; biographies, memoirs, and correspondence of literary people and their associates; and primary bibliographies. Not included are volumes in general reference series, literary criticism, and bibliographies of criticism.

Ackerman, Robert. *J. G. Frazer: His Life and Work.* New York: Cambridge University Press, 1988.

Assouline, Pierre. *Gaston Gallimard: A Half-Century of French Publishing.* San Diego: Harcourt Brace Jovanovich, 1988.

Bartlett, Lee. *William Everson: The Life of Brother Antoninus.* New York: New Directions, 1988.

Bergman, Ingmar. *The Magic Lantern: An Autobiography.* Translated by Joan Tate. New York: Viking, 1988.

Bogard, Travis, and Jackson R. Bryer, eds. *Selected Letters of Eugene O'Neill.* New Haven & London: Yale University Press, 1988.

Brian, Denis. *The True Gen: An Intimate Portrait of Ernest Hemingway by Those Who Knew Him.* New York: Grove, 1988.

Butscher, Edward. *Conrad Aiken: Poet of White Horse Vale.* Athens: University of Georgia Press, 1988.

Carey, Gary. *Anita Loos: A Biography.* New York: Knopf, 1988.

Carpenter, Humphrey. *A Serious Character: The Life of Ezra Pound.* Boston: Houghton Mifflin, 1988.

Clarke, Gerald. *Capote: A Life.* New York: Simon & Schuster, 1988.

Crabbe, Kathryn W. *Evelyn Waugh.* New York: Continuum, 1988.

de Courcel, Martine. *Tolstoy: The Ultimate Reconciliation.* New York: Scribners, 1988.

Dickenson, Donna. *George Sand: A Brave Man, the Most Womanly Woman.* New York: Berg/St. Martin's Press, 1988.

Donaldson, Scott. *John Cheever: A Biography.* New York: Random House, 1988.

Eliot, Valerie, ed. *The Letters of T. S. Eliot: Volume I (1898-1922).* San Diego: Harcourt Brace Jovanovich, 1988.

Ellmann, Richard. *Oscar Wilde.* New York: Knopf, 1988.

Feibleman, Peter. *Lilly: Reminiscences of Lillian Hellman.* New York: Morrow, 1988.

Fitzgerald, Penelope. *Charlotte Mew and Her Friends.* Reading, Mass.: Addison-Wesley, 1988.

Frazer, Russell. *Young Shakespeare.* New York: Columbia University Press, 1988.

Gates, Henry Lewis, Jr. *The Signifying Monkey: A Theory of Afro-American Literary Criticism.* New York: Oxford University Press, 1988.

Gay, Peter. *Freud: A Life for Our Times.* New York: Norton, 1988.

Gelderman, Carol. *Mary McCarthy: A Life.* New York: St. Martin's Press, 1988.

Gilbert, Sandra M., and Susan Gubar. *No Man's Land: The Place of the Woman Writer in the Twentieth Century, Volume I, The War of the Words.* New Haven: Yale University Press, 1988.

Gombrowicz, Witold. *Diary: Volume One.* Edited by Jan Kott. Translated by Lillian Vallee. Evanston, Ill.: Northwestern University Press, 1988.

Gordon, Lyndall. *Eliot's New Life.* New York: Farrar, Straus & Giroux, 1988.

Gornick, Vivian. *The Durrell-Miller Letters, 1935-80.* New York: New Directions, 1988.

Hamilton, Ian. *In Search of J. D. Salinger.* New York: Random House, 1988.

Henrickson, Louise Levitas, with Jo Ann Boydston. *Anna Yezierska: A Writer's Life.* New Brunswick, N.J.: Rutgers University Press, 1988.

Holroyd, Michael. *Bernard Shaw: The Search for Love, 1856-1898.* New York: Random House, 1988.

Honan, Park. *Jane Austen: Her Life.* New York: St. Martin's Press, 1988.

Kahn, E. J., Jr., *Year of Change: More about "The New Yorker" & Me.* New York: Viking, 1988.

Kaplan, Fred. *Dickens: A Biography.* New York: Morrow, 1988.

Kazan, Elia. *Elia Kazan: A Life.* New York: Knopf, 1988.

Kelly, Richard J. *We Dream of Honour: John Berryman's Letters to His Mother.* New York: Norton, 1988.

Kelvin, Norman, ed. *The Collected Letters of William Morris, Volume Two: 1881-1888.* Princeton: Princeton University Press, 1988.

Kjetsaa, Geir. *Fyodor Dostoyevsky: A Writer's Life.* Translated by Siri Hustvedt and David McDuff. New York: Elisabeth Sifton Books/Viking, 1988.

Lehmann, John. *Christopher Isherwood: A Personal Memoir.* New York: Holt, 1988.

Maddox, Brenda. *Nora: The Real Life of Molly Bloom.* Boston: Houghton Mifflin, 1988.

Meade, Marion. *Dorothy Parker: What Fresh Hell is This?* New York: Villard, 1988.

Morgan, Ted. *Literary Outlaw: The Life and Times of William S. Burroughs.* New York: Holt, 1988.

Nolan, Christopher. *Under the Eye of the Clock: The Life Story of Christopher Nolan.* New York: St. Martin's Press, 1988.

O'Connor, Garry. *Sean O'Casey: A Life.* New York: Atheneum, 1988.

Oppenheimer, Judy. *Private Demons: The Life of Shirley Jackson.* New York: Putnam's, 1988.

Paton, Alan. *Journey Continued: An Autobiography.* New York: Scribners, 1988.

Petitfils, Pierre. *Rimbaud.* Charlottesville: University Press of Virginia, 1988.

Pritchett, V. S. *Chekhov: A Spirit Set Free.* New York: Random House, 1988.

Rampersand, Arnold. *The Life of Langston Hughes, Volume II, 1941-1967: I Dream a World.* New York: Oxford University Press, 1988.

Roberts, David. *Jean Stafford: A Biography.* Boston: Little, Brown, 1988.

Rollyson, Carl. *Lillian Hellman: Her Legend and Her Legacy.* New York: St. Martin's Press, 1988.

Roth, Philip. *The Facts: A Novelist's Autobiography.* New York: Farrar, Straus & Giroux, 1988.

Rowse, A. L. *The Poet Auden: A Personal Memoir.* New York: Holt, 1988.

Schom, Alan. *Emile Zola: A Biography.* New York: Holt, 1988.

Silverthorne, Elizabeth. *Marjorie Kinnan Rawlings: Sojourner at Cross Creek.* Woodstock: Overlook Press, 1988.

Thomas, D. M. *Memories and Hallucinations: A Memoir.* New York: Viking, 1988.

Timms, Edward, and Naomi Segal. *Freud in Exile: Psychoanalysis and Its Vicissitudes.* New Haven: Yale University Press, 1988.

Timms, Edward, and Peter Collier, eds. *Visions and Blueprints: Avant-Garde Culture and Radical Politics in Early Twentieth-Century Europe.* New York: Manchester University Press/St. Martin's Press, 1988.

Tomalin, Claire. *Katherine Mansfield: A Secret Life.* New York: Knopf, 1988.

Townsend, Kim. *Sherwood Anderson.* Boston: Houghton Mifflin, 1988.

Tynan, Kathleen. *The Life of Kenneth Tynan.* New York: Morrow, 1988.

Walker, Margaret. *Richard Wright, Daemonic Genius.* New York: Warner Books, 1988.

Wehr, Gerhard. *Jung: A Biography.* Boston: Shambhala, 1988.

Welsh, Alexander. *Copyright to Copperfield: The Identity of Dickens.* Cambridge: Harvard University Press, 1988.

West, Rebecca. *Family Memories: An Autobiographical Journey.* Edited by Faith Evans. New York: Viking, 1988.

Wilson, A. N. *Tolstoy.* New York: Norton, 1988.

Necrology

Leonie Adams–27 June 1988
Charles Addams–29 September 1988
Clarus Backes–23 October 1988
John Ball–15 October 1988
Ellin Berlin–30 July 1988
Raymond Carver–2 August 1988
Edward Chodorov–9 October 1988
Allen Churchill–16 January 1988
William R. Cox–7 August 1988
I. A. L. Diamond–21 April 1988
Robert Duncan–3 February 1988
Eleanor Estes–15 July 1988
Charles E. Feinberg–1 March 1988
Melvin Frank–13 October 1988
Rose Franken–22 June 1988
Elwin S. Gelsey–12 December 1988
Noel Gerson–20 November 1988
Sheilah Graham–17 November 1988
Miriam Gurko–3 July 1988
Nancy Hale–24 September 1988
Hamish Hamilton–25 May 1988
Colin Higgins–5 August 1988
Lawrence Hill–14 March 1988
John Clellon Holmes–30 March 1988
Geoffrey Household–4 October 1988
John Houseman–31 October 1988
Daniel Lewis James–18 May 1988
Marghanita Laski–6 February 1988
Jay Leyda–18 February 1988

Irving Mansfield–25 August 1988
Harold Matson–5 January 1988
Theodore Morrison–27 November 1988
Jane S. Nickerson–10 January 1988
Ursula Nordstrom–11 October 1988
Paul Osborn–12 May 1988
Peggy Parish–18 November 1988
Alan Paton–12 April 1988
Henri Peyre–9 December 1988
Miguel Piñero–21 June 1988
Emeric Pressburger–5 February 1988
J. Saunders Redding–2 March 1988
Paul R. Reynolds–10 June 1988
Adela Rogers St. Johns–10 August 1988
Harold Salemson–25 August 1988
Michael J. Shaara–5 May 1988
Robert Shaplen–15 May 1988
Leon Shimkin–25 May 1988
Joseph Shipley–11 May 1988
Max Shulman–28 August 1988
Clifford D. Simak–25 April 1988
Sir Sacheverell Sitwell–1 October 1988
Terrence L. Smith–7 December 1988
Frederick Ungar–16 November 1988
Iris Vinton–6 February 1988
Hyatt Waggoner–13 October 1988
Edward van Westerborg–7 May 1988
Monroe Wheeler–14 August 1988
Charles Willeford–27 March 1988

Contributors

Gay Wilson Allen ....*Raleigh North Carolina*

Roger Allen ....*University of Pennsylvania*

Richard R. Centing...*Ohio State University*

Anne Hobson Freeman...*University of Virginia*

George Garrett ....*University of Virginia*

George L. Geckle ....*University of South Carolina*

R. S. Gwynn..*Lamar University*

Mark Heberle...*University of Hawaii at Manoa*

Howard Kissel ....*New York Daily News*

Jeffrey Meyers..*University of Colorado at Boulder*

Gerald Petievich...*San Marino, California*

John Henry Raleigh ....*University of California, Berkeley*

Steven Serafin............................*Hunter College of the City University of New York*

David R. Slavitt ....*Philadelphia, Pennsylvania*

Margaret Slythe...*Dulwich College*

Cumulative Index

Dictionary of Literary Biography, Volumes 1-79
Dictionary of Literary Biography Yearbook, 1980-1988
Dictionary of Literary Biography Documentary Series, Volumes 1-6

Cumulative Index

DLB before number: *Dictionary of Literary Biography,* Volumes 1-79
Y before number: *Dictionary of Literary Biography Yearbook,* 1980-1988
DS before number: *Dictionary of Literary Biography Documentary Series,* Volumes 1-6

B

Cumulative Index

C

D

E

F

G

H

I

J

K

L

M

N

P

Q

R

S

Cumulative Index

Y

Z

Cumulative Index

continued from front endsheets

71: *American Literary Critics and Scholars, 1880-1900*, edited by John W. Rathbun and Monica M. Grecu (1988)

72: *French Novelists, 1930-1960*, edited by Catharine Savage Brosman (1988)

73: *American Magazine Journalists, 1741-1850*, edited by Sam G. Riley (1988)

74: *American Short-Story Writers Before 1880*, edited by Bobby Ellen Kimbel, with the assistance of William E. Grant (1988)

75: *Contemporary German Fiction Writers*, Second Series, edited by Wolfgang D. Elfe and James Hardin (1988)

76: *Afro-American Writers, 1940-1955*, edited by Trudier Harris (1988)

77: *British Mystery Writers, 1920-1939*, edited by Bernard Benstock and Thomas F. Staley (1988)

78: *American Short-Story Writers, 1880-1910*, edited by Bobby Ellen Kimbel, with the assistance of William E. Grant (1988)

79: *American Magazine Journalists, 1850-1900*, edited by Sam G. Riley (1988)

80: *Restoration and Eighteenth-Century Dramatists*, First Series, edited by Paula R. Backsheider (1989)

Documentary Series

1: *Sherwood Anderson, Willa Cather, John Dos Passos, Theodore Dreiser, F. Scott Fitzgerald, Ernest Hemingway, Sinclair Lewis*, edited by Margaret A. Van Antwerp (1982)

2: *James Gould Cozzens, James T. Farrell, William Faulkner, John O'Hara, John Steinbeck, Thomas Wolfe, Richard Wright*, edited by Margaret A. Van Antwerp (1982)

3: *Saul Bellow, Jack Kerouac, Norman Mailer, Vladimir Nabokov, John Updike, Kurt Vonnegut*, edited by Mary Bruccoli (1983)

4: *Tennessee Williams*, edited by Margaret A. Van Antwerp and Sally Johns (1984)

5: *American Transcendentalists*, edited by Joel Myerson (1988)

6: *Hardboiled Mystery Writers*, edited by Matthew J. Bruccoli and Richard Layman (1988)

Yearbooks

1980, edited by Karen L. Rood, Jean W. Ross, and Richard Ziegfeld (1981)

1981, edited by Karen L. Rood, Jean W. Ross, and Richard Ziegfeld (1982)

1982, edited by Richard Ziegfeld; associate editors: Jean W. Ross and Lynne C. Zeigler (1983)

1983, edited by Mary Bruccoli and Jean W. Ross; associate editor: Richard Ziegfeld (1984)

1984, edited by Jean W. Ross (1985)

1985, edited by Jean W. Ross (1986)

1986, edited by J. M. Brook (1987)

1987, edited by J. M. Brook (1988)

1988, edited by J. M. Brook (1989)

Concise Series

The New Consciousness, 1941-1968 (1987)

Colonization to the American Renaissance, 1640-1865 (1988)

Realism, Naturalism, and Local Color, 1865-1917 (1988)

The Twenties, 1917-1929 (1989)